Legal Ethics and Human

David Luban is one of the world's leading scholars of legal ethics. In this collection of his most significant papers from the past twenty-five years, he ranges over such topics as the moral psychology of organizational evil, the strengths and weaknesses of the adversary system, and jurisprudence from the lawyer's point of view. His discussion combines philosophical argument, legal analysis, and many cases drawn from actual law practice, and he defends a theory of legal ethics that focuses on the lawyer's role in enhancing human dignity and human rights. In addition to an analytical introduction, the volume includes two major previously unpublished papers, including a detailed critique of the US government lawyers who produced the notorious "torture memos." It will be of interest to a wide range of readers in both philosophy and law.

David Luban is University Professor and Professor of Law and Philosophy at Georgetown University.

Cambridge Studies in Philosophy and Law

GENERAL EDITOR
Gerald Postema
(University of North Carolina, Chapel Hill)

ADVISORY BOARD
Jules Coleman (Yale Law School)
Antony Duff (University of Stirling)
David Lyons (Boston University)
Neil MacCormick (University of Edinburgh)
Stephen Munzer (U.C.L.A. Law School)
Philip Pettit (Princeton University)
Joseph Raz (University of Oxford)
Jeremy Waldron (Columbia Law School)

Other books in the series:

Jeffrie G. Murphy and Jean Hampton: *Forgiveness and Mercy*
Stephen R. Munzer: *A Theory of Property*
R. G. Frey and Christopher W. Morris (eds.): *Liability and Responsibility: Essays in Law and Morals*
Robert F. Schopp: *Automatism, Insanity, and the Psychology of Criminal Responsibility*
Steven J. Burton: *Judging in Good Faith*
Jules Coleman: *Risks and Wrongs*
Suzanne Uniacke: *Permissible Killing: The Self-Defense Justification of Homicide*
Jules Coleman and Allen Buchanan (eds.): *In Harm's Way: Essays in Honor of Joel Feinberg*
Warren F. Schwartz (ed.): *Justice in Immigration*
John Fischer and Mark Ravizza: *Responsibility and Control*
R. A. Duff (ed.): *Philosophy and the Criminal Law*
Larry Alexander (ed.): *Constitutionalism*
R. Schopp: *Justification Defenses and Just Convictions*
Anthony Sebok: *Legal Positivism in American Jurisprudence*
Arthur Ripstein: *Equality, Responsibility and the Law*
Steven J. Burton: *The Path of the Law and its Influence*
Jody S. Kraus and Steven D. Walt: *The Jurisprudential Foundations of Corporate and Commercial Law*
Brian Leiter: *Objectivity in Law and Morals*
Christopher Kutz: *Complicity*
Peter Benson (ed.): *The Theory of Contract Law*

Walter J. Schultz: *The Moral Conditions of Economic Efficiency*
Stephen R. Munzer: *New Essays in the Legal and Political Theory of Property*
Mark C. Murphy: *Natural Law and Practical Rationality*
Philip Soper: *The Ethics of Deference*
Gerald J. Postema: *Philosophy of the Law of Torts*
Alan Wertheimer: *Consent to Sexual Relations*
Timothy MacKlein: *Beyond Comparison*
Steven A. Ketcher: *Norms in a Wired World*
Mark R. Reiff: *Punishment, Compensation, and Law*
Larry Alexander: *Is There a Right of Freedom of Expression?*
Larry May: *Crimes Against Humanity*
Larry Laudan: *Truth, Error, and Criminal Law*
Mark C. Murphy: *Natural Law in Jurisprudence and Politics*
Douglas E. Edlin: *Common Law Theory*
W. J. Waluchow: *A Common Law Theory of Judicial Review*

Legal Ethics and Human Dignity

David Luban

Georgetown University

CAMBRIDGE UNIVERSITY PRESS
Cambridge, New York, Melbourne, Madrid, Cape Town, Singapore, São Paulo, Delhi

Cambridge University Press
The Edinburgh Building, Cambridge CB2 8RU, UK

Published in the United States of America by Cambridge University Press, New York

www.cambridge.org
Information on this title: www.cambridge.org/9780521118248

First published 2007
Fourth printing 2009
This digitally printed version 2009

A catalogue record for this publication is available from the British Library

ISBN 978-0-521-86285-1 hardback
ISBN 978-0-521-11824-8 paperback

for
Deborah Rhode

Contents

Acknowledgments

The essays in this book were written over many years, and I have presented them to a great many audiences. To acknowledge all the people whose comments, criticisms, and questions improved these papers is impossible. Even those whose names I know would number in the dozens.

Several debts, though, run deeper than help on individual papers. David Wasserman had the biggest philosophical influence on these papers, talking me through many of the arguments and a great deal of the social psychology that figures in the later chapters. Patrick Byrne has doubled as my relentless sparring partner and enthusiastic booster for more than twenty years. Julie O'Sullivan has changed the way I teach and think about law. Robin West has, over many years, become something akin to my alter ego. And Deborah Rhode, to whom this book is dedicated, has been both a great friend and an ideal co-author. Laboring with me through the four editions of our textbook, she has taught me most of the legal ethics I know.

Since I arrived at Georgetown, Carrie Menkel-Meadow and Mike Seidman have been steady sources of ideas and moral support. I've also gotten a great deal of help from my other Georgetown legal ethics colleagues Jeff Bauman, Heidi Feldman, Mike Frisch, Mitt Regan, Phil Schrag, and Abbe Smith – and, like all of them, I have drawn inspiration from the late Father Robert Drinan. Among legal ethics scholars elsewhere, Robert Gordon, Michael Kelly, Thomas Shaffer, and William Simon have had particular impact on the ideas in this book, through disagreement as well as agreement.

Equally important have been my clinical colleagues. Mike Millemann, one of the finest and most dynamic lawyers I've ever known, first fired my enthusiasm for clinical ethics teaching; at the University of Maryland, I also cut my teeth partnering in clinical ethics classes with Barbara Bezdek and Homer LaRue. At Georgetown, I have done half-a-dozen tours of duty in the Center for Applied Legal Studies (CALS), working side by side with student-lawyers and their advisors on political asylum cases. I owe a great deal to my CALS teammates Karen Bouton, Mary Brittingham, Anna Gallagher, Andrea

Goodman, David Koplow, Michele Pistone, Jaya Ramji-Nogales, Phil Schrag, Rebecca Storey, Virgil Wiebe, and Diane Uchimiya, as well as to our amazing students. None of them will take it amiss, I think, if I add that the greatest debt is to CALS's clients. All of them are human rights refugees, whose dignity, courage, and resourcefulness have opened my eyes to a great deal about my own country, about the wider world, and about what is best and worst in the rule of law. Above all, they have opened my eyes to the resilience of the human spirit.

Several chapters of the book originated during my year as a Fellow of the Woodrow Wilson International Center for Scholars, an ideally collegial host. I wrote chapters 4 and 5 – the two new chapters of the book – during my visiting year at Stanford Law School, where Barbara Fried and Mark Kelman gave me especially helpful comments. Chapter 5 benefited greatly from an ongoing dialogue with Marty Lederman. I also wish to thank Colonel Bill Mayall and Captain John Yeager, who invited me on half-a-dozen occasions to present material from this book to multinational classes of military officers at the Industrial College of the Armed Forces in the National Defense University. The acute comments of the officers worked their way into the final versions of several chapters.

I would also like to thank Judy Areen and Alex Aleinikoff, my deans at Georgetown, for the tremendous support they've given me, both institutional and intellectual; Kathleen Sullivan and Larry Kramer for making possible the visit at Stanford Law School during which I finished this book; Gerald Postema, editor of Cambridge Studies in Philosophy and Law, who advised me on the early stages of the project; Hilary Gaskin, Cambridge University Press's philosophy editor, for moving the project along; and two anonymous readers for the Press whose comments helped in the final revisions. Tselane Holloway and Mary Ann Rundell turned the papers into a revisable manuscript.

I owe an enormous debt of gratitude to my students, who have always been my main source of inspiration. Among the Georgetown students, special thanks goes to Brian Shaughnessy, my friend and workout partner.

Above all, I must thank my family – my children, Daniel and Rachel, now old enough to spot the flaws in my arguments, and my wife Judy Lichtenberg, who has tolerated my endless kvetching about writing deadlines with nearly superhuman love and patience. As a philosopher in her own right, Judy read and commented on nearly every chapter in this book, and shared ideas on a daily basis for enough years that I barely know whose are whose. Their love makes everything else possible.

Several of the papers collected here were given as named lectures, and I wish to thank the host institutions and sponsors. I will also give information and acknowledgments for the initial publication of these chapters.

Chapter 1, "The Adversary System Excuse," was the Catriona Gibbs Memorial Lecture at Queen's University Law School in Kingston, Ontario.

It appeared in my anthology *The Good Lawyer: Lawyers' Roles and Lawyers' Ethics*, Rowman & Allanheld [now Rowman & Littlefield], 1984. The current version incorporates an excerpt from "Rediscovering Fuller's Legal Ethics," Georgetown Journal of Legal Ethics, vol. 11, no. 4, pp. 801–29 (1998), also in Willem J. Witteveen and Wibren van der Burg, eds., *Rediscovering Fuller: Essays on Implicit Law and Institutional Design* (Amsterdam University Press, 1999), pp. 193–225.

Chapter 2, "Lawyers as Defenders of Human Dignity (When They Aren't Busy Attacking It)," was the Van Arsdell Lecture on Litigation Ethics at the University of Illinois School of Law. It appeared in University of Illinois Law Review, vol. 2005, no. 3, pp. 815–46 (2005).

Chapter 3, "Natural Law as Professional Ethics: A Reading of Fuller," Social Philosophy and Policy, vol. 18, no. 1, pp. 176–205 (2001), reprinted in Ellen Frankel Paul, Fred D. Miller, Jr., and Jeffrey Paul, eds., *Natural Law and Modern Moral Philosophy* (Cambridge University Press, 2001), pp. 176–205.

Chapters 4 and 5 were written for this volume, but include brief excerpts from "Liberalism, Torture, and the Ticking Bomb," in Karen Greenberg, ed., *The Torture Debate in America* (Cambridge University Press, 2005).

Chapter 6, "Contrived Ignorance," was my inaugural lecture as Frederick J. Haas Professor of Law and Philosophy at Georgetown University Law Center. I also delivered it as the Blankenbaker Lecture at the University of Montana School of Law. It appeared in the Georgetown Law Journal, vol. 87, no. 4, pp. 957–80 (1999).

Chapter 7, "The Ethics of Wrongful Obedience," originated as the Keck Foundation Award Lecture to the Fellows of the American Bar Foundation; it was also delivered as the Condon-Faulkner Lecture at the University of Washington School of Law and in the Kennedy School lecture series at Harvard University. It appeared in Deborah L. Rhode, ed., *Ethics in Practice* (Oxford University Press, 2000), pp. 94–120.

Chapter 8, "Integrity: Its Causes and Cures," Fordham Law Review, vol. 72, no. 2, pp. 279–310 (2003). Written for a symposium on integrity in the law in honor of John D. Feerick.

Chapter 9, "A Midrash on Rabbi Shaffer and Rabbi Trollope," Notre Dame Law Review, vol. 77, no. 3 (2002), pp. 889–923. This paper was written for a *Propter Honoris Respectum* for Thomas L. Shaffer.

Introduction

When I was growing up in a middle-class, Midwestern, mid-century family, I knew only one lawyer, my parents' solo-practitioner friend Cyril Gross. Gross joined us for holiday dinners, and every few years my father consulted him professionally on small, uncontentious matters of probate or property. Gross was a genial bachelor with a sense of humor and a sardonic glint in his eye that made him a little intimidating. He kept up with world news and knew what was going on in our city; that made him a welcome guest for my civic-minded and intellectually inclined father. Even as a child, I could tell that Gross was more sophisticated than most of the adults I knew, but he fitted in seamlessly with the civil servants and small business people in our circle of the Milwaukee Jewish community. In fact, he *was* a small business person, nothing more and nothing less, who lunched at Benjy's Delicatessen to shoot the breeze, over corned-beef sandwiches, with the insurance brokers and furniture dealers who were his clients.

This is a book about legal ethics that focuses on the lawyer's role in enhancing or assaulting human dignity. That may sound like an awfully grandiose way to describe professionals like Cyril Gross whose activities are usually pretty mundane, and which have to do with money far more often than dignity. Isn't it only a small handful of lawyers – heroic defenders of the downtrodden – whose job consists of fighting for human dignity?

Not really. Although lawyers who fight for human rights certainly deserve admiration, fighting for dignity is not the only way of enhancing it. Lawyers are the primary administrators of the rule of law, the point of contact between citizens and their legal system. Lawyers like Cyril Gross make law's empire run (or not) on the ground. If the rule of law is a necessary condition for human rights and human dignity, lawyers in all fields will play a vital role in securing these goods. And the ethical character of the legal profession – the commitment of lawyers to the rule of law and the human dignity it helps secure – will determine whether the rule of law is anything more than a slogan.

Who are the lawyers?

Lawyers come in varying shapes and sizes. We may have a distorted image of lawyers, shaped by the hunks and hotties of TV dramas and Hollywood films. Distorted, but not completely false. Dispensing equal parts office sex and moral conundrums, shows like *LA Law* and *The Practice* have done a respectable job of teaching academic legal ethics to television viewers, because many of their plots come straight from actual cases passed along to the scriptwriters by lawyer-consultants. I expect that millions of people now know some fine points about the attorney–client privilege because they watch television. The office sex is probably exaggerated (I wouldn't know), and the climactic courtroom face-offs are absurd. For that matter, real-life clients of urban law firms are mostly businesses, not the individual clients of the TV shows. Basically, though, the shows do a reasonable job of dramatizing law firms and lawyers who are trying to do the right thing, with a few human, all-too-human lapses, in a hard-bitten world. From my vantage point as a law teacher, they are often lawyers I can imagine my students becoming, facing dilemmas straight out of the cases in my ethics textbook. But they bear almost no resemblance to Cyril Gross, or to most other lawyers I know.

We have other images of lawyers as well. There are the flamboyant criminal defense lawyers like Johnnie Cochran, and the rich Southern plaintiffs' lawyers in their custom-made suits, cowboy boots, and private jets – veteran villains of a thousand lawyer-bashing Wall Street Journal editorials. And their poorer cousins trolling for torts on late-night television, with phony-looking shelves of law books as the backdrop; and grandstanding US Attorneys announcing high-profile arrests. Popular culture does not, I think, offer a similarly well-etched stereotype of business lawyers in corporate counsels' offices and high-end law firms. Their practice is too unfamiliar, too invisible, and, for most people, too anesthetic to give rise to stereotypes. Neither do we know the corporate defense bar, except in occasional Hollywood movies that caricature them as robotic teams of interchangeable creeps in suits.

These different kinds of lawyers – visible and invisible, fictional, semifictional, and real – seem to have nothing much in common; and it has become a truism among legal sociologists and commentators that today we have many bars, not one bar, segmented by subspecialty and by the wealth and class of their clients.

In fact, however, all these lawyers have a good deal in common. They all went to law school, where they studied nearly identical basic curricula from a more or less uniform set of textbooks. As theorist Melvin Eisenberg observes, these textbooks teach "national law" – a construct that isn't really the law of any specific jurisdiction, but rather combines representative principles into a kind of legal Esperanto that provides what real Esperanto was supposed to: a common language.[1] All the lawyers learn the same basic techniques of reading legal texts, what law professors call "thinking like a lawyer." All are taught by professors who are, increasingly, drawn from national law schools and who teach national law in roughly the same way. All the lawyers in every state take the same state bar examination, and many states' bar exams test on "national law" as well as the state's specific variant of it. Most states require the same ethics exam (the Multistate Professional Responsibility Examination), which tests national law. And so, beneath their diversity, the lawyers inhabit a single, profession-wide interpretive community, with the same overall understanding of what makes law law. This fact allows us to speak coherently of a single legal profession. To an important extent, the uniformity of legal training is an indispensable material condition for maintaining the rule of law.

The rule of law and human dignity

We often speak about the rule of law as an abstract and highfalutin ideal. But the rule of law is no meaningless abstraction once we spell it out in tangible, everyday terms. When we do, it often turns out to mean something as mundane as the most humdrum cases of ordinary lawyers like Cyril Gross. For example: my neighbor, who came to the United States from Russia in the early 1990s, went back to Russia a few years later to sell her apartment. "The big difference between here and Moscow," she said, "is that in Moscow I can't deal with government offices by telephone. The answer you get to even the simplest question will be completely different depending on who answers the phone and how they feel that day. My sister owns a business. She says it's easier dealing with the mafia than the government, because at least when you pay the mafia protection money, they don't come back the next day saying it wasn't enough." So, among other things, the rule of law means getting questions answered on the telephone without having to worry about it. Or, as we might put it in more general terms, the rule of law presupposes an underlying uniformity and stability of official behavior. Private lawyers who explain the law to clients, and monitor or prod officials, help maintain

---

[1] Melvin Eisenberg, *The Concept of National Law and the Rule of Recognition*, 29 Fla. St. U. L. Rev. 1229 (2002). I borrow the image of Esperanto from Richard Posner, who did not mean it as a compliment. In an influential judicial opinion, Posner criticized a consolidated multi-state class action lawsuit in which "the district judge proposes ... a single trial before a single jury instructed in accordance with no actual law of any jurisdiction – a jury that will receive a kind of Esperanto instruction, merging the negligence standards of the 50 states and the District of Columbia." In re Rhone-Poulenc Rorer, Inc., 51 F.3d 1293, 1300 (7th Cir. 1995). Unlike Posner, I follow Eisenberg in viewing "legal Esperanto" as an important material condition for the rule of law.

uniformity and stability; obviously, so do government lawyers who write the regulations, protocols, and training manuals for officials.

In Kosovo, where one of my legal colleagues went to work for the UN "building rule of law capacity," the rule of law meant something equally mundane: getting municipal judges to take down their provocative Albanian flags from the courtrooms when Serbs were litigants, and teaching the foreign police enough about Kosovar law that they knew what evidence to collect when they investigated crimes.

In the United States, as in other rule-of-law regimes, we take thousands of minor institutional niceties like these for granted. We assume that inflammatory foreign flags will not hang in the courtroom. We assume that officials will answer questions over the telephone and that police will know what evidence to collect. We tend to reserve rule-of-law rhetoric for more exalted issues of due process. We think, for example, of the military lawyers appointed by the Pentagon to represent Guantánamo Bay detainees before military commissions where the rules are a travesty of fairness. These were not docile defenders of government policies. Instead, they challenged every aspect of the military commissions in every court they could find, denouncing their own employer in the press and fighting all the way to the Supreme Court.[2] I have met two of them – career Judge Advocate General's Corps officers facing the ultimate gut check, who rose to the challenge in extraordinary ways, and lost their promotions because they defended their clients too well.

Yet, to observe the rule of law in everyday life, we will do better looking at humdrum real-estate transactions or business contracts – say, a contract between a chain of gas stations and a paper company to provide paper towels for gas station bathrooms (an example used by the legal philosopher Lon Fuller).[3] For Fuller, law is not a body of statutes or doctrines; rather, it is the activity of lawyers as "architects of social structure." Law enhances human dignity by knitting together thousands of details that make it possible for ordinary people to accomplish ordinary business smoothly. Fuller's perspective on what lawyers do strongly pervades many of the arguments that follow. From this perspective, the rule of law depends on how Cyril Gross did his job, not just how heroic human rights lawyers do theirs. In an important sense, the pervasive, inconspicuous work of ordinary lawyers on humdrum cases makes the heroic work possible. It creates the baseline of regularity that allows us to see outrages for what they are. And, of course, it maintains the legal institutions that heroic human rights lawyers rely on for their successes and even for their physical safety.

[2] See Jonathan Mahler, *Commander Swift Objects*, N. Y. Times Mag., June 13, 2004.

[3] Lon L. Fuller, *The Lawyer as Architect of Social Structure*, in The Principles of Social Order: Selected Essays of Lon L. Fuller 265 (Kenneth I. Winston ed., 1981).

Obviously, the connection between the rule of law and the enhancement of human dignity is neither tight nor direct. Legal positivists remind us that there is no necessary connection between legality and morality. Laws and legal systems can be brutal, inhuman, and oppressive. All legal systems have been so at one time or another, and even the most enlightened systems still contain pockets of oppressiveness – and not only among anachronistic statutes left over from yesteryear. In what way, then, does the rule of law enhance human dignity? If the law is bad, won't law's rule be bad as well?

That is the wrong question. No technology of governance provides a magic bullet against brutality and oppression. The right question is how the rule of law stacks up against alternatives. Suppose we ask whether a brutal dictator will prefer to operate under the rule-of-law requirements of regularity, transparency, and constraint, or a regime of arbitrariness, secrecy, and unfettered discretion. I think the answer is obvious. Although no logical inconsistency exists between the rule-of-law virtues and substantively horrible laws, oppression is far more easily accomplished outside the rule of law than within, and it would be puzzling for an oppressor to bind himself to the rule of law.[4] Transparency may itself discourage brutality by exposing it to outside condemnation.

In practical terms, when states institute the rule of law, they transfer power to lawyers. To those who believe we are being smothered under a vast parasitic swarm of lawyers, this may seem like a problem, not a solution. I disagree completely. Historically, an independent bar, like an active and free press, has often formed an important counterweight to arbitrary authority. In his famous discussion of the American legal profession, Tocqueville observed that when a prince entrusts to lawyers "a despotism taking its shape from violence ... he ... receives it back from their hands with features of justice and law."[5] Fussy lawyerly formalism may be tedious and exasperating, but it domesticates power. Lawyers are trained to debate and interpret law by looking at its possible rational purposes, and this form of discourse also helps blunt the edges of oppression. As Fuller wrote, "when men are compelled to explain and justify their decisions, the effect will generally be to pull those decisions toward goodness, by whatever standards of ultimate goodness there are."[6] Furthermore, lawyers acting as architects of social structure – by drafting contracts, by incorporating businesses, by writing by-laws for organizations – contribute to the flourishing of civil society

---

[4] John Finnis makes this point in his exposition of Fuller. Finnis, Natural Law and Natural Rights 273–74 (1980).

[5] 1 Alexis de Tocqueville, Democracy in America 266 (J. P. Mayer ed., George Lawrence trans., Doubleday 1969).

[6] Lon L. Fuller, *Positivism and Fidelity to Law – A Reply to Professor Hart*, 71 Harv. L. Rev. 630, 636 (1958).

institutions that are themselves counterweights to oppressive state authority. Although the correlation between the rule of law and human dignity can fail in innumerable instances, human dignity has been better served in nations with mature legal systems and independent legal professions.

One theme of this book, then, is that ordinary law practice by ordinary lawyers deserves attention because it is central to the rule of law. I develop this theme most prominently in chapters 3 and 4. A second theme, developed and argued in chapter 2, is that familiar dilemmas in legal ethics can best be understood as defenses or assaults on human dignity – and, conversely, that one way to give content to the concept of human dignity is to examine how it emerges when people engage with lawyers and the legal system. In chapter 2, I examine four issues of legal ethics – the right to counsel, the duty of confidentiality, lawyers' paternalism toward clients, and the duty of pro bono service – and draw from them a naturalized account of human dignity as a relationship among people in which they are not humiliated. Non-humiliation plays a key role in my understanding of human dignity. Drawing on Avishai Margalit's idea that a decent society is one whose institutions do not humiliate people, I argue that human dignity should best be understood as a kind of conceptual shorthand referring to relations among people, rather than as a metaphysical property of individuals. Agents and institutions violate human dignity when they humiliate people, and so non-humiliation becomes a common-sense proxy for honoring human dignity.[7] This account, I believe, fits well with Fuller's ideas about human dignity and the rule of law that chapter 3 explores.

Chapter 5, by contrast, turns to the dark side of lawyers and human dignity. It examines the work of the "torture lawyers" – US government lawyers whose secret memoranda loopholed the law to provide cover for the torture of War on Terror prisoners. Although this is a much more time-bound, fact- and law-specific topic than the more philosophical subjects treated in the remainder of the book, it seems impossible to write about legal ethics and human dignity without discussing one of the most egregious cases in recent memory of lawyers twisting law to assault human dignity. It demonstrates that fussy lawyerly formalism does not always domesticate power, particularly when the lawyers can keep their handiwork secret. In the same chapter, however, I argue that the torture lawyers reached the results they did only by betraying their own craft values – a backhanded acknowledgment that the connection between legal ethics and human dignity is more than wishful thinking or happenstance.[8]

[7] Avishai Margalit, The Decent Society 1 (Naomi Goldblum trans., 1996). Margalit's idea draws on a traditional theme in Jewish ethics, and I develop it in those terms in chapters 2 and 8.

[8] This discussion draws on a more extended analysis of the most notorious of the torture memos, along with a philosophical examination of what makes torture the ultimate assault on human

Organizational evil

It seems entirely possible that the torture lawyers, sealed up in the echo chambers of the Justice Department and the Pentagon, never visualized the Abu Ghraib photos. For that matter, junior lawyers in the Office of Legal Counsel, told to research particular points of law or draft small bits of the argument in the torture memos, may not have grasped the significance of the entire enterprise. Or they may simply have shut their eyes to it. These possibilities raise the next major theme treated in this book – a theme that has preoccupied me for many years. This is the subject of *organizational evil*: the ways in which organizations – be they law firms, corporations, bureaucracies, or armies – can subdivide moral responsibility out of existence by parceling out tasks and knowledge so that no individual employee owns the action. Organizational evil does not require crooks and thugs. It can be done, as C. S. Lewis says, by "quiet men with white collars and cut fingernails and smooth-shaven cheeks who do not need to raise their voice."[9] Hannah Arendt once wrote that where ancient political thought distinguished rule by the one, the few, and the many, modern bureaucracies are "rule by nobody." She added that in rule by nobody, responsibility vanishes, and the outcome can be tyranny without an identifiable tyrant.[10] Obviously, Arendt had in mind the "writing-desk perpetrators" of totalitarian regimes, but the moral problem posed by divided responsibility and fragmented knowledge doesn't require lurid or atrocious examples.[11]

As I now conceptualize it, the problem of divided responsibility actually encompasses at least three distinct moral issues: the responsibility of supervisors who contrive to maintain their own ignorance of what their subordinates are doing; the responsibility of subordinates ordered to do wrong; and the more general problem of complicity, the subtle ways in which

dignity. David Luban, *Liberalism, Torture, and the Ticking Bomb*, in The Torture Debate in America 35 (Karen J. Greenberg ed., 2005) – an expanded version of an essay published first in 91 Virginia L. Rev. 1425 (2005), and excerpted in Harper's Magazine, March 2006, at 11–16.

[9] C. S. Lewis, The Screwtape Letters and Screwtape Proposes a Toast, at x (Collier, 1962).

[10] Hannah Arendt, On Violence 81 (1970).

[11] See Luban, *Making Sense of Moral Meltdowns*, which appears in slightly different versions in Lawyers' Ethics and the Pursuit of Social Justice: A Critical Reader 355 (Susan D. Carle ed., 2005), and Moral Leadership: The Theory and Practice of Power, Judgment, and Policy 57 (Deborah L. Rhode ed., Stanford University Press 2006). The latter version focuses on business executives, the former on lawyers. I first addressed the problem of divided responsibility in an essay written at the fortieth anniversary of the Nuremberg trials, and then at greater length in a paper co-authored with Alan Strudler and David Wasserman. Luban, *The Legacies of Nuremberg*, 54 Soc. Res. 779 (1987), reprinted in my book Legal Modernism (1994); Luban, Strudler, and Wasserman, *Moral Responsibility in the Age of Bureaucracy*, 90 Mich. L. Rev. 2348 (1992).

organizational members aid and abet each other in wrongdoing, sometimes simply by providing mutual moral support or encouraging group-think. Chapters 6 and 7 ("Contrived Ignorance" and "The Ethics of Wrongful Obedience") examine the first two of these problems, while chapter 8 considers one aspect of the problem of complicity: the way in which we unconsciously align our own moral compass with the prevailing direction of the people around us, who are watching us and doing exactly the same thing.[12] All three chapters address problems that range far wider than legal ethics, but the examples I use to focus discussion are drawn from law-firm practice, and chapter 8 was originally written for a post-Enron conference on integrity in corporate law and business. A bit perversely, I argue that the quest for integrity might be the problem, not the solution, because – as numerous social psychology experiments suggest – we often harmonize our practices and principles by gerrymandering the principles to rationalize the practices.

At this point, of course, the topic has strayed very far from the modest, constructive contributions to the rule of law of the Cyril Grosses of the world. Significantly, Gross was a solo practitioner, not a stressed-out senior associate in a thousand-lawyer law firm or the general counsel of an aggressive Enron-like corporation whose officers think that laws are just red tape and deadweight. Demographers of the legal profession note that the trend over time has been for firms to get larger, for a higher proportion of lawyers to work in large firms, and for young lawyers to work in large organizations in even higher proportions.[13] While sole practitioners like Gross still compose a third of the profession, their number is diminishing and so is their proportion of total lawyer income. I don't mean to romanticize solo practitioners, who are not all the salt of the earth; and Fuller's praise of lawyers as architects of social structure obviously applies to lawyers in large organizations, perhaps far more than to solo practitioners. Nevertheless, the movement of the legal profession to large and increasingly bureaucratized organizations means that the pathologies of organizational morality become increasingly important. The dark themes of chapters 5 through 8 must counterbalance the rosier picture of the legal profession I paint in chapters 2 through 4.

---

[12] For a more general treatment of complicity, see Christopher L. Kutz, Complicity: Ethics and Law for a Collective Age (2000). My own thinking about this subject has also been strongly influenced by Sanford H. Kadish, *Complicity, Cause and Blame: A Study in the Interpretation of Doctrine*, 73 Cal. L. Rev. 323 (1985).

[13] See Clara N. Carson, The Lawyer Statistical Report: The US Legal Profession in 2000 7–10 (2004); After the JD: First Results of a National Study of Legal Careers 27 (NALP Foundation/ABF 2006).

The adversary system and moral accountability

The most elementary problem of divided responsibility facing lawyers results from the adversarial structure of common-law legal systems. Chapter 1, "The Adversary System Excuse," is the oldest paper in the book (I published it as a working paper in 1980). It was my first significant foray into legal ethics, and formed the core of my first major book on the subject. I include it here because the present book explores different themes and implications of its argument – and also because I have modified the argument significantly.

My target in "The Adversary System Excuse" is a view of legal ethics that in *Lawyers and Justice* I called the "standard conception of the lawyer's role," but that I now call *neutral partisanship*. Neutral partisanship sees lawyers as hired guns, whose duty of loyalty to their clients means they must, if necessary, do everything the law permits to advance their clients' interests – regardless of whether those interests are worthy or base, and regardless of how much collateral damage the lawyer inflicts on third parties. Thomas Babington Macaulay asked rhetorically "whether it be right that a man should, with a wig on his head, and a band round his neck, do for a guinea what, without those appendages, he would think it wicked and infamous to do for an empire."[14] Proponents of neutral partisanship don't regard Macaulay's question as merely rhetorical, and their answer is yes. They see lawyers as agents of their clients, professionally obligated to do whatever the client wants done if the law permits it. After all, the client is entitled to do anything within his legal rights, and a lawyer who agrees to represent him takes on the responsibility of serving as the client's proxy.

Not only are lawyers their clients' partisans and proxies, but professionalism requires that lawyers remain morally neutral toward lawful client ends, refraining from waving a censorious finger at the client or pulling their punches out of moral squeamishness. (Hence the label "neutral partisanship.") If so, lawyers acting in their professional role cannot be held morally accountable for client ends and the means they use to pursue them. Neutral partisanship is non-accountable partisanship.

These are very aggressive claims, and I argue that they are false. As Macaulay suggests, they imply that lawyers have a role morality that can differ dramatically from morality outside the role, what we might call "common morality." How can that be? Moral accountability is not something we can put on and take off like a barrister's wig. If a lawyer acting on a client's behalf ruins innocent people, can she really excuse herself by saying, "It's not my doing, it's my client's doing" or "It's the law's doing"? Excuses like these sound like a hit man's rationalizations.

[14] Thomas Babington Macaulay, *Francis Bacon*, in 2 Critical and Historical Essays 317 (1926).

Often, lawyers say it's the adversary system's doing. The adversary system pits interest against interest and lawyer against lawyer in a contest to determine whose right gets vindicated. As Monroe Freedman pointed out in *Lawyers' Ethics in an Adversary System* – one of the pillars of the modern legal ethics literature – the adversary system requires advocates to hew to their clients and let adversaries and others take care of themselves, even when gross injustice results.

"The Adversary System Excuse" argues that the excuse is only as good as the adversary system itself, and the adversary system is not nearly as good as its defenders believe. Defenders offer an idealized picture of a system designed to elicit maximum input from the contesting parties. In reality, the parties labor prodigiously to keep the bad evidence out, or, better still, to manipulate the system so their adversaries never get their day in court. One issue on which I break decisively from Fuller is his defense of the adversary system, which in my view fails.[15] We ought to retain the adversary system because it isn't demonstrably worse than its alternatives. But if that is the highest praise we can offer, the adversary system cannot underwrite lawyers' blanket disclaimer of moral accountability for the damage they do. Even though I have largely followed Fuller's boosterism about the constructive work that lawyers do, the failure of the adversary system excuse makes my overall account of legal ethics considerably less sunny than Fuller's. To-gether, the problem of organizational evil and the excessive attachment of the legal profession to neutral partisanship sometimes lead lawyers to assault rather than enhance human dignity.

In one significant respect, however, I have modified the essay's critique of the adversary system. If the weakness of the adversary system lies in the incentives it creates for lawyers to hide or exclude evidence, its strength appears when lawyers argue points of law that do not rely on evidence. Here, the virtues of free and full debate can indeed manifest themselves, and a commitment to rational discussion of law speaks in favor of the adversary system. Stuart Hampshire, in two of the most significant philosophical books in recent years, argues forcefully that we have no image of procedural justice more basic than hearing all sides of arguments, and I accept his argument.[16]

---

[15] I discussed his defense briefly in the original version of "The Adversary System Excuse," then returned to it in greater depth in *Rediscovering Fuller's Legal Ethics*, published concurrently in 11 Geo. J. Legal Ethics 801 (1998) and Rediscovering Fuller: Essays on Implicit Law and Institutional Design 193 (Willem J. Witteveen and Wibren van der Burg eds., University of Amsterdam Press, 1999). In this book, I have substituted an excerpt from the later paper for the original discussion.

[16] See Hampshire, Justice Is Conflict (2000); Hampshire, Innocence and Experience (1990). I have discussed Hampshire's splendid books in a pair of untitled reviews, one in 88 J. Phil. 317 (1991), the other in 112 Ethics 156 (2001).

Outside this context, however, the critique of the adversary system implies that lawyers cannot duck moral accountability. In *Lawyers and Justice* I argued that if lawyers are morally accountable for their representations, they can no longer passively acquiesce in the agent's role. They must become moral activists, using law practice to further justice. Much of the book focused on public interest law practice on behalf of progressive causes. Here, I pursue the critique of neutral partisanship in a different direction. The conclusion of "The Adversary System Excuse" is, carefully stated, that often lawyers' moral obligations will differ very little from those of a non-lawyer in similar circumstances. But it may not be easy to figure out what the non-lawyer's responsibilities are. As philosopher Richard Wasserstrom observed thirty years ago, neutral partisanship allows lawyers to inhabit a simplified moral world.[17] Take it away and the simplicity vanishes. In fraught, adversarial situations, we will often have a hard time figuring out which principles apply ("Turnabout is fair play," or "Two wrongs don't make a right"? "Turn the other cheek," or "Fight fire with fire"?), or how to weigh them against each other. Real cases, with real people, usually have bad behavior on all sides. Eliminating the stripped-down, simplified moral code of neutral partisanship lands lawyers back in the same messy, dilemma-ridden, ambiguous moral world as everyone else.

The messiness of moral life

The messiness of moral life forms the primary topic of my last chapter, which explores legal ethics through a reading of Anthony Trollope's *Orley Farm*. *Orley Farm* is partly about legal ethics, and it explores situations of intense moral ambiguity, where self-deception runs rampant, where good people do bad things for mixed motives, bad people sometimes have right on their side, and even the best people have flaws, sometimes nearly unforgivable ones. Significantly, Trollope's lawyers act as neutral partisans (broadly speaking) for more complex reasons than those underlying the adversary system excuse, and their partisanship can seem both noble and base. Concluding the book in this way, I aim to remind readers that criticizing excuses, or pointing to the importance of broad values like human dignity, barely scratches the surface of moral judgment in a messy world. The chapter also pays homage to Thomas Shaffer, a legal ethicist whose work I greatly admire. Shaffer is best known for his eloquent writing on legal ethics and religion, and the chapter allows me to situate some of my views about moral complexity, human dignity, and non-humiliation within my own understanding of Jewish ethics.

---

[17] Richard A. Wasserstrom, *Lawyers as Professionals: Some Moral Issues*, 5 Human Rights 1, 8 (1976).

An anonymous reader of these papers noticed that I seem "often on the fence, and more ambivalent as to the lawyer's proper role in the later papers than in the earlier ... One would hope for a clearer stance from one who has spent his entire career writing in this area." At first, I was stung by these comments. On reflection, I believe the anonymous reader is asking for something that moral philosophy delivers at its peril: crisp principles to resolve difficult moral dilemmas in ambiguous situations where values collide and every result is an unhappy one for somebody. Philosophical analysis serves its purpose when it exposes bad arguments and inadequate rationalizations like the adversary system excuse. But moral theories and the principles they generate are too abstract to be directly useful in practical deliberation. In the words of Oliver Wendell Holmes, Jr., general propositions do not decide particular cases. Furthermore, in their mature forms the moral theories incorporate exceptions and refinements introduced to take care of troublesome counter-examples. Once their purity is breached in this way, it begs the question to use the theories to resolve hard practical dilemmas, because there is no *a priori* way to tell whether the dilemma is itself a counter-example that the theory should accommodate rather than dissolve. Novelists like Trollope remind you that there are more things in heaven and Earth than are dreamt of in your philosophy.

Readers of *Lawyers and Justice* may regard the present book as more complacent and conservative in its overall approach. Instead of focusing on moral activists using law as an instrument of social reform, I now emphasize the ordinary work of ordinary lawyers. Fred Schauer has perceptively described Fuller's work as "insider jurisprudence."[18] Is that true of the present book as well?

I don't see it that way. My admiration for public interest lawyers has not diminished a whit. But they represent a very small segment of the legal profession; and in any case, the ideal of moral activism applies to all lawyers, not just public interest lawyers. Moral activism means accepting rather than denying moral responsibility for law practice, and therefore embracing the prospect that sometimes lawyers must confront their clients about the injustice of their causes. The argument of this book seems to me fully continuous with that of *Lawyers and Justice*, although here I place less emphasis on public interest law and more on the constructive work lawyers do in more routine practice.

Nevertheless, after two-and-a-half decades teaching in law schools I can hardly deny being an insider. Although I am not myself a lawyer and have no law degree, spending a career among lawyers and law students has given me a broader and far more sympathetic appreciation of the profession than I had when I began writing about it in 1980. An important turning point occurred

---

[18] Frederick Schauer, *Fuller's Internal Point of View*, 13 Law & Phil. 285 (1994), 305.

in 1992, when my University of Maryland colleague Michael Millemann invited me to partner with legal clinic lawyers as an "ethics consultant" and co-teacher. This invitation began a multi-year involvement in clinical education over a variety of issues: landlord–tenant law, special education placements, and criminal defense. (For readers unfamiliar with law-school clinics: they involve students representing real clients, typically low-income clients, in real cases, under the supervision of expert law teachers.) I continued this involvement at Georgetown, teaching the classroom component of a clinical ethics course, and participating in Georgetown's political asylum clinic. As a non-lawyer, I obviously could not join the student-lawyers and their advisors in representing clients, but my consulting and teaching role provided a participant's point of view far different from that of a philosophical commentator from the sidelines. Ethical questions that seemed straightforward from the spectator's point of view suddenly seemed far more difficult and ambiguous. I thought frequently about a story I once heard involving a famous mathematical decision theorist who was contemplating a job offer at another university. When a friend suggested that he use his own methods to decide what to do, he supposedly snapped, "Don't be silly. This is real." It seemed clear that without understanding the participant's perspective, the philosophical spectator runs the risk of glib, abstract moralism. On the other hand, participants labor under tremendous psychological pressure that distorts judgment in their own favor and that of their clients. Neither perspective seems reliable. Good judgment, it seems, must somehow integrate, or at least alternate between, the outsider's and insider's perspectives (a conclusion that Millemann and I reached in a 1995 article).[19] The difficulty of doing this no doubt explains some of the "fence sitting" that my reader complained about; but it also generated many of the ideas in several of the book's chapters.[20]

---

[19] For description and reflection, see David Luban & Michael Millemann, *Good Judgment: Ethics Teaching in Dark Times*, 9 Geo. J. Legal Ethics 31 (1995).

[20] There is another, more philosophical reason for my greater attachment to the insider's perspective in the present book. In a review essay of *Lawyers and Justice*, David Wasserman pointed out a significant difficulty in the argument – an equivocation between balancing role morality against common morality (Wasserman calls the balancing approach a "sophisticated act consequentialism") and an approach that gives some presumption or priority to the demands of the role. David Wasserman, *Should a Good Lawyer Do the Right Thing? David Luban on the Morality of Adversary Representation*, 49 Md. L. Rev. 392, 395–404 (1990). Reflecting on this problem, I came to believe, based on an argument of moral psychology, that the latter is the better approach. It is simply impossible to maintain coherency in the role without giving some, defeasible, priority to its demands. Luban, *Freedom and Constraint in Legal Ethics: Some Mid-Course Corrections to* Lawyers and Justice, 49 Md. L. Rev. 424, 434–52 (1990). This correction marks a small but significant departure from the conclusion of "The Adversary System Excuse," that lawyers' moral responsibilities are no different from those of non-lawyers in analogous situations. Nowadays, I prefer to treat the role obligation as a baseline

A note on the text

I originally wrote the chapters as separate essays, all but two previously published. Chapter 1 dates back over twenty-five years, but the remainder were written over the last decade or so. I have revised all of them, several quite extensively.

Returning to old work is at best a mixed pleasure. I rediscovered some arguments and ideas I had forgotten about. More often, I found substantive errors and stylistic excesses that were sometimes excruciating to read. How could I have thought that? How could I have said it in print? How could I have imagined that this juvenile witticism was clever? In places, my views have evolved over time. Some of the essays floated offhand speculations – trial balloons – that I took up more systematically in subsequent papers, only to discover in the process that my original idea wasn't quite right the way I originally stated it.

The result was a stack of papers that included inconsistencies of both substance and style. How to proceed? One can take two approaches to anthologizing previously published work. The easy way leaves it intact, on the theory that the anthology's main purpose is to make scattered, hard-to-find essays available in a single location. Here, I chose the alternative approach: revising and trying to get it right this time around. More than that, I have tried to knit the essays together into a single connected set of arguments. To that end, I have regularized terminology, reconciled inconsistencies, added cross-references, removed redundancies, and shifted material around to more natural points in the argument. In some essays I replaced outdated examples with fresher ones, and bad formulations with what I trust are better ones. In a few places, I substituted pieces of other essays, not included in this book, which had improved on less satisfactory versions of the arguments in the original. (These substitutions are indicated in the notes.) The only major repair I have not attempted is systematically updating references to the scholarly literature. The literature on legal ethics is voluminous, and it seemed on the whole that it would not be worth the trouble to multiply footnotes. I must therefore ask forgiveness from authors whose important work on the same problems is not cited in these pages because it appeared after my essay was published.

I have, however, indulged in substantial self-citation. Normally, self-citation is an unattractive practice. But over the years I have written papers

---

presumption, which can be overridden by strong moral reasons to break the role. Where the former conclusion could be read as discounting professional obligations entirely when they conflict with common morality, I now give more presumptive weight to professional obligations.

that space doesn't permit me to include in this book, which offer more detailed treatment of ideas that appear here in abbreviated form. With some effort, I could have incorporated the more detailed treatments. But to save this book from bloat, it seemed simpler to refer readers to papers where I develop subjects merely alluded to here.

I

The ethics in legal ethics

1

The adversary system excuse

It is not the lawyer's responsibility to believe or not to believe – the lawyer is a technician ... Law is an adversarial profession. The other side is out to get your client. Your job is to protect your client and the nonsense they hand out in these ethics courses today – if the young people listen to this kind of nonsense, there isn't going to be such a thing as an intelligent defense in a civil or criminal case.[1]

A conscience ... put out to lease is not conscience but the evasion of it, except for that specious semblance of conscience which may be discerned in one's blind obedience to the authority that happens to be in command.[2]

Introduction

Holding forth at table in 1831, Samuel Taylor Coleridge turned to the behavior of lawyers. "There is undoubtedly a limit to the exertions of an advocate for his client," he said, for "the advocate has no right, nor is it his duty, to do that for his client which his client *in foro conscientiae* has no right to do for himself."[3] Thirteen years later, William Whewell elaborated the same point:

Every man is, in an unofficial sense, by being a moral agent, a Judge of right and wrong, and an Advocate of what is right ... This general character of a moral agent, he cannot put off, by putting on any professional character ... If he mixes up his character as an Advocate, with his character as a Moral Agent ... he acts immorally. He makes the Moral Rule subordinate to the Professional Rule. He sells to his Client,

[1] Roy Cohn, interview, Nat'l L. J., Dec. 1, 1980, at 46.
[2] Aurel Kolnai, *Erroneous Conscience*, in Ethics, Value and Reality 7 (Bernard Williams & David Wiggins eds., 1978).
[3] Samuel Taylor Coleridge, *Duties and Needs of an Advocate*, in The Table Talk and Omniana of Samuel Taylor Coleridge 140–41 (T. Ashe ed., George Bell and Sons, 1888).

not only his skill and learning, but himself. He makes it the Supreme Object of his life to be, not a good man, but a successful Lawyer.[4]

Whewell's position is not commonly acknowledged to be valid. George Sharswood, whose 1854 *Legal Ethics* is the ancestor of the current ABA Model Rules of Professional Conduct, wrote: "The lawyer, who refuses his professional assistance because in his judgment the case is unjust and indefensible, usurps the functions of both judge and jury."[5] A lawyer is not to judge the morality of the client's cause; it is irrelevant to the morality of the representation. That, I think, is the official view of most lawyers: the lawyer's morality is distinct from, and not implicated in, the client's. Murray Schwartz labels this the "Principle of Nonaccountability":

When acting as an advocate for a client ... a lawyer is neither legally, professionally, nor morally accountable for the means used or the ends achieved.

Add to this the "Principle of Professionalism":

When acting as an advocate, a lawyer must, within the established constraints upon professional behavior, maximize the likelihood that the client will prevail[6]

and you get what is usually taken to be the professional morality of lawyers. Gerald Postema calls it the "standard conception of the lawyer's role"; William Simon says that these principles (which he titles the "Principle of Neutrality" and the "Principle of Partisanship") define partisan advocacy.[7] Borrowing Simon's terminology, we may call the view of legal ethics captured by them *Neutral Partisanship*. Shortly after introducing these principles, Schwartz raises two points about them:

It might be argued, that the law cannot convert an immoral act into a moral one, nor a moral act into an immoral one, by simple fiat. Or, more fundamentally, the lawyer's nonaccountability might be illusory if it depends upon the morality of the adversary system and if that system is immoral ... If either [of these challenges] were to prove persuasive, the justification for the application of the Principle of Nonaccountability to moral accountability would disappear.[8]

---

[4] 1 William Whewell, The Elements of Morality, Including Polity 258–59 (John W. Parker, 1845).

[5] George Sharswood, A Compend of Lectures on the Aims and Duties of the Profession of the Law 84 (T. & J. W. Johnson, 1854).

[6] Murray Schwartz, *The Professionalism and Accountability of Lawyers*, 66 Calif. L. Rev. 669, 673 (1978).

[7] Gerald J. Postema, *Moral Responsibility in Professional Ethics*, 55 NYU L. Rev. 63, 73 (1980). William Simon, *The Ideology of Advocacy: Procedural Justice and Professional Ethics*, 1978 Wisc. L. Rev. 29, 36–37.

[8] Schwartz, *Professionalism and Accountability*, supra note 6, at 674.

Schwartz raises these issues but does not address them. My aim in this chapter is to meet them head-on. I shall argue (1) that a lawyer's nonaccountability does depend on the adversary system; (2) that the adversary system is not a sufficient basis for it; and (3) thus, that while the Principle of Professionalism may be true, the Principle of Nonaccountability is not.

This, I believe, will defend the morality of conscience – the position of Coleridge and Whewell – against the claim that professional obligation can override it.

Institutional excuses

On February 7, 1973, Richard Helms, the former director of the Central Intelligence Agency, lied to a Senate committee about American involvement in the overthrow of the Allende government in Chile. Santiago proved to be Helms's Waterloo: he was caught out in his perjury and prosecuted.[9] Helms claimed that requirements of national security led him to lie to Congress. We can only speculate, however, on how the court would have viewed this excuse, for in fact the case never came to trial; Helms's lawyer, the redoubtable Edward Bennett Williams, found an ingenious way to back the government down. He argued that national security information was relevant to Helms's defense and must be turned over to Helms, thereby confronting the government with the unpleasant choice of dropping the action or making public classified and presumably vital information. The government chose the first option and allowed Helms to plead guilty to a misdemeanor charge.[10]

I don't know if anyone ever asked Williams to justify his actions; had anyone attempted to do so, they would presumably have been told that Williams was simply doing his job as a criminal defense attorney. The parallel with Helms's own excuse is clear – he was doing his job, Williams was doing his – but it is hard to miss the irony. Helms tried to conceal national security information; therefore he lied. Williams, acting on Helms's behalf, threatened to reveal national security information as part of a tactic that has come to be called "graymailing." One man's ends are another man's means. Neither lying nor graymailing (to say nothing of destabilizing elected regimes) is morally pretty, but a job is a job and that was the job that was. So, at any rate, runs the excuse.

---

[9] Mitchell Rogovin, *"Graymail": Shaded Variant of a Darker Hue*, Legal Times of Washington, March 26, 1979; see Lawrence Meyer, *Justice Dept. is Examining Helms' Testimony on CIA*, Wash. Post, February 12, 1975, at A1, A12.

[10] Joe Trento, *Inside the Helms File*, Nat'l. L.J., Dec. 22, 1980, at 1.

We may want to reject these "good soldier" excuses or we may find them valid and persuasive. That is the issue I shall address here. A second gray-mailing example will warm us to our topic:

In instances [of merger cases involving firms in competition with each other] in which the [Federal Trade] commission's legal case looked particularly good and none of the usual defenses appeared likely to work, the staff was confronted several times with the argument that if they did not refrain from prosecution and allow the merger, one of the proposed merger partners would close down its operations and dismiss its employees ... Of course, the mere announcement of the threat to close the plant generates enormous political pressure on the prosecutor not to go forward. Ought lawyers to be engaged in such strategies for the purpose of consummating an other-wise anticompetitive and illegal transaction involving the joinder of two substantial competitors?[11]

On the lawyers' advice, the firms played a nice game of chicken: closing down by stages, they laid off a few workers each day until the FTC cried uncle.

What could justify the conduct of these lawyers? A famous answer is the following statement of Lord Henry Brougham:

An advocate, in the discharge of his duty, knows but one person in all the world, and that person is his client. To save that client by all means and expedients, and at all hazards and costs to other persons, and, amongst them, to himself, is his first and only duty; and in performing this duty he must not regard the alarm, the torments, the destruction which he may bring upon others. Separating the duty of a patriot from that of an advocate, he must go on reckless of consequences, though it should be his unhappy fate to involve his country in confusion.[12]

This speech, made in his 1820 defense of Queen Caroline against King George IV's charge of adultery, was itself an act of graymail. Reminiscing years later, Brougham said that the king would recognize in it a tacit threat to reveal his secret marriage to a Catholic, a marriage that, were it to become public knowledge, would cost him his crown.[13] Knowing this background of Brougham's oft-quoted statement might make us take a dim view of it; it has, nevertheless, frequently been admired as the most eloquent encapsulation of the advocate's job.

Brougham's statement invites philosophical reflection, for at first blush it is equally baffling to utilitarianism, and moral rights theory, and Kantianism.

---

[11] Daniel Schwartz, *The "New" Legal Ethics & the Administrative Law Bar*, in The Good Lawyer: Lawyers' Roles and Lawyers' Ethics 247–48 (David Luban ed., Rowman & Allanheld, 1983).

[12] 2 Trial of Queen Caroline 8 (J. Nightingale ed., J. Robins & Co., Albion Press, 1820–21).

[13] David Mellinkoff, The Conscience of a Lawyer 188 (1973).

The client's utility matters more than that of the rest of the world put together. No one else's moral rights matter. Other people are merely means to the client's ends.[14] Moral theory seems simply to reject Brougham's imperatives. Nor does the Biblical morality of the Golden Rule and the twin injunctions to love your neighbor as yourself and love the stranger as yourself (Lev. 19:18, 34) look with greater kindness on the proposition that an advocate knows only one person in all the world, and that person is his client.

They are, however, universalizable over lawyers, or so it is claimed. The idea seems to be that the role of lawyer, hence the social institutions that set up this role, reparse the Moral Law, relaxing some moral obligations and imposing new ones. In the words of an Australian appellate court, "Our system of administering justice necessarily imposes upon those who practice advocacy duties which have no analogies, and the system cannot dispense with their strict observance."[15]

The system of which the court speaks is the so-called "adversary system of justice." My main question is this: Does the adversary system really justify Brougham's position? I hope that the example of Helms and his lawyers has convinced you that a more general issue is lurking here, the issue of what I shall call *institutional excuses*. We can state the general question this way: Can a person appeal to a social institution in which he or she occupies a role in order to excuse conduct that would be morally culpable were anyone else to do it? Plausibly, examples exist in which the answer is yes: we do not call it murder when a soldier kills a sleeping enemy in wartime, although it is surely immoral for you or me to do it. There are also cases where the answer is no, as in the job "concentration camp commandant" or "professional strikebreaker." Here, we feel, the immorality of the job is so great that it accuses, not excuses, the person who holds it.

This suggests that an important feature of a successful institutional excuse is that the institution is itself justified. I think that is partly right, but I do not think it is the whole story: I shall argue that the *kind* of justification of the institution that can be offered is germane to the success of the excuses it provides.

The adversary system and the two principles

Sometimes a lawyer pursuing a case finds herself compelled to do something outrageous. Graymailing is one example. A second is the Lake Pleasant bodies case, in which lawyers Frank Belge and Frank Armani, having been

---

[14] See Edward Dauer & Arthur Leff, *Correspondence: The Lawyer as Friend*, 86 Yale L. J. 573, 581 (1977).

[15] Tukiar and the King, 52 Commw. L. R. 335, 347 (Austl., 1934), quoted in Mellinkoff, The Conscience of a Lawyer, supra note 13, at 273.

told by their client Robert Garrow of two murders he committed, found and photographed the bodies but kept the information to themselves for half a year – this despite the fact that the father of one of the victims, knowing that Armani was representing an accused murderer, personally pleaded with him to tell him if he knew anything about his daughter.[16]

Such spectacular examples could be multiplied, but I think the point is made. A more important point is that the spectacular examples are not the only problem – they only dramatize it. I dare say that all litigators have had cases where, in their heart of hearts, they wanted their client to lose or wished that a distasteful action did not need to be performed. The problem is that (recollecting Brougham's words) "to save that client ... [the lawyer] must not regard the alarm, the torments, the destruction which he may bring upon others."[17] On the face of it, this is as terse a characterization of amorality as one could hope to find. Of course, that was not Brougham's intention; he meant to be stating a moral ideal. If so, however, it is reminiscent of Nietzsche's description of the old Teutonic code: "To practice loyalty and, for the sake of loyalty, to risk honor and blood even for evil and dangerous things."[18] Loyalty outweighs the evil of the cause – except, of course, that it does nothing of the sort. Evil remains evil, and loyalty to evil remains just that: loyalty to evil.

Lawyers phrase the ideal as "zealous advocacy," and the current ABA Model Rules of Professional Conduct enjoin lawyers to "act with commitment and dedication to the interests of the client and with zeal in advocacy on the client's behalf."[19] This means that a lawyer should "take whatever lawful and ethical measures are required to vindicate a client's cause or endeavor.[20] It sounds nicer than Zarathustra or Brougham, but in fact there is no difference: the zealous advocate is supposed to press the client's interests to the limit of the legal, regardless of the "torments or destruction" this wreaks on others.

---

[16] For Armani's riveting account of this celebrated case, see Tom Alibrandi & Frank H. Armani, Privileged Information (1984).

[17] The damages to all concerned in the Lake Pleasant bodies case were considerable: the parents of the victims were anguished, the public aghast, the tourism business in Lake Pleasant harmed because of the unsolved disappearances, Garrow convicted and sentenced to thirty-five-years-to-life, Belge and Armani nearly ruined. In a surreal twist, Armani discovered during Garrow's trial that, during his serial-rape spree, Garrow had at one point been stalking Armani's daughter. Garrow eventually escaped from prison, and the frightened Armani revealed to the police Garrow's preferred method for evading capture – something Garrow had described in the same confidential conversations with Armani and Belge that they had risked all to protect. The police used the confidential information Armani gave them to locate Garrow. They shot him dead. Ibid.

[18] Friedrich Nietzsche, Thus Spoke Zarathustra, in The Portable Nietzsche 171 (Walter Kaufmann ed. and trans., Viking Press, 1954).

[19] ABA Model Rules of Professional Conduct, Rule 1.3, cmt [1].   [20] Ibid.

Nor does the phrase "lawful and ethical" mitigate this. Lawyers understand "ethical" to refer to the law governing professional ethics, not law-independent moral principles, and the Model Rules carefully explain that a lawyer's representation of the client "does not constitute an endorsement of the client's political, economic, social or moral views or activities" – a version of Schwartz's Principle of Nonaccountability that disclaims lawyer responsibility for the moral character of client representation.[21] As for "lawful," the law is inherently double-edged: any rule imposed to limit zealous advocacy (or any other form of conduct, for that matter) may be used by an adversary as an offensive weapon. In the words of former Judge Marvin E. Frankel, "the object always is to beat every plowshare into a sword."[22] The rules of discovery, for example, initiated to enable one side to find out crucial facts from the other, are used nowadays to delay trial or impose added expense on the other side; conversely, one might respond to an interrogatory by delivering to the discoverer several tons of miscellaneous documents, to run up their legal bills or conceal a needle in a haystack. Rules barring lawyers from representations involving conflicts of interest may equally be used by adversaries to drive up the other side's costs by having their counsel disqualified; civil discovery rules sanctioning lawyers for frivolous litigation documents can be invoked by adversaries to punish their foes and intimidate them into abandoning their claims. The general problem of double-edgedness is described by the novelist Yasunari Kawabata:

When a law is made, the cunning that finds loopholes goes to work. We cannot deny that there is a certain slyness ... a slyness which, when rules are written to prevent slyness, makes use of the rules themselves.[23]

It is not just the rules governing lawyer conduct that are double-edged – double-edgedness is an essential feature of any law because any restraint imposed on human behavior in the name of just social policy may be used to restrain behavior when circumstances make this an unjust outcome. This is the unbridgeable gap between formal and substantive justice. David Mellinkoff gives these examples:

The law intended to stop sharpers from claiming money that is not owed (the Statute of Frauds) may sometimes defeat a just debt, because the claim was not in writing.
    The law intended to stop a man from holding off suit until defense becomes impossible – memories grown dim, witnesses dead or missing – (the Statute of Limitations) may sometimes defeat a just suit, because it was not filed fast enough.

[21] ABA Model Rules 1.2(b).   [22] Marvin Frankel, Partisan Justice 18 (1980).
[23] Yasunari Kawabata, The Master of Go 54 (Edward Seidensticker trans., Alfred A. Knopf, 1972).

The law intended to prevent designing grown-ups from imposing on children (the defense of infancy) may defeat a just claim, because the man who signed the contract was 20 instead of 21.

The law intended to give a man, for all his misfortunes, a new start in life (the bankruptcy laws) may defeat a widow's just claim for the money she needs to live on.[24]

The double-edgedness of law underlines the moral problem involved in representing a client "zealously within the bounds of the law." If on the one hand this means forwarding legal claims that are morally dubious, as in Mellinkoff's examples, on the other it means pushing claims to the limit of the law and then a bit further, into the realm of what is "colorably" the limit of the law.[25] "Zeal" means zeal at the margin of the legal, and thus well past the margin of whatever moral and political insight constitutes the "spirit" of the law in question.[26] The limits of the law inevitably lie beyond moral limits, and zealous advocacy always means zeal at the margin.

It is at this point that the adversary system looms large, for it provides the institutional excuse for the duty of zealous advocacy. Each side of an adversary proceeding is represented by a lawyer whose sole obligation is to present that side as forcefully as possible; anything less, it is claimed, would subvert the operation of the system. The 1969 ABA Code of Professional Responsibility states the matter quite clearly: "The duty of a lawyer to his client and his duty to the legal system are the same: to represent his client zealously within the bounds of the law."[27]

Everything rides on this argument. Lawyers have to assert legal interests unsupported by moral rights all the time. Asserting legal interests is what they do, and everyone can't be in the right on all issues. Unless zealous advocacy could be justified by relating it to some larger social good, the lawyer's role would be morally impossible. That larger social good, we are told, is justice, and the adversary system is supposed to be the best way of attaining it.

Indeed, it is misleading to call this Justification by the Adversary System an *argument*. It is more like a presupposition accepted by all parties before the arguments begin. Even lawyers with nothing good to say about the legal system in general believe that their current actions are justified or excused by the nature of the adversary system.

---

[24] Mellinkoff, The Conscience of a Lawyer, supra note 13, at 152.

[25] The ABA Code of Professional Responsibility – the predecessor to the Model Rules – is especially clear on this point. See EC 7–1 to 7–5.

[26] A pioneering article exploring the implications for legal ethics of the law's malleability at the margins is David B. Wilkins, *Legal Realism for Lawyers*, 104 Harv. L. Rev. 469 (1990).

[27] ABA Code of Professional Responsibility, EC 7–19.

The point deserves to be labored a bit, for the universal acceptance among lawyers of the Justification by the Adversary System is a startling thing, a marvelous thing, a thing to behold. It can go something like this: one talks with a pragmatic and hard-boiled attorney. At the mention of legal ethics, he smiles sardonically and informs one that it is a joke (or that it just means obeying the ethics rules, nothing more). One presses the subject and produces examples such as the buried bodies case. The smile fades, the forehead furrows, he retreats into a nearby phone booth and returns moments later clothed in the Adversary System, trailing clouds of glory. Distant angels sing. The discussion usually gets no further.

This portrait is drawn from life, but I do not tell the story just to be snide. It is meant to suggest that discussions of the adversary system usually stop where they ought to start, with a chorus of deeply felt but basically unexamined rhetoric.

What, then, is the adversary system? We may distinguish narrow and wide senses. In the narrow sense, it is a method of adjudication characterized by three things: an impartial tribunal of defined jurisdiction, formal procedural rules, and most importantly for the present discussion, assignment to the parties of the responsibility to present their own cases and challenge their opponents'.[28] The attorneys are their clients' agents in the latter task. The duty of a lawyer in an adversary proceeding is therefore one-sided partisan zeal in advocating his or her client's position. This in turn carries with it familiar collateral duties, the most important of which are *disinterestedness* (protected through prohibitions on conflicts of interest) and *confidentiality*. Each of these is best viewed as a prophylactic designed to enhance the quality of partisan advocacy: forbidding lawyers who have conflicts of interest from advocating a client's cause is meant to forestall the possibility of diluted zeal, and forbidding lawyers from divulging clients' confidences and secrets is meant to encourage clients to give their lawyers information necessary for effective advocacy. These duties of zeal, disinterestedness, and confidentiality – what might be called the Three Pillars of Advocacy – form the core of an attorney's professional obligations.

The structure of the adversary system, then – its fission of adjudication into a clash of one-sided representations – explains why Schwartz's Principle of Professionalism holds. But it explains the Principle of Non-accountability as well. If advocates restrain their zeal because of moral compunctions, they are not fulfilling their assigned role in the adversary proceeding. But, if lawyers must hold themselves morally accountable for

---

[28] Schwartz, *Professionalism and Accountability*, supra note 6, at 672; Lon L. Fuller, *The Adversary System*, in Talks on American Law 30–32 (Harold J. Berman ed., 1961); Martin Golding, *On the Adversary System and Justice*, in Philosophical Law 105 (Richard Bronaugh ed., 1978).

what they do in the course of the representation, they will be morally obliged to restrain their zeal whenever they find that the means used or the ends achieved in the advocacy are morally wrong. Therefore, or so the syllogism goes, the structure of adversary adjudication must relieve them of moral accountability, and that is how the adversary system entails Schwartz's Principle of Nonaccountability – how, that is, the adversary system underwrites an institutional excuse for moral ruthlessness.

All this holds (if hold it does) only within the context of adjudication. Lawyers, however, commonly act as though Schwartz's two principles characterized their relationship with clients even when the representations do not involve the courtroom.[29] Thus, there is a wide sense of the adversary system in which it is defined by the structure of the lawyer–client relationship rather than by the structure of adjudication.[30] When lawyers assume Schwartz's two principles in negotiations and counseling as well as in courtroom advocacy, and attribute this to the adversary system, they are speaking of it in the wide sense.

Lawyers often equivocate between the narrow and wide conceptions, appealing to the virtues of adversary adjudication in order to justify ruthless behavior on behalf of clients in nonlitigation contexts. Getting paid by the client, of course, makes it easier to ignore the difference between courtroom and other activities: $800 an hour has been known to buy a lot of Professionalism and will even stand in quite nicely for Moral Nonaccountability, especially around the first of the month – and an hour is an hour, in or out of court. Rather than pursue this equivocation, however, I shall ask if an institutional excuse can be based on the adversary system conceived in the narrow sense. If problems crop up even there, certainly they will be worse outside of a legitimately adversarial institution.

Criminal versus noncriminal contexts

I have suggested that the adversary system excuse may be only as good as the adversary system. The question of how good that is, however, is often ignored by discussions that stop where they ought to start. Indeed, there is a tendency to treat reservations about the adversary system as assaults on the American Way. Monroe Freedman's *Lawyers' Ethics in an Adversary*

---

[29] Indeed, one of Schwartz's reasons for writing *The Professionalism and Accountability of Lawyers,* supra note 6, was to propose a reform according to which the principles do not apply in the context of negotiation.

[30] A sophisticated attempt to characterize the principles of lawyers' ethics through the nature of the lawyer–client relationship rather than the adversary system is Charles Fried, *The Lawyer as Friend: The Moral Foundations of the Lawyer–Client Relation,* 85 Yale L.J. 1060 (1976). See also Charles Fried, Right and Wrong 167–94 (1978).

System, for example, is among the best and best-known modern books on lawyers' ethics.[31] Freedman argues powerfully that the duty to put a perjurious client on the stand, or brutally cross-examine a witness known by the lawyer to be telling the truth, follows from the adversary system.[32] His candid willingness to accept these intuitively unappealing implications of the adversary system is entirely admirable, as is Freedman's courageous defense of the civil liberties of criminal defendants. But *Lawyers' Ethics in an Adversary System* defends the adversary system primarily by contrasting the nonadversarial systems in "totalitarian states" such as Cuba and Bulgaria with American concern for the "dignity of the individual."[33] The argument is that zealous adversary advocacy of those accused of crimes is the greatest safeguard of individual liberty against the encroachment of the state. The good criminal defense lawyer puts the state to its proof in the most stringent and uncompromising way possible. Better, we say, that a hundred criminals go free than that one person be wrongly convicted.[34]

---

[31] Monroe Freedman, Lawyers' Ethics in an Adversary System (Indianapolis: Bobbs-Merrill, 1975).

[32] The fact that the ethics rules of most US jurisdictions forbid the former tactic, but not the latter, does not diminish the force of Freedman's argument for the former. In brief, he argues that the duty of a lawyer to investigate her client's case thoroughly, the duty to keep what she learns confidential, and the duty of candor toward courts (requiring the lawyer to blow the whistle on client perjury) are inconsistent: the lawyer can fulfill at most two of the three. Neutral partisanship strongly supports the duty to investigate and the duty of confidentiality (without which, so the argument goes, the client will be chilled from telling the lawyer what she needs to know to represent the client with suitable adversary zeal). Hence, the duty of candor must go. I criticize this argument in *Lawyers and Justice*, at 197–201 – but that is because I disagree with Freedman about the centrality of the duty of confidentiality.

[33] Freedman, Lawyers' Ethics in an Adversary System, supra note 31, at 2, 4.

[34] John Griffiths suggests that this way of thinking reflects "little more than the concerns of the middle class in connection with the rare occasions on which it has to fear prosecution." *Ideology in Criminal Procedure or A Third "Model" of the Criminal Process*, 79 Yale L. J. 359, 415 (1970). It is clear, of course, that despite the official rhetoric of the bar indigent criminal defendants do not often get the zealous advocacy the rhetoric promises; it is hard to see, though, why it would not benefit them if they did get it, and thus why it is a strictly "middle-class" concern. See generally David Luban, *Are Criminal Defenders Different?*, 91 Mich. L. Rev. 1729 (1993). Griffiths's point seems to be that treating the exceptional case of genuine zeal as a paradigm simply reinforces a false liberal political philosophy "assuming the inevitability of a state of irreconcilable hostility between the individual and the state," Griffiths at 413 – a political philosophy that is "middle class." I find Griffiths's view of liberalism implausible, but in any case, the liberal abstraction is a rather good first approximation of the relationship between individual defendants and state. Maurice Nadjari, lecturing his fellow prosecutors, told them that their "true purpose is to convict the guilty man who sits at the defense table, and to go for the jugular as viciously and rapidly as possible . . . You must never forget that your goal is total annihilation" (quoted in Frankel, *Partisan Justice*, supra note 22, at 32). If that isn't "irreconcilable hostility," what is?

I think this is right as far as it goes, but as a general defense of the adversary system it is beside the point for two related reasons. The first is that it pertains only to criminal defense and thus is irrelevant to the enormous number of civil cases tried each year. The latter are in a way much more morally troubling. It inflicts no tangible harm on anyone when a criminal evades punishment or, as is much more common, receives a lighter sentence, through good legal representation. This is not to deny that people may be legitimately outraged when a guilty criminal walks out of jail sooner than justice may seem to demand. But no one's life is made materially worse off. However, when A wins an unjust personal injury claim against B, every dollar in A's pocket comes out of B's. A's lawyer, in my book, has a lot of explaining to do.

This point is worth emphasizing. Many people assume that the paradigm of the morally dubious representation is the defense of the guilty criminal, the defense that gets a murderer back out on the street. This, I suspect, reflects a perception of the justice system as primarily concerned with protecting the lives and property of Decent People (meaning us) from You Know Who (meaning you know who). It is You Know Who that needs watching, not the real-estate speculator, the slumlord, the redliner, the discriminatory employer, the finance company, the welfare officials who won't give recipients their due, or the police.

It is this public preoccupation with crime and criminals, I think, that leads writers like Freedman and David Mellinkoff to focus their justifications of Broughamesque advocacy on criminal defense. They are reacting to an assault from the Right, an assault that sees the rights of the accused as a liberal invention leading to anarchy. Now, emphasizing the role of lawyers in safeguarding individual liberty may indeed be the best defense against the Law and Order attack on lawyers. Criminal defense is, so to speak, the "worst-case scenario," and it might be assumed that any defense of advocacy that works there works everywhere else as well.

In fact, and this is my second point, criminal defense is a very special case in which the zealous advocate serves atypical social goals. The point is one of political theory. The goal of zealous advocacy in criminal defense is to curtail the power of the state over its citizens. We want to handicap the state in its power even legitimately to punish us. And so the adversary system – more specifically, zealous criminal defense – is justified, not because it is a good way of achieving justice, but because it is a good way of keeping the state honest, and we have excellent reasons for wanting this. The argument, in other words, does not claim that the adversary system is the best way of obtaining justice. It claims just the opposite, that it is the best way of impeding justice in the name of more fundamental political ends, namely, keeping the government's hands off people. Nothing, of course, is wrong with that; indeed, I believe that Brougham's imperative may well hold in criminal defense. My point is merely that criminal defense is an exceptional part of the legal system, one that aims at protection rather than justice.

One might adopt Aristotelian language and say that the "final cause" of the adversary system is different in criminal and in noncriminal contexts. In the latter, the primary end of adversary adjudication is legal justice, the assignment of rewards and remedies on the basis of parties' behavior as prescribed by legal norms. The adversary method is supposed to yield accurate accounts of past behavior and legitimate interpretations of the law. In the criminal context, on the other hand, the protection of accused individuals against state overreaching is just as central a goal as attaining legal justice. The criminal justice system aims to defend our life, liberty, and property against those who would wrongfully take them. But that can include the state abusing its prosecution power just as easily as it can include murderers, kidnappers, and thieves.[35] We don't want the state to push its powers to the limit, because it is too easy in that case to exceed the limit. Instead, the system of rights – including the right to a defense lawyer – should leave generous margins of safety against prosecutorial overreaching. Criminal justice is not the same as legal justice, because a properly functioning criminal justice system will focus just as stringently on overprotecting the rights of the accused as it will on convicting the guilty. (This suggests one qualification to what I have just said: some noncriminal matters, such as administrative hearings, can raise the same issues of state versus subject and should be treated similarly. To take a striking example, a deportation proceeding – a non-criminal hearing before an administrative court – can be a de facto death penalty trial, if it results in sending an asylum-seeker back to political murder and torture in her home country. The reader should therefore read "criminal context" as an abbreviation for "criminal and quasi-criminal contexts."[36])

It seems, then, that focusing on the adversary system in the criminal context obscures the issue of how it works as a system of justice, and for this reason I shall talk only about arguments attempting to vindicate it as a system of justice. There are two sorts of arguments: those claiming that the adversary system is the best way of accomplishing various goals (consequentialist arguments), and those claiming that it is intrinsically good

[35] John Hasnas forcefully explicates this point in *Once More unto the Breach: The Inherent Liberalism of the Criminal Law and Liability for Attempting the Impossible*, 54 Hastings L. J. 1, 49–51 (2002).

[36] Indeed, once we recognize that powerful private organizations can pose threats to individuals under their control as serious as those posed by the state, we might expand the notion of quasi-criminal contexts to include a variety of civil matters pitting individuals against menacing Goliaths. I defend this expansion – which I label the "progressive correction to classical liberalism" – in *Lawyers and Justice*, at 58–66.

(nonconsequentialist arguments). To begin, we shall look at three versions of the former: (1) that the adversary system is the best way of ferreting out truth, (2) that it is the best way of defending people's legal rights, and (3) that by establishing checks and balances it is the best way of safeguarding against excesses.

Consequentialist justifications of the adversary system

Truth

The question whether the adversary system is, all in all, the best way of uncovering the facts of a case at bar sounds like an empirical question. I happen to think that it is – an empirical question, moreover, that has scarcely been investigated, and that is most likely impossible to answer. This last is because one does not, after a trial is over, find the parties coming forth to make a clean breast of it and enlighten the world about what *really* happened. A trial is not a quiz show with the right answer waiting in a sealed envelope. We can't learn directly whether the facts are really as the trier determined them because we don't ever find out the facts.

The kind of empirical research that can be done, then, is laboratory simulations: social psychology experiments intended to model the adversary proceeding. Obviously, there are inherent limitations on how closely such experiments can correspond to actual trials, no matter how skillfully they are done. In fact, the only experiments of the sort I know of are those of Thibaut, Walker, and their associates, and these are far from perfect modelings of the adversary and "inquisitorial" – meaning French- and German-style – systems that they are comparing.[37] Even so, the results are instructive: they show that in some situations the adversary system works better while in others the inquisitorial system does, and furthermore, that the participants cannot tell which situation they are in. This would hardly surprise us: it would be much more astounding to discover a greater difference in veracity between the Anglo-American and continental systems, for surely such a difference would after so many centuries have become a commonplace in our folklore.

Given all this, it is unsurprising to discover that the arguments purporting to show the advantages of the adversary system as a fact-finder have mostly been nonempirical, a mix of *a priori* theories of inquiry and armchair psychology.

---

[37] John Thibaut & Laurens Walker, Procedural Justice: A Psychological Analysis (1975). For critique, see Mirjan Damaska, *Presentation of Evidence and Fact-Finding Precision*, 123 U. Penn. L. Rev. 1083 (1975).

Here is one, based on the idea, very similar to Sir Karl Popper's theory of scientific rationality, that the way to get at the truth is a wholehearted dialectic of assertion and refutation.[38] If each side attempts to prove its case, with the other trying as energetically as possible to assault the steps of the proof, it is more likely that all of the aspects of the situation will be presented to the fact-finder than if it attempts to investigate for itself with the help of the lawyers.

This theory is open to a number of objections. First of all, the analogy to Popperian scientific methodology is not a good one. Perhaps science proceeds by advancing conjectures and then trying to refute them, but it does not proceed by advancing conjectures that the scientist believes to be false and then using procedural rules to exclude probative evidence.[39]

The two adversary attorneys are each under an obligation to present the facts in the manner most consistent with their client's position – to prevent the introduction of unfavorable evidence, to undermine the credibility of opposing witnesses, to set unfavorable facts in a context in which their importance is minimized, to attempt to provoke inferences in their client's favor. The assumption is that two such accounts will cancel out, leaving the truth of the matter. But there is no earthly reason to think this is so; they may simply pile up the confusion.

This is particularly likely in cases turning on someone's sanity or state of mind. Out comes the parade of psychiatrists, what Hannah Arendt once called "the comedy of the soul-experts."[40] Needless to say, they have been prepared by the lawyers, sometimes without knowing it. A clinical law teacher explained to a class that when you first contact a psychiatrist and sketch the facts of the case, you mention only the favorable ones. That way, he or she has an initial bias in your favor and tends to discount the unfavorable facts when you finally get around to mentioning them.

The other side, of course, can cross-examine such a witness to get the truth out. Irving Younger, in his time the most popular lecturer on trial tactics in

---

[38] Karl Popper, Conjectures and Refutations: The Growth of Scientific Knowledge iv, 33–65, 114–19, 352, 355–63 (1963). See Fuller, *The Adversary System*, supra note 28; Marvin Frankel, *The Search for Truth: An Umpireal View*, 123 U. Penn. L. Rev. 1031, 1036 (1975); and Monroe Freedman, *Judge Frankel's Search for Truth*, 123 U. Penn. L. Rev. 1060, 1060–61 (1975).

[39] Popper, of course, has his critics. Among the classics are Imre Lakatos, *Falsification and the Methodology of Scientific Research Programmes*, in Criticism and the Growth of Knowledge (Imre Lakatos & Alan Musgrave eds., 1970); Paul Feyerabend, Against Method (New Left Books, 1975) and Science in a Free Society (New Left Books, 1978). Feyerabend, who loved playing the epistemological bad boy, argued in both these books that in fact scientists *do* make progress by misrepresentation and suppression of evidence. But his view is widely rejected, and anyway he does not claim that truth is the outcome of the process.

[40] Hannah Arendt, Eichmann in Jerusalem: A Report on the Banality of Evil 26 (rev. edn. 1964).

the country, tells how. Among his famous "Ten Commandments of Cross-Examination" are these:

- Never ask anything but a leading question.
- Never ask a question to which you don't already know the answer.
- Never permit the witness to explain his or her answers.
- Don't bring out your conclusions in the cross-examination. Save them for closing arguments when the witness is in no position to refute them.[41]

Of course, the opposition may be prepared for this; they may have seen Younger's three-hour, $425 videotape on how to examine expert witnesses. They may know, therefore, that the cross-examiner is saving his or her conclusions for the closing argument. Not to worry! Younger knows how to stop an attorney from distorting the truth in closing arguments. "If the opposing lawyer is holding the jury spellbound ... the spell must be broken at all cost. [Younger] suggests the attorney leap to his or her feet and make furious and spurious objections. They will be overruled, but they might at least break the opposing counsel's concentration."[42]

My guess is that this is not quite what Sir Karl Popper had in mind when he wrote, "The Western rationalist tradition ... is the tradition of critical discussion – of examining and testing propositions or theories by attempting to refute them."[43]

A skeptic, in fact, might try this scientific analogy: a beam of invisible electrically charged particles – charge and origin unknown – travels through a distorting magnetic field of unknown strength, then through an opposite field of unknown, but probably different, strength. The beam strikes a detector of undeterminable reliability, from which we are supposed to infer the nature and location of the beam's source. That is the adversary system at its worst.

There is, however, one legal context in which the Popperian defense of the adversary system approximates reality and in which the adversary system is indeed strongly justified. When lawyers debate purely legal questions – particularly in appellate argument, where both sides work from a fixed record and no new evidence can be introduced – we find the kind of give and take that critical rationalists favor.

It makes sense to assign each advocate the task of arguing one side's interpretation of the law as forcefully as possible, and doing everything possible to undermine the adversary's arguments. With no facts to hide and everything out in the open, only the arguments and counter-arguments remain. Judges invariably attest that the better the advocates arguing before

[41] Frank Moya, *The Teacher Takes the Final Exam*, Nat'l. L. J., Nov. 17, 1981, at 22.
[42] Ibid.   [43] Popper, Conjectures and Refutations, supra note 38, at 352.

them, the better decisions they make. Adversary advocacy helps ensure that no arguments or objections get overlooked.[44]

Now, the same thing will often be true when lawyers argue over the interpretation of evidence in a trial of facts, so it may appear that my defense of the adversary system of arguing questions of law proves too much, and provides a defense for adversary arguments about facts as well. To the extent that the lawyers are arguing the interpretation of evidence in the record, that is true. But the problems with the adversary system I have highlighted lie in the fact that trial lawyers view one of their main jobs as keeping damaging information out of the record, or – as in Younger's recommendation that lawyers disrupt their adversaries' closing arguments – clouding the decision-making process. Consider, for example, complaints by the president of a lawyers' organization about a recent American innovation in which jurors are permitted to question witnesses directly. "You work very hard to keep certain information out of the trial. Then all of your finesse and art and technique are thrown out the window when a juror comes in and asks, 'Where were you on the night in question?' "[45] It is hard to defend adversary fact-finding on the ground that it is the best way of ensuring that judges and juries get the most information, when the lawyer's "finesse and art and technique" consists of keeping awkward facts out of court.

Even worse, adversarial tactics sometimes include efforts to ensure that cases never even make it to the stage of fact-finding. Defense counsel for corporate defendants use procedural delays to exhaust their opponents' funds. When they can, lawyers resort to intimidation tactics. A particularly egregious example occurred repeatedly during litigation over the Dalkon Shield, an intrauterine contraceptive device that pharmaceutical manufacturer A. H. Robins marketed during the 1970s to over three million women. Because of a design flaw, the Dalkon Shield caused an estimated 66,000 miscarriages and sterilized thousands of women by infecting them with pelvic inflammatory disease (PID). Faced with staggering liability exposure, Robins and its counsel decided on a scorched-earth defense. One tactic of Robins's counsel

---

[44] Stuart Hampshire argues powerfully that open adversarial argument such as we find in appellate advocacy is actually the form that justice takes in our world of plural, conflicting values. See Hampshire, Justice Is Conflict (2000); Hampshire, Innocence and Experience (1990). I have discussed Hampshire's splendid books in a pair of untitled reviews, one in 88 J. Phil. 317 (1991), the other in 112 Ethics 156 (2001); and I draw on his views in Luban, *Taking Out the Adversary: The Assault on Progressive Public Interest Lawyers*, 91 Cal. L. Rev. 209 (2003). Hampshire has powerfully influenced my views on the virtues of open adversary argument, although I believe that he errs by neglecting the incentives the adversary system creates for avoiding open argument by hiding facts and imposing costs and burdens on adversaries.

[45] Bill Miller, *Making a Case For Questions From Jurors; Process, Rare Now, Is Judicial Trend of Future, Backers Say*, Wash. Post, May 26, 1997, at A1.

soon acquired the nickname "the dirty questions list." Defense lawyers taking depositions asked plaintiffs very specific, very graphic questions about intimate details of their personal hygiene and sexual practices – questions that one plaintiff described as "more like an obscene phone call" than a legal interrogation. Firm lawyers argued that the "dirty questions" were relevant to the lawsuits because they might reveal alternative sources of PID infection. The questions mainly served, however, to intimidate plaintiffs into dropping their lawsuits or settling them for inadequate amounts. The message was clear that they might have to answer the same questions in open court. Among other things, defense lawyers asked plaintiffs for the names of all their past and present sexual partners ("besides your husband"), with the clear implication that the partners' names might be revealed and their testimony elicited for purposes of impeaching plaintiffs' answers to the "dirty questions" about what they like to do in bed. Potential plaintiffs filed affidavits indicating that they had dropped their own lawsuits because of the questions other plaintiffs had been asked.[46]

A similar example is the rise of the so-called "SLAPP suit" – "Strategic Lawsuit Against Public Participation." In a typical SLAPP suit, citizens protesting corporate policies or actions are sued for defamation or tortious interference with business. Some of the alleged defamation has been based on speech as innocuous as testifying against a real-estate developer at a zoning hearing, complaining to a school board about incompetent teachers, or collecting signatures on a petition. Although 80 percent of SLAPP suits are dismissed before trial, the aim of the suits is not legal victory but intimidation. Defendants faced with the prospect of ruinous legal bills and the risk of substantial personal liability agree to cease protest activities in return for withdrawal of the SLAPP suits.[47]

The point of these examples is plain: you cannot defend the adversary system on the basis of its truth-finding function when it licenses (or even requires) behavior designed to ensure that the truth never comes out, because litigants are intimidated into abandoning legitimate cases.

One final difference between "pure" argument, paradigmatically appellate argument of legal issues, and the adversary system of fact-finding appears in the ethics rules themselves. Ordinarily, lawyers are required to keep facts confidential, and in the adversary system they must never reveal damaging facts to a court unless they are compelled to do so. Matters are very different when we turn from facts to law. Here, the fundamental rule requires lawyers "to disclose to the tribunal legal authority in the controlling jurisdiction known to the lawyer to be directly adverse to the position of the

---

[46] Ronald J. Bacigal, The Limits of Litigation: The Dalkon Shield Controversy 19–20 (1990).
[47] George W. Pring & Penelope Canan, SLAPPs: Getting Sued for Speaking Out (1996).

client and not disclosed by opposing counsel."[48] This rule, which law students and lawyers often find counter-intuitive ("why should I do my adversary's legal research for them?"), highlights what makes argument about legal questions different. The idea is to ensure that judges reach the best resolutions they can of questions of law. Their resolutions, after all, become precedents. Getting to the best resolutions requires total transparency, and if my adversary has overlooked a favorable case on point, the rule requires me to throw myself on the sword by telling the judge about the case, to ensure that the judge does not overlook it. By contrast, we have seen that adversarial advocacy on factual matters places lawyers at war with transparency.

There is a sophisticated response to these arguments, which was offered in 1958 by Lon Fuller and John Randall in a semi-official report by a conference of the ABA and the AALS (the law schools' association). In the *Joint Conference Report*, Fuller and Randall argue that even though the adversary system apparently requires lawyers to obscure the truth on behalf of their clients, the system is actually more likely to arrive at the truth than an inquisitorial alternative in which the judge (or jury) rather than the lawyer conducts the inquiry. They base the argument on the psychological impossibility of a single mind formulating the strongest version of two contradictory positions:

> Any arbiter who attempts to decide a dispute without the aid of partisan advocacy ... must undertake not only the role of judge, but that of representative for both of the litigants. Each of these roles must be played to the full without being muted by qualifications derived from the others. When he is developing for each side the most effective statement of his case, the arbiter must put aside his neutrality and permit himself to be moved by a sympathetic identification sufficiently intense to draw from his mind all that it is capable of giving ... When he resumes his neutral position, he must be able to view with distrust the fruits of this identification and be ready to reject the products of his own best mental efforts. The difficulties of this undertaking are obvious. If it is true that a man in his time must play many parts, it is scarcely given to him to play them all at once.[49]

This argument, plausible though it appears on the surface, should set off an alarm in the minds of readers, because what Fuller and Randall claim is psychologically impossible turns out to be daily practice in civil law systems – and Fuller was a good enough comparativist to have known better.[50] Sybille

---

[48] Model Rules of Professional Conduct 3.3(a)(2).

[49] Lon Fuller & John D. Randall, *Professional Responsibility: Report of the Joint Conference of the ABA/AALS*, 44 ABAJ 1159, 1160 (1958). Cited hereafter as *Joint Conference Report*.

[50] Fuller's colleagues Benjamin Kaplan and Arthur von Mehren published pioneering articles on German civil procedure in the *Harvard Law Review* the same year that the Hart–Fuller debate

Bedford, who observed trials in several countries, wrote this about a German criminal trial:

It was a strange experience to hear this presentation of a case by both sides, as it were, in one; not a prosecution case followed by a defence case, but an attempt to build the whole case ... as it went. A strange experience ... to hear all questions, probing questions and soothing questions, accusatory and absolving questions, questions throwing a favourable light and questions having the opposite effect, flow from one and the same source, the bench ...[51]

What Mrs. Bedford found "strange" she nevertheless found extremely effective as well; and there is not a shred of evidence that continental systems are worse fact-finders than their Anglo-American counterparts. Perhaps a trained judge *can* play all parts at once.[52] If so, then where is the error in Fuller and Randall's argument?

One problem is that it begs the question. When Fuller and Randall write, "Each of these [representative] roles must be played to the full without being muted by qualifications derived from the others," they presuppose that inquiry proceeds best by unmuted adversary presentation – in which case, of course, an inquisitorial investigation becomes by definition a mere copy of the real thing. Isn't it equally possible, however, that a decision-maker can form a more reliable picture if the opposed positions *are* muted by qualifications derived from each other? After all, the strongest form of each side's case may be strongest because it is exaggerated and misleading. Sometimes the opponent may be able to smoke out the distortions and half-truths, but there will inevitably be cases in which the decision-maker simply cannot sort

appeared, and there can be little doubt that Fuller, who had a strong interest in German legal thought, knew their work. Benjamin Kaplan, Arthur T. von Mehren, & Rudolf Schaefer, *Phases of German Civil Procedure I*, 71 Harv. L. Rev. 1193 (1958); Kaplan, von Mehren, & Schaefer, *Phases of German Civil Procedure II*, 71 Harv. L. Rev. 1443 (1958). There is, however, reason to believe that Fuller was deeply suspicious of continental procedure. See Fuller, *The Adversary System*, supra note 28, at 36.

[51] Sybille Bedford, The Faces of Justice: A Traveller's Report 117 (Simon & Schuster, 1961).

[52] Of course one might respond that continental systems actually are adversarial. Judges don't proceed in a vacuum; rather, they work from written, partisan submissions by the litigants' attorneys.

This response is unconvincing. The judges still take the active role in questioning witnesses and eliciting further submissions and further evidence; and the lawyers assume a role considerably more passive than their American counterparts. (To offer one telling example, German ethics rules discourage lawyers from interviewing witnesses and forbid lawyers from preparing them, whereas an American lawyer who does not prepare witnesses for trial has done an inadequate job.) The German judge takes the written submissions as a beginning point, but need not confine the inquiry to those submissions. If Fuller's argument were sound, it would apply to the half-inquisitorial, half-adversarial systems of continental procedure.

through the exaggerations, strategic omissions, and false implications, and as a result decides wrongly.

In addition, Fuller and Randall's argument proves too much: it proves the impossibility not merely of reliable inquisitorial investigation, but of partisan advocacy as well! Any skilled lawyer preparing a case tries to anticipate the strongest arguments available to the adversary, preferably in their most devastating form. When she sizes up her witnesses, she puts herself in her opponent's shoes and probes for weaknesses in the witness's story; she digs for damaging information the opponent might unearth about the witness. Then she tries to construct counter-arguments to the opponent's best shot, and to anticipate counter-arguments to her counter-arguments. In short, she employs precisely the mental progression – from sympathetic identification with her own position, to detachment from it, to distrust of it, then back again – that Fuller claims is psychologically impossible for the inquisitorial judge.

The *Joint Conference Report* employs two additional psychological arguments against inquisitorial tribunals. The first is that the adversary system will "hold the case ... in suspension between two opposing inter-pretations of it," so the finder of fact won't jump to hasty conclusions.[53] The inquisitorial judge, by contrast, inevitably forms preliminary conceptions of the case, and will quite naturally become so invested in these working hypotheses that he may hang on to them even after they turn out to be false leads.

The second argument is that if the judge and not the lawyer had to "absorb" the embarrassment of her initial theory of the case being exploded in court, she would be "under a strong temptation to keep the hearing moving within the boundaries originally set for it"; that would turn a fair trial into a mere "public confirmation for what the tribunal considers it has already established in private."[54]

These arguments, unlike the previous one, have a well-confirmed psychological basis. The theory of cognitive dissonance holds that when we perform an action, our beliefs become more congruent with the action. An inquisitorial judge, pursuing her theory of the case, will call witnesses, request evidence, ask questions. To abandon the line of inquiry is tantamount to admitting that she has been wasting everyone's time. Here, she eliminates cognitive dissonance by continuing to believe that her theory of the case is plausible even when it should be abandoned.

The problem with the argument, of course, is that the shortcomings of inquisitorial procedure don't necessarily put it at a comparative disadvantage to adversarial procedure. The adversary system has its own epistemic short-comings, which derive from the fact that zealous advocates can sometimes

---

[53] *Joint Conference Report*, supra note 49, at 1160.   [54] Ibid. at 1161.

hide facts successfully to win a weak case. In addition, many "inquisitorial" courts use multi-judge panels, which mutes the psychological distortions of cognitive dissonance: if one judge becomes overly invested in a fruitless line of inquiry, the other judges can take the reins.

Ultimately, the *Joint Conference Report* seems to take as a premise the idea that truth is served by self-interested rather than disinterested investigation. "The lawyer appearing as an advocate before a tribunal presents, as persuasively as he can, the facts and the law of the case *as seen from the standpoint of his client's interest*" [emphasis added].[55] The emphasized phrase is accurate, but it gives the game away. For there is all the difference in the world between "the facts seen from X's standpoint" and "the facts seen from the standpoint of X's interest." Of course it is important to hear the former – the more perspectives we have, the better informed our judgment. But to hear the latter is not helpful at all. It is in the murderer's *interest* not to have been at the scene of the crime; consequently, the "facts of the case as seen from the standpoint of [the] client's interest" are that the client was elsewhere that weekend. From the standpoint of my *interest*, the world is my cupcake with a cherry on top; from the standpoint of yours, its streets are paved with gold and you own the streets. Combining the two does not change folly to truth.

All this does not mean that the adversary system may not in fact get at the truth in many hard cases. I suppose that it is as good as its rivals. But, to repeat the point I began with, nobody knows how good that is.[56]

Legal rights

It is sometimes said, however, that the point of the adversary system is *not* that it is the best way of getting at the truth, but rather the best way of defending individuals' legal rights. Freedman points out that if the sole purpose of a trial were to get at the truth we would not have our Fourth, Fifth, and Sixth Amendment rights; that improperly obtained evidence cannot be used against us and that we cannot be required to testify against ourselves indicate that our society considers other values more central than truth.[57]

---

[55] Ibid. at 1160.

[56] For related arguments expressing skepticism about the truth-finding function of the adversary system, see Golding, *On the Adversary System and Justice*, supra note 28, at 106–12; and Alan H. Goldman, The Moral Foundations of Professional Ethics 112–16 (1980). Geoffrey Hazard, the Reporter who drafted the ABA Model Rules of Professional Conduct, acknowledges that "there is no proof that the adversary system of trial yields truth more often than other systems of trial; that ... is an article of faith, because there is no way to conduct a reliable experiment." *Rules of Legal Ethics: The Drafting Task*, 36 Record of the Assoc. of the Bar of the City of N.Y. 93 (March 1981).

[57] Freedman, Lawyers' Ethics in an Adversary System, supra note 31, at 3–4.

And, according to the theory we shall now consider, these other values have to do with legal rights.[58]

The argument is that the best way to guarantee that an individual's legal rights are protected is to provide him or her with a zealous adversary advocate who will further the client's interest.

This argument, we should note, is slightly different from Freedman's, according to which counsel by a zealous advocate is not merely the best way of defending one's legal rights, but is itself one of those rights. That, of course, would make the adversary system necessary for the defense of legal rights, but only in the tautological sense that taking away counsel infringes a person's right to counsel and you can't defend a right by infringing it. Freedman suggests that adversary advocacy is a constitutional value, but this is not obvious.[59] The Constitution makes no explicit mention of the adversary system. In fact, US courts of equity used inquisitorial procedure that only gradually metamorphosed into adversary procedure, not completing the process until the fusion of equity courts and law courts in the twentieth century.[60] Now, it may be, as Theodore Koskoff says, a "fact, so basic that the Constitution does not even mention it, that our system of justice is an adversary system."[61] Certainly the Supreme Court has asserted many times that we have an adversary system.[62] But the Court has also explicitly held that due process can be satisfied through non-adversarial procedures, and its assertion that we have an adversary system means only that under an adversary system, due process requires adversary advocacy.[63] It is clear that the Court tolerates tinkering with the adversary format – for example, the

---

[58] It should be noted that values other than truth and legal rights are also implicated in trial procedure. For example, in a personal injury negligence case evidence that the defendant has repaired the site of an accident after it happened is not admissible, even though it would indirectly establish that the defendant really had been negligent. The reason for this policy is that to do otherwise would discourage the repair and so enhance a menace to the public. It is thus an oversimplification to suggest that the whole purpose of the trial process is to protect the interests of the court (by getting at the truth) or of the parties. The public interest is also involved.

[59] Freedman, Lawyers' Ethics in an Adversary System, supra note 31, at 8. See also James L. Oakes, *Lawyer and Judge: The Ethical Duty of Competency*, in Ethics and Advocacy 60 (The Roscoe Pound-American Trial Lawyers Foundation, 1978), who argues that the adversary system is required by Article III and Amendments V, VI, and VII of the Constitution.

[60] For an instructive and sophisticated discussion of this nearly forgotten fact of American legal history, see Amalia D. Kessler, *Our Inquisitorial Tradition: Equity Procedure, Due Process, and the Search for an Alternative to the Adversarial*, 90 Cornell L. Rev. 1181 (2005).

[61] Theodore Koskoff, *Introduction* to The American Lawyer's Code of Conduct Public Discussion Draft ii (The Roscoe Pound-American Trial Lawyers Foundation, 1980).

[62] See, for example, Hickman v. Taylor, 329 US 495, 514 (1946); or Herring v. New York, 422 US 853, 857–58 (1974).

[63] Mathews v. Eldridge, 424 US 319 (1976); Lassiter v. Dep't. of Social Services, 452 US 18 (1981).

Court approved modified discovery rules that require lawyers to turn over more information, even though three justices complained that the new rules are "contrary to the nature of our adversary system."[64] While the Sixth Amendment certainly gives persons accused of crimes the right to counsel, it says nothing about the rules of engagement. If we used a nonadversarial system, the Sixth Amendment right could be fulfilled by giving the accused a nonadversary advocate.

The argument we are considering is rather that, right to counsel aside, adversary advocacy is the best defense of our *other* legal rights. The no-holds-barred zealous advocate tries to get everything the law can give (if that is the client's wish) and thereby does a better job of defending the client's legal rights than a less committed lawyer would do.

Put this way, however, it is clear that the argument trades on a confusion. My legal rights are *everything I am in fact legally entitled to*, not *everything the law can be made to give*. For obviously a good lawyer may be able to get me things to which I am not entitled, but this, to call a spade a spade, is an example of infringing my opponent's legal rights, not defending mine. The "dirty questions list" and SLAPP suits are adversarial tricks of the trade used to do opponents out of their legal deserts.

It might be replied that looking at it this way leaves the opponent's lawyer out of the picture. Of course, the reply continues, no one is claiming that a zealous adversary advocate is attempting to *defend* legal rights: he or she is attempting to *win*. The claim is only that the clash of two such adversaries will in fact defend legal rights most effectively.

But what reason do we have to believe this, other than a question-begging analogy to eighteenth-century economic theories of the Invisible Hand, theories that are themselves myth rather than fact? Every skill an advocate is taught is bent to winning cases no matter where the legal right lies. If the opponent manages to counter a lawyer's move with a better one, this has precisely nothing to do with legal rights. In the Middle Ages lawsuits were sometimes tried by combat between hired champions. Each was charged with defending the legal right of his employer, but surely the fact that one swordsman successfully filleted the other did not mean that a right was established. Of course, judicial combat did not involve argument *about* rights. But neither does graymailing, "dollaring to death," driving up opponents' costs by getting their law firms disqualified, peremptorily challenging jurors because they seem too smart, or even masking bad arguments with what Titus Castricius called "the orator's privilege to make statements that are untrue, daring, crafty, deceptive and sophistical, provided they have some semblance

---

[64] Supreme Court of the United States, Amendments to the Federal Rules of Civil Procedure, 146 F.R.D. 401, 507 (1993) (Scalia, J., dissenting, joined by Souter, J. and Thomas, J.).

of truth and can by any artifice be made to insinuate themselves into the minds of the persons who are to be influenced."[65]

It is obvious that litigators pride themselves on their won–lost record. The *National Law Journal* describes "the world's most successful criminal lawyer – 229 murder acquittals without a loss!" and describes the Inner Circle, a lawyer's club whose membership requirement is winning a seven-figure verdict.[66] (That was before the day of the nine- or ten-figure verdict.) You never know, of course – maybe each of these cases really had legal right on its side. And when a coin comes up heads 229 times in a row it may be fair, but there *is* another explanation. Lawyers themselves do not see the point of what they do as defending their clients' legal rights, but as using the law to get their clients what they want.

It is true, of course, that one way for society to guarantee that lawyers do their best to defend their clients' rights is to commit them to defending every claim a client has to a right, whether valid or not. That kind of overkill is reassuring to each client, of course. But suppose we look at it from the point of view of the whole process, rather than of the individual clients. It is hard to see then why an adversary system is the best defender of legal rights. Why not, for example, a system in which both attorneys are committed to defending the legal rights of both parties, if they seem to be getting trampled? I am not recommending such a system: my point is only that we have no reason at all to believe that when two zealous advocates slug it out, the better case, rather than the better lawyer, wins.

Let me be clear about the objection. It is not that the flaw in the adversary system is overkill on the part of morally imperfect, victory-hungry lawyers. The objection is that under the adversary system an *exemplary* lawyer is required to indulge in overkill to obtain as legal rights benefits that in fact may not be legal rights.

At this point an objection can be raised to my argument. The argument depends on a distinction I have drawn between *what a person is in fact legally entitled to* and *what the law can be made to give*. But this is a suspect distinction because it is based on the notion that there are legal entitlements other than what the law in fact gives. American realism, the dominant jurisprudential theory of the twentieth century, was primarily responsible for throwing cold water on the notion of entitlements-in-themselves floating around in some sort of noumenal never-never land. The law is nothing other than what the courts say it is.

The objection fails, however, for it cuts the ground out from under itself. If legal rights are strictly identical with what the courts decide they are, then it

[65] The Attic Nights of Aulus Gellius (John C. Rolfe trans., 1954), I. vi. 4–5 (quoted in Golding, *On the Adversary System and Justice*, supra note 28).

[66] Advertisement, Nat'l. L. J., June 2, 1980, at 30.

is simply false that the adversary system is the best defender of legal rights. *Any* system whatsoever would defend legal rights equally well, as long as on the basis of that system courts decided cases.

There is, however, a legitimate insight concealed in the realist objection. Whether or not legal rights are anything beyond what the courts say they are, it is the courts that are charged with adjudicating them. And – the point continues – if lawyers were given discretion to back off from zealous advocacy, they would have to prejudge the case themselves by deciding what the legal rights actually are in order to exercise this discretion. Lawyers would be usurping the judicial function.

Now, it must be said that this insight cannot be used to defend the innumerable tactics lawyers use to force favorable settlements of cases outside of court (dirty questions, SLAPP suits, delaying tactics); if anything, the argument should condemn such practices inasmuch as they preempt the adjudicatory process. Nor does it militate against requiring lawyers to disclose adverse information and arguments, since doing so does not usurp the judicial function. But I do not wish to focus on these points, for I think that the insight contains an important argument for the adversary system that we have not yet considered.

Ethical division of labor

This argument is no longer that the excesses of zealous advocacy are excused by the promotion of truth or the defense of legal rights. Rather, it is that they are excused by what Thomas Nagel calls "ethical division of labor." He says, in a discussion of the peculiarly ruthless and result-oriented role morality of public officials,

that the constraints of public morality are not imposed as a whole in the same way on all public actions or on all public offices. Because public agency is itself complex and divided, there is a corresponding ethical division of labor, or ethical specialization. Different aspects of public morality are in the hands of different officials. This can create the illusion that public morality is more consequentialist or less restrictive than it is, because the general conditions may be wrongly identified with the boundaries of a particular role. But in fact those boundaries usually presuppose a larger institutional structure without which they would be illegitimate. (The most conspicuous example is the legitimacy conferred on legislative decisions by the limitation of constitutional protections enforced by the courts.)[67]

The idea is that behavior that looks wrong from the point of view of ordinary morality can be justified by the fact that other social roles exist

[67] Thomas Nagel, *Ruthlessness in Public Life*, in Public and Private Morality 85 (Stuart Hampshire ed., 1978).

whose purpose is to counteract the excesses resulting from role-behavior. Zealous adversary advocacy is justified by the fact that the other side is also furnished with a zealous advocate; the impartial arbiter provides a further check.

This is in fact one of the most commonly heard defenses for pugnacious advocacy: "He had a lawyer, too"; "I'm not supposed to do his lawyer's job for him"; or quoting Sharswood once again, "The lawyer, who refuses his professional assistance because in his judgment the case is unjust and indefensible, usurps the functions of both judge and jury."[68]

The idea is really a checks-and-balances theory, in which social engineering or "wise legislation" is supposed to relieve some of the strain on individual conscience. A functionary in a well-designed checks-and-balances system can simply go ahead and perform his duties secure in the knowledge that injuries inflicted or wrongs committed in the course of those duties will be rectified by other parts of the system.

Will this do the trick? The answer, I am afraid, is no. Suppose that a lawyer is about to embark on a course of action that is unjustified from the point of view of ordinary morality, such as attempting to win an unfair, lopsided judgment for a client from a hapless and innocent party. Or think of our second graymailing example, in which lawyers for a corporation involved in a merger advise their client to fire employees a few at a time to blackmail federal authorities into permitting the merger to go forward. A zealous adversary advocate will do whatever she can to avoid the opposing counsel's attempt to foil her designs. For that reason, she surely cannot claim that the existence of the opposing counsel morally justifies these actions. Certainly the fact that a man has a bodyguard in no way excuses you for trying to kill him, particularly if you bend all your ingenuity to avoiding the bodyguard.

The problem is this. The checks-and-balances notion is desirable because if other parts of the system exist to rectify one's excesses, one will be able to devote undivided energy to the job at hand and do it better. It is analogous to wearing protective clothing in a sport such as fencing: knowing that your opponent is protected, you can go all out in the match. But in the adversary system the situation is different, since the attorney is actively trying to get around the checks and balances. Here the analogy is to a fencer who uses a special foil that can cut through the opponent's protective clothing. To put the point another way, the adversary advocate attempts to evade the system of checks and balances, not to rely on it to save her opponents.

There is another problem with the notion of ethical division of labor. It attempts to justify a system of roles by the fact that the system is self-correcting, in other words that injuries perpetrated by one part of the system will be rectified by another. Rectification, however, carries with it high

---

[68] Sharswood, A Compend of Lectures, note 5 above, at 84.

transaction costs in terms of money, time, worry, energy, and (generally) an arduous passage through the bureaucratic straits. These transaction costs create a general background "noise" in the system, a penalty imposed on one simply for becoming embroiled in it. This can be justified only if the system itself is justified, but then the checks-and-balances argument seems merely to gild the lily. Had we found a justification for the adversary system on other grounds, we would not have needed to turn to the ethical division-of-labor argument to begin with.

Division-of-labor arguments raise a very troubling and difficult topic. The structure of bureaucratic institutions such as the legal system lends itself to divided responsibility. Those who write the rules, those who give the orders, and those who carry them out each have some basis for claiming that they are not at fault for any wrong that results. But this is unacceptable. If moral agency divides along lines of institutional authority, it seems to me that every agent in the institution will wind up abdicating moral responsibility. It is for this reason that division-of-labor arguments must walk a thin line between the legitimate notion that different roles have different duties and the unacceptable notion that moral responsibility is itself diminished or "divided down" by institutional structure. In chapters 6 and 7 we shall examine more closely the ways in which institutional structure serves, in an illusory way, to divide down moral responsibility.[69]

A final division-of-labor argument exists which is different from those we have just been considering. This is the general line of argument of the *Joint Conference Report*. It is based on a point emphasized by the realists, namely that lawyers spend very little of their time or attention on actual litigation. Mostly they are involved in other activities: document-drafting, deal-making, negotiation, giving advice, and so forth. The *Joint Conference Report* seizes on this fact to argue for a separation of lawyerly functions, with a corresponding separation of norms of professional behavior in accord with the nature of those functions. The report restricts no-holds-barred zeal to the role of advocate, a role that, to repeat, lawyers do not occupy very much of the time. The real key to the lawyer's function in society, according to the report, lies not in litigation but in wise counsel and airtight draftsmanship, which make litigation unnecessary. As to the morally troubling cases, the lawyer is permitted or even required to advise the client against "a course of conduct technically permissible under existing law, though inconsistent with its underlying spirit and purpose."[70] This the lawyer does by reminding the client of the "long-run costs" of such conduct.[71]

---

[69] See also David Luban, Alan Strudler, & David Wasserman, *Moral Responsibility in the Age of Bureaucracy*, 90 Mich. L. Rev. 2348 (1992).

[70] *Joint Conference Report*, supra note 49, at 1161.   [71] Ibid.

I do not think we need to take this argument very seriously, for it trades on a sleight-of-hand and a key omission. The sleight-of-hand lies in the tricky phrase "long-run costs." Costs to whom? Society at large? I suppose some clients engaged in morally shady projects may be dissuaded by being told how they are harming society, but surely these are just the people least likely to listen. Perhaps the long-run costs are to the client, costs in the form of loss of respect in the community, hard feelings, inability to do business with people in the future, etc. But why suppose that these inevitably accompany morally unworthy litigation? It is a commonplace that we live in a litigious society, and the fact that a person or corporation makes effective use of an arsenal of legal weapons is not often held against him. We have, for better or worse, learned to expect such behavior, and ruthless, hard-driving entrepreneurship that eagerly goes to the legal mat is more likely to win respect than enmity if it is successful. You'd be surprised (or maybe not) what a lot of money will do to make people like an amoral wheeler-dealer. The *Joint Conference Report's* ominous rumbling about long-run costs is Panglossian piety, which harmonizes society's loss with the client's, when in fact society's loss is often the client's gain.

The argument also omits the key point that, after lawyers have offered their "quiet counsel," they will still have to press forward with the representation if the client won't be dissuaded. Perhaps the lawyer can say that she gave morality the old college try, and her heart is pure. Our worry, however, was not about impure hearts, but about dirty hands. And those haven't become any cleaner.

Thus, the division of functions within a lawyer's own professional life fares no better than the division of functions within the legal system as a whole: neither is sufficient to provide the moral timbering of adversary advocacy.

Nonconsequentialist justifications of the adversary system

It may be thought, however, that assessing the adversary system in consequentialist terms of how it will get some job done misses the point. Some social institutions, such as participatory democracy, are justifiable despite the fact that – maybe even because – they are inefficient. The moral standing of such institutions has a noninstrumental basis.

I wish to consider two nonconsequentialist justifications of the adversary system. The first and perhaps boldest is an attempt to justify the adversary system in the wide sense: it is the argument that the traditional lawyer–client relation is an intrinsic moral good. The second is a cluster of related arguments: that adversary adjudication is a valued and valuable tradition, that it enjoys the consent of the governed, and that it is thus an integral part of our social fabric.

Adversary advocacy as intrinsically good

When we seek out the services of a professional, it seems to me that we generally see more to the relationship than a mere *quid pro quo*. Perhaps this is because the *quo* may be of vital importance to us; perhaps it is because a lot of *quid* may be required to hire those services. In any event, we have the sense of entrusting a large chunk of our life to this person, and the fact that he or she takes on so intimate a burden and handles it in a trustworthy and skillful manner when the stakes are high seems commendable in itself. Nor does the fact that the professional makes a living by providing this service seem to mitigate the praiseworthiness of it. The business aspect moves along a different moral dimension: it explains how the relationship came about, not what it involves.[72] Finally, our being able to bare our weaknesses and mistakes to the professional and receive assistance without condemnation enhances our sense that beneficence or moral graciousness is at work here. Our lawyer, *mirabile dictu*, forgives us our transgressions.

Feelings such as these are quite real; the question is whether they have merely subjective significance. If they do not, if they mean something more, that may show that Schwartz's two principles, and thus the adversary system and the behavior it countenances, are themselves positive moral goods. Such arguments are, in fact, frequently made: they are based on the idea that providing service is intrinsically good. No finer statement of this exists, in my opinion, than Mellinkoff's. He sees the paradigm client as the "man-in-trouble."

Cruelty, oppression, deception, unhappiness, worry, strain, incomprehension, frustration, bewilderment – a sorcerer's bag of misery. These become the expected. Then the saddest of all human cries: "Who will help me?" Try God, and politics, and medicine, and a soft shoulder, sooner or later a lawyer. Too many do.

The lawyer, as lawyer, is no sweet kind loving moralizer. He assumes he is needed, and that no one comes to see him to pass the time of day. He is a prober, an analyzer, a scrapper, a man with a strange devotion to his client. Beautifully strange, or so it seems to the man-in-trouble; ugly strange to the untroubled onlooker.[73]

Charles Fried thinks of the lawyer as a "special-purpose friend" whose activity – enhancing the client's autonomy and individuality – is an intrinsic moral good.[74] This is true even when the lawyer's "friendship" consists in assisting the profiteering slumlord to evict an indigent tenant or enabling the wealthy debtor to run the statute of limitations to avoid an honest debt to an old (and less well-off) friend.

[72] Fried, *The Lawyer as Friend*, supra note 30, at 1075.
[73] Mellinkoff, The Conscience of a Lawyer, supra note 13, at 270.
[74] Fried, *The Lawyer as Friend*, supra note 30, at 1068–73.

I mention Mellinkoff's and Fried's arguments together because, it seems to me, they express similar ideas, while the unsavory consequences Fried draws from his argument expose the limitations of Mellinkoff's. Both arguments attempt to show that a lawyer serving a client is engaged in an intrinsic moral good. Mellinkoff's, however, really shows something much weaker, that a lawyer serving a man-in-trouble is (even more cautiously: can be) engaged in an intrinsic moral good. If the client is Fried's profiteering slumlord or unscrupulous debtor, we are confronted with no man-in-trouble, and the intuitions to which Mellinkoff's argument appeals disappear. Indeed, if these were the typical clients, the real men-in-trouble – the victims of these predators – might be better off taking their chances in the war of all against all than seeking to have their "autonomy" vindicated legally. The trouble with Mellinkoff's argument is that he makes clients look more pitiable than many really are.

Fried, on the other hand, bites the bullet and argues that it is morally good to represent the man-in-no-trouble-in-particular, the man-who-troubles-others. The slumlord and the graymailing, anticompetitive multiglomerate are nobly served by a special-purpose friend who helps extract that pound of flesh. Fried constructs a "concentric-circles morality" in which, beginning with an absolute right to self-love based on our own moral standing, we work outward toward those closest to us, then to those whose connections are more remote. Fried argues that the abstract connection between a remote person (even a person-in-trouble) and the agent exercises too slight a claim on the agent to override this inclination toward concrete others. This justifies lavishing special care on our friends, even at the expense of "abstract others"; and because lavishing care is morally praiseworthy, once we grant that a lawyer is a special-purpose friend of his client, we are home free with the intrinsic moral worth of the lawyer–client relation.

Several of Fried's critics focus on the fact that the friendship analogy is question-begging: Fried builds enough lawyerly qualities into his concept of friendship that the argument becomes circular; in the words of Edward Dauer and Arthur Leff, "a lawyer is like a friend ... because, for Professor Fried, a friend is like a lawyer."[75] It does seem to me, however, that the analogy captures some of the legitimate notion of professionals as devoted by the nature of their calling to the service of their clients. Fried's analogy contains a large grain of truth.

This does not, however, vindicate the adversary system. For the friendship analogy undercuts rather than establishes the Principle of Nonaccountability. Most of us are not willing to do grossly immoral things to help our friends, nor should we be. Lord Brougham's apology may be many things, but it is

---

[75] See Dauer and Leff, *Correspondence: The Lawyer as Friend,* supra note 14, at 577–78; Simon, *The Ideology of Advocacy,* supra note 7, at 108–9.

not a credo of human friendship in any of its forms. Fried realizes the danger, for he confesses that

not only would I not lie or steal for ... my friends, I probably also would not pursue socially noxious schemes, foreclose the mortgages of widows or orphans, or assist in the avoidance of just punishment. So we must be careful lest the whole argument unravel on us at this point.[76]

The method for saving the argument, however, proves disappointing. Fried distinguishes between *personal* wrongs committed by a lawyer, such as abusing a witness, and *institutional* wrongs occasioned by the lawyer, such as foreclosing on widows. The latter are precisely those done by the lawyer in his or her proper role of advancing the client's legal autonomy and – pre-established harmony? – they are precisely the ones that are morally accep-table. That is because the lawyer isn't really doing them; the system is.

This last distinction has not been very popular since World War II, and Fried takes pains to restrict it to "generally just and decent" systems, not Nazi Germany. With this qualification, he can more comfortably assert: "We should absolve the lawyer of personal moral responsibility for the result he accomplishes because the wrong is wholly institutional."[77]

This last sentence, however, is nothing but the assertion that institutional excuses work for lawyers, and this should tip us off that Fried's argument will be useless for our purposes. For consider: our whole line of argument has been an attempt to justify the adversary system by showing that the tradi-tional lawyer–client relation is an intrinsic moral good. Now it seems that this can be established by Fried's argument only if we are permitted to cancel the moral debit column by means of an institutional excuse; but that can work only if the institution is justified, and we are back where we started.

Part of the problem is that Fried considers the wrong institution: the context of the lawyer's behavior is not simply the system of laws in general, which he assumes to be just and decent, but the adversary system in particular with its peculiar requirement of one-sided zeal at the margin. It is the adversary system and not the system of laws that shapes the lawyer–client relationship.

The more fundamental problem, however, is that Fried takes the lawyer to be the mere occasion rather than the agent of morally-bad-but-legally-legit-imate outcomes. The system did it; it "was just one of those things difficult to pre-visualize – like a cow, say, getting hit by lightning."[78]

This is false in three respects. First, because it discounts the extent to which the lawyer has had a creative hand in advocating the outcome, at times

---

[76] Fried, Right and Wrong, supra note 30, at 191.   [77] Ibid. at 192.
[78] Galway Kinnell, The Book of Nightmares 43 (1971).

even reversing the law – a skilled lawyer, after all, argues, advocates, bargains, and persuades. Second, because the system is not an abstract structure of impersonal role-descriptions but a social structure of interacting human beings, so that the actions of its agents *are* the system. Third, because the lawyer is indeed acting *in propria persona* by "pulling the levers of the legal machinery."[79] Fried's imagery seems to trade on a Rube Goldberg insight: if the apparatus is complex enough, then the lever-puller doesn't really look like the agent. But that cannot be right. I chop the broccoli, whether I do it with a knife or merely push the button on the blender. The legal levers are pulled by the lawyer: no one else can do it.

The social fabric argument

The remaining arguments are distinct but closely related. They are two variants of the following idea, which may be called the "social fabric argument": *Regardless of whether the adversary system is efficacious, it is an integral part of our culture, and that fact by itself justifies it.* The first variation derives from democratic theory: it claims that the adversary system is justified because it enjoys the consent of the governed. The second variation comes from conservative theory: it claims that the adversary system is justified because it is a deeply rooted part of our tradition.

According to the social fabric argument, the moral reason for staying with our institutions is precisely that they are *ours.* We live under them, adapt our lives and practices to them, assess our neighbors' behavior in their light, employ them as a standard against which to measure other ways of life. Traditional institutions bind us – morally and legitimately bind us – because we assimilate ourselves to our tradition (Variation 2). In the language of political theory, we *consent* to them (Variation 1). They express who we are and what we stand for.

This way of looking at the adversary system is quite different from the claim that it promotes the discovery of truth, or the protection of legal rights, or the rectification of wrongs. Those arguments are consequentialist in character: they attempt to justify the adversary system on the basis of what *it* does. The social fabric argument justifies it on the basis of what *we* do, or who we are. Let us look at the variants.

The *consent argument* claims that the adversary system forms part of the social contract. The adversary system is justified because it enjoys the consent of the governed, the highest moral compliment that can be paid to it in a democracy. An immediate problem with the argument, however, is that we obviously do not *explicitly* consent to the adversary system. Nobody asked us,

---

[79] Slightly paraphrased from Fried, Right and Wrong, supra note 30, at 192; and *The Lawyer as Friend*, supra note 30, at 1085.

and I don't suppose anyone intends to. If the argument is to work, the consent must be *tacit* consent, and then we are entitled to wonder how we can tell that it has been given. One test is simply that, over an extended period of time, we have incorporated the institution into our shared practices. Michael Walzer makes this suggestion: "Over a long period of time, shared experiences and cooperative activity of many different kinds shape a common life. 'Contract' is a metaphor for a process of association and mutuality."[80]

There is a problem with this account, however: just because people do not have the energy, inclination, or courage to replace their institutions we should not conclude that they want them or approve of them. But unless they want them or approve of them, people's endurance of institutions does not make the institutions morally good. The verb "consent" can mean either "put up with" or "actively approve." Only the latter has the moral force required to show that the institution is a positive moral good, but only the former is revealed by the mere existence of "our common life."

To see this, recall the original point of consent theory – classically, the theory that we incur political obligations and forfeit political rights only through our own consent. The intuition behind consent theory is that human beings are morally autonomous. For classic consent theorists such as Locke, this autonomy was expressed in the concept of natural right, but other conceptual vocabularies capture the same idea. In each version, regardless of vocabulary, consent theory assumes that coercion is *prima facie* wrong and that this *prima facie* wrongness may normally be overridden only by the fact that we have consented to submit to coercive institutions. It offers a theory of governmental legitimacy that assumes government is illegitimate until proven otherwise, and that specifies the standard form of such proof: demonstration of the consent of the governed.

Such a demonstration – and this is the important conclusion of the preceding paragraph – shows that a coercive institution is *not illegitimate*, that it is *acceptable*. It does not show that it is *good* and thus does not provide an argument in favor of it. Think of this analogy: you ask me for a two-week extension on repaying some money you owe me. I grant the extension – I consent to it. That shows that you *may* wait two more weeks before repaying me, but it does not show that you *should* wait two more weeks, or that it is good for you to wait two more weeks.

Thus, the most we get from tacit consent arguments, such as Walzer's appeal to our "common life," is a demonstration that we are not obliged to dismantle the adversary system. To get anything stronger we must appeal to a different concept in democratic theory from consent: we must show that

---

[80] Michael Walzer, Just and Unjust Wars: A Moral Argument with Historical Illustrations 54 (1977).

people *want* the adversary system. In Rousseau's language, we must show that having an adversary system is our "general will."

Does the adversary system pass such a test? The answer, I think, is clearly no. Few of our institutions are trusted less than adversary adjudication, precisely because it seems to license lawyers to trample the truth, and legal rights, and common morality. David Mellinkoff begins *The Conscience of a Lawyer* with a history of lawyer-hating that is quite eloquent in this regard. At one point he notes: "The full force of the complaint is not alone the denial of truth, even coupled with avarice, but that with a God-given talent the lawyer stands in the way of every man's birthright, the right to justice. The lawyer, in John Stuart Mill's phrase, is ready to 'frustrate justice with his tongue.' "[81] Is this because of the adversary system? Indeed it is, for it is the adversary system that makes zealous advocacy of the client's interests the pillar of professional obligation. The *Joint Conference Report* puts it best:

At the first meeting of the Conference the general problem discussed was that of bringing home to the law student, the lawyer and the public an understanding of the nature of the lawyer's professional responsibilities. All present considered that the chief obstacle to the success of this undertaking lay in "the adversary system" ... Those who had attempted to teach ethical principles to law students found that the students were uneasy about the adversary system, some thinking of it as an un-wholesome compromise with the combativeness of human nature, others vaguely approving of it but disturbed by their inability to articulate its proper limits ... Confronted by the layman's charge that he is nothing but a hired brain and voice, the lawyer often finds it difficult to convey an insight into the value of the adversary system.[82]

Even law students, then, are suspicious of the adversary system (though not for long). There is irony here: the need to justify the adversary system lies, according to the *Joint Conference Report*, in the fact that no one seems to trust it or the conduct it countenances; our current argument purports to justify it by claiming that we all tacitly approve of it. The argument fails.

Seeing that it fails and why can motivate the second variation, which we may call the *tradition argument*. Consent theorists assume that we have no political obligations except those we consent to, but as Hume noted, "would these reasoners look abroad into the world, they would meet with nothing that, in the least, corresponds to their ideas, or can warrant so refined and philosophical a system."[83] On the contrary, as Hume argued, people

---

[81] Mellinkoff, The Conscience of a Lawyer, supra note 13, at 12.

[82] *Joint Conference Report*, supra note 49, at 1159.

[83] David Hume, *Of the Original Contract*, in Essays, Literary, Moral and Political 272 (George Routledge & Sons, n.d.).

commonly consent to institutions because they take themselves to be obligated to them, rather than the other way around. We feel that traditional institutions lay claim to us, even when they themselves originated through violence or usurpation.

The power of the past to move us and bind us is enormous; compared with such deep feelings, the ideas of consent theory seem shallow and alien to human experience. This criticism is most familiar in Burke (though it is implicit in Hume as well):

Society is indeed a contract ... but the state ought not to be considered as nothing better than a partnership agreement in a trade of pepper and coffee, callico or tobacco, or some such low concern, to be taken up for a little temporary interest, and to be dissolved by the fancy of the parties ... It is ... a partnership not only between those who are living, but between those who are living, those who are dead, and those who are to be born. Each contract of each particular state is but a clause in the great primaeval contract of eternal society ... The municipal corporations of that universal kingdom are not morally at liberty at their pleasure, and on the speculations of a contingent improvement, wholly to separate and tear asunder the bonds of their subordinate community, and to dissolve it into an unsocial, uncivil, unconnected chaos of elementary principles.[84]

A Burkean argument for the adversary system would appeal to its place in our traditions and claim that we are under a moral obligation to spurn "speculations of a contingent improvement" that would tear this tradition apart. There is much to be said for Burkean argument, if for no other reason than its rejection of a shallow and philistine conception of progress.[85] But it does not apply to the adversary system.

In the first place, it ignores the fact that there is no constant tradition: common law constantly modifies the adversary system.[86] Indeed, the adversary advocate is a recent invention within that changing tradition. In England, criminal defense lawyers were not permitted to address the courts until 1836;[87] in the United States, criminal defendants were not guaranteed counsel until 1963.[88] Civil litigants still have no guarantee of counsel, even in quasi-criminal matters such as a state's attempt to take a child from its

[84] Edmund Burke, Reflections on the Revolution in France 110 (Anchor Books, 1973) (1791).
[85] My view here is heavily influenced by Walter Benjamin's brilliant but gnomic *Theses on the Philosophy of History*, in Illuminations (Hannah Arendt ed., Harry Zohn trans., 1969). See particularly Thesis XV, at 261. For a particularly eloquent version of the Burkean argument in law, see Anthony T. Kronman, *Precedent and Tradition*, 99 Yale L.J. 1029 (1990).
[86] Particularly instructive on this point is Kessler's examination of the inquisitorial process used by courts of equity in both Great Britain and eighteenth- and nineteenth-century America. Kessler, *Our Inquisitorial Tradition*, supra note 59.
[87] Mellinkoff, The Conscience of a Lawyer, supra note 13, at 47.
[88] Gideon v. Wainwright, 372 US 335 (1963).

parent.[89] Moreover, it is simply false that the "neutral partisanship" norm governs every aspect of litigation. Ethics codes and case law insist that public prosecutors should seek justice, not victory.[90] Admittedly, prosecutors often forget this and play the hardest of hardball to win convictions; but that simply illustrates the extent to which the adversary system excuse has permeated litigator culture in defiance of formal rules and the cultural norms they reflect. All in all, it is hard to see the adversary system as "a clause in the great primaeval contract."

In the second place, the adversary system is an ancillary institution compared with those with which Burke was concerned. In William Simon's words,

I think the argument will seem rather out of proportion to the subject. It's one thing to talk about the dangers of utopian change when you're talking about ripping the whole society apart to restructure it from top to bottom. But there are plenty of ways of abolishing adversary ethics which from a larger point of view are really just marginal social reforms which, whether good or bad, hardly suggest the likelihood of Burkean dangers. It's like making a Burkean argument against no-fault or social security.[91]

The Burkean argument is in effect a demurrer to the demand that we justify the adversary system: it suggests that the system is too central to the "great primaeval contract" to be put to the justificatory test. To this argument the reply is simply that the tradition does not clearly incorporate the adversary system, and that the system is too marginal for us to let Burkean considerations permit the demurrer.

The adversary system excuse

Pragmatic justification

So far the course of argument has been purely negative, a persecution and assassination of the adversary system. By this time you are entitled to ask

---

[89] Lassiter v. Dep't of Social Services, 452 US 18 (1981).

[90] See, e.g., Model Rule 3.8 cmt [1] ("A prosecutor has the responsibility of a minister of justice and not simply that of an advocate"); ABA Model Code of Professional Responsibility EC 7–13 ("The responsibility of a public prosecutor differs from that of the usual advocate; his duty is to seek justice, not merely to convict"); ABA Standards Relating to the Administration of Criminal Justice: The Prosecution Function (3rd edn. 1992), Standard 3–1.2(c) ("The duty of the prosecutor is to seek justice, not merely to convict"); Berger v. United States, 295 US 78, 88 (1935) ("The United States Attorney is the representative not of an ordinary party to a controversy, but of a sovereignty whose obligation to govern impartially is as compelling as its obligation to govern at all; and whose interest, therefore, in a criminal prosecution is not that it shall win a case, but that justice shall be done").

[91] Letter to the author, January 31, 1981.

what I propose putting in its place. The answer is: nothing, for I think the adversary system is justified.

I do not, let me quickly say, have an argumentative novelty to produce. It would be strange indeed for a social institution to be justified on the basis of virtues other than the tried and true ones, virtues that no one had noticed in it before. My justification is rather a version of the tradition argument, but purged of its ideological overtones. I shall call it the "pragmatic justification" or "pragmatic argument" to suggest its affinity with the relaxed, problem-oriented, and historicist notion of justification associated with American pragmatism. The justification is this:

> First, the adversary system, despite its imperfections, irrationalities, loopholes, and perversities, seems to do as good a job as any at finding truth and protecting legal rights. None of its existing rivals is demonstrably better, and some, such as trial by ordeal, are demonstrably worse. Indeed, even if one of the other systems were slightly better, the human costs – in terms of effort, confusion, anxiety, disorientation, inadvertent miscarriages of justice due to improper understanding, retraining, resentment, loss of tradition, you name it – would outweigh reasons for replacing the existing system.
>
> Second, *some* adjudicatory system is necessary.
>
> Third, it's the way we have done things for at least a century.

These propositions constitute a pragmatic argument: if a social institution does a reasonable enough job of its sort that the costs of replacing it outweigh the benefits, and if we need that sort of job done, we should stick with what we have.

A cynic might say that the insight underlying a pragmatic justification is twofold: first, what has been called the Law of Conservation of Trouble, and second, the principle that the devil you know is better than the devil you don't. The suspicion is that even if the adversary system murders truth (and legal rights and morality) in its characteristic way, whatever we replace it with will do so in new and unexpected ways. Why, then, go through the trauma of change?

That this is a very relaxed sort of justification may be seen from the fact that it works equally well for the inquisitorial system in France and Germany. A pragmatic justification is weak as well because it crumbles in the face of a demonstration that, contrary to what we believe, the institution is awful enough to replace. The argument, in other words, does not really endorse an institution – it only endures it.

Accepting a pragmatic justification of the adversary system, it should be added, does not commit one to a blanket conservatism. One can believe that our society should be drastically changed or that our legal system is scandalously unjust and still accept that a changed society or overhauled legal system should utilize adversary adjudication. Thus, while the argument leads to a conservative conclusion, it does so in a piecemeal, nonideological way, and the conclusion extends no further than the institution for which the argument is offered.

In my opinion, many of our social institutions are like the adversary system in that they admit only of pragmatic justification. Some are not intended to serve any positive moral good; some serve it badly. That these institutions are not worth replacing may be a measure of nothing more than social lethargy and our inability to come up with a better idea; my point is that this is a real reason. A pragmatic argument is logically weak – it justifies institutions without showing that they are better than their rivals, or even that they are particularly good – but in practice it is overwhelmingly powerful. Institutions, like bodies, obey Newton's First Law.

Pragmatic justification and institutional excuses

Because this is so typical of institutions it is worth asking about the effect of pragmatic argument on the moral obligations of institutional functionaries (such as lawyers). The position I want to press is roughly that a social institution that can receive only a pragmatic justification is not capable of providing institutional excuses for immoral acts. To do that, an institution must be justified in a much stronger way, by showing that it is a positive moral good. A pragmatic argument, by contrast, need show only that it is not much more mediocre than its rivals.

Let me spell this out by criticizing what I shall call the Transitivity Argument, which goes as follows:

1. The institution is justified.
2. The institution requires its functionary to do A.
3. Therefore, the functionary is justified in doing A.

This plausible-looking defense of institutional excuses can be criticized by denying the first premise; however, I am accepting the pragmatic justification of the adversary system and thus accepting the premise. Or it could be criticized by attacking the second premise: thus, Richard Abel and William Simon have argued that the role-morality of lawyers is so riddled with contradictions that it is impossible to derive any coherent set of professional requirements from it.[92] My strategy, however, is to deny that the

---

[92] Abel, *Why Does the ABA Promulgate Ethical Rules?* 59 Texas L. Rev. 639 (1981); Simon, *The Ideology of Advocacy,* supra note 7.

conclusion follows from the premises. The institutional obligation is only a *prima facie* obligation, and the weaker the justification of the institution, the weaker the force of this obligation in overriding other morally relevant factors.

To get the argument underway, let us look at the way an institutional excuse might work when the institution is strongly justified, when it is a positive moral good.

Consider, as an example, a charitable organization whose sole function is to distribute food to famine-stricken people in impoverished areas of the world. We will call this the *institution*. Division of labor within it creates different jobs or *institutional tasks*, each of which has specified duties or *role-obligations*. These may be quite general: the logistics officer, for example, might have as his role-obligation procuring means of transporting food. To carry out the role-obligation, he must perform various actions, call them the *role-acts*.

Let us suppose that to get food to a remote village the logistics officer must obtain trucks from a local, very powerful gangster, P. As it happens, P is involved in a number of unsavory activities, including a plan to murder a local man, because P wants to sleep with the man's wife. Imagine further that the logistics officer overhears P dispatching a murderer to kill the man that very night, that P discovers that the logistics officer has overheard him, and that P tells the officer that if the man is warned and escapes, P will not provide the trucks.

The officer faces a terrible moral dilemma. Other things being equal, he is under a moral obligation to warn the man. Let us, at any rate, suppose that this is so. But here, if anywhere, we may wish to permit an institutional excuse. Suppose the officer complies with P's demand. Asked to justify this, he says, "My job is more important." This is an institutional excuse, the structure of which may be spelled out as follows: he points out that the role-act of complying with P is required by his role-obligation, which in turn is necessary to perform the institutional task, which (finally) is justified by the positive moral good of the institution – the saving of many innocent lives.

The general problem, which creates the dilemma, is that the propositions *The institution is a morally good one* and *The institution imposes role-obligations on its officers some of which may mandate morally bad role-acts* can both be true.

In such a case, the institutional excuse, fully spelled out, will take the form I have indicated: the agent justifies the role-act by showing that it is required by the role-obligation, justifies the obligation by showing that it derives from the institutional task, justifies the institutional task by appealing to the structure of the institution, and justifies the institution by demonstrating its moral goodness.

Let us apply this form of argument to a legal example. Freedman uses it in his analysis of the Lake Pleasant bodies case.[93] The lawyers' role-act (preserving the defendant's confidence) was required by the general duty of confidentiality (the role-obligation). This is justified by arguing that the duty is required in order to guarantee adequate criminal defense (the institutional task). That argument maintains that without confidentiality, defendants will not tell their lawyer what the lawyers need to know to conduct an adequate defense. The next step asserts that an adequate defense is a requirement of the adversary system, and this in turn, or so it is claimed and so I have agreed, serves the positive moral good of preserving individual rights against the encroachment of the state.

I am *not* claiming that an institutional excuse is inevitably appropriate when the institution is strongly justified. You and I may differ in our assessment even of the humanitarian aid worker and Lake Pleasant examples. I am claiming only that in such cases a difficult moral dilemma exists, from which an institutional excuse offers one possible way out.

If, on the other hand, an institution can be justified only pragmatically, the sides of the dilemma do not have equal weight and the institutional excuse collapses. For in that case it reads as follows:

It is true that I am morally wronging you. But that is required by my role-obligations, which are essential to my institutional task, which is necessary to the structure of the institution, which is justified

because it is there;
because it's the way we do things around here;
because it's not worth the trouble to replace it.

This, I think, will not do. The excuse rests on an elephant that stands on a tortoise that floats in the sky. But the sky is falling.

Compare this well-known example with the Lake Pleasant case. A youth, Spaulding, badly injured in an automobile wreck, sued for damages. The conscientious defense lawyers had their own doctor examine the youth; the doctor discovered a life-threatening aortic aneurism, apparently caused by the accident, that Spaulding's own doctor had not found. Spaulding was willing to settle the case for $6,500, but the defense lawyers realized that if the youth learned of the aneurism he would demand a much higher amount. The defense lawyer concealed the information and settled for $6,500.[94] How could this be justified? Presumably, the argument would have to track

[93] Freedman, Lawyers' Ethics in an Adversary System, supra note 31, chap. 1.
[94] Spaulding v. Zimmerman, 116 N.W. 2d 704 (1962). For background and discussion on this case, see Roger C. Cramton & Lori P. Knowles, *Professional Secrecy and Its Exceptions*: Spaulding v. Zimmerman *Revisited*, 83 Minn. L. Rev. 63 (1998). Among other things,

Freedman's defense in the Lake Pleasant case, but the final step would be missing. In this case the adversary system is not strongly justified by the liberal argument about keeping the state's hands off people accused of a crime. No one is accused of a crime in this case. Uncharitably put, the basis of confidentiality here is the need to save money for an insurance company. Charitably put, it is that the adversary system is weakly justified – justified because it is there. That may be a reason to risk one's own life on a mountain, but it is not a reason to risk Spaulding's life in a law office.

It might be objected to this line of criticism that the pragmatic argument for the adversary system is a strong justification for it, even in noncriminal cases. After all, what better justification of the system can there be than saying that it performs a necessary function as well as any of its competitors? What absolute yardstick is used to measure it and find it wanting?

The answer to these questions has already been given in our discussion of the difference between the criminal and noncriminal contexts. In the non-criminal context, the primary end of adversary adjudication is the assignment of rewards and remedies on the basis of parties' behavior as prescribed by legal norms: legal justice, rather than protection from the state, is the pre-ponderant goal. The adversary method is supposed to yield accurate accounts of facts and legitimate interpretations of the law. *That* is the absolute yard-stick: if the adversary system yields legal justice, it is a positive moral good. But, as I have argued, we have no reason to believe that it does yield legal justice in the hard cases.

An analogy may clarify this point. Scientists at times accept and use a theory because it is the best account going, even though they do not have much confidence in its truth. Such a theory is pragmatically justified in much the same way as the adversary system: it is as good as its competitors, some theory is necessary, and it is there. It's just that most scientists in the field

---

Cramton and Knowles learned (a) that Zimmerman's defense counsel were (as is common) working for Zimmerman's insurance carrier; (b) that they made the decision not to reveal Spaulding's aortic aneurism without consulting either Zimmerman or the insurer; (c) that the reason Spaulding's inexperienced attorney did not request the defense physician's report was not sheer negligence, but rather that he feared it would lead to disclosure of one of his own physician's reports, which he thought might prevent the court from approving the settlement because it suggested waiting a year to see how bad Spaulding's brain injuries were; and (d) that the judge refrained from criticizing defense counsel in part because counsel's law partner was his close friend.

The denouement of *Spaulding v. Zimmerman* is worth recounting. Several years after the settlement, Spaulding discovered the aneurism when he went in for his draft physical. He had life-saving surgery to repair the damage, and then moved successfully to have the settlement in the case set aside (which is how it came before the Minnesota Supreme Court). But the ending was not entirely happy: because of the delay between the settlement and the surgery, Spaulding suffered a terrible side-effect, losing the power of speech.

predict that the theory will turn out to be false – and for that reason it is weakly, not strongly, justified.[95]

The general point is that some practices carry absolute criteria of success. The criterion of success for a scientific theory is truth; the criterion of success for mountain-climbing is getting to the top and back. Other practices carry criteria that are merely relative (the fastest runner in the world is *ipso facto* a successful runner). A pragmatic argument strongly justifies only the latter sort of practices, but, if I am right, the adversary system is of the former sort.

Let us return to the two confidentiality examples and, more generally, to the adversary system excuse. As we have seen, the adversary system establishes an institutional role, whose functional requirements become role-obligations on those who inhabit the roles. There is a general presumption that lawyers will represent their clients faithfully and keep confidences. But the presumption that lawyers must fulfill their role-obligations may be overcome by sufficiently weighty values on the other side. What if fulfilling the role-obligation breaches some other moral obligation, such as the obligation to reveal information that could save Spaulding's life? An institution anchors a moral excuse only to the extent that it has moral heft. If the institution is justified only because it is there, it possesses only the minutest quantum of force to excuse an otherwise immoral act. The Transitivity Argument fails.

Another way to see this, derived from a point made by Gerald Postema and Bernard Williams, can also be offered.[96] Suppose that the Transitivity Argument were valid. Then it would not be immoral for lawyers to engage in ruthless, rights-violating activity. They would therefore have no occasion for moral regret at their actions. But – and this is Postema's and Williams's point – we want agents in "dirty hands" situations to feel regret at what they must do, because otherwise they will not develop the sort of moral character that enables them to judge when they should refrain from ruthless action. It follows that we should accept the Transitivity Argument only if we are willing to accept lawyers who are incapable of turning off their own adversariality. But that would be an absurd thing to want, because such a lawyer would be unable to draw adequate lines in *any* sort of situation that requires normative judgment, and that is inconsistent with what it takes to practice law at all.

The basic problem with the Transitivity Argument is that it exempts officers of an institution from ordinary moral requirements that conflict with

---

[95] I am indebted to Victoria Choy for pointing out this analogy to me.

[96] Gerald Postema, *Moral Responsibility in Professional Ethics*, 55 NYU L. Rev. 63, 79–80 (1980); Bernard Williams, *Politics and Moral Character*, in Public and Private Morality, supra note 66, at 61–65.

role-obligations, even though the institution itself is in place only because we have done it that way for a long time. The result is to place conformity to existing institutions beyond the very possibility of criticism. This, however, is no longer justified conservatism: rather, it is fetishism of tradition.

Pragmatic arguments do not really praise institutions; they merely give reason for not burying them. Since their force is more inertial than moral, they create insufficient counterweight to resolve dilemmas in favor of the role-obligation. An excuse based on institutions justified in this way is simply a "good soldier" argument with little more to be said.

Conclusion and peroration

It is time to summarize.

Perhaps the best way to see the import of the arguments I have been offering is not as an attack on the adversary system (for, after all, I have not suggested that it should be replaced) so much as an attack on an ideology consisting of these ideas:

1. The adversary system is the most powerful engine of justice ever devised.
2. It is a delicately poised instrument in which the generation of just outcomes depends on the regular functioning of each of its parts.
3. Hence the pursuit of justice morally obligates an attorney to assume a one-sided Broughamesque role.
4. The adversary system, in consequence, institutionally excuses lawyers from ordinary moral obligations conflicting with their professional obligations.
5. Broughamesque advocacy is, moreover, a cornerstone of our system of political liberties, for it is the last defense of the hapless criminal-accused against the awesome power of the state. To restrict the advocate is to invite totalitarianism.

I have argued against the first four of these propositions. About the fifth a more cautious conclusion is in order. The argument it offers, that the criminal defense lawyer "must not regard the alarm, the torments, the destruction which he may bring upon others" (Brougham, again), is rather persuasive, but only because of two special features of the criminal context: that we have political reasons for handicapping the government in its role as enforcer, and that the criminal defendant comes closest to the paradigm of the man-in-trouble. The argument, then, countenances adversarial ruthlessness as a blanket policy only in criminal and quasi-criminal defense, and thus only in these situations is the adversary system fully available as an institutional excuse.

What does all this mean in noncriminal contexts, where this institutional excuse based on liberal fear of the state is unavailable? The answer, very simply, is this. The adversary system possesses only slight moral force, and thus appealing to it can excuse only slight moral wrongs. Anything else that is morally wrong for a nonlawyer to do on behalf of another person is morally wrong for a lawyer to do as well. The lawyer's role carries no moral privileges and immunities.

This does not mean that zealous advocacy is immoral, not even when it frustrates the search for truth or violates legal rights. Sometimes frustrating the search for truth may be a morally worthy thing to do, and sometimes moral rights are ill served by legal rights. All I am insisting on is that the standards by which such judgments are made are the same for lawyers and for nonlawyers. If a lawyer is permitted to puff, bluff, or threaten on certain occasions, this is not because of the adversary system and the Principle of Nonaccountability, but because, in such circumstances, anyone would be permitted to do these things. Nothing justifies doing them on behalf of a predator.

But, it will be objected, my argument leads to a paradox, for I have claimed to offer a vindication, albeit a weak one, of the adversary system, and therefore of the duties of partisan advocacy that it entails. Am I not saying that a lawyer may be professionally obligated to do A and morally obligated not to do A?

That is indeed the conclusion, but there is no contradiction here. The adversary system and the system of professional obligation it mandates are justified only in that, lacking a clearly superior alternative, they should not be replaced. This implies, I have argued, a presumption in favor of professional obligation, but one that any serious and countervailing moral obligation rebuts. Thus, when professional and serious moral obligation conflict, moral obligation takes precedence. When they don't conflict, professional obligations rule the day. The Principle of Professionalism follows from the fact that we have an adversary system; the Principle of Nonaccountability does not. The point of elaborating the former is to tell the lawyer what, in this system, professionalism requires – to insist that it requires zeal, for example, even when cutting corners might be more profitable or pleasant. Professionalism can tell lawyers not to cut corners; my point is that it cannot mandate them to cut throats. When serious moral obligation conflicts with professional obligation, the lawyer must become a civil disobedient to professional rules.

Not that this is likely to happen. Lawyers get paid for their services, not for their consciences. But so does everyone else. As we do not expect the world to strike a truce in the war of all against all, we should not expect lawyers to do so. Shen Te, the Good Woman of Setzuan in Brecht's play, says: "I'd like to be good, it's true, but there's the rent to pay. And that's not all: I sell myself for a living. Even so I can't make ends meet, there's too much competition."[97]

That, of course, is the way the world is, and criticizing an ideology won't change the world. The point of the exercise, I suppose, is merely to get our moral ideas straight: one less ideology is, after all, one less excuse.

[97] Bertolt Brecht, The Good Woman of Setzuan 24 (Eric Bentley trans., Grove Press, 1947).

2

Lawyers as upholders of human dignity (when they aren't busy assaulting it)

The many grounds for the excellence of human nature reported by many men failed to satisfy me – that man is the intermediary between creatures, the intimate of the gods, the king of the lower beings, by the acuteness of his senses, by the discernment of his reason, and by the light of his intelligence the interpreter of nature, the interval between fixed eternity and fleeting time, and (as the Persians say) the bond, nay, rather, the marriage song of the world, on David's testimony but little lower than the angels. Admittedly great though these reasons be, they are not the principal grounds, that is, those which may rightfully claim for themselves the privilege of the highest admiration.

Pico della Mirandella, *Oration on the Dignity of Man* (1486)[1]

A few months ago I had dinner with a litigation partner from a famously combative Washington law firm that specializes in white-collar defense – a firm that has often been the last resort of officials in trouble. She asked me what I was working on, and I told her that I've been thinking about human dignity and its connection with law. I halfway expected the neutral, wary response that practical people often have toward rarefied philosophical issues – the cautious response appropriate when your dinner companion explains that he's been brooding over the Good, the True, and the Beautiful. Instead, she smiled and replied, "That's extremely interesting to me, because defending human dignity is what I do every single day."

Her response came spontaneously and without a moment's hesitation. It seemed like a remarkable thing to say. After all, "defending human dignity" is an awfully abstract, intellectualized way to describe work that is as concrete and sordid as the penitentiaries my friend keeps her clients out of. Her adversaries would hardly use the phrase to describe the smashmouth litigation tactics her firm is famous for. I expect, however, that many lawyers, and not just litigators, will agree with her. And, on reflection, I've come to recognize

---

[1] Trans. Elizabeth Livermore Forbes, in The Renaissance Philosophy of Man 233 (Ernst Cassirer, Paul Oskar Kristeller, John Herman Randall, Jr. eds., 1948).

that it is precisely concern for human dignity which lies at the bottom of arguments in legal ethics that have occupied me for more than twenty years. In this chapter I revisit some of these arguments, and use them to test a pair of working hypotheses: First, that what makes the practice of law worthwhile is upholding human dignity; second, that adversarial excesses are wrong precisely when they assault human dignity instead of upholding it.

Of course, the concept of human dignity raises profound philosophical puzzles, and we can't simply help ourselves to the phrase without undertaking to study what it means – or if indeed it means anything at all. Like Pico della Mirandella five centuries ago, the grounds for human dignity reported by many people (including, by the way, Pico della Mirandella) "fail to satisfy me." The concept of human dignity sprouts from theological roots offered by the Abrahamic religions. The familiar grounds for asserting human dignity are that humanity is created in God's image, that humans have dominion over the rest of nature, and that man consists of spirit. All of these are essentially articles of faith beyond proof or disproof, and I don't believe they can be rationally reconstructed into secular counterparts. Rationalist proofs that we have immortal souls have not survived the philosophical criticisms of Kant, Nietzsche, or for that matter Aristotle. In any event, immortality would confer dignity on the soul only if the soul already possessed dignity on other grounds – immortal cockroaches would have no more dignity than their cousins who are not immortal, but merely very hard to get rid of. And, unfortunately, the picture of the human psyche emerging from scientific psychology seems more humiliating than it is dignifying.[2] More controversially, the philosophical identification of human dignity with autonomy is, or so I shall argue, wrongheaded.

It seems to me that all these efforts fail because they try to zero in on some metaphysical property of humans that makes us the crown of creation, the paramount mortal links in the Great Chain of Being. I suspect that human dignity is not a metaphysical property of individual humans, but rather a property of relationships between humans – between, so to speak, the dignifier and the dignified. To put it another way, "human dignity" designates a *way* of being human, not a *property* of being human. It may even be the name of more than one way of being human.

But that jumps the gun. Here, I want to approach the question "What is human dignity?" modestly and inductively, by looking at several examples of arguments that claim to connect what lawyers do with the defense of human dignity.

---

[2] It is a picture of creatures who, over a wide range of cases, unconsciously falsify reality and change their own values whenever that is necessary to maintain an essential belief in their own inherent goodness. See chapters 7 and 8 of this book.

Admittedly, there is something rather absurd about approaching a great and deep philosophical question by peering into the corridors of law firms. But I take my litigator friend very seriously. There is nothing absurd about connecting human dignity with legal personality and legal rights; and it is legal personality and legal rights that lawyers construct and demolish. By examining arguments about what lawyers do, I hope we can get some sense of what the term 'human dignity' means in them, and in that way tease out a picture of what lawyers and those who study them mean when they invoke human dignity.

I have a more ambitious aim, however, than examining a handful of arguments about lawyers. The notion of human dignity plays something of a cameo role in discussions of legal ethics, although this book argues that it is a lot more central than many writers appreciate. However, it plays an enormous, central, role in the contemporary law of human rights. All of the most vital documents in the twentieth-century law of human rights gives human dignity pride of place. The UN Charter's Preamble states the aim of reaffirming "faith ... in the dignity and worth of the human person . ." Article 1 of the Universal Declaration of Human Rights begins, "All human beings are born free and equal in dignity and rights." The Charter of Fundamental Rights of the European Union begins with an Article 1 entitled "Human Dignity" that reads simply: "Human dignity is inviolable. It must be respected and protected." And Principle VII of the Helsinki Accords asserts a philosophical proposition: that all human rights "derive from the inherent dignity of the human person."[3]

The phrase "inherent dignity of the human person" is, of course, a vague one, and the framers of these instruments left it vague intentionally. When the Universal Declaration was drafted, it seemed initially like a good idea to include philosophers and theologians from all over the world to help clarify its basic concepts. Predictably, however, they quickly fell into sectarian squabbling. The drafters ended by negotiating language that finessed the metaphysical and theological questions at issue.[4] In one famous incident, Eleanor Roosevelt – the chair of the committee drafting the Declaration – hosted a tea for two of its most prominent members, Charles Malik (from Lebanon) and Peng-chun Chang (from China). Both were US-trained philosophers and each was a remarkable figure in his own right. At the tea, however, they fell to debating the foundations of human rights (Malik's Thomism against Chang's Confucianism). Roosevelt's fascination quickly turned to alarm, as she realized the bottomless political pit into which philosophical controversy might

---

[3] See generally Oscar Schachter, *Human Dignity as a Normative Concept*, 77 AJIL 848 (1983).

[4] Johannes Morsink, The Universal Declaration of Human Rights: Origins, Drafting, and Intent 284–302 (1999). See also Mary Ann Glendon, A World Made New: Eleanor Roosevelt and the Universal Declaration of Human Rights (2001).

consign the Declaration. She maneuvered skillfully and successfully to leave metaphysics out of the deliberations. The result was a document that remains strategically silent about what key terms like 'human dignity' are supposed to mean – strategically, because of course it leaves everyone to fill in their own meaning.

Is this the counsel of wisdom? Roosevelt thought so, and we have no reason to doubt her political judgment. But a concept that can mean anything means nothing, and it seems to me that the invocation of human dignity in human rights documents does no conceptual work in explaining what rights everyone ought to have. If anyone denies, for example, that the rights to free speech or to paid maternity leave are genuine human rights – and both of these appear in major human rights instruments despite the fact that some nations deny their validity – how can the case be argued pro or con if human rights are supposed to derive from human dignity, even though the concept of human dignity has intentionally been bled of content? The answer, of course, is that the case gets argued politically and diplomatically. Perhaps that is the best we can hope for. If so, however, then the invocation of human dignity in the instruments turns out to be empty rhetoric – a conceptual wheel unattached to the rest of the machinery.

I would hope that we can do better than this – that we can come up with an understanding of human dignity that doesn't beg too many important questions, but that nevertheless has enough content that it can actually be useful in the critique of existing practices. This is obviously a much bigger task than understanding how lawyers defend human dignity (when they aren't busy assaulting it). But I mean to undertake the smaller task as one step toward the larger – toward understanding human dignity in all its manifestations, not just those that pertain to our entanglements with the legal profession.

Human dignity and the right to counsel: Alan Donagan's argument

Let us begin with the most basic question about lawyers in their role as courtroom advocates: Why should litigants have them? The answer that, over the years, has appealed to me the most rests on a principle stated by the late philosopher Alan Donagan: "No matter how untrustworthy somebody may have proved to be in the past, one fails to respect his or her dignity as a human being if on any serious matter one refuses even provisionally to treat his or her testimony about it as being in good faith."[5] An immediate corollary to this principle is that *litigants get to tell their stories and argue their understandings of the law*. A procedural system that simply gagged a litigant and refused even to consider her version of the case would be in effect

---

[5] Alan Donagan, *Justifying Legal Practice in the Adversary System*, in The Good Lawyer: Lawyers' Roles and Lawyers' Ethics 130 (David Luban ed., 1984).

treating her story as if it didn't exist, her point of view as if it were literally beneath contempt.

Once we accept that human dignity requires litigants to be heard, the justification for the advocate becomes clear. People may be poor public speakers. They may be inarticulate, unlettered, mentally disorganized, or just plain stupid. They may know nothing of the law, and so they are scarcely in a position to argue its interpretation, or to utilize such basic procedural rights as objecting to their adversary's leading questions. Knowing no law, they may omit the very facts that make their case, or focus on pieces of the story that are irrelevant or prejudicial.[6] Their voices may be nails on a chalkboard or too mumbled to understand. They may speak dialect, or for that matter know no English. None of this should matter: human dignity doesn't depend on whether you are stupid or smooth. Hence the need for an advocate. Just as a non-English speaker must be provided with an interpreter, the legally mute should have – in the very finest sense of the term – a mouthpiece.[7]

Thus, Donagan's argument connects the right to counsel with human dignity in two steps: first, that human dignity requires litigants to be heard, and second, that without a lawyer they cannot be heard. Of course, the argument represents an abstraction from reality. In real life, advocates create their theories of the case and assemble the arguments and evidence without caring much whether their theory is the client's theory. Clients, for their part, generally won't have a theory of the case, and what interests them is the outcome, not the fidelity with which their lawyer represents their own version of reality. This is not a decisive objection. The law forces an artificial and stylized organization on to the way stories have to be told; by trial-time, any legally coherent telling of the client's story will bear only scant resemblance to its raw version. And, precisely if the client is inarticulate, unreflective, or simply stupid, the lawyer's version of the client's story will be stronger, cleaner, and more nuanced than the client's own version. The lawyer will read between the lines, and perhaps imbue the story with more subtlety than the client ever could. It seems to me that this does not disqualify the story from being, in an important sense, the client's story. I acknowledge, nevertheless, that if the lawyer embellishes too much, at some point the story ceases to be the client's and becomes instead the lawyer's fictionalized version of the client's story. The difference is a matter of degree, not of kind, but that makes it no less real. For the moment, I will postpone exploring the

---

[6] When Clarence Earl Gideon defended himself against a breaking and entering charge because he couldn't afford a lawyer, he spent most of his time trying to prove that on the night of the crime he was not drunk, which was irrelevant to the charge, and completely overlooked the real weaknesses in the state's case. How was he supposed to know any better? Anthony Lewis, Gideon's Trumpet 59–62 (1964).

[7] See Luban, Lawyers and Justice: An Ethical Study 85–87 (1988).

implications of this point for our discussion of human dignity; but I take it up again shortly.

If the advocate is the client's mouthpiece or (to use a less offensive word) *voice*, telling the client's story and interpreting the law from the client's viewpoint, it follows that advocacy has its limits. The lawyer may not knowingly tell a false story, and perhaps under some circumstances this prohibition includes willful blindness whereby a lawyer affirmatively takes steps to avoid knowing that the story is false.[8] As Donagan puts it, the story has to have the minimum of credibility necessary so that it *can* be provisionally taken as a good-faith account. Decades ago, Lon Fuller and John Randall drafted a quasi-official statement of the principles of adversary ethics, and argued that a lawyer "trespasses against the obligations of professional responsibility, when his desire to win leads him to muddy the headwaters of decision, when, instead of lending a needed perspective to a controversy, he distorts and obscures its true nature."[9] I suspect that almost every trial lawyer would disagree with this conclusion; but, on the terms of Donagan's argument, it seems to me largely correct.[10]

At this point, let us return to the principle underlying Donagan's argument:

No matter how untrustworthy somebody may have proved to be in the past, one fails to respect his or her dignity as a human being if on any serious matter one refuses even provisionally to treat his or her testimony about it as being in good faith.

What does the phrase 'human dignity' signify in this principle? Apparently, honoring a litigant's human dignity means suspending disbelief and hearing the story she has to tell. So, in this context, having human dignity means, roughly, *having a story of one's own*.

I add the words "of one's own" to emphasize the first-personal, subjective character of the story. Fuller once described the advocate's job as displaying the case "in the aspect it assumes when viewed from that corner of life into which fate has cast his client."[11] The client's story is not just the story in which she figures; it is the story she has to tell. It is *about* her in both senses of the term: she is its subject-matter, and she is its center. It revolves

---

[8] See chapter 6 of this book.

[9] Lon L. Fuller & John Randall, *Professional Responsibility: Report of the Joint Conference of the ABA-AALS*, 44 ABAJ 1159, 1161 (1958).

[10] But there remains plenty of room for controversy about how far the defender's leeway to mislead extends. See David Luban, *Are Criminal Defenders Different?*, 91 Mich. L. Rev. 1729, 1759–62 (1993).

[11] Lon L. Fuller, *The Adversary System*, in Talks on American Law 31 (Harold Berman ed., Vintage, 1961).

about her, just as, to terrestrials, the Sun revolves about the Earth (no more and no less).[12]

Now, subjectivity is (if you'll pardon the word-play) an elusive subject. As Wittgenstein observed, my subjectivity is not, properly speaking, part of the world at all: it is the limit of the world, just as my eye is the limit of my visual field rather than a part of it.[13] If I were to compose a book that enumerated every fact in the world, including every fact about me, about D. L., my subjectivity would appear nowhere in it. The book (Wittgenstein suggests we entitle it *The World As I Found It*) would record every fact about D. L. except that *I* am D. L.[14]

Intuitively, it seems plain that, elusive or not, our own subjectivity lies at the very core of our concern for human dignity. To deny my subjectivity is to deny my human dignity. Obviously, only a psychotic or a solipsist really thinks "the world revolves around me." But, tautologically, my world revolves around me; tautologically, that is, I am the one necessary being in my world. This is what some have called the "egocentric predicament."[15] Human dignity is in some sense a generalization from the egocentric predicament: human beings have ontological heft because each of us is an 'I', and I have ontological heft. For others to treat me as though I have none fundamentally denigrates my status in the world. It amounts to a form of humiliation that violates my human dignity. Hence Donagan's principle: to honor a litigant's dignity as a person requires us to hear the story she has to tell, because to ignore and exclude her treats her as though her subjectivity and the point of view it inhabits are totally insignificant.

It seems here that I am explaining human dignity through a metaphysical theory. Subjectivity gives us ontological heft, ignoring someone's subjectivity denies that she has ontological heft, and that humiliates her. The trouble is that – as I indicated – subjectivity is not really a metaphysical fact about us; it appears nowhere in the Big Book of Facts, *The World As I Found It*.[16] So I want to propose another way of accommodating our key intuitions, and that is by reversing the order of explanation. Certain ways of treating

---

[12] My own thinking about stories has been deeply influenced by Hannah Arendt's discussion in The Human Condition 181–88 (1958); the present idea at 184. See Robert P. Burns, A Theory of the Trial (1999), which analyzes trials as narrative structures.

[13] Ludwig Wittgenstein, Tractatus Logico-Philosophicus 117 (D. F. Pears & B. McGuiness trans., 1961) (1921), 5.632, 5.633, 5.6331.

[14] Ibid., 5.631, at 117. My formulation of this point derives both from Wittgenstein and from Thomas Nagel, The View From Nowhere 55–56 (1986).

[15] The term originates in Ralph Barton Perry, *The Ego-Centric Predicament*, 7 J. Phil., Psych. & Scientific Methods 5 (1910) (now J. Phil.).

[16] A Kantian would say that subjectivity in the sense described here is a transcendental fact, not an empirical fact. See, e.g., Immanuel Kant, Critique of Pure Reason (1781/1787), *A346/ B404, *A355, *B426–27.

people humiliate them; humiliating people denies their human dignity. One of those humiliations consists in presuming that some individuals have no point of view worth hearing or expressing, and that is tantamount to denying the ontological heft of their point of view. Instead of beginning with a metaphysical theory of subjectivity, identifying subjectivity with human dignity, and using that to explain why humiliating people violates human dignity, I am proposing that we begin with the proposition that humiliating people denies their human dignity. We then explain what human dignity is by trying to isolate characteristic features of humiliation – in this case, treating a person's story and viewpoint as insignificant. In effect, an explanation along these lines begins with a relationship between people – between the dignifier and the dignified – called "honoring (or respecting) human dignity." Human dignity as such becomes a derived term – derived from the relation – rather than a primitive term. By taking Donagan's argument at face value, we arrive at a common-sense or, as a philosopher might say, a "naturalized" account of human dignity as *having a story of one's own*, and the wrong of denying human dignity as humiliation. The courtroom advocate defends human dignity by giving the client voice and sparing the client the humiliation of being silenced and ignored.

That brings us back to an earlier question. What about the advocate who constructs a story that has nothing to do with the client's? Consider an example offered by William Simon. A man is arrested while placing a stolen television into his car, and charged with possession of stolen goods. He tells the police that he bought it from a stranger on the street and had no idea it was stolen. At trial, he does not testify, but his lawyer wishes to argue the client's version of how he obtained the television. The lawyer, cross-examining the arresting officer, elicits the admission that the defendant was placing the television in the back seat of the car, not the trunk. Arguing to the jury, the lawyer points out that if the defendant knew the television was stolen, he would be unlikely to put it in plain sight. The fact that he was placing it in the back seat rather than the trunk strongly suggests his innocence. But, unbeknownst to the jury and the prosecutor – yet known to the lawyer – the defendant didn't have a key to the trunk.[17]

Here, the lawyer has constructed a client story that is, we will assume, a fabrication that the client has not told in good faith. Criminal defenders will justify the lawyer's tactic by the following argument: the lawyer has not lied, but merely shown that the evidence supports the client's version of the story. Given this evidence, the jury should acquit, because if the evidence reasonably supports an innocent alternative, it cannot prove guilt beyond a reasonable doubt. All the lawyer has done is dramatize the reasonable doubt instead of arguing for it in an abstract matter. That seems like an entirely

[17] William H. Simon, The Practice of Justice: A Theory of Lawyers' Ethics 171–72 (2000).

legitimate way to make the case for reasonable doubt. Every litigator knows that it takes a story to beat a story. Arguing abstractly for reasonable doubt will never shake a jury's preconceptions.

I think this is a good argument, and it illustrates one of the things skilled advocates do: they construct and promote theories of the case consistent with the evidence even if the theories have nothing to do with reality. If so, then at least this function of the advocate has nothing to do with telling the client's story or providing voice to the legally mute. And so this function of the advocate seemingly has nothing to do with defending the client's human dignity, at least according to Donagan's argument that I have endorsed.

In fact, however, it does. The reason lies deeply embedded in the unique character of criminal law. To honor the defendant's human dignity – in the sense we have been exploring, namely to presume initially that the defendant has a good-faith story to tell – requires us to presume innocence if the defendant claims innocence. That by itself does not tell us what the burden of proof should be that overcomes this presumption. The choice of proof beyond a reasonable doubt arises because criminal conviction carries moral condemnation with it.[18] Because we presume innocence, we must be extremely careful to avoid mistaken moral condemnation. Hence we apply the "beyond a reasonable doubt" standard. In essence, this standard says that if a good-faith story of innocence could be constructed from the evidence, it violates the human dignity of the defendant to convict – even if that story is untrue. And the advocate defends her client's human dignity either directly, by telling his story, or indirectly, by demonstrating that a good-faith story of innocence could be constructed from the evidence.

This is a more complex account of the criminal defender's role than our initial idea of the advocate as the client's voice. The defender does serve as the client's voice if the client wants his story told. But if he does not, the defender still protects the client's human dignity by demonstrating that the evidence is consistent with the presumption of innocence. I take it that this dual role of the advocate as defender of human dignity derives from the fact that criminal conviction carries with it moral condemnation, that is, loss of stature. Outside the criminal process, losing a lawsuit can still carry moral stigma – think of losing a sexual harassment lawsuit, for example – but it does not quite carry the communal condemnation that criminal conviction does. And so, while civil litigators strive mightily to blow smoke in the eyes of the fact-finder if that serves their clients' interest, I think they can scarcely claim that doing so has anything much to do with defending the human dignity of their clients.

---

[18] Henry M. Hart, Jr. argued in his classic *The Aims of the Criminal Law*, 23 Law & Contemp. Probs. 401 (1958) that the sole distinguishing feature of criminal law is the element of moral condemnation attached to criminal punishment. I adopt this view here.

Paternalism toward clients

The idea of advocates as voices for those who might otherwise be legally mute has obvious relevance to the issue of lawyers' paternalism toward clients. I use the term "paternalism" to refer to interfering with someone else's liberty for their own good. In the present context, the term refers even more specifically to a lawyer's refusal to do what the client wants because it would harm the client.

Consider the case *Jones v. Barnes*.[19] Barnes, convicted of robbery, wanted his court-appointed appellate lawyer Melinger to include some specific arguments in his brief. Even though the arguments were not frivolous, Melinger refused to include them, and when Barnes's conviction was affirmed, he raised an "ineffective assistance of counsel" claim. The US Supreme Court rejected the claim, and Chief Justice Burger's opinion offered frankly paternalistic reasons for the rejection. Good appellate advocates understand that less is more, and freighting a brief with bad arguments simply detracts from the best arguments in the brief. To give clients control over tactics "would disserve the very goal of vigorous and effective advocacy."[20]

Justices Brennan and Marshall replied in dissent that "today's ruling denigrates the values of individual autonomy and dignity ... The role of the defense lawyer should be above all to function as the instrument and defender of the client's autonomy and dignity."[21] Rather clearly, the concept of dignity at work is very close to the one we have been examining. Respect for the client's dignity consists in getting the lawyer to articulate the client's arguments – how the law and trial looked to the client. Perhaps the client's argument was that his trial lawyer was ineffective because the lawyer bullied him out of his intention to testify; or perhaps he was incensed that the police tricked him into revealing where the stolen loot was hidden by taunting him about his manhood. Perhaps he simply wishes to argue that the one-eye-witness rule is insufficient to establish his identity; or, as in Barnes's case, he wishes to argue that his trial counsel prepared inadequately for the trial and failed to challenge inflammatory remarks by the prosecutor. All of these arguments are sure losers, but none of them is frivolous, and it might matter greatly to the client that Melinger included them in his brief. These arguments represent the client's story about why he was wrongfully convicted, and to dismiss them as Melinger did is an affront to Barnes's dignity as a human being and a story-bearer.

Justices Brennan and Marshall refer to "the values of individual autonomy and dignity." And one important question for us to consider is whether autonomy and dignity are related values – indeed, whether perhaps they are the same thing, or, more precisely, whether the best analysis of human dignity

[19] 436 US 745 (1983).   [20] Ibid. at 754.   [21] Ibid. at 763.

will identify it with autonomy. That would be a familiar and attractive analysis. Familiar, because it has roots deep in the history of philosophy, beginning with Renaissance writers such as Pico della Mirandella (who identifies human dignity with freedom of choice), and including, most famously, Kant.[22] Attractive, because as we all know, Americans are in love with freedom of choice. Legal historian Lawrence Friedman, analyzing contemporary American legal culture, refers to us as "the Republic of Choice."[23] The fact that we don't like someone else telling us what to do suggests that the offensive feature of paternalism lies in its violation of autonomy – that paternalism offends human dignity because autonomy *is*, or is the basis of, human dignity.

Before proceeding, it is important to observe that Kant's concept of autonomy differs greatly from what contemporary Americans ordinarily call freedom of choice. Etymologically, 'auto-nomy' means self-legislation: giving laws to oneself and acting according to them. This was what Kant meant by autonomy, and the word entered the vocabulary of morals and law primarily through the Kantian philosophy. Kant modeled morality on legislation, and conceived of the moral agent as one who acts on moral laws rather than inclinations, thus as one who asks about each proposed action, "If I were a legislator, could I will the maxim commending this action as a universal law?"[24]

That is surely not what we mean by 'autonomy' when we think of freedom of choice in the ordinary sense prevailing in American culture. Freedom of choice means doing whatever I want; that is, not having to do what others want me to do, or even to consider except in a calculating way what others

---

[22] Pico imagines God addressing Adam: "The nature of all other beings is limited and constrained within the bounds of laws prescribed by Us. Thou, constrained by no limits, in accordance with thine own free will ... shalt ordain for thyself the limits of thy nature ... With freedom of choice and with honor ... thou mayest fashion thyself in whatever shape thou shalt prefer. Thou shalt have the power to degenerate into the lower forms of life, which are brutish. Thou shalt have the power, out of thy soul's judgment, to be reborn into the higher forms, which are divine." Pico adds, "Who would not admire this our chameleon?" Pico della Mirandella, *Oration on the Dignity of Man*, supra note 1, at 225. Immanuel Kant, Foundations of the Metaphysics of Morals 60–61 (Robert Paul Wolff ed., Lewis White Beck trans., 1969) (1785), Ak. 434–36.

[23] Lawrence M. Friedman, The Republic of Choice: Law, Authority, and Culture (1990).

[24] In Paton's by now standard typology, my formulation in this sentence combines Formula III of the categorical imperative, the Formula of Autonomy ("So act that your will can regard itself at the same time as making universal law through its maxim") with Formula IIIa, the Formula of the Kingdom of Ends ("So act as if you were always through your maxims a law-making member in a universal kingdom of ends"). H. J. Paton, The Categorical Imperative: A Study in Kant's Moral Philosophy (Harper & Row 1965), paraphrasing from Kant, Foundations of the Metaphysics of Morals, supra note 22, at 4 Ak. 434 and 4 Ak. 438. I prefer Beck's translation of *Reich* as "realm" rather than "kingdom," however, because Kant conceived of the *Reich der Zwecke* as a republic, not a kingdom.

might wish. Freedom of choice means consumer sovereignty. It means don't tread on me. It means my way or the highway. The difference between this and Kantian autonomy could not be sharper. For Kant, autonomy lies in the power to act on the basis of duty rather than inclination, whereas in American culture, with its strong libertarian streak, it means the power of acting on inclination rather than duty. Kantian autonomy represents freedom achieved through stoic self-control and self-command; it means reasoned self-restraint. Freedom of choice represents casting off restraints. Donagan, a profound student of Kant, complained with some justice that the latter conception of autonomy is a "vulgarity" – but, be that as it may, it is popular culture's favorite vulgarity.[25]

However, I want to reject the identification of human dignity with autonomy in either Kant's form or the consumer-sovereignty form. Autonomy focuses on just one human faculty, the will, and identifying dignity with autonomy likewise identifies human dignity with willing and choosing. This, I believe, is a truncated view of humanity and human experience. Honoring someone's human dignity means honoring their being, not merely their willing. Their being transcends the choices they make. It includes the way they experience the world – their perceptions, their passions and sufferings, their reflections, their relationships and commitments, what they care about. Strikingly, the experience of caring about someone or something has a phenomenology very different from that of free choice. When I care about something, it chooses me – we sometimes say "it grabs me" – rather than the other way around. Caring lacks the "affect of command" that Nietzsche thought was definitive of the autonomous will.[26] And yet what I care about is central to who I am, and to honor my human dignity is to take my cares and commitments seriously. The real objection to lawyers' paternalism toward their clients is not that lawyers interfere with their clients' autonomous choices, but that they sometimes ride roughshod over the commitments that make the client's life meaningful and so impart dignity to it.[27]

Consider a particularly troubling case, that of Theodore Kaczynski, the Unabomber. Kaczynski, a mathematician-turned-recluse, came to believe that technological society is destroying humanity. In his secluded mountain cabin in Montana, he fashioned bombs and mailed them to technologists, academics, and businessmen whose activities he thought were emblematic of technological society. After years of murdering and maiming his victims, Kaczynski anonymously contacted major newspapers and told them that he

[25] Donagan, supra note 5, at 129.

[26] Friedrich Nietzsche, Beyond Good and Evil §25, at 19 (Walter Kaufmann trans., 1966) (1886).

[27] This is the view of paternalism that I develop in David Luban, *Paternalism and the Legal Profession*, 1981 Wisc. L. Rev. 454. See generally Harry G. Frankfurt, Importance of What We Care About: Philosophical Essays (1988).

would halt the bombings if they would publish his 35,000-word manifesto against modernity, *Industrial Society and Its Future.* Remarkably, they did. Kaczynski was captured when his own brother read the manifesto, suspected the identity of its author, and turned him in in return for a promise by the government (later broken) that it would not seek the death penalty.[28]

Kaczynski's lawyers, both of them first-rate federal public defenders, decided to put on a mental defense. The problem was that they couldn't get Kaczynski to go along. He didn't even want to be interviewed by a psychiatrist. He had his own theory of how he would win acquittal: his lawyers would move to exclude all the evidence seized from his cabin because the search was illegal, and without that evidence the government had no case.[29]

Of course, the chance that the court would exclude the evidence was approximately zero – a mathematician like Kaczynski would say that the chance was "epsilon" – and Kaczynski's optimism about the strategy was a product of legal naivete if not of mental disturbance. But independently of his faith in the exclusion strategy, Kaczynski simply abominated the prospect of a mental defense. As he wrote in his manifesto, "Our society tends to regard as a 'sickness' any mode of thought or behavior that is inconvenient for the system, and this is plausible because when an individual doesn't fit into the system it causes pain to the individual as well as problems for the system. Thus the manipulation of an individual to adjust him to the system is seen as a 'cure' for a 'sickness' and therefore as good."[30] In a letter to the judge, he wrote, "I do not believe that science has any business probing the workings of the human mind, and ... my personal ideology and that of the mental-health professions are mutually antagonistic."[31]

But he was confronted by relentless pressure from his lawyers, from his brother, and from an anti-death-penalty consultant his brother hired to help "manage" Kaczynski.[32] His lawyers reassured him that the psychiatric evidence would be used only at the penalty stage if he was convicted, not at the guilt stage; and Kaczynski, convinced that the case would never get to the penalty stage because he would be acquitted, relented and spoke to the psychiatrist.[33] Apparently, his lawyers also reassured him that the main reason they wanted him to speak with a psychiatrist was to gather evidence to refute media assertions that he was demented.[34]

---

[28] See William Finnegan, *Defending the Unabomber*, The New Yorker, March 16, 1998, at 52.
[29] Ibid. at 57.
[30] Theodore Kaczynski, The Unabomber's Manifesto: Industrial Society and Its Future, para. 155 (1995), available at <www.panix.com/~clays/Una/una5.html#section20>.
[31] Quoted in US v. Kaczynski, 239 F.3d 1108, 1123 (9th Cir. (2001) (Reinhardt, J., dissenting).
[32] Finnegan, supra note 28, at 54.   [33] 239 F.3d at 1111.
[34] Ibid. at 1122–23 (Reinhardt, J., dissenting).

But then they double-crossed him. At the last minute, they announced that at the guilt phase they would undertake the mental defense – the only one that might save his life. Stunned and helpless, Kaczynski demanded to represent himself rather than let his lawyers put on the mental defense. He wrote to the judge,

> It is humiliating to have one's mind probed. [My lawyers] calculatedly deceived me in order to get me to reveal my private thoughts, and then without warning they made accessible to the public the cold and heartless assessments of their experts ... to me this was a stunning blow ... [and] the worst experience I ever underwent in my life ... I would rather die, or suffer prolonged physical torture, than have the [mental] defense imposed on me in this way by my present attorneys.[35]

Subsequently, he attempted suicide. But if Kaczynski was in a bind, Judge Burrell was in one as well. If he let Kaczynski represent himself, a headline-grabbing trial would turn into a gruesome travesty in which a team of professional prosecutors mowed down an unrepresented, mentally disturbed defendant and secured the death penalty, which it would have been the judge's unhappy responsibility to impose. The judge denied Kaczynski's *Faretta* motion (a motion to represent himself) on the unlikely ground that Kaczynski was simply manipulating to postpone his trial – although, as Kaczynski rightly pointed out, he had nothing to gain by delaying the trial because he was already in prison. Faced with the alternative of the mental defense and a plea bargain, Kaczynski pleaded guilty, and received a sentence of life without parole.

Could Kaczynski have had any respectable reasons for rejecting the psychiatric defense, or was his behavior simply his illness talking? The answer, I think, is that his reasons were perfectly comprehensible and respectable. The mental defense would discredit what he regarded as his life's principal contribution to human welfare, the manifesto that he had killed to get into print. If the manifesto were discredited, then his intellectual justification for his terrorism would evaporate. The defense would paint him, in Kaczynski's own words, as nothing more than a "grotesque and repellent lunatic" – in the eyes of millions.[36] Where is the dignity in that?

Let me make clear that I am not defending Kaczynski, who remorselessly blew off the limbs and took the lives of innocent people. In my view, that makes him an evil man. Nor am I denying that he may be suffering from some form of mental illness. But the manifesto he wrote is a coherent work of social theory, certainly as coherent as many essays by respectable philosophers, and more coherent by far than most anarchist rants on the internet. And his motivation for wanting to avoid the mental defense is equally

---

[35] Ibid. at 1123.   [36] Ibid. at 1121.

coherent, and expressed with substantial eloquence. He did not want to be portrayed as a grotesque and repellent lunatic, for then millions of people would dismiss his life's work as grotesque and repellent lunacy. The thought that he would prefer death or torture to abject humiliation is hardly insane. By failing to respect his wishes, his attorneys demolished his human dignity.

Their defenders might protest. Doesn't the fact that Kaczynski was willing to permit the mental defense in the penalty phase of his trial indicates that he preferred humiliation to death? The only reason that he rejected the mental defense in the guilt phase was his delusion that he did not need it to win acquittal.

I think the explanation is different. Police interrogators often wear suspects down until they sign false confessions simply to make the interrogation stop. I think that, in the same way, Kaczynski's lawyers simply wore him down, and he finally agreed to the psychiatric interview to humor them and get them to stop. They are, after all, topnotch, relentless advocates, and Kaczynski stated that he was utterly exhausted.[37]

When Kaczynski's counsel overrode his resistance and humiliated him in the eyes of millions, it seems to me that they did wrong. But the wrong they did has nothing special to do with Kaczynski's autonomy. True, he had chosen to forgo a mental defense and they took away his choice. But the important wrong they did to him was not to take away his choice of defense, as though the choice of how to be convicted matters a great deal. It was that they made nonsense of his deepest commitments, of what mattered to him and made him who he was. That was their sin against human dignity. Autonomy has little to do with it.

In the aftermath of his trial, Kaczynski wrote:

Perhaps I ought to hate my attorneys for what they have done to me, but I do not. Their motives were in no way malicious. They are essentially conventional people who are blind to some of the implications of this case, and they acted as they did because they subscribe to certain professional principles that they believe left them no alternative. These principles may seem rigid and even ruthless to a non-lawyer, but there is no doubt my attorneys believe in them sincerely.[38]

Condescending? No doubt. Kaczynski paints his counsel as narrow-minded professional automata. Given the portrait they painted of him – as a schizophrenic, not a terrorist – this seems like poetic justice.

---

[37] Ibid. at 1124.
[38] Michael Mello, *The Non-Trial of the Century: Representations of the Unabomber*, 24 Vt. L. Rev. 417, 502 (2000).

Human dignity, confidentiality, and self-incrimination

As a third example of the grounding of lawyers' responsibilities in concern for human dignity, let us next consider the attorney–client privilege and the related duty of lawyers to keep client confidences. The familiar justification of these doctrines lies in the concern that without confidentiality, clients will be chilled from telling their lawyers what the lawyers need to know to represent them. Champions of confidentiality often point to this argument to demonstrate the close connection between confidentiality and the core rationale of advocacy – based, I have just argued, in concern for human dignity. What good is the right to an advocate who can help me tell my story if I am afraid to reveal to my advocate the very story that she is supposed to help me tell?

However, this is a weak, almost self-contradictory argument for confidentiality. After all, the only reason that I need confidentiality is my fear that without it my advocate can be compelled to reveal whatever story I tell her. The fear, in other words, is not that abolishing confidentiality will make my lawyer an ineffective mouthpiece. The fear is that it will make her all too effective, a perfect conduit of a story that I would prefer never gets told at all. The "mouthpiece" rationale behind advocacy seems on its face to provide an argument for abolishing confidentiality, not for preserving it.

Perhaps because they understand this, defenders of confidentiality usually invoke a utilitarian, systemic argument in addition to the one based on human dignity. Only if advocates know in advance the strengths and weaknesses of their case can they investigate properly and frame the strongest arguments; and a properly functioning adversary system requires investigation and strong arguments.

This, too, however, is a weak argument, because confidentiality and the attorney–client privilege can be used to keep crucial information out of the system as well as to ensure that it gets into the system. A doctrine that frustrates the search for truth can scarcely be defended on the ground that it's good for the adversary system. Almost 200 years ago, Jeremy Bentham argued that abolishing the attorney–client privilege would not harm the innocent, who have nothing to fear from the truth, and thus that the privilege helps only the guilty.[39] Bentham's argument is too glib, because we can easily imagine cases in which innocent people might not realize that they are innocent, and be chilled from telling their counsel the very facts that exonerate them. But cases of this sort are likely to be too few to undermine Bentham's conclusion that confidentiality is a bad bet on utilitarian terms. His fundamental point is that, from the point of view of truth and justice we would be

---

[39] Jeremy Bentham, 5 Rationale of Judicial Evidence, Specially Applied to English Practice, 302–11 (London, Hunt & Clarke, 1827).

better off if miscreants' lawyers spilled the beans. Why not change the doctrine of confidentiality to compel the lawyers to sing? In that case, either the truth would come out, or miscreants would be chilled from revealing the damning facts to their lawyers and alerting the lawyers that they will have to contrive some method to make truth look like lies and fiction look like fact.

Indeed, confidentiality can actually harm the innocent. Precisely because everyone knows that lawyers must keep the secrets of dishonest clients as well as honest ones, those who deal with lawyers may mistrust and discount the reliability of what they say on behalf of clients. This harms the innocent client who wants what her lawyer says to be trusted.[40] As Richard Painter has shown, it may actually help business clients trying to reassure nervous potential lenders if lawyers and clients waive confidentiality, in effect contracting around the protections it offers.[41]

So far, then, we find only reasons to abandon confidentiality and the attorney–client privilege, not to defend them. Let us try again. Suppose the attorney–client privilege and the duty of confidentiality were eliminated from the legal system, and consider the situation faced by a client with something to hide. The client faces a trilemma of unpleasant choices. First, he can elect not to tell his story to his lawyer, because he is afraid the lawyer might be compelled to reveal it. Second, he can lie to his lawyer. Either way, silence or lies, the client loses much of the benefit that having an advocate was supposed to provide. Or, finally, he can reveal the story to his lawyer, knowing that doing so amounts to revealing it to the world at large. If the story concerns a crime he has committed, revealing it to his lawyer amounts to vicarious self-incrimination, because without the attorney–client privilege the lawyer can be compelled to testify about whatever the client has told her. All three choices are disastrous: the first two abrogate the right to counsel, while the third abandons the right against self-incrimination.

At this point, in fact, the argument becomes isomorphic to a parallel argument in the debate about the privilege against self-incrimination (which, by the way, Bentham also opposed on utilitarian grounds). The confidentiality trilemma exactly parallels the US Supreme Court's analysis in the 1964 opinion *Murphy v. Waterfront Commission.*[42] According to the unanimous Court, abolishing the privilege against self-incrimination is inhumane because it would confront the witness with "the cruel trilemma of self-accusation, perjury or contempt."[43] That is: if the witness refuses to testify,

[40] See Daniel R. Fischel, *Lawyers and Confidentiality*, 65 U. Chi. L. Rev. 1, 18–19 (1998).

[41] Richard W. Painter, *Toward a Market for Lawyer Disclosure Services: In Search of Optimal Whistleblowing Rules*, 63 Geo. Wash. L. Rev. 221 (1995).

[42] 378 US 52 (1964).

[43] Ibid. at 55. The concurring opinions do not differ from the Court's opinion about the rationale of the privilege.

he can be jailed indefinitely for civil contempt; if he testifies truthfully, he incriminates himself; and if he testifies falsely he commits perjury. The confidentiality and self-incrimination trilemmas involve the same trio of options: self-destructive silence, self-incriminating revelation, and lying.

Murphy's cruel-trilemma argument – and, indeed, the entire rationale of the self-incrimination privilege – is controversial.[44] For, one might ask, why recognize a privilege that (like attorney confidentiality) often helps the guilty escape conviction? And what is so cruel about compulsory self-incrimination? Obviously, self-incrimination is bad for the witness because it might convict him of a crime; but we typically suppose that convicting the guilty is socially valuable rather than cruel, even if the guilty find it disagreeable. Perhaps criminal punishment is inherently cruel; but if so, it would be cruel whether the witness were incriminated by his own testimony or by the testimony of others. Once we conclude that punishing crimes through imprisonment is not unacceptably cruel, it seems peculiar to throw up our hands in horror at the lesser cruelty of compelled testimony, which seems trivial by comparison with jail. Nor, finally, is there anything intrinsically repugnant about the act of self-incrimination. After all, if a remorseful defendant voluntarily confesses his crime we should praise him for accepting responsibility; in any event, we would hardly condemn him for confessing. What cruelty is *Murphy* talking about?

Professor Akhil Amar believes that the cruelty *Murphy* worries about is "psychological," the angst of the hard choice.[45] But, as Amar and other commentators rightly observe, this worry seems excessive, and oddly inconsistent with our willingness to countenance other psychologically wrenching criminal investigation techniques. Witnesses can be and are compelled to testify against their friends or members of their immediate families; if anything, compulsory betrayal is more "ruthlessly callous" than compulsory self-incrimination.[46] Moreover, prosecutors have little compunction about immunizing foot-soldiers in criminal gangs to compel their testimony even when the witnesses run the risk of being murdered or having their families murdered if they sing.[47] Now *that* is an agonizing choice. If the law is so concerned about psychological cruelty, why permit practices like these?

The answer, I believe, is that the cruelty of compelled self-incrimination is at bottom not psychological. In fact, the *Murphy* Court makes no mention of

---

[44] Some scholars, notably Professor David Dolinko, have carefully dissected the arguments for the privilege against self-incrimination and concluded that none of them really works. David Dolinko, *Is There a Rationale for the Privilege Against Self-Incrimination?*, 33 UCLA L. Rev. 1063 (1986).

[45] Akhil Reed Amar, The Constitution and Criminal Procedure: First Principles 65 (1997).

[46] Ibid. at 214 n. 130.   [47] Dolinko, supra note 44, at 1094–95.

psychology – but it does say that compulsory self-incrimination would contradict "our respect for the inviolability of the human personality."[48] That sounds like a more abstract and philosophical concern than worry about the witness's unpleasant psychological experiences. It is, in fact, a concern about violating human dignity.

The basic idea is that although it is sometimes permissible to injure someone, for example by punishing him, it is immoral to make him do it to himself. You do not make the inmate lock himself in his cell each night, just as you do not punish a naughty child by making her throw away her favorite toys – even if locking up the prisoner or taking away the child's toys are acceptable punishments when administered by an appropriate outside authority.[49]

This intuitive idea seems right. However, it may not suffice to explain the cruelty of compelled self-incrimination. As David Dolinko points out, what revolts us about compelling people to administer punishments to themselves is the element of deliberate sadism. The sole point seems to be humiliating the victim. By contrast, the point of compelling testimony is not humiliating the witness, but finding out the truth. Absent the aspect of deliberate humiliation, we might find no special affront to human dignity in compulsory self-incrimination.[50]

I think that Dolinko is right that compelled self-punishment violates human dignity because it humiliates the victim. But he is wrong that compelled self-incrimination does not likewise humiliate the witness. In both practices, the humiliation lies in enlisting a person's own will in the process of punishing her, splitting her against herself. To see this, begin with the actual language of the self-incrimination clause, which states that no person "shall be compelled in any criminal case to be a witness against himself."[51] The crucial phrase "witness against himself" indicates a kind of splitting or division within the self – one half, the person with an interest in evading condemnation; the other, the witness who disinterestedly provides whatever information the state requires. A witness fulfills a civic obligation. Even if it is unpleasant or inconvenient to testify, she must do so for the good of the community, if necessary under compulsion of subpoena. Temporarily, at any rate, the witness becomes the eyes and ears of the community, and aims at a collective rather than a personal or individual good.

To be a witness against yourself means to assume the disinterested outsider's stance toward your own condemnation. This represents an extraordinary kind of self-alienation, as if the only interest you have in the matter is the state's interest in ascertaining the truth and apportioning blame. Being a witness against yourself divides you in two, one the individual with an

---

[48] 378 US 52, 55 (1964).   [49] Dolinko, supra note 44, at 1104–7.   [50] Ibid. at 1105–6.
[51] US Constitution, Amendment V.

interest in evading condemnation, the other the state's representative; and compelling you to be a witness against yourself subordinates the former to the latter. In effect, it treats the individual as insignificant – as if his subjectivity simply doesn't exist or doesn't matter. Even if humiliation is not the purpose of compelling someone to be a witness against himself, as it is in forcing someone to administer his own punishment, humiliation is the outcome.

It might be thought that the real issue in self-incrimination is what it does to the witness's autonomy – his natural right (the Lockean language seems appropriate here) to reject the state and the community and the law, and to say, in effect, "You can lock me up if you want to, but you won't get me to help you do it." Michael Green likens the witness to a prisoner of war who refuses to give any information except his name, rank, and serial number.[52] In the same vein, Michael Seidman relates the following story from a criminal trial. An aggressive prosecutor was cross-examining a defendant with an alibi, hectoring him with trick questions to make him seem like a liar. As the barrage of questions continued, the defendant "stood up, straightened himself to his full height, and said in words that will live as long as the English language is spoken, 'Fuck this shit!' " He was convicted, and went to prison. Seidman comments: "But in a deeper sense, he was a truly free man. They had his body, but they couldn't touch his soul."[53] Saying "Fuck this shit!" to the state, one might think, is the autonomy right that the self-incrimination clause means to defend: the right spares the witness the need for the heroic melodrama that Seidman's client engaged in.[54]

Although this is an attractive argument, I don't in the end think it succeeds, and I don't think autonomy is the real issue.[55] I have already argued that identifying human dignity with autonomy represents a deep philosophical mistake. But even those enamored of autonomy must recognize that in the context of self-incrimination the appeal to autonomy proves too much. If the self-incrimination privilege protects a supposed natural right to flip the

[52] Michael S. Green, *The Privilege's Last Stand: The Privilege Against Self-Incrimination and the Right to Rebel Against the State*, 65 Brook. L. Rev. 627, 634, 716 n. 245 (1999). See also Louis Michael Seidman, *Points of Intersection: Discontinuities at the Junction Between Criminal Law and the Welfare State*, 7 Journal of Contemporary Legal Issues 97, 131 (1996), which spells out a version of this argument by observing that compulsory self-incrimination is tantamount to forced consent to one's own punishment.

[53] Louis Michael Seidman, *Some Stories About Confessions and Confessions About Stories*, in Law's Stories 162–63 (Peter Brooks & Paul Gewirtz eds., 1996).

[54] Of course, I am not suggesting that Seidman's client was testifying against his will.

[55] Indeed, I don't think that autonomy is the reason for the law of war that allows prisoners of war to maintain their silence. The value this rule defends is loyalty to one's own state, in one sense the opposite of individual autonomy; and the rule exists because it is in belligerent states' reciprocal interest to recognize it, a point that has no parallel when the individual is at war with the state.

bird at the state *sub silentio*, then how can we explain the practice of sub-poenaing witnesses to testify against their will about other people? Remember the paradox at the heart of the self-incrimination privilege: the law is willing to compel people to bear witness against others when they passionately wish not to do so; and the law is willing to use hard means to bring criminals to justice. But the law is unwilling to bring criminals to justice by the hard means of compelling them to bear witness against themselves. It is the combination of the two – the inner split, the self-alienation, at the heart of compelled witnessing against yourself – that generates the humiliation that the self-incrimination clause means to spare us. Autonomy has to do with individual will, which the law reserves the power to override to serve important social goals. Self-alienation goes to something more basic than will – it goes to protecting the self, which the law must never override on pain of violating human dignity.

Consider next that there is no right to remain silent in a noncriminal case, even if the stakes are enormous. This shows that the point of the self-incrimination clause is not to spare people the burden of testifying against their own important interests.[56] The privilege concerns only one specific interest – the interest in avoiding criminal condemnation. The difference cannot be that criminal punishments are harsher than the stakes in non-criminal matters, for that is not invariably true. If the difference does not lie in the tangible consequences, then it must lie in the moral element of criminal punishment: the fact that criminal conviction joins a tangible penalty with condemnation. Noticing this helps identify more exactly the split in the self that compulsory self-incrimination creates. Making the witness testify enlists his will in the process of his own moral condemnation. It is not exactly a compulsory *mea culpa*, because the witness testifies to facts, not to guilt; but it is a compulsory *mea inculpare*, and that seems just as humiliating.

American law recognizes the special affront to human dignity that comes from forced confession in only one context, when the confession is itself insincere. I am referring to the curious practice known as the *Alford* plea, in which a defendant accepts a plea bargain but denies factual guilt.[57] The background is this. When a defendant accepts a plea bargain and enters a guilty plea, the judge is responsible for ascertaining that the guilty plea is voluntary. The judge will ask the defendant if he truly admits to the elements of the crime. But what if he doesn't? What if he has accepted the plea bargain

---

[56] Holmes was not wrong when he said, "No society has ever admitted that it could not sacrifice individual welfare to its own existence." The Common Law 37 (Mark DeWolfe Howe ed., Harv. Univ. Press 1963) (1881). That includes liberal societies that preserve the privilege against self-incrimination. Holmes went on, "If conscripts are necessary for its army, it seizes them, and marches them, with bayonets in their rear, to death." Ibid.

[57] North Carolina v. Alford, 400 US 25 (1970) (holding that such a plea was not coerced within the meaning of the Fifth Amendment).

only because he is afraid of what will happen if he goes to trial? Confronted with a strong capital murder case against him, Alford accepted a life-saving plea bargain, but said to the judge,

I pleaded guilty on second degree murder because they said there is too much evidence, but I ain't shot no man, but I take the fault for the other man. We never had an argument in our life and I just pleaded guilty because they said if I didn't they would gas me for it, and that is all.[58]

Alford was convicted. The question raised in his appeal was whether his plea was voluntary.

The Court said yes. The outcome was probably a foregone conclusion, because the Supreme Court was not going to throw out the practice of plea-bargaining, nor was it going to say that Alford should have lied under oath. The remaining alternative was to condone guilty pleas in which defendants deny their factual guilt.

This result may be the *reductio ad absurdum* of the view that plea-bargaining is morally acceptable. But, supposing for the sake of argument that the practice of plea-bargaining is acceptable, *Alford* pleas may be seen as a requirement of human dignity, because without them defendants would be placed in a "cruel dilemma" of rejecting life-saving plea bargains or disowning their own stories by stating in public that they are guilty when they believe they are not. Notice that the *Alford* plea makes no difference in the defendant's sentence – it actually makes no practical difference at all. The sole rationale seems to be protection of the defendant's dignity.

After this prolonged detour through the privilege against self-incrimination, let us return to confidentiality and the attorney–client privilege. Eliminate the attorney–client privilege, and the defendant's three choices are vicarious self-incrimination, lying to her lawyer, or telling her lawyer little or nothing. Either of the latter two choices effectively forgoes the very right to counsel that we have seen is closely tied to respecting human dignity. Thus, each horn of the trilemma violates the defendant's human dignity in one way or another. Furthermore, as we have analyzed these violations, our understanding of human dignity has become clearer and fuller. Human dignity consists in having one's own story to tell. It consists as well in not subsuming one's own point of view – one's own story – to the impersonal needs of the legal system.

Of course, a complete discussion of the human dignity defense of lawyer confidentiality would have to address many other issues. One issue is why on this argument the constitutional privilege not to bear witness against yourself applies only in criminal cases, but the attorney–client privilege applies in all

---

[58] Ibid. at 29.

cases. Another issue concerns exceptions to the attorney–client privilege and confidentiality, topics of perennial debate. These I defer to another occasion.

I do wish, however, to highlight one conclusion that is likely to be controversial. Because, in my view, the rationale for lawyer confidentiality and the attorney–client privilege is to protect the human dignity of the client, it should apply only when the client is a flesh-and-blood person. In *Lawyers and Justice*, I argued that the organizational attorney–client privilege should be abolished, because organizational clients are not subjects with human dignity, and the privilege costs society too much by facilitating corporate coverups.[59] This argument, which I naively regarded as among the strongest in my book, attracted no subsequent discussion, not even criticism. Apparently, my recommendation was too fanciful to take seriously. Yet in the years since I published it, events have amply confirmed my worries. One such event was the collapse of the savings-and-loan industry in the late 1980s, a catastrophe that required the services and confidentiality of lawyers every step of the way. Judge Stanley Sporkin's blistering opinion in the Lincoln Savings and Loan case, with its famous question "Where were the attorneys?", was prompted because Sporkin understood all too well that the lawyers knew everything but said nothing.[60]

The second major event was the gradual unveiling of Big Tobacco's secrets through a combination of whistleblowing and litigation. One of the striking revelations was how successfully Big Tobacco's lawyers had abused the attorney–client privilege as an information-concealing device. Now some might say that the tobacco case shows that sooner or later even the best-kept secrets will come out, so there is no need to pare back the corporate attorney–client privilege. Eventually a Merrell Williams or a Jeffrey Wigand will blow the whistle. It doesn't have to be a lawyer.[61]

---

[59] Lawyers and Justice, at 225. Many observers have commented on the so-called "Black Hole" problem. See, e.g., Michael L. Waldman, "Beyond *Upjohn*: The Attorney–Client Privilege in the Corporate Context," 28 Wm. & Mary L. Rev. 473, 496 (1987). Suppose that a CEO wants to do an internal investigation without the risk of being compelled to reveal what is found. The CEO puts a lawyer in charge. Every conversation between the lawyer and employees is privileged, and the lawyer's report to the CEO is likewise privileged. The lawyer becomes a black hole of information: information goes in but it does not come out. One version of the black-hole problem that emerged in both the Dalkon Shield and tobacco litigation concerned scientific studies of product safety supervised by lawyers rather than by executives, in order to maintain the privilege. Medical studies ordered and supervised by lawyers are my idea of a nightmare.

[60] "Where were these professionals … when these clearly improper transactions were being consummated? … Where also were the … attorneys when these transactions were effectuated?" Lincoln Sav. & Loan Ass'n v. Wall, 743 F. Supp. 901, 920 (D.D.C. 1990).

[61] The number of tobacco informants turned out to be not insignificant. See generally David Kessler, A Question of Intent (2001).

But I think the lesson is the opposite. The privilege was an essential tool in suppressing information for forty years. The corporate attorney–client privilege has turned out to be a bad utilitarian bet for society; and the "deontological" human dignity defense of the privilege cannot be invoked on behalf of an artificial person with no soul to divide against itself, no body to imprison, no subjectivity to ignore and humiliate.

Human dignity as non-humiliation

At this point we are in a position to draw some preliminary conclusions about what it means to have human dignity, as the concept has emerged so far. It means, first, being the subject of a story, no matter how humdrum or commonplace that story is. And honoring human dignity means assuming that someone has a story that can be told in good faith, hence listening to it and insisting that it be told. Second, we have learned that to have a story means more than to be an autonomous chooser. It means being the subject of experience, and it means existing in a web of commitments, however detestable or pathetic those commitments may be. And honoring human dignity means refraining from overriding those commitments for paternalistic reasons. Third, our discussion of confidentiality and the right against self-incrimination shows that having human dignity means being an individual self who is not entirely subsumed into larger communities. Not only are we subjects of a story, it is *our* story, and human dignity requires that we not be forced to tell it as an instrument of our own condemnation.

Underlying all these themes, I think, lies a single root idea. Whatever the metaphysical basis of human dignity – indeed, whether or not human dignity even has a metaphysical basis – at the very least honoring human dignity requires not humiliating people.[62] Indeed, I would propose this as a condition or criterion that any theory of human dignity must satisfy: it must entail nonhumiliation as a theorem.

What is the intuitive connection between human dignity and non-humiliation? Begin with the notion of dignity. Oscar Schachter, reflecting on the phrase "dignity and worth of the human person" used in human rights documents, suggests that *dignity* and *worth* are synonyms.[63] I disagree. Schachter has focused on one lexical meaning of "dignity," namely intrinsic worth. But another, more prominent, meaning treats "dignity" as a

---

[62] Readers of Avishai Margalit's The Decent Society 1 (Naomi Goldblum trans., 1996), will recognize it as the source of my proposal. Margalit's thesis is straightforward: whatever the good society may turn out to be, the decent society is simply one whose institutions do not humiliate people. My analysis of dignity and humiliation differ at some points from Margalit's.

[63] Schachter, supra note 3, at 849.

status-concept. Dignity goes with rank; an indignity occurs when someone is treated below their rank. And the effect of indignity is humiliation, which is connected semantically as well as etymologically with the word 'humbling' and its cognates. The difference between the two is this: I am humbled when I am *rightly* taken down a peg – when my own inadequacies, made visible to all, reveal me as a lesser sort than I have represented myself as (to others or to myself). I am humiliated when I am *wrongly* taken down a peg – when others treat me as a lesser sort than I really am.[64] Humiliation is an affront to my dignity.

Dignity, as a concept connected with social rank or prestige, will vary in its concrete meaning from society to society. What about human dignity? Evidently, it must refer to the prestige conferred simply by being human. To violate someone's human dignity means to treat them as if they were a being of lower rank – as an animal, as a handy but disposable tool, as property, as an object, as a subhuman, as an overgrown child, as nothing at all.[65] The phrase "death with dignity," as used in discussions of the right to die, incorporates this way of reading the concept. To die with dignity means to go out with my boots on, not to be maintained as a "ghost in the machine," a frail, drugged simulacrum of myself hooked up to respirators and catheters and intravenous tubes. The gross diminution of my stature amounts to a loss of dignity, a humiliation.

In our discussion of lawyers as defenders of human dignity, the specific indignity at issue was treating people as though their own subjective stories and commitments are insignificant. Everyone is a subject, everyone's story is as meaningful to her or to him as everyone else's, and everyone's deep commitments are central to their personality. To treat someone's subjectivity as insignificant treats her as a being of lower status; and that turns out to be the specific form humiliation takes when we analyze the right to counsel, the

---

[64] I recognize that this is not the only legitimate sense of the word "humiliation." Sometimes we simply use it as a synonym for "extreme embarrassment," which can be deserved as well as undeserved. (Consider the sentence, "He humiliated himself.") Similarly, being humbled is sometimes used as a synonym for being defeated at a contest. Thus, my uses of these words are narrower than ordinary usage.

William Ian Miller argues that humiliation (in distinction from shame and embarrassment) always involves puncturing someone's pretenses. Humiliation in Miller's sense can be justified (when the victim of humiliation is putting on airs, is pretentious, is a pompous ass who needs to be put in his place, like Malvolio in *Twelfth Night*) or unjustified (when the victim is not putting on airs, when the humiliation is done out of cruelty or thoughtlessness, like children making fun of the retarded child in their school.) I am reserving the word for the unjustified kind of humiliation, and using the term "being humbled" for the justified kind. See William Ian Miller, Humiliation 137–41, 146–48 (1995).

[65] Margalit defines humiliation as "the rejection of a human being from the 'Family of Man' – that is, treating humans as nonhuman, or relating to humans as if they were not human." The Decent Society, supra note 62, at 108.

right against self-incrimination, and the lawyer's duty of confidentiality. I do not assert that disregarding another person's subjectivity or commitments is the only form that human indignity can take – but I do assert that the wrong of disregarding another's subjectivity and commitments lies in the humiliation it inflicts by treating the other beneath their human status.

Pro bono and its critics

To further elaborate on how the practice of law can uphold – or assault – human dignity, I want to fasten on the notion of dignity as nonhumiliation and discuss the pro bono obligations of lawyers. To facilitate the discussion, I will use that time-honored literary device, the foil – a published article that approaches the issue of pro bono in what seems to me exactly the wrong way.

My foil is an essay by two professors, Charles Silver and Frank Cross, that ingeniously criticizes the very idea that lawyers ought to perform pro bono service.[66] They don't deny that "all persons of means should be charitable, especially to widows, orphans, the handicapped, and others whose poverty results from circumstances that are largely or wholly beyond their control."[67] But they believe that legal services simply are not as important to the poor as "money, hot meals, home repairs, medical assistance, transportation, and help with chores ... Lawyers should provide the forms of charity that poor people need most, especially gifts of cash."[68] Thus, Silver and Cross reject the duty to do legal service for the poor not because they are skeptical of duties to the poor but because "poor people would rather have other things."[69]

To illustrate their point, they pose a rhetorical question: "Query: Would a poor person waiting for help at a legal aid office rather have twenty hours of a lawyer's time ... or $3000? ... Three thousand dollars would be a lot of money for so poor a person to pass up."[70]

Silver and Cross seem to think that offering the money, which the poor person can spend as she wishes, pays more honor to her autonomy than offering her legal services on a take-it-or-leave-it basis. My intuition runs differently, and not only because I do not identify dignity with autonomy. I would like us to imagine Silver and Cross staffing the intake desk at the legal aid office. Four clients are sitting in the waiting room, thumbing the old *People* magazines and the cheaply printed "Know Your Rights!" pamphlets. A bored toddler is tugging at her mother's dress. Absently, she pushes the

---

[66] Charles Silver & Frank B. Cross, *What's Not to Like About Being a Lawyer?*, 109 Yale L. J. 1443 (2000) (reviewing Arthur L. Liman, Lawyer: A Life of Counsel and Controversy).
[67] Ibid. at 1479.   [68] Ibid. at 1478.   [69] Ibid. at 1483.   [70] Ibid. at 1484.

toddler's hand away. Then the lawyers call her name. She sweeps up the toddler and goes in to speak with the professors:

> *Prospective Client #1:* The city is trying to terminate my parental rights and take my child away. Can you help me?
> *Silver and Cross:* That's a twenty-hour job. We won't represent you, but we'll give you $3,000.

They are honoring her autonomy. Which does she prefer, the money or the child? It's her call.

After she leaves, clutching the child to her, the next client comes in:

> *Prospective Client #2:* Immigration is trying to deport me back to my home country. I'll be arrested if I'm sent back, maybe tortured and killed. Can you represent me at my asylum hearing?
> *Silver and Cross:* Oh, sure. But that will take at least forty hours to do right. Tell you what: We'll give you $6,000 instead. That should get you across the Canadian border in style!

Next comes Client Number Three:

> *Prospective Client #3:* Last week my boyfriend beat me up and broke my arm. Now he's threatening to kill me. My cousin told me that you could help me get a court order to keep him away.
> *Silver and Cross:* We could. It would take about four hours. But what if we give you $600 instead? Now you can buy a gun and take yourself out to dinner with the change.

And now the last:

> *Prospective Client #4:* My landlord is trying to evict me, and I haven't got the money for a new apartment. He has no right to evict me – I've always been a good tenant and paid the rent on time. He just doesn't like me. My eviction hearing is next week. Can you help me?
> *Silver and Cross:* Here's the money for a new apartment.

It's been a good day's work at the alms factory. Instead of foisting legal services on clients, they have honored the clients' autonomy by giving them money they can spend on anything they wish. The professors apparently believe that the four prospective clients will be grateful for their response. My own prediction is rather different. Even if Prospective Client Number Four will be happier with the money for a new apartment than with legal assistance, I suspect she will also be angered and humiliated by the offer.

The imaginary dialogues dramatize a few points that Silver and Cross overlook. First, whether the client prefers legal services or cash depends on

how urgent the legal problem is. Second, how much the case is worth to the
lawyer may have nothing to do with how much it matters to the client. Third,
not all legal woes translate into monetary equivalents.

Of course, nothing prevents the clients from taking the money and
spending it on legal services – in effect, retaining someone other than Cross
and Silver to do the legal work. But the fact that some or all of these clients
will undoubtedly prefer to spend the money on legal services demonstrates
that Cross's and Silver's question about whether legal aid clients would rather
have lawyers or money is not merely rhetorical.

Though they are important, these points do not bear on the question of
human dignity. The next point does, however. Even if the client's legal
problem concerns only money, as in the eviction case, it may matter enor-
mously to her how she gets the money. The reason has to do with the entirely
different social meanings of help and handouts. Handouts accentuate the
helplessness and dependency of the recipient. They do nothing good for a
person's self-respect.

Help is different. All of us need help sometimes for some things, so there
is no sense that getting help demeans us. When you help someone cope with a
problem, you create a sense of shared enterprise. Your implicit aim is to
reduce their dependency by removing a stumbling-block. By contrast, substituting handouts for help seems very much like bribing the recipient to go
away. Handouts accentuate social distance. Handouts humiliate.

Consider an instructive Biblical passage from the book of Leviticus:

When you reap the harvest of the land, you shall not reap right into the edges of your
field; neither shall you glean the loose ears of your crop; you shall not completely strip
your vineyard nor glean the fallen grapes. You shall leave them for the poor and the
alien.[71]

One important point to notice about this passage is that it sets out a duty, not
just something that you do if you are nice. In fact, the rabbinic Hebrew word
for giving to the needy – *tzedakah* – derives from *tzedek*, the word for
"justice."[72]

---

[71] Lev. 19:9–10. This commandment appears in the chapter of Leviticus that the rabbis regarded
as the moral core of the Bible – the so-called Law of Holiness (*kedushim*), the same chapter
that contains the laws "Love your neighbor as yourself" (Lev. 19:18) and "Love the stranger as
yourself" (Lev. 19:34).

[72] However, Maimonides' analysis of the word *tzedakah* downplays this link. He distinguishes
two senses of justice. The first, giving people what they have by right (his example is returning
a pledge to the poor) is not called *tzedakah*. Instead, the word is reserved for fulfilling justice-
duties that are connected with moral virtue, "such as remedying the injuries of all those who
are injured." We might use the English word 'philanthropy' – etymologically, 'love of man' –
except that Maimonides carefully distinguishes *tzedakah* from *chesed* (loving-kindness). His

The second point to notice about the duty to leave gleanings for the poor and the foreigner is that it is not a commandment to give handouts. It does not say, "After the harvest, give some grain to the poor begging at your gates." Instead, the commandment is to leave something for the poor to gather for themselves. The poor will gain their living by work – indeed, by the same kind of work as any other harvester. It is a commandment to help the poor in a way that, to the highest degree possible, maintains their self-respect and makes their lives normal. It is a commandment to do *tzedakah* in a manner that honors human dignity, that spares the gleaner humiliation. As the twelfth-century rabbi Maimonides puts it, "Whoever gives *tzedakah* to a poor man ill-manneredly ... has lost all the merit of his action even though he should give him a thousand gold pieces."[73]

The views of Maimonides, who thought more deeply about the duty to give than any other author I know, are instructive, and his analysis of benevolence, which includes a subtle classification of modes of giving into eight degrees, highest to lowest, is one of the most celebrated passages in the rabbinic literature. His teaching centers overwhelmingly around the concern that gifts to the poor should never humiliate recipients or perpetuate their dependency. For that reason, Maimonides argued for the superiority of anonymous giving;[74] he thought that giving too little, but graciously, is better than giving an adequate amount grudgingly;[75] he maintained that gifts bestowed before the poor person asks are better than those given after;[76] and

---

emphasis is on the duty and virtue aspects of *tzedakah*, not the emotional and motivational aspects. And, according to Maimonides, this implies that the connection between *tzedakah* and justice is that by performing *tzedakah* one does justice to one's own soul, not to the beneficiary. Nevertheless, the fact remains that Maimonides insists that *tzedakah* is a duty, not a grace. 2 Moses Maimonides, Guide of the Perplexed 631 (Shlomo Pines trans., Univ. Chi. Press 1963) (1197), Part 3, ch. 53, reprinted in A Maimonides Reader 351 (Isadore Twersky ed., 1972).

[73] Moses Maimonides, Mishneh Torah, "Gifts to the Poor," Book 7, ch. 10, §7, in A Maimonides Reader, supra note 72, at 136.

[74] Ibid., §§8–10, at 137. Giving in which neither donor nor recipient knows each other's identities is the seventh (second-highest) stage of Maimonides' eight-stage classification. Just below that is giving in which the donor is unknown to the recipient – as in the case of "the great sages who would go forth and covertly throw coins into poor people's doorways"; and below that is giving in which the recipient is unknown to the donor, as in the case of "the great sages who would tie their coins in their scarves which they would fling over their shoulders so that the poor might help themselves without suffering shame." Ibid., §§9–10. Why is unknown-recipient *tzedakah* ranked lower than unknown-donor *tzedakah*? Presumably, the answer lies in the fact that when the recipient knows the donor she will feel beholden; when the donor is unknown, the recipient can consort with anyone in the community on an equal footing.

[75] Ibid., §§13–14, at 137. Giving "morosely" is the first, or lowest, of the eight degrees, while giving graciously, but too little, is second-lowest.

[76] Ibid., §§11–12, at 137. Giving before being asked is the fourth stage, while giving only after the poor person asks is the third.

he regarded giving that promotes the self-sufficiency of the recipient, for example by making him one's business partner, as the highest form of benevolence.[77] Particularly relevant to pro bono is Maimonides' careful specification that, if a gift cannot be anonymous, the giver should bestow it "with his own hand."[78] Bestowing the gift with your own hand matters because it removes the suspicion that, while you are willing to help the recipient, you aren't willing to associate with her.[79]

How do these ideas play out in the context of legal services? The four imaginary dialogues dramatize the way that offering money in place of legal assistance humbles and humiliates the would-be client. To start with the obvious, to offer money when someone asks for legal services is to treat a potential client like an actual beggar. Secondly, legal problems often concern rights, and treating people as rights-bearers by offering legal help dignifies them in a way that treating them as needs-bearers, by offering them cash, does not.[80] A rights-bearer is, after all, a legal *person*, with ontological heft that others are obligated to respect. Rights connect with human dignity in a way that needs do not. A lawyer who offers pro bono assistance recognizes the client as a person, not a panhandler.

Now Silver and Cross might reply that giving cash to poor people who request pro bono services actually treats them with greater respect than restricting your gift to in-kind services. The reason is one we have already

---

[77] Ibid., §7, at 136–37. "The highest degree, exceeded by none, is that of the person who assists a poor Jew by providing him with a gift or a loan or by accepting him into a business partnership or by helping him find employment – in a word, by putting him where he can dispense with other people's aid."

[78] Ibid., §11.

[79] It is worth noting that Maimonides' rules for recipients partake of the same themes of dignity, equality, and independence. He offers three fundamental rules: first, that dependence on the community's benevolence should be a last resort, and one should be willing to work hard and even endure some hardship before asking for aid. Second, and related, obtaining aid by deception is forbidden. Third, and perhaps most interesting and surprising, is that a needy person who *rejects* essential aid has sinned – he is "a shedder of blood, guilty of attempts on his own life." There is a difference between enduring hardship to avoid the shame of dependence and stiff-necked, false pride. One suspects that Maimonides included the third rule in part for strategic reasons. Maimonides was the greatest rabbi – as well as the greatest physician and lawyer – of his time. (On learning this, my wife remarked, "His mother must have been so happy!") Maimonides served as the court physician of the caliph in Cairo, and wrote legal opinions for Jewish communities all over the world. His codification of the religious law, the Mishneh Torah, became the model for the Shulchan Arech, the authoritative code still used by rabbinic courts. In addition, he wrote medical, astronomical, and philosophical treatises. So great was his celebrity that he has been known ever since by the acronym "Rambam" (*R*abbi *M*oses *ben M*aimon). Backed by Maimonides' authority, the needy can henceforth regard their acceptance of aid as a duty, not a weakness.

[80] This is an important theme of Patricia J. Williams, The Alchemy of Race and Rights: The Diary of a Law Professor (1991).

seen: if it's really legal services poor people want, they can use the cash to hire a lawyer. If not, they can use the money for something more important. Giving cash leaves the decision up to them.[81]

I remain skeptical, however. Is the donor-lawyer giving the would-be client money to hire a different lawyer? If so, the message seems to be, "I don't want to have to deal with you, so here's some money so you can go away and find another lawyer." Maimonides' injunction that a giver should provide aid "with his own hand" comes ineluctably to mind.

Or, alternatively, is the donor saying to the would-be client, "Here's some money. You can either use it to hire me to represent you, or you can spend it on whatever else you think is more important"? This alternative is certainly better than the last – but it still transforms the nature of the encounter from a professional consultation into an occasion for handouts. Instead of a lawyer–client relationship, the offer creates a patron–client relationship. No longer is the client a person with rights at stake. Now her rights are subsumed into the category of her needs. Furthermore, now the client must regard her legal problem as fungible with all her other needs, which diminishes its significance and underlines the fact that a poor person finds desperation wherever she looks. Imagine a physician making a similar offer to an impoverished person who shows up at the physician's office with, say, a broken wrist: "Sure, I could set your wrist for free, which is actually $1,000-worth of medical treatment. But instead, I'll give you $1,000. That way, you can decide whether to spend it on getting your wrist set, or else live with the broken wrist while you take care of something even more urgent." How much humiliation should a poor person have to put up with?

I do not suggest that pro bono legal assistance is always morally superior to cash assistance. Blanket generalizations in either direction are absurd. Every poverty lawyer can call to mind clients who needed money more than anything a lawyer could do for them; I suspect that every poverty lawyer has at one time or another chafed under the ethics rule forbidding lawyers to offer humanitarian financial assistance to their litigation clients.[82] What I am suggesting is that, even when all a client wants from a lawyer is help in obtaining money, ignoring the legal problem and giving the client money creates a sorry excuse for a moral relationship. Helping those in need is an interaction, not an action, and Silver and Cross neglect the question of what kind of interactions cash transfers rather than legal services would be likely to create. They are, it seems to me, humiliating transactions. The lawyer who offers legal services may not be offering what the client needs most urgently. But the offer honors the client's human dignity in a way that cash on the barrel-head never can.

---

[81] I am grateful to David Hyman for pointing out this argument to me.
[82] Model Rules of Professional Conduct, Rule 1.8(e).

II

The jurisprudence of legal ethics

3

Natural law as professional ethics: a reading of Fuller

Introduction

In Plato's *Laws*, the Athenian Stranger claims that the gods will smile only on a city where the law is despot over the rulers and the rulers are slaves of the law.[1] This passage is the origin of the slogan "The rule of law not of men," an abbreviation of which forms our phrase "the rule of law." From Plato and Aristotle, through John Adams and John Marshall, down to us, no idea has proven more central to Western political and legal culture.[2] Yet the slogan turns on a very dubious metaphor. Laws do not rule, and "the rule of law not of men" is actually a specific form of rule by men (including, nowadays, a few women). These rulers are not slaves to anything. Furthermore, the construction of the slogan – rule of law and *not* of men – has unfortunate connotations. It suggests that the personal qualities of the human rulers required to secure the rule of law are nothing more than forbearance and disinterestedness – a resolution to stay out of law's way.

What if the rule of law is more demanding than this? What if it turns out to be a particularly elaborate and technically ingenious form of the rule of (let me say) men and women? What if the rule of law establishes a moral relationship between those who govern and those whom they govern? Furthermore, what if sustaining this relationship requires moral attitudes and virtues on the part of the governors that are not simply disinterested forbearance, and not simply the moral attitudes and virtues required of everyone?

---

[1] Plato, The Laws of Plato (Thomas L. Pangle trans., 1980) *715d.

[2] Aristotle offers a similar phrase in the *Politics*. 2 The Complete Works of Aristotle 2042 (Jonathan Barnes ed., 1984), at *1287a1–b1. John Adams introduced the phrase "government of laws, and not of men" into America in his 1774 "Novangelus Paper" (no. 7), reprinted in 4 The Works of John Adams 106 (Charles Francis Adams ed., 1969). From there it migrated into the Massachusetts constitution of 1780 and eventually into Justice Marshall's opinion in *Marbury v. Madison*, 5 US 137 (1803). Fred R. Shapiro, The Oxford Dictionary of American Legal Quotations 319 (1993).

In that case, the rule of law would turn out to rely on the specifically professional ethics of the lawmakers. One might be tempted to call this "political ethics," the ethics of rulers. But that is not quite right. Rulers are not identical with lawmakers. Rulers make decisions and devise policies, but decisions and policies are not yet laws. Embodying decisions and policies in the form of laws is a tricky business, technically difficult in exactly the same way that embodying private parties' intentions in a legal contract is difficult – and the people who carry out each of these lawmaking tasks are (what else?) *lawyers*. Thus, the rule of law relies on the professional ethics of lawyers (even if they do not call themselves lawyers or belong to the bar).

Finally, what if the professional ethics of lawyer-lawmakers – the moral relationship and attitudes and virtues required by the rule of law – cohere better with laws enhancing human dignity than with laws assaulting it, because enacting laws that assault human dignity tends to undermine the moral relationship that sustains the rule of law? If this were the case, we would be entitled to assert that the rule of law morally constrains the content of laws. This sounds like a natural law theory. We could call it a theory of the "morality of law," provided we understood that the phrase refers to the morality of *lawmakers*, and only derivatively to the morality of laws. We would have a theory of natural law as professional ethics.

What I have just described is the unfamiliar argument of a very familiar book, Lon Fuller's *The Morality of Law* (hereafter *ML*), first published in 1964.[3] (Note that in what follows, my page citations to *ML* refer to the revised edition, published in 1969.) I call the argument unfamiliar because readers have typically treated *ML* as a book on general jurisprudence, not on professional ethics, and have neglected its moral theory to focus on what they regard as analytical claims about "the concept of law." But "the concept of law" is H. L. A. Hart's title, not Fuller's.[4]

As Fuller himself observed in 1969 (*ML* 188), this misunderstanding is perfectly natural given the state of play in legal theory when he first published *ML*. For several years, he had been engaged in a debate with Hart, beginning

---

[3] I will use the following abbreviations for works of Fuller which I cite repeatedly: *ML* = The Morality of Law (rev. edn. 1969); *LQI* = The Law in Quest of Itself (Northwestern University Press, 1940); *PSO* = The Principles of Social Order: Selected Essays of Lon L. Fuller (Kenneth I. Winston ed., 1981); *PFL* = *Positivism and Fidelity to Law – A Reply to Professor Hart*, 71 Harv. L. Rev. 630 (1958); *RFCL* = *Reason and Fiat in Case Law*, 59 Harv. L. Rev. 376 (1946); *RN* = *A Rejoinder to Professor Nagel*, 3 Natural Law Forum 83 (1958).

The present chapter examines, from a different perspective, themes I discuss in *Redis-covering Fuller's Legal Ethics*, published concurrently in 11 Geo. J. Legal Ethics 801 (1998) and Rediscovering Fuller: Essays on Implicit Law and Institutional Design 193 (Willem J. Witteveen & Wibren van der Burg eds., University of Amsterdam Press, 1999).

[4] H. L. A. Hart, The Concept of Law (2nd edn. 1994).

with their fam   *Review*.[5] Hart weighed in
next in *The Co*   :d in chapter 3 of *ML*. Hart
returned the co   and Fuller responded in the
new appendix 1   *'L*. Subsequent readers have
naturally assur   debating the same issue of
whether legal r   ral norms – an issue framed
by Hart in his   debate.

On this assumption, *ML* gets read approximately as follows. The central argument of *ML* begins with the famous parable "Eight Ways to Fail to Make Law," found in chapter 2. The parable does two things. First, it provides an analysis of the rule of law into the eight familiar canons that Fuller calls "principles of legality." These hold that laws should exhibit (1) generality (i.e., legislating through rules rather than case-by-case directives), (2) publicity, (3) prospectivity, (4) clarity, (5) logical consistency, (6) feasibility – that is, obeyability in practice, (7) constancy through time, and (8) congruence between the rules as announced and their actual administration (*ML* 39). Second, the parable argues that when these canons are violated, the result is not bad law, but no law at all. The eight canons, then, are necessary conditions on the concept of law. They are also, or so Fuller claims, an "inner morality of law"; because they have to do with the promulgation of laws, not with their content, this inner morality is a "procedural natural law." There is also a substantive natural law, but Fuller leaves the connection between the procedural and substantive branches of natural law obscure. And that's about it.

How do those who read Fuller this way react to his argument? They generally like his analysis of the rule of law, which ranks alongside comparable efforts by John Rawls and Joseph Raz.[7] Many accept the idea that without these canons there can be no law at all; however, most reject the claim that the canons represent principles of morality, inner or otherwise, rather than principles of effectiveness. It is this latter claim that forms the crux of the issue between Fuller and Hart, and the dominant view seems to be that Fuller was wrong.

Undoubtedly, that latter claim is important. But reading Fuller in the manner described above slides over his treatment of substantive natural law, and treats the first chapter of *ML*, on ethical theory, as if it does not exist. As a result, the argument about professional ethics with which I began simply disappears from the reading entirely. And that is too bad, because in important ways (not every way) Fuller's argument is right.

---

[5] H. L. A. Hart, *Positivism and the Separation of Law and Morals*, 71 Harv. L. Rev. 593 (1958). Fuller's reply is *PFL*, cited in full in note 3 above.

[6] H. L. A. Hart, *Book Review* – The Morality of Law, 78 Harv. L. Rev. 1281 (1965).

[7] John Rawls, A Theory of Justice 235–43 (1971); Joseph Raz, *The Rule of Law and Its Virtue*, 93 Law Quarterly Rev. 195 (1977).

The word "law" means the life work of the lawyer

Fuller never disguises his intentions. He says in *ML* that he will offer only one definition of law: "the enterprise of subjecting human conduct to the governance of rules" (*ML* 106). His title, *The Morality of Law*, then, must be paraphrased thus: "the morality of the enterprise of subjecting human conduct to the governance of rules." Fuller explicitly calls attention to the fact that his definition classifies law as an activity rather than, say, a set of propositions of law, or a distinctive kind of social norm. The activity of *subjecting* human conduct to rules, unlike the activity of governing one's own conduct in accordance with rules, is performed specifically by the rule-designer. "So when I speak of legal morality, I mean just that. I mean that special morality that attaches to the office of law-giver and law-applier."[8] He labels this a "role morality," and likens it to the distinctive ethics of lawyers – it is "no mere restatement of the moral principles governing human conduct generally, but ... special standards applicable to the discharge of a distinctive social function" (*ML* 193; see also *PSO* 201). In the second edition of *ML*, Fuller complains that "no modern positivist elevates to a central position in his thinking any limitations contained in 'the law job' itself" (*ML* 192). The "law job" is performed by the lawyer, whom he elsewhere calls the "architect of social structure" (*PSO* 50–52, 253, 264–70). This makes clear that *ML* is a book about professional ethics – specifically, the professional ethics of those lawyers Fuller refers to as lawgivers and law-appliers.[9]

This way of thinking about law was already evident in 1940, when Fuller first discussed natural law and positivism in *The Law in Quest of Itself*.

---

[8] Lon L. Fuller, *A Reply to Professors Cohen and Dworkin*, 10 Villanova L. Rev. 660 (1965). He employs similar phrasing at *ML* 206.

[9] I do not mean that Fuller literally thought that all legislators are professional lawyers. He understood, of course, that nonlawyer legislators decide on what should become law before turning it over to lawyers for drafting. He emphasized that the lawmaking job has a technical side, because embodying policies in effective rules is difficult in exactly the way that embodying parties' intentions in a well-wrought contract is difficult. Negotiating these difficulties is precisely the special craft of lawyers. Fuller also argued that the technical aspect of lawmaking imposes substantive constraints on what policies can be embodied in laws, because human activity "always involves a reciprocal adjustment between ends and means." Lon L. Fuller, *The Philosophy of Codes of Ethics*, 74 Electrical Engineering 916 (1955). See Fuller's *Means and Ends* in *PSO*, at 52–58. Not every conceivable end can be turned into workable law. In this sense, all legislation requires the exercise of lawyerly skills, even when the legislator is not a lawyer. The reciprocal adjustment of ends and means likewise implies that a transactional lawyer papering a deal shapes it rather than serving as a mere scrivener: lawyering requires the exercise of legislative skills, even when the lawyer is not a legislator. It follows that the roles of legislators and of lawyers are closer than appears at first sight, and this overlap matters to Fuller – it is one of the points of his King Rex parable. Hence my talk of lawyers in the text.

After rehearsing the definitions of law offered by several philosophical schools, he considers the obvious concern that debates among them amount to little more than terminological hairsplitting. Here is how he responds:

Yet if in these definitions the word "law" means the life work of the lawyer, it is apparent that something more vital than a verbal dispute hinges on the choice between them. Surely the man who conceives his task as that of reducing the relations of men to a reasoned harmony will be a different kind of lawyer from one who regards his task as that of charting the behavior of certain elderly state officials. (*LQI* 3–4)

"*The word 'law' means the life work of the lawyer.*" This is not just a rhetorical hook to capture the interest of the law-school audience to which he was lecturing. It is, in paraphrase, the very definition he employs in *ML*.

In the second sentence of the quotation from *LQI*, Fuller offers his own characterization of natural law, or rather, of the activity of the natural-law lawyer: "reducing the relations of men to a reasoned harmony." On its face, this is strikingly different from the most common understanding of natural law in analytic jurisprudence. Analytic philosophers of law tend to regard natural law and positivism as competing theses about the relation between legal and moral propositions. Jules Coleman's careful definition is a good example: on his account, positivism is the "proposition that there exists at least one conceivable legal system in which the rule of recognition does not specify being a principle of morality among the truth conditions for any proposition of law."[10] Natural law, then, is the view that in every conceivable legal system, the rule of recognition (the rule by which we recognize valid laws) specifies that being a principle of morality is among the truth conditions for any proposition of law.

Fuller characterizes natural law as a way of conducting a practical activity – "reducing the relations of men to a reasoned harmony" – rather than as a philosophical thesis about the truth conditions of propositions of law. For Fuller, there is not really a thesis associated with natural law at all (*RN* 84). Of course, Fuller believes that there is a characteristic morality associated with the "law job" (*ML* 192). But this marks an important shift in emphasis. Where other writers on all sides of the positivism/natural-law debate understand the phrase "the morality of law" to refer to the morality of *laws*, for Fuller it refers to the morality of *lawmaking*.

This usage, which is quite consistent in Fuller's work, is bound to create confusions for those who assume that the phrase "the morality of law" refers not to the moral code of the rule-designer but rather to the moral content of

---

[10] Jules L. Coleman, *Negative and Positive Positivism*, in Ronald Dworkin and Contemporary Jurisprudence 31 (Marshall Cohen ed., 1983). This is Coleman's definition of "negative" (that is, minimal) positivism.

legal rules. In particular, it means that when positivists deny that the law has any necessary moral content, Fuller tends to hear them asserting that no moral code governs lawgiving, a claim that he finds preposterous. Positivists, however, do not really intend to make this claim. Similarly, when Fuller insists that there is a morality to law, his critics assume that he is making a conceptual claim about the necessary connection between legal rules and morality, rather than arguing that lawmaking is a profession with a distinctive professional ethics. But it is the latter that Fuller means.

I said earlier that Fuller classifies lawgivers and law-appliers (legislators and judges) together with lawyers.[11] This will seem puzzling until we realize that Fuller invariably has in mind transactional lawyers, not litigators (who, he observes, are a small minority of the legal profession [*PSO* 252–53]). As noted above, Fuller views the lawyer as an "architect of social structure"; he regards litigation, the recourse when social structure fails, as a poor – even perverse – focus for understanding what makes lawyers' work important. It would be like trying to understand an educator's work by focusing on the process of disciplining classroom troublemakers, or trying to understand marriage by examining divorce.[12]

Three characteristics of the transactional lawyer make him the paradigm jurist in Fuller's eyes. First, his job is to facilitate interaction between two or more private parties – and facilitating interaction is, for Fuller, the principal aim of law. Second, although the transactional lawyer advises his client, sometimes quite forcefully – he is not merely a mouthpiece or a scrivener – he understands that the client, not the lawyer, is the person who has to do the interacting after the deal is made. This is the fundamental moral fact about the relationship. Third, the transactional lawyer facilitates the interaction by drawing up a framework of rules – a contract, the transactional equivalent of a piece of legislation.[13]

---

[11] On this point, see also Kenneth I. Winston, *Legislators and Liberty*, 13 Law & Phil. 393 (1994).

[12] These analogies are mine, not Fuller's. Although transactional lawyers must anticipate possible litigation, "battening down the hatches against possible future litigation" (*PSO* 253) cannot be their principal job as they draft contracts. The clients are trying to get something done, not merely avoid losses when their projects shipwreck. Fuller more than once quotes Aquinas' dictum that if the highest duty of a captain were to preserve his ship, he would keep it in port forever. Aquinas, Summa Theologiae, I-II, q. 2, a. 5, quoted at *PSO* 56, *ML* 185.

I discuss Fuller's conception of lawyers' work more fully in *Rediscovering Fuller's Legal Ethics*, supra note 3, at 810–19.

[13] Fuller argues, strikingly, that the terms contained *in* a contract are just as much law as the rules governing the formation of contracts. *PSO* 174–75. He is a legal pluralist – someone who believes that there are many legal systems in a society, not just the big legal system administered by the state: on this account, both private actors and the state can make law. Fuller argues explicitly for legal pluralism at *ML* 123–29.

Excellences as powers: "Sin is a sinking into nothingness"

When we fully appreciate that *The Morality of Law* is a book about professional ethics rather than a traditional treatise on jurisprudence, we can better understand why Fuller begins the book with a chapter on ethical theory, and why the chapter opens with contrasting definitions of 'sin', rather than, say, justice or injustice. Talk about sin would be strange if the subject were the morality of laws, rather than the morality of lawmaking. Because Fuller is focusing on the latter, however, he is interested in the ways lawyers can sin against the enterprise in which they are engaged. To an unusual extent, Fuller personalizes jurisprudence: he sees acts of legislation and interpretation as products of lawgivers and law-appliers, products whose quality depends crucially on the people who make them.

Fuller's moral theory turns on a distinction between the *morality of duty* – "the most obvious demands of social living" (*ML* 9) – and the *morality of aspiration* – "the morality of the Good Life, of excellence, of the fullest realization of human powers" (*ML* 5). Several points stand out.

1. There is, first of all, the idea that aspiration has a morality. This is hardly an obvious point. Many of our aspirations fall under the general heading of things that it would be nice to do, but there is nothing especially moral about the category of the "that-would-be-nice." It would be nice if I could play the piano, speak German, throw softball strikes, and work the exercises in the old mathematics textbooks that have been hibernating on my shelf since college. All these things being among my interests, it is natural to think of them as aspirations. But it would be odd for anyone to take me to task for my failings at piano, German, fast pitch softball, and mathematics, and equally odd for me to feel ashamed about them. In contrast, speaking of moral failings implies, at the minimum, a dimension of blame and shame: moral failings are among those failings that do deserve criticism (from both oneself and others). Otherwise, why call them *moral* failings? From a moral outlook centered on rights and duties, "mere" aspiration is a non-moral phenomenon; Fuller's claim to the contrary marks out a distinctive moral position.

2. Kant believed that we lie under a duty to improve ourselves; this and the duty to promote others' happiness are the principal obligations he elaborates in the "Doctrine of Virtue."[14] These two duties roughly correspond with Fuller's categories, but Fuller rejects the reduction of aspiration to duty (*ML* 5). Instead, he finds that criticism appropriate to the morality of

---

[14] See generally Immanuel Kant, The Doctrine of Virtue, in The Metaphysics of Morals (Mary Gregor trans., Cambridge University Press, 1991). The treatise is divided into two principal sections: "On Duties to Oneself as Such" and "Duties of Virtue to Others." See also Marcia Baron, *Kantian Ethics*, in Marcia Baron, Philip Pettit, & Michael Slote, Three Methods of Ethics: A Debate 13–21 (1997).

aspiration involves terms like "failure" and "shortcoming, not ... wrong-doing," as well as assertions that one has not engaged in "conduct such as beseems a human being functioning at his best" (*ML* 5; see also *ML* 3). In other words, the morality of aspiration employs the vocabulary of human excellence – what philosophers call 'aretaic' concepts – rather than 'deontic' concepts, the vocabulary of right or wrong action. In that sense, the morality of aspiration lies very close to contemporary virtue ethics, the view that places aretaic concepts at the heart of moral theory.[15]

3. When is it appropriate to treat aspirations morally, rather than merely as things it would be nice to do? Fuller never explicitly addresses this question, but the use to which he puts the distinction suggests one important answer: *our aspirations have a moral dimension whenever other people's well-being depends on them.* Paradigmatically, this will be true in the sphere of work, and specifically in the professions. It is hardly coincidental that aretaic concepts evolved in Greek thought to characterize warriors, whose excellences and failures meant the difference between prosperity and disaster for those who relied on them.[16] In more peaceable societies, we continue to think "aretaically" when we choose a surgeon or a lawyer. We want something more than dutifulness, which after all is merely the requirement for avoiding malpractice liability. We want someone who strives for professional excellence and attains it. We criticize professionals who fail for want of excellence, along with those who do not even strive for it. This is moral criticism, and it is based in the morality of aspiration.

Even when no one else's well-being depends directly on our work (as is true, for example, in the writing of philosophy), the morality of aspiration applies in a derivative way. It would (merely) be nice if I could play the piano; playing the piano is, for me, a nonmoral aspiration. But, as a writer on philosophical topics, it is a more serious failing that my German is not good enough to read Kant or Hegel. If my philosophizing is slipshod, that is an even more serious failing. Here, the morality of aspiration applies.

---

[15] For an alternative approach to Fuller's theory, see Wibren van der Burg, *The Morality of Aspiration: A Neglected Dimension of Law and Morality*, in Witteveen & van der Burg, supra note 3, at 174–80. Van der Burg focuses on Fuller's claim that the moralities of duty and aspiration lie on a single continuum (*ML* 9–10), but I believe that this was a mistake on Fuller's part. The continuum image implies that there will be some point above which everything is aspiration and below which everything is duty. However, ideals such as always doing my duty, never being negligent or unfair for even a single second, or leading a perfectly blameless life belong simultaneously to the morality of duty and to the morality of aspiration: to deviate from these ideals violates the morality of aspiration because we can only aspire to such superhuman perfection; but by definition each deviation also violates a duty. Hence, the continuum metaphor must be incorrect. For this reason, I emphasize the categorical differences between aspiration and duty.

[16] A. W. H. Adkins, Merit and Responsibility: A Study in Greek Values 30–60 (1960).

In general, it seems, aspiration "goes moral" when our aspirations tie in to serious commitments, when they move from the amateur to the professional. Fuller is in love with the idea of professionalism. He celebrates the virtues of excellence in work; in this respect, his nearest literary counterpart is Primo Levi in *The Monkey's Wrench* and *The Periodic Table*.[17] Thus, the third point that emerges from Fuller's "two moralities" discussion – alongside the ideas that aspiration has a morality, and that its morality is a kind of virtue ethics – is the thought that professional ethics includes the morality of aspiration as one of its central features.

4. Next, consider the quotation with which Fuller begins the first chapter of *ML*: "Sin is a sinking into nothingness" (*ML* 3).[18] The absence of excellence, of virtue, is not badness so much as nonbeing. This is a familiar Platonic and Augustinian idea, and I think it is quite false as a general account of evil. It makes a great deal of sense, however, when applied to aretaic concepts such as "virtue" (a word that for Fuller has the "original sense of power, efficacy, skill, and courage" [*ML* 15]). If a lawyer is not doing any of the things a good lawyer does, she is not merely practicing law badly. She is not practicing law at all. Virtues are functional excellences, and a professional role is defined by its functions; take away enough of the professional virtues, and the result is simply not recognizable as the professional role.

It should be clear why these four major points are important to understanding Fuller's jurisprudential argument. I have been claiming that Fuller's morality of law is a set of excellences that belong to the professional ethics – the role-morality – of lawmakers. This is specifically true of the inner morality of law, Fuller's eight canons of lawmaking. It is significant, after all, that Fuller introduces the canons with the parable of King Rex, who aimed "to make his name in history as a great lawgiver" (*ML* 34) – an entirely aretaic ambition. As Fuller tells the story, moreover, Rex's failures led him after each failure to reflect not on the concept of law, but on his own personal failings – further evidence that Fuller's focus is on the legislator, not the legislation.[19] If sin is a sinking into nothingness, then we can understand Fuller's famous conclusion that Rex "never even succeeded in creating any

---

[17] Primo Levi, The Monkey's Wrench (William Weaver trans., Penguin, 1987); Primo Levi, The Periodic Table (Raymond Rosenthal trans., Schocken, 1984).

[18] "Der Sünde ist ein Versinken in das Nichts." Significantly, Fuller says he may have imagined this quotation, an admission that suggests how central it is to his outlook.

[19] Consider, for example, these statements found in the parable: "His first move was to subscribe to a course of lessons in generalization" (*ML* 34); "Rex undertook an earnest inventory of his personal strengths and weaknesses" (*ML* 35); "Continuing his lessons in generalization, Rex worked diligently " (*ML* 35); "Recognizing for the first time that he needed assistance . . ." (*ML* 36); "By now, however, Rex had lost his patience with his subjects" (*ML* 36); "Reflecting on the misadventures of his reign, he concluded . . ." (*ML* 37).

law at all, good or bad" (*ML* 34) in a somewhat nonstandard light. It becomes an observation about the role morality of lawgiving rather than an analytical claim about necessary conditions on the very concept of law. Fuller is simply pointing out that whatever King Rex did when he issued directives in a fashion that entirely lacked the characteristic excellences of the lawgiver's craft, he was not subjecting human conduct to the governance of rules. He was not making law.

These observations derive from a more general point about what I will call *purposive* concepts – concepts that define objects by the functions they serve in fulfilling purposes. For example, 'light switch' is a purposive concept: it defines objects by their function of turning lights on and off.[20] Fuller's fundamental insight into purposive concepts is that to identify an object purposively is implicitly to specify a standard of success and failure. Fuller puts this strikingly when he writes that the concept of a steam engine "overlaps mightily" with the concept of a good steam engine (*LQI* 10–11). 'Steam engine' is a purposive concept: what makes devices steam engines is their ability to convert steam power to usable mechanical energy. What a steam engine is good for and what a steam engine is "overlap mightily."

This point carries the important consequence that when we use purposive concepts in descriptions, we are automatically evaluating as well as describing. Take a simple example. Touring a house, I notice an odd-looking bump on the wall. It can be wiggled from side to side, but wiggling it does nothing whatsoever. I'm puzzled. Suddenly I recognize that the bump is a broken light switch. This is one single recognition, not two: to identify the bump as a light switch is simultaneously to identify it as a defective light switch. If I have no idea that a light switch that does not turn the lights on or off is defective, I lack the concept 'light switch' altogether.[21]

The way that Fuller usually phrases this point is to say that the *is* and the *ought* cannot be sharply distinguished, or that they merge. This is a maddeningly elusive way of putting things, and even Fuller recognized that "phrases like 'a merger of fact and value' are unsatisfactory" (*RN* 83). The reason such phrases are unsatisfactory is that they wrongly suggest that to describe something as a steam engine is already to describe it as a good steam engine. This is certainly not what Fuller means to say. Substitute the word 'law' for 'steam engine' and this sort of misinterpretation is disastrous.

---

[20] Defining objects purposively is a special case of functional definition. It is not the only case, of course, because there are also functional concepts defining objects by the roles they play in nonpurposive processes. For chemists, "catalyst" is a functional concept, but it is not purposive, because chemical reactions are not purposes.

[21] Fuller argues that omitting the purpose in descriptions of purposive objects makes them misdescriptions. Lon L. Fuller, *Human Purpose and Natural Law*, 3 Natural Law Forum 68 (1958).

As I interpret them, such phrases instead assert that to recognize something as a steam engine or a light switch is already to recognize what it ought to do, to recognize a built-in standard of success or failure. Success or failure at what? At being a steam engine or a light switch – at being what it is, one might say. Purposive concepts are *aspirational* concepts – and now we recognize that Fuller's morality of aspiration is intimately connected with his analysis of purposive concepts, and hence with the is/ought distinction.

This point can be turned around. If an object is so bad at converting steam power to mechanical energy or turning lights on and off that we cannot even recognize it as *unsuccessfully* doing these things, then we will be unable to recognize the object as a steam engine or light switch at all. The worse things get at fulfilling the purposes of steam engines and light switches, the closer they get to the threshold between being a bad steam engine or light switch and not being a steam engine or light switch at all. Sin is a sinking into nothingness.

One more point about the evaluative dimension of purposive concepts turns out to be crucial to Fuller's understanding of the morality of law. There is nothing distinctively moral about converting steam power to usable mechanical energy or turning lights on and off – so the "merger of *is* and *ought*" in these examples is not quite a merger of fact and value. Matters are different, however, when the purposively defined entity is a person defined through her social or occupational role ("parent," "physician," "lawyer," "lawmaker"), and the means by which she fulfills the role's purposes create a long-term moral relationship with other people. In such cases, the standard of success implicit in the purposive concept is not just fulfillment of the occupation's ends narrowly conceived. Instead, the standard of success is fulfillment of these ends in a manner consistent with the moral relationship, for if the role-occupier chronically betrays the moral relationship, the other parties will dissolve it. Under this standard, a relationship that originates only as a means to an end becomes incorporated into the end itself.

"The citizen's role as a self-determining agent"

According to Fuller, when a lawmaker systematically violates any of the canons of the internal morality of law – the role-morality of his or her job – the result is not law (*ML* 39). What, then, if not law, is it? Fuller seems to think that there are two characteristic answers to this question. His first answer emerges when he discusses the Nazi legal system or other criminal legal systems. In this discussion, he leaves little doubt that he considers these systems as nothing more than Hart's illegitimate "gunman writ large" – examples of raw power disguised as law.

However, violating the eight canons need not always be illegitimate in the way that the gunman writ large is illegitimate. Fuller's second answer is that law must be distinguished from "managerial direction" (*ML* 207) – a form of governance that is perfectly legitimate in many everyday contexts, but that involves no commitment to the canons of generality or congruence between official action and declared rule.[22] Managerial direction is a form of governance, but it is not the enterprise of subjecting human conduct to the governance of rules, because managerial directives are not necessarily rules: a manager can deviate from his own general directives whenever circumstances require.

Usually, when Fuller asserts that governance that systematically violates the eight canons is not law, the way to understand the phrase "not law" is as an abbreviation for "not law but tyranny" or "not law but managerial direction."[23] (The distinction between tyranny and managerial direction is that in the latter, but not the former, subordinates share their superiors' aims.) For Fuller, the "identification of law with every conceivable kind of official act" (*ML* 169) is a conceptual mistake that leads to misunderstandings about the morality of law.[24]

In particular, Fuller argues that governing the conduct of others through law rather than managerial direction is itself a morally freighted choice. According to Fuller, it implies "a certain built-in respect for [the] human dignity" of those subject to the law ("the governed," as I shall call them for short), in a way that managerial direction does not.[25] This is the case for several reasons.

First, it recognizes that the form of governance will not be moment-by-moment direct supervision. Governance through general rules, unlike managerial direction, presumes a measure of respect for the moral powers of the governed. "To embark on the enterprise of subjecting human conduct to the governance of rules involves of necessity a commitment to the view that man is, or can become, a responsible agent, capable of understanding and following rules, and answerable for his defaults" (*ML* 162). Elsewhere,

---

[22] Fuller mistakenly asserts that the issue of nonretroactivity never arises in managerial direction, because no manager would ever order someone today to do something yesterday (*ML* 209). However, a manager might find it quite expedient to change a policy retroactively. For example, a manager might decide to deduct the costs of tools that workers damage from their paychecks, and it is easy to imagine circumstances in which the manager might wish to make this policy retroactive. If the terms of employment do not protect workers from policies like this, and if there is no labor union to fight the policy, we can readily imagine that the manager will be successful. Thus, Fuller's point should have been that in a managerial context, there is no necessary moral commitment to prospectivity.

[23] The one notable exception is the King Rex parable itself. There, the hapless king is neither a manager nor a tyrant – he is merely an incompetent.

[24] Here (and in other places) my reading is influenced by Jeremy Waldron, *Why Law – Efficacy, Freedom, or Fidelity?*, 13 Law & Phil. 259 (1994).

[25] Fuller, *A Reply to Professors Cohen and Dworkin*, supra note 8, at 665.

Fuller makes the Wittgensteinian point that legal rules cannot explicitly exclude all aberrant interpretations in advance, and concludes that relying on the governed to follow rules presupposes shared "notions of the limits of legal decency and sanity."[26] Governance through rules implies that the governed and the governors belong to the same interpretive community and have roughly equivalent powers of intellect and will.

Second, governance through general rules, unlike specific directives, presupposes the autonomy of the governed. "The law does not tell a man what he should do to accomplish specific ends set by the lawgiver; it furnishes him with baselines against which to organize his life with his fellows ... Law provides a framework for the citizen within which to live his own life" (*PSO* 234).[27] Elsewhere, Fuller describes "the view of man implicit in legal morality" (*ML* 162) as "the citizen's role as a self-determining agent" (*ML* 166). To be a lawgiver rather than a command-giver is to treat the citizen as a self-determining agent.

Governing through general rules also implies a certain impersonality in the relationship between governors and governed. Each individual falls under a rule only as a member of a general class, and each action is likewise judged only on the basis of general characteristics. What matters is *what* we are and do, not *who* we are – our deeper identity remains outside law's purview. Government through general rules contrasts starkly with the patrimonial familiarity that breeds contempt; law treats us as '*Sie*' rather than '*du*', as '*vous*' rather than '*tu*'.

Third, governance through rules, unlike the gunman writ large, assumes a measure of self-enforcement and self-monitoring on the part of the governed. Governance through rules, which is relatively cumbersome, would be unnecessary if an enforcer were always present. Although a tyrant can dominate a hostile population using a surprisingly small number of police – by making it extremely dangerous to even attempt to organize resistance that could overwhelm the police force – governance through rules presumes at least the passive cooperation of the governed (*ML* 216).[28]

---

[26] Lon L. Fuller, Anatomy of the Law 63 (1968).

[27] Fuller makes the same point in *ML*: "Law furnishes a baseline for self-directed action, not a detailed set of instructions for accomplishing specific objectives." *ML* 210. He also uses the "baseline" terminology to make the converse point, namely that not only does law presuppose the goal-setting freedom of the governed, but that the goal-setting freedom of the governed requires law. "To live the good life ... requires the support of firm base lines for human interaction, something that – in modern society at least – only a sound legal system can supply." *ML* 205. He elaborates this latter point in *Freedom – A Suggested Analysis*, 68 Harv. L. Rev. 1305 (1955).

[28] For an illuminating explanation of how even widely hated police states can maintain their dominance using a surprisingly small number of enforcers, see Russell Hardin, One for All: The Logic of Group Conflict 29–32 (1995).

Respect for the governed, respect for the autonomy of the governed, and trust in the governed – these are the three overlapping moral values underlying a governor's choice of law, rather than managerial direction or tyranny, as the specific form of governance. Fuller's point, then, seems to be that embarking on the enterprise of subjecting human conduct to the governance of rules creates a certain kind of moral relationship between governor and governed. It is, specifically, a relationship in which a governor abjures the streamlined efficiency of managerial direction in favor of trusting the governed to understand and follow general rules on their own.

Once we see this point, a puzzling passage from *The Morality of Law* begins to make sense. Many of Fuller's critics complain that Fuller's eight principles of legality are merely conditions of efficacy, not moral principles. They accept that Fuller's King Rex parable demonstrates that governors must follow the eight canons if they want people to obey their laws. These critics argue, however, that this is true whether the laws in question are good or evil, and thus that the canons themselves have nothing to do with morality. To illustrate the point, Hart observes that there are also rules of effective poisoning. Dworkin makes the same point with blackmail and genocide; Marshall Cohen, with murder; and Schauer, more recently, with lynching.[29]

Fuller responds strangely: "I must confess that this line of argument struck me at first as being so bizarre, and even perverse, as not to deserve an answer" (*ML* 201). But what is so bizarre and perverse about it? Fuller himself insists that his eight canons are principles of efficacy (*ML* 155–56); indeed, when he introduced the idea of an internal morality of law in his 1958 reply to Hart, he argued for its canons solely on grounds of efficacy (*PFL* 644–45).

What strikes Fuller as perverse about the accusation that he has confused morality with efficacy is that he regards the choice to govern through law rather than managerial direction as a sacrifice of efficacy for moral ends (*ML* 202–3). To put the point another way: while Fuller agrees that the principles of legality are instrumentally necessary to make governance by law effective (*ML* 155–56), he thinks that governing by law rather than managerial direction represents a sacrifice of expediency in the name of principle. The ultimate justification of the principles of legality is therefore moral, not instrumental. Fuller finds the poisoning and blackmail analogies perverse because they

---

[29] Hart, *Book Review* – The Morality of Law, supra note 6, at 1286; Ronald Dworkin, *Philosophy, Morality, and Law – Observations Prompted by Professor Fuller's Novel Claim*, 113 U. Penn. L. Rev. 668, 676 (1965); Ronald Dworkin, *The Elusive Morality of Law*, 10 Villanova L. Rev. 631, 634 (1965); Marshall Cohen, *Law, Morality, and Purpose*, 10 Villanova L. Rev. 640, 651 (1965); Frederick Schauer, *Fuller's Internal Point of View*, 13 Law & Phil. 285, 302–4 (1994).

assume that an evildoer would for some mysterious reason choose as an instrument of evil a relatively ineffective tool – a tool, moreover, that is relatively ineffective because it displays precisely the kind of moral regard for its victim that an evildoer lacks.[30]

Consider, by analogy, a professor's decision to teach a large class through the Socratic method of eliciting the classroom material by questioning students rather than by straight lecture. (The analogy is mine, not Fuller's.) The Socratic method is much less efficient than lecturing, and much harder to do well. It sacrifices coverage of material, it frequently frustrates and puzzles students, and it makes classroom progress hostage to the commitment and capabilities of the class. Why, then, would a teacher choose the Socratic method? The principal reason is that teachers wish to train their students in the art of analyzing issues for themselves, along with the art of explaining their own thinking, in public, on their feet. The point of Socratic teaching is to cultivate the students' active powers, even at the cost of efficiency. This is very similar to what Fuller takes to be the point of governance through law: to cultivate activity rather than passivity, to enhance rather than restrict the citizens' powers of self-determination, even though self-determination is unruly and therefore inefficient.

Socratic teaching is also subject to characteristic abuses that are quite analogous to the abuse of law by tyrants. When a teacher really has a lecture idea in mind, but tries to elicit it through Socratic questioning, she will find herself compelled to deal brusquely with student answers that do not take the discussion where she wants it to go. She will cut corners to guide the discussion, and students will quickly perceive that they are involved in a Socratic shell game of guessing what the teacher has in mind, not in cultivating their own powers. They will rightly view this as a betrayal of the teacher–student relationship: the teacher here is merely pretending to respect the students' intellectual autonomy and cultivate their powers. In reality, she is dominating them.[31]

---

[30] As I read Fuller's argument, it is precisely the argument offered by John Finnis in his exposition of Fuller: "Adherence to the Rule of Law (especially the eighth requirement, of conformity by officials to pre-announced and stable general rules) is always liable to reduce the efficiency for evil of an evil government, since it systematically restricts the government's freedom of maneuver." Finnis, Natural Law and Natural Rights 274 (1980). Thus, "[a] tyranny devoted to pernicious ends has no self-sufficient *reason* to submit itself to the discipline of operating consistently through the demanding processes of law, granted that the rational point of such self-discipline is the very value of reciprocity, fairness, and respect for persons which the tyrant, *ex hypothesi*, holds in contempt." Ibid. at 273.

[31] A famous philosophy professor (no names, please) was a legendary practitioner of the Socratic shell game, and generations of students parodied his teaching with the following dialogue. *Professor:* I'm thinking of a number between 1 and 500. Mr. A, please tell me the number. *Student A:* 15? *Professor:* No. Ms. B? *Student B:* Um, is it 96? *Professor* (fiercely): Ms. B, I asked you to name the number between 1 and 500 I am thinking of. Do you really think you've

Does Fuller mean to deny, then, that a lawmaker may have domination on his mind? Not at all.[32] His conclusion is substantially more interesting than that. Fuller argues that *every* exercise of social power requires some reciprocity. Even a blackmailer has to exercise some restraint; otherwise, his victim might elect to reveal his own shameful secret in order to bring the bite to an end. Here, Fuller observes, we can imagine the blackmailer pleading with the victim not to do this, and promising to be less greedy in the future (*PSO* 195–96). Elsewhere, Fuller suggests that a tyrant will find that domination will be easier if he enlists his subjects' cooperation by enhancing their freedom and happiness.[33] If a lawmaker persistently abuses his relationship with the governed, he will be unable to count on the governed to interpret and follow rules; therefore, a decision to govern through rules rather than orders, perhaps undertaken initially because the order-giver cannot be everywhere at once, imposes moral constraints on the order-giver. The more that the power-holder turns tasks over to the subordinate for his own convenience, the more he makes himself dependent on the agency and independence of the subordinate. In that case, reciprocity tends toward at least rough equality, and one-way projection of authority becomes two-way interaction.[34]

Fuller describes his theory as an *interactional* view of law (*ML* 221), because in his view the choice of law over managerial direction implies a moral relationship between governors and the governed based on mutuality (*ML* 209, 216).

Government says to the citizen in effect, "These are the rules we expect you to follow. If you follow them, you have our assurance that they are the rules that will be applied to your conduct." When this bond of reciprocity is finally and completely ruptured by government, nothing is left on which to ground the citizen's duty to observe the rules. (*ML* 39–40)

---

answered my question? Mr. C, tell us the number. *Student C*: 216. *Professor*: That is correct. Ms. B, now do you see your mistake?

The professor was widely regarded as an unforgivable intellectual bully.

[32] "I have never asserted that there is any logical contradiction in the notion of achieving evil, at least some kinds of evil, through means that fully respect all the demands of legality." Fuller, *A Reply to Professors Cohen and Dworkin*, supra note 8, at 664.

[33] See Lon Fuller, *Freedom as a Problem of Allocating Choice*, 112 Proc. Am. Phil. Soc'y. 105 (1968).

[34] Although this is not the place to discuss this point in any detail, Fuller has offered a version of Hegel's master/slave argument from the *Phenomenology of Spirit*. There, Hegel describes the evolution of relationships of *pure dependency* (of the slave on the master, who holds the power of life and death over him) to relationships of *reverse dependency* (as the master comes to rely on the slave, who takes over the active role, playing Jeeves to the master's increasingly infantile and incompetent Bertie Wooster) and, later, to relationships of *reciprocity*. G. W. F. Hegel, The Phenomenology of Spirit 111–19 (A. V. Miller trans., Oxford University Press, 1977).

This is an entirely different moral relationship than that of managerial direction – "the basic relation of order-giver and order-executor" (*ML* 209) – although even managerial direction creates *some* reciprocity. Interestingly, Fuller insists that within the managerial context, the canons of clarity, consistency, feasibility, constancy through time, and publicity really are principles of efficacy and nothing more (*ML* 208–9); the clear implication of this point is that he believes that these canons have a different status in the context of law. There, they are professional virtues of the lawgiver, part and parcel of the mutual respect that Fuller believes is at the heart of the relationship between a lawmaker and those whom she governs.

In what sense are canons like clarity, noncontradictoriness, or constancy through time professional virtues of the lawgiver? Consider a group of people who wish to go into business together, and who retain a lawyer to draw up a partnership agreement that reconciles the divergences that inevitably exist among their interests. The partners are entrusting their joint venture to the lawyer; they are counting on the lawyer's professional ability to craft an agreement that will provide a workable architecture for their enterprise. If the partnership agreement turns out to be unclear, self-contradictory, or incapable of execution, this is betrayal, not just incoherence or "inefficacy."[35] The partners will suffer for the lawyer's fecklessness. Those who claim that Fuller's canons merely represent conditions of efficacy appear to overlook this point when they emphasize that a ruler who violates the canons will be unable to accomplish his aim, as though the point of the ruler's activity is only to accomplish his own aim, rather than the aims of those he rules. It is this, perhaps, that leads Fuller repeatedly to accuse his critics of viewing government "as a one-way projection of authority" (*ML* 204).

We can be more specific about how the eight canons are virtues of lawmaking. The two most fundamental – the canons that distinguish the lawgiving enterprise from managerial control – are the canons of generality and congruence between rules and their enforcement. The former insists that governors give directions in the form of general rules; the latter demands that they treat those rules as binding on themselves as well as on the governed, in

---

[35] Indeed, all of these infirmities are breach-of-contract defenses at common law: they void at least the afflicted clauses of the instrument. When we notice this, and recall that Fuller was a contracts scholar, it is tempting to argue that Fuller derived the canons by asking himself what conditions are necessary for a valid social contract between governors and the governed. Recall in this connection the passage quoted above, in which government "makes an offer" to citizens: "These are the rules we expect you to follow. If you follow them, you have our assurance that they are the rules that will be applied to your conduct." This sounds a great deal like a social contract. It is noteworthy as well that when Fuller discusses total failure to abide by the canons, he writes: "It results in something that is not properly called a legal system at all, *except perhaps in the Pickwickian sense in which a void contract can still be said to be one kind of contract.*" *ML* 39, emphasis added.

the sense that they will not depart from the rules they have announced.[36] The commitment to bind the governed only through general rules that also bind the lawmaker establishes the moral relationship of reciprocity between governors and the governed. These two canons are moral commitments that define the enterprise as lawgiving rather than something else.

The remaining six canons fall into two natural groupings: precepts of *clear communication* and precepts of *reasonable expectation*. Once the lawmaker has undertaken to govern through general rules binding on both her and the governed, she must announce the rules to the governed, and she must ensure that her rules are ones that the governed may reasonably be expected to follow. Rather obviously, the canons of clarity and publicity are aspects of clear communication, while the canons of constancy and feasibility are aspects of reasonable expectation. The remaining canons – prospectivity and logical consistency – may be regarded as aspects of both clear communication and reasonable expectation. A rule requiring me to do something today is not adequately communicated if it is not issued until tomorrow, nor is it reasonable to expect me to abide by it; likewise, a self-contradictory rule conveys nothing (because anything follows from a contradiction), and cannot be obeyed.

The burden of understanding and complying with rules falls on those whom the rules govern; the reciprocal relationship between governors and the governed places a corresponding burden on the governor to make the rules understood and capable of being complied with. That, ultimately, is why clear communication and reasonableness are moral virtues of the lawmaker.

" 'Discovery' in the moral realm"

Why does Fuller call his view "natural law"? Fuller energetically rejects the traditional idea that natural law represents "higher law" (*RFCL* 379, *ML* 96, *RN* 84), and indeed he suspects that the appeal to higher law is an unfortunate residue from positivism (*PFL* 656, 659–60). Strikingly, he attributes *no* authority to laws as such: like a good legal realist, he argues that judges should treat statutes and precedents simply as "one [more] of the realities the judge must respect in making his decisions" (*RFCL* 380) – in other words, as constraints within which judicial problem-solving must maneuver, not as authorities to which judges must defer. If Fuller had never employed the term "natural law" in connection with his views, we might be hard-pressed to guess that his is a natural-law jurisprudence.

---

[36] A manager may also issue orders in the form of general directives – rules – but remains at liberty to depart from the directives when circumstances require. In the terminology of Rawls's *Two Concepts of Rules*, the manager adopts a "summary conception" of rules, whereas the lawmaker adopts a "practice conception." John Rawls, *Two Concepts of Rules*, in Collected Papers 34–39 (Samuel Freeman ed., 1999).

Fuller's pronouncements about natural law do not help much. "I discern ... one central aim common to all the schools of natural law, that of discovering those principles of social order which will enable men to attain a satisfactory life in common. It is an acceptance of the possibility of 'discovery' in the moral realm that seems to me to distinguish all the theories of natural law from opposing views" (*RN* 84). Talk of the possibility of discovery in the moral realm makes it sound as if Fuller equates natural-law theory with moral realism. But moral realism, the thesis that moral judgments are objective and referential, is not distinctive to natural law. Positivists, who believe that law can and should be open to moral criticism, can accept the realist thesis without difficulty. Indeed, many of the positivists were utilitarians, and utilitarians hold that judgments of right and wrong – claims about which actions are utility-maximizing and which are not – are objective and referential.

Elsewhere, Fuller cautions that "for many the term 'natural law' still has about it a rich, deep odor [...] [RFLT 1]79). But all it really signifies, he says, is

that there are external criteria found in the conditions required for successful group living, that furnish some standard against which the rightness of decisions should be measured ... Certainly it would never occur to him [the natural lawyer] to describe the natural law he sought to discover ... and felt bound to respect as a "brooding omnipresence in the skies." Rather, for him it would be a hard and ... worthy reality that challenged his best intellectual efforts to capture it. The ... attitude ... would not be that of one doing obeisance before an altar, but more like that of a cook trying to find the secret of a flaky pie crust. (RFLT 179)

Once again, there is nothing here that a utilitarian positivist could not enthusiastically embrace. Like Fuller, the utilitarian positivist is an ethical naturalist, who believes that deciding what the law ought to be is hard intellectual work, with external standards of success determined in large part by empirical facts about nature and human nature.

I believe, however, that once we think of Fuller's theory as the professional ethics of lawmaking, we find a coherent answer to the question of what makes it a natural-law theory: it derives moral requirements of the lawmaker's job from features unique to the lawmaking enterprise. Unlike other natural-law theories, however, the morality implicit in Fuller's concept of law is the morality of lawmaking, not of the law made.

Fuller complains that positivists neglect the distinctive role-morality of lawmaking: "If the lawgiver enacts what Hart calls 'iniquitous' laws, he sins of course against general morality, but there is no special morality applicable to his job itself" (*ML* 193). This description is plainly true of utilitarianism, which regards a job as nothing more than a causal path connecting an agent's input to output in the form of utility, the way that a transmission connects an auto's engine to its wheels. The utilitarian would regard the role morality of a job as nothing more than an application or instantiation of the principle of utility. For Fuller, however, it is a fallacy "to assume that moral precepts retain the same meaning regardless of the social context into which they are projected" (*ML* 207); he accuses both utilitarians and Kantians of this fallacy (*PSO* 201). What both overlook, Fuller argues, is that when you take on a job, intending to pursue it in a way that respects general morality, you discover that the job creates moral expectations of its own (*PSO* 200–1). Fuller's arguments about the morality of law are meant to show that lawmaking has its own distinctive virtues (conformity to the eight canons) and its own distinctive moral outlook (respect for the self-determining agency of the governed), both of which follow from the nature of the lawmaking enterprise and not directly from general morality.

This is what Fuller has in mind when he writes about discovery in the moral realm. He is not tendering a general commitment to moral realism, but rather making the more specific claim that institutions, particularly legal institutions, although they are entirely human creations, have moral properties of their own – properties that their designers may never have intended or even thought about, and that are connected only indirectly to general morality. Identifying the morality of institutions, the virtues and vices of participating in them, is a matter of discovery, not invention – a matter of reason rather than fiat.

I think Fuller is right. We can observe these phenomena in the evolution of games like baseball. Games are in one sense an entirely positivist creation: the rules define the game, and presumably, if the rules permit a practice, engaging in it cannot be cheating. One might argue that the game would be better if the rules forbade certain practices – in positivist terms, that the game as it is isn't the game as it ought to be. But as long as the rules do not favor one team over the other, abiding by these rules cannot be criticized on the ground that it is not a fair way to play baseball. So goes the positivist argument.

Yet in actuality, the rules of baseball have been modified repeatedly over the years because, as the game develops, it becomes clear that some behavior permitted by the rules really is cheating. Fielders intentionally miss infield pop-ups when there are runners on first and second base, in order to get an easy double play; pitchers make the ball curve by spitting on it; base runners block batted balls with their bodies to prevent fielders from making a play; hitters peek at the catcher to see whether he is setting up for an inside or an outside pitch; batters with two strikes against them intentionally swing and miss at wild pitches so they can run safely to first base when the ball flies past the catcher. All of these practices were at one time permitted by the rules, and the first three were banned – not because the game would be better if they were banned (though this is true), but because it became clear that missing infield flies to get the cheap double play, throwing the spitter, and interfering with batted balls were forms of cheating. These were moral discoveries about baseball-playing, of just the kind that Fuller claims to have made about lawmaking. They are part of the natural law of an artificial institution. Interestingly, no rule currently forbids batters from peeking at the catcher to see where he is setting up. However, if the opposing players catch him in the act, the batter will be hit by a pitch his next time up, and no one will complain, because even the batter knows he deserves it. He has violated the natural law of baseball.[37] The same goes for the batter with two strikes against him who swings at a wild pitch: one writer recalls that when he did this in high school, his own teammates shunned him afterward.[38]

One might object that these practices are cheating, not because they violate the "natural law of baseball," but merely because the written rules did not do a good enough job of codifying the game as it was supposed to be played. But no one knew *a priori* how baseball was supposed to be played; refining the rules was not merely a means to the end of preserving the original intent of baseball's framers. The discovery that throwing the spitball is a form of cheating was simultaneously a discovery about the point of the contest between batter and pitcher. The relationship is dialectical, not hierarchical.

One important point should be added about the concept of role-morality that Fuller invokes. As Fuller understands the role-morality of lawyers, it consists of role-derived duties over and above those contained in "general morality" (Fuller's term for morality in its universal dimension, apart from specific social roles). Thus, in addition to the demands of general morality, the lawgiver has a duty to issue laws that accord with the eight canons, and that respect the self-determining agency of those subject to the law. Fuller seems to assume that these special role-related duties supplement general morality but do not contradict it. Here, at any rate, he does not consider the difficulties that arise when role-morality contradicts general morality – for

---

[37] See Keith Hernandez & Mike Bryan, Pure Baseball: Pitch by Pitch for the Advanced Fan 125–27 (1995). Interestingly, Hernandez (an all-star first baseman) states both that the peeker deserves to be hit by a pitch *and* that peeking is neither cheating nor bad sportsmanship. That is because Hernandez believes that nothing, not even practices forbidden by the rules, is unfair if the other team or the umpires have a fair opportunity to catch and punish the players who engage in it. His is a legal realist view of cheating, desert, and self-help, quite distinct from both natural law and positivism.

[38] Ted Cohen, *There Are No Ties at First Base*, 79 Yale Rev. at 321–22 (1990). "[My team-mates] did not care for what I had done ... They regarded me as someone who did not really grasp the nature of the game. I thought that in knowing the rules I knew the game; they knew the game in some other way." Ibid. at 322. I am grateful to David Brink for calling Cohen's hilarious essay to my attention.

example, when the adversarial role-morality of neutral partisanship compels lawyers to further morally obnoxious client ends or to utilize lawful but morally repugnant means. Alan Goldman registers the difference between these two categories of role-related obligations by distinguishing duties that are "weakly role differentiated" from those that are differentiated strongly: the former are duties different from, but not inconsistent with, general morality, while the latter are duties that contradict general morality.[39] A lawyer's duty to maintain a separate bank account for client funds is weakly role-differentiated; the duty to defend a client's unjust cause is strongly role-differentiated.

Fuller gives only a slight indication that he recognizes the problems raised by strong role-differentiation. My own view, as argued in chapter 1 (and at greater length in *Lawyers and Justice*) is that neutral partisanship – and, more generally, strongly differentiated role-obligations in other professions – can be defended only within narrow contexts such as criminal defense. Unless the professional institutions have powerful justification, and the role-obligations are essential to the functioning of those institutions, role-morality does not prevail over general morality. It is unclear whether Fuller would disagree, for while he strongly defends the adversary system, he also argues that lawyers within it have violated its role-morality if they "muddy the headwaters of decision" – a cryptic qualification that may well rule out most of the problematic tactics required by neutral partisanship (for example, using tactics of delay and intimidation to force adversaries to drop legitimate claims).[40]

As the earlier chapters of this book demonstrate, the legitimacy of a strongly differentiated role-morality raises crucial questions of legal ethics. But the legitimacy of weakly differentiated role-morality – professional obligations that supplement rather than contradict general morality – raises no such questions. And Fuller's view of the natural law of lawmaking focuses only on the latter kind of role-morality. Or so Fuller seems to believe. In the final section of this chapter I shall return to this question, and suggest that he may well have been over-optimistic in his faith that the lawyer's role-morality inevitably upholds human dignity. As I suggested in the previous chapter, adversarial law practice may well lead lawyers to assault human dignity rather than enhancing it.

The progressive positivists' critique of natural law

I now turn to criticisms of Fuller's view. In his review of *The Morality of Law*, Hart wonders whether he and Fuller are perhaps "fated never to

---

[39] Alan H. Goldman, The Moral Foundations of Professional Ethics 2–3 (1980).

[40] Lon L. Fuller & John Randall, *Professional Responsibility: Report of the Joint Conference of the ABA-AALS*, 44 ABAJ 1159, 1161 (1958).

understand each other's work,"[41] and on one central issue it seems clear that Fuller and his positivist critics talk past each other. This is the curious issue of which theory provides its adherents with the morally superior point of view on the law. The issue is curious, of course, because ordinarily we think that theories should be chosen on the basis of whether they are correct, not whether they morally improve their adherents. Nevertheless, the argument turns out to be an important one both for Fuller and for his critics.[42]

Let us put it most directly. Fuller repeatedly accuses positivists of being statists, "overprimed with power" (*PSO* 277); theirs, he says, is "the view that identifies the lawyer's work with established state power" (*PSO* 252). And repeatedly, progressive positivists like Fred Schauer, Neil MacCormick, and Robin West level the identical accusation of statism against natural lawyers.[43] (By *progressive positivists*, I mean positivists who deny *per se* moral authority to the legal status quo and therefore to the state.) According to Schauer, "the classical natural law theorist" believes "that the very existence of a legal system provides ... assurance that the legal system has been designed either to incorporate moral criteria or to produce morally desirable ends."[44]

This argument between natural lawyers and progressive positivists originates in one of the most important passages in Hart's half of the debate with Fuller. In *Positivism and the Separation of Law and Morals*, Hart accuses natural lawyers of having only "half digested the spiritual message of liberalism."[45] Natural lawyers understand that in the face of evil enactments by the state, individual conscience should prevail over the duty to obey. This is the spiritual message of liberalism. But natural lawyers have only half-digested it, because it seems that the only way they can license disobedience is by denying that evil enactments are law. Apparently, they cannot shake off the idea that law must be obeyed. In legal philosopher Donald Regan's

---

[41] Hart, *Book Review* – The Morality of Law, supra note 6, at 1281.

[42] See Philip Soper, *Choosing a Legal Theory on Moral Grounds*, in Philosophy and Law 31–48 (Jules Coleman & Ellen Frankel Paul eds., 1987).

[43] See Frederick Schauer, *Positivism Through Thick and Thin*, in Analyzing Law: New Essays in Legal Theory 65 (Brian Bix ed., 1998); Schauer, *Fuller's Internal Point of View*, supra note 29, at 305–12; Schauer, *Constitutional Positivism*, 25 Conn. L. Rev. 797, 805–7 (1993); Schauer, *Positivism as Pariah*, in The Autonomy of Law: Essays on Legal Positivism 31 (Robert P. George ed., 1996); Neil MacCormick, *A Moralistic Case for A-Moralistic Law*, 20 Valparaiso L. Rev. 1, 10–11 (1985); Robin West, *Three Positivisms*, 78 B. U. L. Rev. 791 (1998); and Robin West, *Natural Law Ambiguities*, 25 Conn. L. Rev. 831 (1993). West, it should be noted, expounds the progressive positivist view sympathetically without wholly endorsing it.

[44] Schauer, *Positivism Through Thick and Thin*, supra note 43, at 70.

[45] Hart, *Positivism and the Separation of Law and Morals*, supra note 5, at 618; Hart, The Concept of Law, supra note 4, at 205–6.

felicitous phrase, they still think that law has a halo.[46] This is the illiberal side of natural law.

Positivists, according to Hart, are morally more clear-headed. They understand that law has no necessary moral content, no halo. They labor under one fewer illusion about where their moral duty lies, and are less likely to accede to bad law merely because it is law. Quoting Schauer once again, "in insisting that the concept of law does no moral work the [progressive positivist] is taking the irreducibly moral position that we ought not to expect our understanding of law and legal institutions to carry any of the moral water when we engage in personal decision-making or institutional design."[47]

It is very curious to find a natural lawyer like Fuller and progressive positivists like Hart and Schauer each accusing the other side of being too statist. In effect, each is trying to outflank the other on the left – which of course leads battlefield adversaries to revolve in a perpetual circle around a point of engagement that neither ever reaches. At least one side in this debate is failing to grasp something about the other's position. In this case, I think, both are.

Let us begin with Fuller's accusation that positivists identify law with "a one-way projection of authority, originating with government and imposing itself upon the citizen" (ML 204). This is only half true, because positivists argue only that legal systems *may* be one-way projections of state authority, not that they *must* be. Even if the accusation were true, though, Fuller wrongly supposes that positivists approve of one-way projections of state authority. Hart's argument, of course, is that when the law authorizes something evil, a liberal positivist will disapprove and disobey.

Next, look at the progressive positivists' moral critique of natural law. Schauer, recall, argues that for classical natural-law theorists, the very existence of a legal system ensures its morality. Why should that be? Schauer does not say, but evidently he believes that the classical theorists contrapose the natural law maxim "unjust law is not law" into the claim that law is just. However, natural lawyers do not actually make this mistake in contraposition. The natural-law maxim is shorthand for "unjust *positive* law is not *genuine* law." This is logically equivalent not to the claim that (all) law is just, but to the claim that positive law that is also genuine law is just.[48]

---

[46] Donald H. Regan, *Law's Halo*, in Coleman & Paul, Philosophy and Law, supra note 42, at 15–30.

[47] Schauer, *Positivism Through Thick and Thin*, supra note 43, at 70.

[48] Among the progressive positivists, West is clear about this. She regards these two ways of reading the natural-law maxim as an ambiguity in natural-law theory, whereas I regard them as a positivist misunderstanding of natural law. As for the logical equivalence, let $P(x)$ mean "x is positive law"; $J(x)$ mean "x is just law"; and $G(x)$ mean "x is genuine law." "Unjust (positive) law is not (genuine) law" gets formalized as "$((x)(P(x) \,\&\, \sim J(x) \rightarrow \sim G(x))$)" (i.e., "anything that is a positive law and an unjust law is not a genuine law"), which is logically equivalent to "$((x)(P(x) \,\&\, G(x) \rightarrow J(x))$)" (i.e., "anything that is a positive law and a genuine law is a just law").

The mere existence of positive law leads to no conclusion whatever about its justice or injustice.

Let me rephrase all this in a more polemical and less logic-chopping manner. Progressive positivists like Hart, MacCormick, and Schauer think that the natural-law maxim will confuse its adherents and make them too impressed with law, too complacent with the status quo, and too likely to obey. But of course, "unjust law is not law" is the traditional argument for disobedience, not for obedience – so who exactly is it who is confused? In its most famous contemporary American incarnation, the natural-law maxim figures prominently in Martin Luther King's *Letter from Birmingham City Jail*, where King invoked it to explain, in the most stirring terms, why he was right to disobey a court order forbidding a 1963 civil rights march.[49] If the progressive positivists think that the natural-law maxim is an invitation to complacency and obedience, then they must believe that King misunderstood the maxim, because he was neither complacent nor obedient. King misunderstood the maxim, apparently, by failing to draw the wrong conclusion from it. Isn't it more likely that the progressive positivists have misunderstood why natural lawyers like King insist that unjust law is not law?

The positivist moral critique of classical natural law misfires in a slightly different way against Fuller's version. The progressive positivists fear that anyone who believes in "the morality of law" will illicitly regard legal enactments as having already passed a preliminary threshold toward moral acceptability. As we have seen, Fuller thinks just the opposite. For Fuller, to call an enactment law entails that it has *extra* moral demands placed on it by virtue of the "morality of law" – the role-morality of lawgiving. Law's halo, on Fuller's account, provides additional grounds for criticizing law, not for obeying it.

In this respect, at any rate, Hart and Fuller were talking past one another. Notice, for example, that when Fuller speaks of "fidelity to law" (in *PFL*) he is generally talking about officials' professional obligation to maintain the legal system in good order, not about the citizen's obligation to obey the law, which is Hart's topic. Fuller asks how German judges, not ordinary Germans, should have responded to the Third Reich, and he answers that fidelity to law – which is *not* the same as obedience to law – should have led them to resist.

In a recent essay, Schauer offers a different criticism of Fuller, one which presents an interesting twist on the progressive positivist argument. Schauer focuses on the fact that Fuller's is "insider jurisprudence," designed and built to help conscientious legal professionals become better lawyers. In the terms I have been urging, it is jurisprudence in the service of professional

---

[49] Martin Luther King, Jr., *Letter from Birmingham County Jail*, reprinted in King, Why We Can't Wait 76 (Mentor, 1964).

ethics. Schauer acutely remarks that "Fuller's perspective flows smoothly from *his* role as a legal theorist explicitly seeing himself located in a law school and speaking to actual or would-be lawyers."[50] Insider jurisprudence presupposes that the professional project has worth, and is worth the efforts of conscientious people to improve it.

Suppose, however, that one is an outsider, whose question is not "What kind of lawyer shall I be?" but "Why should anyone be a lawyer?"[51] An outsider need not begin by supposing that the legal system has any worth at all, but she does need to understand what the legal system is. For the outsider, then, positivism is the superior starting point, for only positivism facilitates the project of "first ... characterizing the legal system, and then ... morally evaluating it."[52]

To illustrate Schauer's point, let our outsider be a visitor newly arrived in a foreign country, who asks someone, "What is the legal system like?" (Perhaps she is thinking about emigrating to the foreign country and going to law school.) And suppose the answer is this: "The judges do whatever the regime tells them to, the regime is repressive, the lawyers are not allowed to disagree with the judges, the laws are vague and change all the time, and the schedule of criminal penalties is a state secret." If a Fullerian overhearing the conversation chimes in, "You see, it isn't a legal system at all!" the outsider will reply, "Call it whatever you like – but the person I just talked with answered the question I am interested in." The outsider has rightfully asked a positivist question and gotten a positivist answer. If the outsider had instead approached the Fullerian to ask, "What is the legal system like?" and received the answer, "There is no legal system here," this answer would be misleadingly coy, and in no way more truthful.

Nor is "There is no legal system here" a caricature of Fuller's way of talking. In his reply to Hart, Fuller quotes a Hitler-era statute against slandering the Nazi Party, deems it a "legislative monstrosity," and then embraces the view of postwar German courts that "saw fit to declare this thing not a law" (*PFL* 654, 655). Schauer's point, I take it, is that there is a straightforward "positivist" sense, glossed over by Fuller, in which the statute is a law (and not, say, a poem). Otherwise, how could Fuller call it a "statute" and declare it a *legislative* monstrosity?

Embedded in Schauer's argument we find a claim that Fuller denies: that the insider's concept of law, which Schauer agrees is and should be a moralized one, is unnecessary to describe a society's legal institutions – a

---

[50] Schauer, *Fuller's Internal Point of View*, supra note 29, at 305.   [51] Ibid. at 308.
[52] Ibid. at 309–10. In *Positivism Through Thick and Thin*, Schauer remarks that he finds it no coincidence that among three of the austerest positivists – himself, Jules Coleman, and David Lyons – "two do not possess law degrees and the third no longer teaches primarily in a law school." Schauer, *Positivism Through Thick and Thin*, supra note 43, at 70 n. 1.

"positivist" description is available. The examples just presented make this seem plausible, but Fuller would not be without a response. It would go, I take it, as follows.[53]

"Lawmaking" is a purposive concept, and the purpose of lawmaking is to subject human conduct to the governance of rules (*ML* 146). Like all purposive concepts, it contains implicit criteria of success and failure. As we have seen, lawmaking creates a moral relationship between governors and the governed, and successfully carrying out the terms of that relationship is part of what succeeding at lawmaking means. It follows that if our outsider can recognize what her informant has described as a legal system at all, she can, and indeed must, recognize it as a deviant legal system. Its servile judges, repressive rulers, gagged lawyers, vague and inconstant rules, and secret punishments represent a gross deviation from the aspirations inherent in the lawmaking enterprise.

Could the positivist resist this conclusion by declining to describe legal systems purposively? This is easier said than done. When the outsider asks, "What is the legal system like?" she must have in mind some concept of what a legal system is, for not just anything can count as a legal system. If the informant answers the outsider's question by saying, "People wander through the countryside gathering grapefruit, which they sell in the marketplace," the outsider would not think, "My, what an unusual legal system." She would instead draw the Davidsonian conclusion that she and her interlocutor are not understanding each other's words properly.[54] And she would draw that conclusion because what the informant has described does not do, badly or otherwise, what legal systems do – thus, her informant cannot be talking about a legal system.

An outsider's description of an alien legal system is implicitly a comparison of that system with her, and our, concept of what a legal system is and is for. Such a concept is an insider's purposive concept. The idea that one can dispense with the internal perspective on legal systems turns out to be untrue, because we need the internal perspective – our understanding of the point of a legal system – in order to recognize a legal system when we encounter one. Even the outsider's viewpoint on a legal system presupposes the priority of the purposive point of view.

---

[53] In the arguments that follow, I am drawing freely from (and modifying in part) *LQI* and *RN*. Interestingly, Ernest Nagel offered an argument very similar to Schauer's thirty-five years earlier. Ernest Nagel, *On the Fusion of Fact and Value: A Reply to Professor Fuller*, 3 Natural L. Forum 79 (1958).

[54] Donald Davidson defended the so-called "principle of charity" in linguistics, a rule of thumb which states that if your translation of a foreigner's utterances implies that the foreigner has crazy beliefs, the fault lies in your translation. Donald Davidson, Inquiries into Truth and Interpretation xvii, 196–97 (1984).

It may t   se arguments overlook the progressive   ich is simply that insider jurisprudence la   man sacrifice you do not turn to the priest -   ts the victim with impeccable concern and   ready. Lawyers, it might be feared, are li   :h invested in their system to seriously cor   nore, lawyers' knowledge is system-speci   desire for epistemic comfort, the fear of tl   rs from grasping that entire continents of   sfunctional.

This may be so, but precisely the same things might be said of nonlawyers. Unjust laws are seldom *only* legal injustices. They typically represent the moral views of dominant or once dominant groups in the larger society – what King, in his Birmingham letter, accurately described as the "numerical or power majority group." Nonlawyers who belong to a system's numerical or power majority group are beneficiaries of the system just as lawyers are, and they are no less likely to confront epistemic vertigo at the prospect of abandoning the familiar evils and the moral beliefs that ratify them.

Perhaps, then, the authentic outsider's standpoint is that of the victims of unjust laws. However, victims are usually cut off from access to information about how their oppressive legal system operates, and in many cases are also denied the basic goods of education. Historically, the great social and legal critics have been insiders or semi-insiders whose lively sense of critical morality allows them to pass beyond their own self-interest and identify with the victims of bad law. I see no reason to suppose that legal insiders will have a weaker sense of critical morality than outsiders. Are legal professionals like Thurgood Marshall or Catharine MacKinnon really at a disadvantage in diagnosing bad law? Worse at it than Malcolm X or Andrea Dworkin? There is no reason to suppose anything of the kind.

"A brutal indifference to justice and human welfare"

And yet there does seem to be something amiss in Fuller's theory, something too quick and easy in the way it concludes that an immoral lawmaker is not just letting down his subjects, but is also betraying the very idea of law. As we have seen, Fuller argues that the enterprise of subjecting human conduct to the governance of rules presupposes a moral relationship between governors and the governed – a moral relationship aimed at promoting the self-determining agency of the governed. From this relationship, it follows that the eight canons are moral excellences, not just rules of efficacy. All this seems like an awful lot to derive from the bare concept of people governing other people through rules. Fuller has pulled a very large rabbit out of a very small hat. His theory seems too good to be true.

I wish to suggest that it *is* too good to be true. Like Schauer, I trace Fuller's over-optimism about the law to his insider perspective. This is not, however, because of the generalized worry about insiders that I have just discussed. The problem is not with insider jurisprudence as such, but with the fact that Fuller's insiders are *lawyers*. Quite simply, the lawyer's role is more problematic than Fuller admits.

At one point, Fuller throws out a challenge to his doubters, rhetorically asking whether "history does in fact afford significant examples of regimes that have combined a faithful adherence to the internal morality of law with a brutal indifference to justice and human welfare" (*ML* 154). He plainly believes that the answer is no, but I begin my argument by suggesting that the answer is yes in almost every regime that has ever existed. This is because almost every regime that has ever existed has legislated expressly to *deny* the self-determining agency of women, and has thereby denied what Fuller claims is the substantive morality imminent in law. Until the most recent times in a bare handful of nations, women have enjoyed few or no political rights, have been classified as property or quasi-property, and have been subjected by law to the tutelage of their husbands and fathers. One might offer analogous examples drawn from the histories of slavery or legally explicit ethnic subjugation. (Would Fuller deny that the American law of slavery adhered rather well to the internal morality of law? On what grounds?) However, I think that the (for all practical purposes) universal legal subjugation of women offers the most striking example of what goes wrong in Fuller's theory.[55]

The important point, it seems to me, is this. Fuller maintains that any legal regime that abides by the eight canons will respect the self-determining agency of those to whom its rules are addressed. So far as it goes, his argument is profound and correct. But it does not go as far as Fuller hoped, because he overlooks an important qualification: those whose self-determining agency law aims to further need not include the entire population subject to the law, because the rules may really be addressed only to a numerical or power majority (to borrow King's words once again). That is, it may well be that the legal edifice of patriarchy aims to enhance the self-determining agency of men. But it does so at the expense of women, who are subject to the tyranny (or, at best, the managerial direction) of their husbands and fathers. Justice for the guys coexists with injustice for women.

---

[55] One might object that regimes of slavery or ethnic/gender subordination violate the canon of generality, and hence they are not genuine rule-of-law regimes. However, generality does not mean that identical laws apply to everyone. It means only that when a rule classifies people, it applies equally to everyone in the specified class. For example, a rule forbidding married women from forming binding contracts without their husbands' permission would satisfy the generality requirement if it applied to all married women.

The crucial condition under which this form of mixed justice and injustice can exist is that the dominant group is able to exert direct control over the subordinate group by virtue of living side by side with them. To take a straightforward illustration, legal regulation of slaveholders, establishing a framework of general rules that advances and respects their self-determining agency, turns out to be wholly consistent with tyrannical or managerial regulation of slaves. In just the same way, patriarchal legal orders enhance the self-determining agency of men in part by enhancing their license to exert unfettered authority over women. The problem, it seems, is that even though both men and women fall under the law's jurisdiction, the law excludes women from the community whose freedom it aims to enhance.

I can find no evidence that Fuller ever considered the catastrophic asymmetry between whom the law binds and whom the law helps, or the implications for his jurisprudence of the law's exclusion of women from the community of freedom. He was certainly aware, though, of the "basic question": "Who is embraced in the moral community?" – that is, "Who shall count as a member of the in-group?" (*ML* 181). He was, after all, writing during the heyday of the civil rights movement.

Within a given political society there are men commonly described as being of different races. These men have lived together for many years … They have together produced a common culture. Is there no moral principle that can imperatively condemn drawing a line between them, and denying to one group access to the essentials on which a satisfactory and dignified life can be built? (*ML* 183)

Fuller recognizes that he needs an affirmative answer to this question, but the one he provides is unsatisfying, except perhaps as rhetoric. He cites the parable of the Good Samaritan and a famous Talmudic aphorism to argue "that we should aspire to enlarge that community [the moral community] at every opportunity" (*ML* 183), because the morality of aspiration "cannot refuse the human quality to human beings without repudiating itself" (*ML* 183). Confusingly, Fuller asserts that these are propositions from the morality of aspiration that are fully as imperative as duties. So far as I can tell, Fuller provides no reason for supposing that the scriptures he cites truly set out the morality of aspiration, or for thinking that cosmopolitan aspirations have the force of duties, or for assuming that cosmopolitanism belongs to the morality of law as Fuller understands it – namely, the professional ethics of lawgivers and law-appliers. Fuller seems to have forgotten his own distinction between criticizing bad laws on general moral grounds, which he disfavors, and criticizing them as violations of the distinctive role-morality of the legislator, a practice of which he approves.

He cannot, for example, really mean that any lawmaker who enacts sexist or racist legislation has violated the role-morality of the legislator's craft. The legislative role-morality surely does not contain an equal protection clause built in *a priori*. If anything, the argument seems more plausible going the other way: perhaps legislators have a role-obligation to enact laws that they find morally objectionable if those laws truly codify the dominant morality of the society.[56] Tennyson's ultracosmopolitan Ulysses ("I am a part of all that I have met"), having returned from his wanderings to govern the cultural backwater of Ithaca, understands that only "slow prudence" will be able "to make mild a rugged people, and thro' soft degrees subdue them to the useful and the good." In the meantime, "I mete and dole unequal laws unto a savage race."[57] Unequal laws, apparently, are all that a savage race can handle, and a conscientious lawmaker will not jump the gun. This argument may be wrong: we have seen that there is a genuine question about whether a professional's role-morality can override the demands of universal morality.[58] But even if the answer is no, the reason is because of the priority of the universal over the particular, not because the demands of universal morality are built into the structure of role-morality *a priori*, for legislators or anyone else.

Fuller is indulging in wishful thinking. He wishes that lawmaking were inherently cosmopolitan, because his argument requires a cosmopolitan solution to the problem of defining the moral community. He confronts a familiar problem in legal ethics. His lawmakers, we have seen, are like transactional lawyers, aiming to facilitate their clients' interactions with a well-crafted structure of rules. But transactional lawyers have clients, and there are limits to how far lawyers can take into account the interests of nonclients. Even when transactions require reciprocity between clients and other parties, each lawyer's primary loyalty runs to her own client – and none of the lawyers may pay attention to the interests of parties who are not part of the transaction at all, regardless of whether the transaction affects those parties' vital interests. The Fullerian legislator is like a transactional lawyer whose "client" is the numerical or power majority in the community; and, as in the case of the lawyer, there is a tension between legislating on behalf of the client's interest and legislating on behalf of everyone's interest.

---

[56] That, at any rate, was Oliver Wendell Holmes's conclusion. "The proximate test of good government is that the dominant power has its way," he wrote, and "legislation ... should modify itself in accordance with the will of the *de facto* supreme power in the community." The first quotation comes from *Montesquieu*, in Oliver Wendell Holmes, Jr., Collected Legal Papers 258 (Peter Smith, 1952); the second, from Oliver Wendell Holmes, Jr., *The Gas-Stokers' Strike*, 7 Am. L. Rev. 582 (1873).

[57] Alfred, Lord Tennyson, *Ulysses*, in Six Centuries of Great Poetry 411–12 (Robert Penn Warren & Albert Erskine eds., 1955), lines 3–4, 18, 36–38.

[58] I have offered an extended treatment of this question in Lawyers and Justice: An Ethical Study, chs. 6 and 7.

In his many writings on the adversarial ethics of the legal profession, Fuller made it clear that he was aware of the problem that advancing client interests may not be in the public interest; but he never found a successful solution to it.[59] That is because no successful solution can be found. Proving that the pursuit of special interests is identical to the pursuit of general interests is like squaring the circle. It is a problem that political philosophers have always wrestled with: Kant argued that the interests of male property-holders are suitably universal, Hegel entered the same claim for bureaucrats, Marx for the proletariat, Gyorgy Lukacs for the Communist Party, and innumerable patriarchs for the menfolk. History has been unusually generous in providing counter-examples to their theories. Civic republican constitutional theorists have in recent years made the claim of universality on behalf of judges.[60] But Fuller is perhaps the only philosopher to do so on behalf of lawyers.[61] That is one of his great strengths; no one, it seems to me, has thought more deeply or perceptively about the services of lawyers in the liberalization of societies and the enhancement of human dignity. But (let's face it) lawyers aren't *that* good.

---

[59] I argue this in detail in *Rediscovering Fuller's Legal Ethics*, supra note 3, at 819–29.

[60] See, for example, Frank I. Michelman, *Foreword: Traces of Self-Government*, 100 Harv. L. Rev. 4 (1986); and Cass R. Sunstein, *Interest Groups in American Public Law*, 38 Stan. L. Rev. 29 (1985).

[61] Talcott Parsons, however, argued that lawyers play a central role in mediating between public interests (represented by the law) and private interests (those of clients). See Talcott Parsons, *A Sociologist Looks at the Legal Profession*, in Essays in Sociological Theory 370 (rev. edn. Free Press, 1954). In some ways, his structural-functionalist argument was anticipated by Tocqueville in his famous chapter on lawyers as the American aristocracy in *Democracy in America*. 1 Alexis de Tocqueville, Democracy in America 263–70 (J. P. Meyer ed., George Lawrence trans., Anchor Books, 1969), ch. 8. For discussion of the Tocqueville–Parsons tradition, see my *The Noblesse Oblige Tradition in the Practice of Law*, 41 Vand. L. Rev. 717 (1988).

4

A different nightmare
and a different dream

Nearly thirty years ago, H. L. A. Hart observed that American jurisprudence "is marked by a concentration, almost to the point of obsession, on the judicial process, that is, with what courts do and should do, how judges reason and should reason in deciding particular cases."[1] Then as now, the figure of the judge dominated American jurisprudence – and wrongly so, in my view. In this chapter I want to explore the hypothesis that a better standpoint for jurisprudence is that of the lawyer, not of the judge. If so, I suggest, legal ethics – regarded by some as a minor and trivial subject – undergoes a remarkable, Cinderella-like transformation to a central spot in how we understand law.

The argument that follows is lengthy but essentially simple. It may be useful to set out its main conclusions here at the beginning. First, taking off from Hart's important insight that a system of rules counts as a legal system only if its institutional actors maintain an internal point of view on the rules, I argue that the most significant actors are not judges, nor, as Hart believes, officials more generally, but lawyers. The lawyer–client consultation is the primary point of intersection between "The Law" and the people it governs, the point at which the law in books becomes the law in action. Second, in singling out lawyer–client consultations as the paradigmatic legal events, I emphasize the role of the lawyer as advisor rather than the lawyer as advocate. Lawyers as advocates must indeed focus on judges and judicial decisions, and their point of view on the law is parasitic on the point of view of judges. The legal advisor occupies a different role, with different ethical standards and different jurisprudential properties. Most discussions of legal ethics emphasize dilemmas of advocacy, but I will suggest that the advisor's role is no less significant. Third, because lawyer–client consultations occur

---

[1] H. L. A. Hart, *American Jurisprudence Through English Eyes: The Nightmare and the Noble Dream*, 11 Ga. L. Rev. 969 (1977).

behind a veil of confidentiality, the integrity of the legal system depends to an enormous degree on the rectitude of the legal advisor. The question "How should lawyers advise clients?" turns out to be at least as important as "How should judges decide cases?"

Among social scientists studying the law, these propositions are old news. In the roughly four decades of active law-and-society scholarship, literally hundreds of studies have argued that law is found outside the courts; and researchers have exhaustively explored law's many locations, formal and informal, including lawyer–client encounters in law offices. Furthermore, many of these studies are keenly aware of the ethical dimension of those encounters.

My fourth conclusion will be less familiar, and less congenial, to legal social scientists. Law-and-society authors typically follow their legal-realist forebears in identifying law with the law in action rather than with the law in books (to use Pound's familiar phrases). They differ from the realists largely in where they locate the action: outside the courts rather than in. For the early realists, the law in action meant judicial behavior, and knowing the law meant predicting what judges will do. In this respect, the realists were not much different than today's law-firm associates, writing memos that analyze statutes by explaining what "courts would say" about them. I will argue that lawyers advising clients about the law's meaning must not deflect their own interpretive responsibility on to hypothetical others, whether those others are courts or non-judicial actors. Instead, their obligation is simply to explain the law in books. So, in the end, I identify law with the law in books, as mediated through the interpretive community of lawyers.

Hart subtitled his essay on American jurisprudence "The Nightmare and the Noble Dream." This arresting phrase refers to the jurisprudential extremes that haunt judge-centered American jurisprudence: the nightmare of unfettered, willful judicial lawmaking, and the noble dream of judicial craft that elaborates the principles inherent in a nation's legal system to fill all gaps in the law. A lawyer-centered jurisprudence also has its nightmare and its noble dream: a nightmare of lawyers who either dominate their clients or capitulate to them, and a noble dream of lawyers who mediate between their clients' interests and the law.

Judge-centered jurisprudence

Before turning to these arguments, we ought to examine the American obsession with judges and judging. I begin where every American lawyer begins, in law school. The curriculum and attitudes of law school form the background conception of law assumed by lawyers, and that is a judge-centered conception. To begin with the mundane, students swiftly learn that American law professors idolize judges, and they especially idolize the justices of the US Supreme Court. Constitutional law reigns supreme in the prestige hierarchy of law-school subjects, and to a far greater extent than other law-school subjects the study of constitutional law means the study of the Court's opinions. "The Court" – there's only one, just as to New Yorkers when you say "the City" there is only one. A Supreme Court clerkship counts among the gold-standard credentials for entering the legal academy (and for entering prestigious law firms, some of which pay six-figure signing bonuses to Supreme Court clerks). In part, of course, that is because the ultra-competitive winnowing process for Supreme Court clerks guarantees that they are among the best and brightest. But equally brilliant law graduates clerk for lesser courts, or don't clerk at all. The Supreme Court clerkship matters because of the aura of The Court and its justices, which somehow clings to the clerks.

The Court sits atop a hierarchy, in power and legal authority most obviously, but also in prestige and charisma. Judges matter, and what powerful judges say matters powerfully. Judges, as somebody or other is always saying (sometimes ironically, often not), are the high priests of justice. Holmes called their opinions "oracles of the law."[2] You pick the religious metaphor – they have all been used, all too often, yet their shopworn banality does nothing to diminish their accuracy. We *do* treat judges as oracles, in the precise sense that we identify the law with their utterances of it.

Thus, when I first attended a colleague's lectures in a jurisprudence course entitled Legal Justice, the guiding question, "What is legal justice?" quickly transformed itself into a different one: "How should judges decide cases?" I do not criticize my colleague's move; when I teach the course – a largely historical survey of a century of American legal theory – I do the same thing.

That is because, deeply embedded in American legal theory, we find nearly everywhere the assumption that the law more or less *is* the set of answers to the question "How should judges decide cases?" In the most influential law review article ever written, Oliver Wendell Holmes, Jr., included what is arguably the most famous one-sentence definition of the law ever penned: "The prophecies of what the courts will do in fact, and nothing more pretentious, are what I mean by the law."[3] John Chipman Gray, a friend and intellectual fellow traveler of Holmes, went so far as to argue that statutes are not laws but sources of law. They become law only when the courts apply them.[4]

From the late nineteenth century on, American legal education has largely been structured along the lines that Holmes's dictum lays down. The standard

---

[2] Oliver Wendell Holmes, Jr., *The Path of the Law*, 10 Harvard L. Rev. 457 (1897).
[3] Ibid. at 461.   [4] John Chipman Gray, The Nature and Sources of the Law 84 (2nd edn. 1921).

law textbook is the casebook, and that means we study law by studying what
the courts have done.[5] Appellate decisions are the paradigm of law. Even
casebooks on statutory subjects make the statutes come to life only through
appellate decisions interpreting them. The subliminal message is that it is
courts and judges that matter, not the legislators who enacted the statute. To
be sure, one of our most familiar political tropes is the lament over the evils
of judicial activism, and the need for courts to defer to legislatures. But legal
education tells us from the very first day that genuine deference is not only
misguided but impossible. That is because, as Morris R. Cohen wrote a
century ago, judges are not phonographs reproducing someone else's music.
They interpret laws, and there is no such thing as a null interpretation.
Cohen's observation is obviously correct. I raise it, however, not to defend
judicial activism but merely to point out that virtually every moment of an
American lawyer's professional education conveys the meta-message that
judges are indeed the active parties in the law. Though no modern writer puts
the point as sharply as Gray, we do continue to treat statutes as mere sources
of law, unactualized potentialities until some court somewhere realizes them
by tendering a decision.

Historians classify Holmes and Gray as legal realists, or proto-realists.
The realists' fundamental theme is that law is what law does, and judges are
the doers – they issue the orders or, in Holmes's imagery, they determine
where the axe will fall. But anti-realism can be just as judge-centered as
Holmes or Gray. The obvious case in point is Ronald Dworkin, for whom
legal philosophy is nothing more than "the general part of adjudication,
silent prologue to any decision at law."[6] Dworkin's conception of "law as
integrity" requires us to view law as a consistent, coherent, and mutually
reinforcing network of principles. Famously, Dworkin expounds his views
using the heuristic device of Hercules, a judge of superhuman synthesizing
powers and an all-inclusive law library. To determine the law of a case
under law-as-integrity, one asks the simple question: "What would Hercules

[5] There is some irony here, because the casebook and the case method of instruction were devised
by Holmes's intellectual antipodes, the arch-formalist Christopher Columbus Langdell. To
Holmes, Langdell's exclusive focus on the logical interconnections among judicial decisions
was "a misspent piece of marvelous ingenuity," and Langdell (whom in a book review Holmes
unflatteringly described as "the greatest living legal theologian") "represents the powers of
darkness." 1 Holmes–Pollock Letters 17 (Mark DeWolfe Howe ed., 1941) (letter of April 10,
1881). The famous first sentence of The Common Law – that the life of the law is not logic but
experience – originally appeared in Holmes's review of Langdell's book. In The Path of the
Law, Holmes tells us that the "man of the future" is the master of statistics and economics, not
the master of doctrine. But his own judicial practice, like his predictive definition of law and his
assertion that reported decisions represent "oracles of the law," are surprisingly conventional in
their orientation toward cases and judges.
[6] Ronald Dworkin, Law's Empire 90 (1986).

decide?" – "WWHD?" And the law itself, the entire system, consists, under Dworkin's conceit, of the set of answers to "WWHD?" Law is nothing but the ideal limit-point of judicial activity. Gray's judge-centeredness pales by comparison with Dworkin's.

Or consider Anthony Kronman's account of good judgment and how lawyers acquire it. Good judgment, in Kronman's view, requires sympathetic identification with alternatives that often represent incommensurable values, combined with the capacity for subsequently detaching yourself from each alternative in order to weigh them.[7] The case method of instruction cultivates lawyers' judgment because, when it is done right, the teacher compels the student to examine each case from the viewpoints of all the parties, articulating the values they represent in the strongest form, then abruptly switching perspectives. Ultimately, the student must come to a decision, and that implies that the judicial point of view takes priority over all others. As Kronman sets it out, we are saved from the slide into moral relativism by assuming the vantage point of "the coldest and most distant, most judicial, eye," which gives us

a broad familiarity with diverse and irreconcilable human goods coupled with an indefatigable willingness to enter the fray, hear the arguments, render judgment, and articulate the reasons that support it, even when all hope of moral certainty is gone. At war with itself, this complex set of attitudes nonetheless describes a recognizable moral ideal, an ideal closest, perhaps, to the public-spirited stoicism implied by the Roman term *gravitas*.[8]

The judge, in Kronman's view, personifies practical wisdom itself, and the judicial standpoint has epistemological priority in articulating "the good of the community represented by the laws."[9]

Ironically, by the end of his life even Hart fell under the sway of judge-centeredness. In his "Postscript" to the second edition of *The Concept of Law* (Hart's late-in-life response to Dworkin), he describes the "rule of recognition" – the complex criterion for identifying law and determining which propositions of law are valid – as "in effect a form of judicial customary rule existing only if it is accepted and practised in the law-identifying and law-applying operations of the courts."[10] Even for Hart, then, the activity of identifying and expounding law has now narrowed to what courts do and should do, how judges reason and should reason in deciding particular cases.

---

[7] Anthony T. Kronman, The Lost Lawyer: Failing Ideals of the Legal Profession 66–74 (1993).
[8] Ibid. at 117–18.   [9] Ibid. at 118.
[10] H. L. A. Hart, The Concept of Law [hereinafter CL] 256 (2nd edn. 1994).

The importance of point of view for jurisprudence

Before examining the arguments that may be offered on behalf of viewing law from the lawyer's or judge's point of view, we must address a more fundamental question: Why does point of view matter at all?

Hart first brought this question to the surface by drawing the distinction between the internal and external points of view on systems of rules. The distinction arises from the elementary fact that insiders to a social practice employ its precepts differently in their practical deliberations than outsiders do. The insider "accepts and uses them as guides to conduct," where the outsider does not – not, at any rate, in the direct way the insider does.[11] The outsider regards the rules as anthropological curiosities, the way that a student of Greek religion regards the rituals and usages of the cult of Athena. In Hart's terminology, this represents the external point of view on a system of rules.

Of course, like the insider, the outsider may at times use the rules as guides to conduct; when in Rome, it is both expedient and courteous to do as the Romans do. But the participant-observer does not obey the rules because she accepts the rules. They have no normative grip on her. The insider's practical reasoning is simple and straightforward: "I do it because the rule prescribes it." The participant-observer reasons more indirectly: "I do it because my hosts respect the rule, and I prefer not to offend my hosts." If the hosts don't care, the guest need not care either. In when-in-Rome cases, there may be no behavioral difference between those who take the internal point of view toward rules and those whose point of view is external. But the relationship between the agent and the system of rules differs dramatically. From the internal point of view, these are *my* rules; from the external point of view, these are *theirs* (not mine). *They* employ them as standards of evaluation and criticism; I don't.

Hart observes that an even more austere external point of view is available, namely that of the mere observer of behavioral correlations, who may not recognize them as instances of rule-governed conduct at all. A Martian visitor to Earth might notice a strong correlation between green stop lights and onrushing traffic, and guide her own patterns of walking accordingly, even before she realizes that human beings are intelligent enough to engage in rule-governed practices.[12] So there are at least two distinct external points of view: the austere external point of view fastens on observable regularities, without necessarily concluding that they represent rules; and the less austere external point of view regards them as rules, but someone else's rules, not one's own. By contrast with both of these, the internal point of view is that of

---

[11] Ibid. at 89.   [12] Ibid. at 90.

someone who regards the rule-system as her own – as a system regulating a practice in which she is a participant.

Notice that in reality we are liable to shift rapidly back and forth between the internal point of view and the (less austere) external point of view. Some rules we obey out of commitment and obligation; some only out of fear of sanctions; some from unreflective habit; and some from a when-in-Rome sense of courtesy or propriety. Hart points out that in the developed legal systems of complex societies it would be unrealistic to suppose that all compliance results from a sense of obligation.[13] But it is crucial to Hart's account that those responsible for the functioning of the legal system adopt the internal point of view toward the rules governing their own practice; and any account that neglects the internal point of view will simply be unable to account for legal systems as we know them.

Hart therefore offers "two minimum conditions necessary and sufficient for the existence of a legal system":[14] first, private citizens must by and large obey the rules "from any motive whatever" – a sense of moral obligation, fear of sanctions, or sheer inertia – and second, the officials of the system must adopt the internal point of view toward at least the rules that apply to officials (what Hart calls "secondary" rules).[15] In other words, the internal point of view can be unevenly dispersed through the society, heavily concentrated among legal officials but rarefied or even non-existent among the general population.

Unfortunately, this conclusion lies in some tension with Hart's overall line of argument. One of his principal targets is the Austinian view of laws as "commands backed by threats," modeling the legal system on the armed robber demanding our money. A fatal problem with the "gunman writ large" model of law, Hart argues, is that the gunman can *oblige* us to hand over our money, but he cannot *obligate* us to do so, and as a result Austin's theory leaves us without a satisfactory account of legal obligation.[16] As Hart elaborates the notion of legal obligation, the main feature Austin omits consists of the internal aspect of rules, the fact that the rules are adopted as standards for judging behavior.[17] Legal obligation can be recognized only by those who take the rules as standards of evaluation and criticism of their own conduct and the conduct of others. To regard rules as obligatory comes from adopting the internal point of view toward them.

[13] Ibid. at 115, 203.

[14] Ibid. at 116. To be picky, if these conditions are truly necessary and sufficient, there is nothing "minimum" about them.

[15] Ibid. at 115–17. Hart phrases this last point by saying that officials must regard the rules "as common standards of official behaviour and appraise critically their own and each other's deviations as lapses." Ibid. at 117.

[16] Ibid. at 82–85.

[17] Ibid. at 88–90; this characterization of the internal aspect of rules comes from 56–57.

If so, however, a legal system in which only officials adopt the internal point of view (and only toward the behavior of other officials) while ordinary citizens obey for any reason, including coercion, simply reproduces the gunman writ large. The only difference lies in the fact that now we confront a many-headed, many-handed gunman – a mafia, perhaps, or a warlord and his minions – rather than a single armed robber. The only thing that converts the mafia into a legal system, on Hart's account, is the fact that the mafiosi take the internal point of view toward the rules they enforce. They regard the rules as obligatory, but, in Hart's terminology, they cannot obligate private citizens to obey, only oblige them to do so. Yet Hart emphatically insists that this, too, is a legal system: "In an extreme case the internal point of view ... might be confined to the official world ... The society in which this was so might be deplorably sheeplike; the sheep might end in the slaughterhouse. But there is little reason for thinking that it could not exist or for denying it the title of a legal system."[18]

Little reason except that it returns us to the very model Hart rejects. He might respond that if the mafia goes to the trouble to create the elaborate system of primary and secondary rules that (Hart shows) exist in all but the most primitive legal systems, and if the mafiosi do indeed adopt the internal point of view toward their rules, to the extent not only of criticizing other mafiosi who deviate, but also of criticizing (and not merely whacking) non-mafioso citizens for their deviations – then they have indeed created a legal system, albeit a pathological one that maintains itself through brute force alone. But it seems far more plausible to say that the mafiosi have created a make-believe legal system, or a parody of a legal system, or that they are aping a legal system. Surely that is how the citizens they lord it over will regard the mafia's congresses, assemblies, rituals, trials, and punishments.[19]

Admittedly, Hart's hypothetical society in which the internal point of view is confined to officials does not have to be a mafia society. It might be one in which the official class, far from being mafiosi, are actually conscientious public servants whose laws are wonderful, and where the citizens fail to share the internal point of view only because of their own wickedness. This, perhaps, is always the fantasy of colonialists, imperialists, and missionaries. But the problem with Hart's argument is not that the society in which only officials take the internal point of view toward law must always be a mafia-like system. The problem is that Hart's conditions do not rule out the mafia system. (In any event, the system with good officials enforcing excellent laws on bad men and women will, in real life, almost certainly need to be

---

[18] Ibid. at 117.

[19] Here I am borrowing a crucial idea from John Finnis: that, as a methodological matter, we should define the concept of a legal system by focusing on central cases of legal systems, not deviant or pathological cases. John Finnis, Natural Law and Natural Right 9–17 (1980).

maintained through force and oppression, so that in the end it will probably differ only slightly from the mafia system.)

It isn't hard to see what has gone wrong here. The mafiosi lack the legitimacy of real legal officials, which is another way of saying that, *pace* Hart, in a genuine legal system it isn't enough for the internal point of view to be confined to the official world. While not all citizens need to adopt the internal point of view toward all the laws all the time, a substantial number of citizens must adopt it toward most laws much of the time.[20] It isn't just the fact of their obedience, but their reasons for obeying, that make a system of primary and secondary rules enforced by an official class into a legal system.

The difference between the mafia "legal" system and a legitimate legal system lies in the fact that, in the former, ordinary citizens regard the law as nothing more than a coercive structure imposed on them by officials. Lon Fuller refers to such structures as "one-way projection[s] of authority," and his fundamental objection to Hart concerns Hart's willingness to accept them as legal systems.[21] Perhaps, however, the distance between Hart and Fuller is not as great as either of them supposes. For, if I am right, Hart's inclusion of one-way projections of authority among legal systems undercuts his own insight about the centrality of the internal point of view in the concept of legal obligation. Acknowledging that ordinary citizens, not officials alone, must for the most part share the internal point of view toward legal rules would push Hart in the direction of three of Fuller's leading ideas: that relations between lawgivers and citizens must be at least minimally reciprocal (or, as Fuller says, "interactional"[22]); that governing through rules rather than commands or directives requires lawgivers and citizens to share "notions of the limits of legal decency and sanity"; and thus that reciprocity requires legal rules to be communicated intelligibly to citizens and to impose reasonable expectations on them.[23] Hart himself explains why: laws, as opposed to "individuated face-to-face orders," require "that the members of society are left to discover the rules and conform their behaviour to them"[24] – the very argument Fuller offers for why officials and citizens must share notions of legal decency and sanity.

---

[20] Oddly enough, given his remark about the sheeplike society, Hart elsewhere recognizes that "if a system of rules is to be imposed by force on any, there must be a sufficient number who accept it voluntarily. Without their voluntary co-operation, thus creating *authority*, the coercive power of law and government cannot be established." Hart, CL, supra note 10, at 201.

[21] Lon Fuller, The Morality of Law 204 (rev. edn. Yale University Press, 1964). See my discussion of Fuller in Chapter 3 above.

[22] Ibid. at 221.

[23] Lon L. Fuller, The Anatomy of the Law 63 (Praeger, 1968). The final requirement generates Fuller's eight canons of lawmaking – see my discussion in Chapter 3 above.

[24] Hart, CL, supra note 10, at 39.

Of course, shared notions of the limits of legal decency and sanity by no means imply shared detailed understandings of the law and legal reasoning. As Hart notes, "ordinary citizens – perhaps a majority – have no general conception of the legal structure or of its criteria of validity. The law which he obeys is something which he knows of only as 'the law'."[25] The ordinary citizen may take an internal point of view toward rules without knowing exactly what those rules prescribe, or even how to find out on his own. That, indeed, is Hart's reason for focusing on officials and insisting that they share "critical common standards" for determining what is and what is not law.[26] It is too much to expect that non-officials share those standards – what Hart calls the rule of recognition – which are technical and recondite.

But what Hart says of ordinary citizens holds for most officials as well. Why should we suppose that pest-control officers, driving examiners, building inspectors, police detectives, and state pension administrators grasp the rule of recognition? Why suppose that the President of the United States grasps it? It seems most likely, in fact, that they have no better knowledge of the structure of precedent or the canons of statutory interpretation than do other, ordinary citizens. The vast majority of officials have little or no legal training.[27]

These observations bring to the surface an assumption so natural it might pass us by: the people in government whom we expect to master the rule of recognition in the legal system are not "officials" in general, but *lawyers* in particular. If other officials know the laws and regulations most pertinent to their jobs, it is because lawyers write the protocols and training manuals that the building inspectors and pest-control authorities follow. Now it may be that these officials, simply by virtue of their job descriptions, adopt an internal attitude toward the protocols they follow. But that is not essential. They may follow the protocols because they have to, or merely by rote. In this respect, most officials differ not at all from ordinary citizens as Hart describes them. The officials who can utilize "critical common standards" for identifying the law will be those with legal training, not the large majority without it.

---

[25] Ibid. at 114.   [26] Ibid. at 115–17.

[27] Within the United States, lawyers in 2002 made up only 1.1 percent of local, state, and federal employees, and it seems plausible that the lawyers form the large majority of legally trained officials. At the local level, in 2002 there were 44,368 lawyers out of 5,415,100 government employees; at the state level, 36,431 lawyers out of 2,436,300 government employees; and at the federal level, 25,688 lawyers out of 1,922,200 government employees, for a total of about 106,500 lawyers out of 9,773,600 government employees. US Bureau of Labor Statistics occupational data, available at <http://data.bls.gov/oep/servlet/oep.nioem.servlet. ActionServlet?Action=empios&Type=Occupation>. If, as seems plausible, government lawyers form the large majority of legally trained government officials, it follows that 98 percent of officials lack legal training.

But of course the 100,000 or so government lawyers in the United States share that training with the more than 600,000 nongovernment lawyers. It seems, then, that what matters is not that these are *government* lawyers, but that they are government *lawyers*. The relevant fact is that they are trained in law – and, equally importantly, the fact that lawyers throughout the nation receive uniform training in the core legal doctrines. Arguably, a necessary precondition for a rule-of-law regime is the existence of a uniformly trained, politically independent, and suitably large and vigorous legal profession.[28] Lawyers are, after all, the primary point of contact between private individuals and institutions and the law.[29]

Must lawyers take the internal point of view on the law? Why can't lawyers hate the legal system, or hate the state? The answer, of course, is that they can. There is nothing self-contradictory in the concept of a radical or oppositional lawyer. It would be a mistake to identify the internal point of view of rules with either psychological or political support for them. Admittedly, Hart's terminology of "accepting rules" and "adopting the internal point of view" sounds like he is talking about psychological states. For Hart, however, adopting the internal point of view toward rules means participating in an interpersonal linguistic practice – a language game – not holding a pro-attitude toward the rules. One takes the internal point of view by engaging in normative practices of evaluation, criticism, and practical argument using the rules.[30]

---

[28] More controversially, one might argue that the existence of a uniformly trained, politically independent, and suitably large legal profession is not only a necessary condition for a rule-of-law regime but a sufficient condition as well. The lawyers will inevitably domesticate the regulatory instruments of the state, and create procedures with the rule-of-law features in which they have been trained.

[29] I am therefore in agreement with Melvin Eisenberg, *The Concept of National Law and the Rule of Recognition*, 29 Fla. St. U. L. Rev. 1229, 1246–47 (2002), who argues, as I do, that in the United States the relevant group who must know the rule of recognition for law is the legal profession. While my argument for this conclusion is somewhat different from Eisenberg's, here I am adopting one strand of his argument: "Finally, for most practical purposes the law is what practicing lawyers say it is; that is, to the extent that private or public actors plan or act on the basis of law, they will normally plan or act on the basis of what their lawyers tell them is the law. Accordingly, the views of practicing lawyers concerning what kinds of rules count as legal rules in rendering such opinions are of vital importance." Ibid. at 1247. See also David Luban, Lawyers and Justice: An Ethical Study xvii (1988): "For practical purposes, the lawyers are the law."

[30] Hart warns that "the internal aspect of rules is often misrepresented as a mere matter of 'feelings' in contrast to externally observable physical behaviour." CL, supra note 10, at 57. In the "Postscript," Hart defines "acceptance" as "the standing disposition of individuals to take such patterns of conduct both as guides to their own future conduct and as standards of criticism ... The internal point of view is that of a participant in such a practice who accepts the rules as guides to conduct and as standards of criticism." Ibid. at 255. This passage makes it clear that the internal point of view is a disposition to engage in certain practices rather than

Plainly, this is what lawyers do in the practice of law, even when they hate the rules. A personal recollection: about thirty years ago, I gave William Kunstler a ride to the airport after he had lost a political case before a federal judge in Cleveland. Kunstler slumped down in the passenger's seat of my Plymouth and muttered, "Nothing's going to change this country except armed struggle." Two hours earlier, Kunstler and the judge had been debating fine points about the First Amendment and the values that the framers had attached to it. You might call this hypocrisy on Kunstler's part, but Hart's key insight about the separation of law and morals is precisely that engaging in practices of legal argument implies nothing about whether you love the law or hate it. Adopting the internal point of view toward rules requires only a reflective critical practice of evaluating the conduct of others by the standards the rules establish – another way of saying "legal argument."[31]

Earlier, we saw that several different external points of view exist: the austerely behaviorist point of view that sees only stimulus–response correlations, not rule-following; the less austere point of view that observes or studies other people's rules; and the point of view of the participant-observer who obeys rules only out of a when-in-Rome sense of propriety, without adopting them as her own rules. We now see that there can be more than one internal point of view as well, ranging between that of ordinary citizens or officials who adopt the law as their own, but know it only as "the law" without having any clear idea how to identify it or argue within its distinctive vocabulary and mode of reasoning, and that of the trained lawyer who maneuvers comfortably within it. The two lie on the ends of a continuum, with no sharp break. Legal reasoning is not rocket science, nor is it an arcane glass bead game played among adepts. Its distinctive methods are continuous with other forms of reasoning; but they are specialized enough, and require enough background knowledge, that lawyers' arguments rather than lay arguments form the central case of the internal point of view.[32]

Locating the internal point of view in the legal profession rather than in the judiciary or in some unspecified category of "officials" goes a long way

a psychological pro-attitude toward rules. Again, Hart writes: "If . . . the courts and officials of the system actually identify the law in accordance with the criteria it [i.e., the constitution] provides, then the constitution is accepted." Ibid. at 293. Here, too, he identifies "acceptance" with participation in an official practice, not with a psychological attitude.

[31] Hart, CL, supra note 10, at 57. Hart's actual phrase is "reflective critical attitude," which is ambiguous between a psychological state and a linguistic practice. But, as I have indicated, I believe that the linguistic practice reading better comports with the rest of Hart's theory.

[32] It is Finnis who notes that even the internal point of view must be internally differentiated, and that some cases of it are more central than others. Finnis, supra note 19, at 13. I argue against the theory that legal reasoning is a self-contained language-game sharply disconnected from everyday discourse in Luban, *Lawyers Rule: A Comment on Patterson's Theories of Truth*, 50 SMU L. Rev. 1613 (1997).

toward solving the previously noted problem with Hart's position, namely that it neglects the interactional, legitimacy-creating character of genuine legal systems (as opposed to ersatz legal systems like mafia rule). Lawyers, representing private clients before the law and advising clients about what the law means, serve a mediating and translating function between public and private interests (a point made long ago by Talcott Parsons).[33] They make the interaction between state and citizen possible. The importance of the lawyer's role, I might add, makes the problem of unequal and inadequate access to legal services a central challenge to the legitimacy of law. But that is another story for another day.[34]

Judge-centeredness

If I am right, we must wonder why American theorists focus so much attention on judges and judicial activity rather than on lawyers and legal advice-giving. I think they shouldn't. In the sections that follow, I examine what I take to be the leading arguments for judge-centeredness. While most of them contain an important grain of truth, we will discover that none is entirely right, and (more significantly) that none is unique to judges. In particular, we shall find that the grains of truth these arguments contain all apply with equal or greater force to one particularly important role of the practicing lawyer: the lawyer as legal advisor.

One explanation of judge-centeredness is that American lawyers have inherited a primarily Judaeo-Christian outlook on legality, and that heritage culturally predisposes us to connect law with judges and judgment. God the lawgiver is likewise the God who judges and punishes transgressions. The Jewish liturgy of the high holy days paints the awesome picture of a God who annually passes His creatures like sheep beneath His staff, examining them and decreeing who shall live and who shall die. Even the angels, all too aware of their own faults, tremble at the Day of Judgment. Christians, too, stand in awe at the thought of Judgment Day.

Yet a moment's thought will show how little the cultural association of divine law with divine judgment has to do with the judicial enunciation of legal meaning. God judges His creatures and their deeds. He does not judge between competing interpretations of what the law commands. God already knows what the law commands; it is only humans who confront legal

---

[33] Talcott Parsons, *A Sociologist Looks at the Legal Profession*, in Essays in Sociological Theory 370, 375, 384 (Free Press, rev. edn. 1954); 1 Alexis de Tocqueville, Democracy in America 275–76 (Philip Bradley ed., 1945). For discussion, see William H. Simon, *Babbitt v. Brandeis: The Decline of the Professional Ideal*, 37 Stan. L. Rev. 565 (1985); and my own paper *The Noblesse Oblige Tradition in the Practice of Law*, 41 Vand. L. Rev. 717 (1988).

[34] See generally Deborah L. Rhode, Access to Justice (2004).

perplexity and ambiguity everywhere. Legal interpretation is therefore a task solely for human beings. Deuteronomy proclaims that the law "is not in heaven, that you should say, 'Who will ascend into heaven for us and bring it to us, that we may hear it and do it?' " (Deut. 30:11–12). The rabbis interpreted "it is not in heaven" to mean that God gave over the interpretation of law to sages and scholars.[35] Sometimes, this meant that rabbinical courts issued rulings. Mostly, however, sages answered legal questions through *tshuvot*, written answers to questions posed – the equivalent of a lawyer's advisory opinion. The same is true in Islamic law, where the term *fatwa* corresponds with the Jewish *tshuvot*: a *fatwa* is an advisory opinion from a religious law specialist, not a judicial ruling. In Christianity, as well, the primary source of legal meaning lies in the word of Jesus the teacher, not in rulings of canon-law courts. Thus, judge-centeredness has little to do with any of these religious and cultural traditions. If anything, religious authorities more closely resemble legal advisors than judges.

Notice that one obvious argument for judge-centeredness will not work. This is the argument that we should focus on judges because judges are the officials whose job it is to settle questions of law. That plainly begs the question. Other officials need to settle questions of law as well. So do citizens trying to write a will, apply for food stamps, or form a corporation; and so do the lawyers they retain to help them. Recent constitutional scholarship has begun to rebel against locating constitutionalism exclusively in the courts and The Court: why shouldn't legislative, executive, or popular understandings of constitutionalism play just as important a role in giving the Constitution meaning? Arguments similar to those of extrajudicial constitutionalists can be marshaled in favor of extrajudicial legalism more generally, and so focusing on judges because judges are the officials to focus on merely argues in a vicious circle. Indeed, it goes too far even to insist that we must focus on officials: it may well be that popular understanding of the law matters more than official understanding. It is not in heaven.

Three other arguments for the centrality of judges are much stronger. First is the realist argument that judges are the power people, whose orders and rulings determine our fate. Right or wrong, what they say *is* the law. Second, and almost the opposite of the realist argument, we find the claim that judicial decisions represent reasoned analysis of the law, which entitles them to special attention based on their intellectual quality. Finally, judges are supposed to be neutral and impartial, unlike citizens, who are entitled to be self-interested, or lawyers, who are supposed to favor their clients. So looking at what the impartial judge does is the best way to find out what the law is rather than what some interested party would like it to be.

---

[35] Babylonian Talmud, Bava Metzia *59b.

The realist argument: judges as the power people

In Holmes's words, "in societies like ours the command of the public force is intrusted to the judges in certain cases, and the whole power of the state will be put forth, if necessary, to carry out their judgments and decrees."[36] That is the reason "why people will pay lawyers to argue for them or advise them": people "want to know under what circumstances and how far they will run the risk of coming against what is so much stronger than themselves."[37] Judicial opinions determine where "the axe will fall."[38]

This is the realist argument, and it obviously has a great deal to be said for it. But, as both realists and their critics quickly realized, the argument has nothing exclusively to do with judges. As Lon Fuller asks, "Why should we stop with judges and exclude commissioners? And for that matter, what of officials whose duties are even further removed from those of a judge, like the sheriff and the sanitary inspector?"[39] It will matter greatly to people whether the prosecutor will proceed to an indictment or drop the charges against them, or whether the sheriff will enforce a judgment of a small claims court, or whether the IRS will audit them. And why stop with officials? The sheriff may balk at enforcing an eviction order that is so wildly unpopular that the friends and neighbors of the person against whom it is entered engage in passive or active resistance to protect their friend. For that matter, a disaffected populace may comply with law in such a grudging, up-to-the-edge manner that they nullify the law in fact – "work to rule" has long been one of labor unions' most effective forms of job action. The passive resistance of Jim Crow Southerners to the courts' desegregation decisions dramatically illustrates the point: these tactics delayed desegregation for two decades. So, following Fuller's line of argument, "must we not extend our definition of law to include the behavior of laymen?" If so, "the realist view approaches perilously close the proposition that the law is the way everyone behaves."[40]

Another way to couch this response is that the power of judges rests on the power of the state more generally, and the power of the state ultimately rests on popular support, or at least popular acquiescence. Ultimately, it is a factual question how much the coercive power of judges matters. Tom Tyler's study of influences on compliance with the law suggests that fear of sanctions

---

[36] Holmes, *The Path of the Law*, supra note 2, at 457.   [37] Ibid.   [38] Ibid.

[39] Lon L. Fuller, *The Law In Quest of Itself* 53 (1940). Fuller quotes one of the realists, Walter Wheeler Cook, who wrote that in Holmes's definition of law as the prophecies of what the courts will do in fact, "the word 'courts' should include some other more or less similar officials." Cook, *The Logical and Legal Bases of the Conflict of Laws*, 33 Yale L.J. 457, 465 n. 31 (1924).

[40] Fuller, The Law In Quest of Itself, supra note 39, at 55.

matters very little – far less than personal morality or gender, and no more than peer opinion and the legitimacy of the legal authorities.[41]

I don't mean to deny the obvious. A single Supreme Court decision can influence the behavior of thousands or even millions of people for decades to come. However, the Fullerian argument reminds us that Court decisions can have this effect only to the extent that those beneath the Court in the hierarchy of authority take up and support the decision rather than passively resisting it or maneuvering around it. From a genuinely realist point of view, the latter phenomena matter at least as much as what the Court does.[42] As I will suggest further on, judges may turn out to be far less important to the functioning of the legal system than practicing lawyers, who transmit the law from its sources to their clients, the law's ultimate destination. If so, then the realist argument will turn out to be an argument for a lawyer-centric rather than a judge-centric conception of law.

As a second point against the realist argument for the primacy of judges, we must bear in mind how atypical and unrepresentative judicial decisions are as legal events. They represent disputes – and, as I shall suggest, that already makes them atypical legal events – and at that only a minute microcosm of the universe of disputes.

Here it is useful to recall the familiar sociologists' image of the "pyramid of disputing" (depicted below).[43] Social life generates perpetual friction over vast numbers of issues, ranging from everyday trivialities to matters of life and death. Only a small subset of these social frictions can be addressed through law. Let this set of legally addressable issues form the base of the pyramid. Out of this incomprehensibly vast mass of legally addressable issues, some will be recognized as such ("named") by the people they affect. The named issues form the smaller second level of the pyramid. But just because I name an issue, it by no means follows that I will raise it or argue

---

[41] Tom R. Tyler, Why People Obey the Law 59–60 (Yale University Press, 1990).

[42] One particularly important way in which court decisions can influence lay behavior occurs when popular culture absorbs the decision (for example, the Supreme Court's *Miranda* decision has plainly entered popular consciousness, and virtually anyone who watches television knows that police have to read suspects their rights when they arrest them). Popular cultural ideas about law, sometimes absorbed from court decisions, can reciprocally influence courts, and the result will be law cycling back and forth between the judicial system and popular culture. For analysis of this phenomenon, see Naomi Mezey, *Law as Culture*, 13 Yale J. L. & Human. 35, 55–57 (2001).

[43] I am unsure where this metaphor originated, but among its earliest appearances are Richard E. Miller & Austin Sarat, *Claims, and Disputes: Assessing the Adversary Culture*, 15 Law & Soc'y Rev. 525, 544–45 (1981) and Marc Galanter, *Reading the Landscape of Disputes: What We Know and Don't Know (and Think We Know) About Our Allegedly Contentious and Litigious Society*, 31 UCLA L. Rev. 4, 11–26 (1983). For another version of the pyramid diagram, see Carrie J. Menkel-Meadow *et al.*, Dispute Resolution: Beyond the Adversarial Model 17 (2004).

about it with anyone else. I will not do so unless I not only name my problem but *blame* someone for it. At that point, my legally addressable issue turns into a dispute. Disputes, a smaller set than recognized legally addressable issues, form the third level of the pyramid.

THE PYRAMID OF DISPUTING

Disputes may proceed no further than a testy conversation, either because I receive redress (the cable company finally agrees to send out some service personnel) or because going further seems not worth the trouble and I decide to "lump it." But people take some of their disputes to lawyers, and those consultations form the fourth level of the rapidly tapering pyramid of disputing. In many of those cases, the dispute ends there, because client or lawyer concludes that legal action wouldn't be worth the trouble.

But sometimes the lawyer and client decide to take legal action, paradigmatically by filing a lawsuit. This takes us to the next level of the pyramid – the moment when the dispute breaks through from the informal into the formal legal system, and legal action commences. At this point, naming and blaming transform into *claiming*.[44]

Very few filed cases proceed to the next level of the pyramid, full-blown adjudication. Only 3 percent of state-court tort cases, for example, and

---

[44] The "naming, blaming, claiming" terminology comes from William L. F. Felstiner, Richard L. Abel & Austin Sarat, *The Emergence and Transformation of Disputes: Naming, Blaming, Claiming* ..., 15 Law & Soc'y. Rev. 631 (1980–81).

3 percent of state criminal filings, are tried to a verdict.[45] Cases may be dropped, or settled, or pleaded out, or withdrawn after a partial adjudication such as an early adverse ruling on a motion, or dismissal by the judge. Even including partial adjudications, the adjudications layer of the pyramid is far smaller than the "filed claims" layer. And the appellate layer is smaller still.

A few numbers help illustrate the shape of the pyramid in the United States. Obviously, determining the size of some layers of the pyramid raises insurmountable measurement problems – we cannot even conjecture, for example, how many informal disputes there are per unit of time. Others, however, can be given rough estimates. Thus, for example, a 1994 ABA study based on 3,000 interviews with moderate- and low-income Americans concluded that half of all households faced legal needs during the twelve-month period of the survey.[46] Given our current population, that would amount to more than 50 million legally addressable issues annually (half of 112 million American households) at the base of the pyramid.[47] Of course, not all of these are actual or potential disputes: legal needs include such noncontentious activities as making a will, incorporating a small business, or obtaining public benefits. But that scarcely matters, because in fact the pyramid's base is much larger. The study excludes all of the legal needs of organizations other than households, and organizations are the most intensive consumers of legal services.[48] The average American household faces one

[45] 1 National State Court Caseload Trends 2 (2004), available at <www.ncsconline.org/D_Research/csp/Highlights/vol1no1.pdf>; US Department of Justice, Bureau of Justice Statistics, Criminal Case Processing Statistics, available at <www.ojp.usdoj.gov/bjs/cases.htm> (visited December 19, 2005). Five percent of criminal convictions result from trial, and a bit more than three-fifths of criminal filings result in conviction.

[46] "Legal need" refers to "specific situations members of households were dealing with that raised legal issues – whether or not they were recognized as 'legal' or taken to some part of the civil justice system." American Bar Association, Consortium on Legal Services and the Public, Legal Needs and Civil Justice: Comprehensive Legal Needs Study 3, 11 (1994), quoted in Deborah L. Rhode & David Luban, Legal Ethics 832 (4th edn. 2004).

[47] US Census Bureau, American Families and Living Arrangements: 2004, Table AVG1, available at <www.census.gov/population/socdemo/hh-fam/cps2004/tabAVG1.csv>.

[48] Although I know of no direct demographic data, indirect data suggest that more than half of American lawyers represent predominantly organizational clients. At last count, about three-fourths of American lawyers were in private practice, and about 40 percent of these practice in firms with more than five lawyers. Clara N. Carson, The Lawyer Statistical Report: The US Legal Profession in 2006 6–8 (2004). Most law firms with more than five lawyers represent primarily business or other organizational clients, so the number of lawyers practicing in these firms (28 percent of American lawyers) provides a rough lower bound on the number of lawyers engaged in primarily organizational practice. The measure is imperfect, because even corporate law firms represent (usually wealthy) individuals as well, and some plaintiffs' law firms, representing primarily individuals, are quite large. On the other hand, lawyers in smaller firms and solo practices also represent a substantial number of business clients. It is plausible to estimate that a third of American lawyers in private practice represent predominantly business or other organizational clients. Another 8 percent of lawyers work for private

legal issue every two years, but government offices and large corporations face dozens or hundreds each week. Even the most cautious estimate, therefore, should number the legally addressable issues at the base of the pyramid in the hundreds of millions annually.

Although we have no reliable way of estimating across the board how many of these issues lead to naming and blaming, or how many legal consultations occur annually, data from several studies show that in one sector – physical injuries – very few result in formal claiming. In the 1990s, large reviews of hospital records in California and New York showed that only 10 percent of patients injured through medical error ever filed malpractice claims.[49] A 1989 Rand Corporation study of liability claiming for nonfatal injuries found that "overall, about one injury in ten led to an attempt to collect liability compensation," including by informal means – that is, by asking for compensation without filing either an insurance claim or lawsuit.[50] Most claiming for physical injuries arises from auto accidents and the workplace, while "in nonwork, non-motor vehicle accidents, only three injuries out of a hundred lead to liability claims."[51] Only 15 percent of the injured subjects contacted a lawyer, while only 8 percent hired a lawyer.[52] The lawyers themselves turned away a fifth of those who contacted them, which implies that about a fourth of those who contacted a lawyer – themselves amounting to only three out of twenty injured persons – decided not to pursue matters legally.[53] In short, the move from the "disputes" level of the pyramid to the "consultations with lawyers" level shrinks the pyramid dramatically, and the further move to "court filings" shrinks it more drastically still.

The high rate of "lumping it" and the low rate of formal claiming still yielded 38 million civil and criminal cases filed in US state courts in 2003. (The state courts represent 98 percent of all court filings.[54]) At this point, the

industries and associations, while another 9 percent are in government. Ibid. at 6. (The US Census statistics cited in note 27, which are a bit more recent than Carson's ABF study, place the number of government lawyers substantially higher than 9 percent.) A consulting firm reports that 140 major corporations average thirty attorneys in their law departments and spend over $1 million annually per attorney. Hildebrandt International 2005 US Law Department Survey, press release available at <www.hildebrandt.com/Documents.aspx?Doc_ID=2342>.

[49] See Paul C. Weiler, Medical Malpractice on Trial 12–13 (1991).

[50] Deborah R. Hensler *et al.*, Compensation for Accidental Injuries in the United States: Executive Summary 19 (Rand Corp., 1991).

[51] Ibid.   [52] Ibid. at 24, Table 6.

[53] Another study of 53,584 contacts between potential clients and contingency fee lawyers in Minnesota found that the lawyers rejected almost 70 percent of the cases. Herbert M. Kritzer, *Contingency Fee Lawyers as Gatekeepers in the Civil Justice System*, 81 Judicature 22, 24 (1997).

[54] Federal court filings that year amounted to 350,000. See Table S-7, <www.uscourts.gov/judbus2004/tables/s7.pdf>. For state filings, see National Center for State Courts, State Court

pyramid of disputing once again narrows significantly, because only a handful of these are tried to a verdict – as we have seen, about 3 percent each of criminal and tort cases. At the next level of the pyramid, we find about 281,000 state-court appeals in 2003 – one appeal for every 135 cases filed.[55] And of these, only 6,400 resulted in signed opinions by the highest court in the state.[56] The ratio is one state supreme court opinion per 44 appeals, or one for every 6,000 cases filed. Federal appeal courts in 2004 terminated 27,000 cases on their merits, four-fifths of them with no opinion or an unpublished opinion.[57] And the United States Supreme Court hears fewer than 100 cases a year.

It is easy to drown in numbers, but the basic point should be clear enough. The mainstay of casebooks consists of appellate opinions, and these represent perhaps 12,000 cases a year out of hundreds of millions of legally significant events – one out of tens of thousands. The litigants, moreover, are not a randomly selected or representative slice of humanity. They are all drawn from the unusual class of people with the money, nerves, and desire to maintain a dispute all the way through appeal. Appellate decisions thus represent only a minute proportion of atypical disputes, and a still smaller proportion of legally significant human interactions.

It might be objected that realists like Holmes were making a conceptual point about the power of judicial decisions, not an empirical one. They were not claiming that courts actually dominate the legal landscape, but that, as a matter of institutional definition and authority, they ought to dominate it. However, this objection robs realism of its interest, which lies in its claim to analyze abstract jurisprudential concepts as actual relationships of power and behavior. Holmes abhorred conceptual points, and aimed to bathe concepts like "legal duty" in cynical acid – to rinse away the moralistic verdigris and reveal the burnished sword that law wields. He certainly did not aim to spin out a peculiar utopian vision of a society in which judges rule.

It will also be objected that, rare or not, judicial decisions powerfully influence social behavior, which (in a familiar academic phrase) takes place "in the shadow of the law." But, as I observed earlier, the extent to which the judicial shadow shapes social behavior depends on how a multitude of agents, intermediate between the judge and the ordinary citizen, take up a judicial

Caseload Statistics, 2004, Table 7, available at <www.ncsconline.org/D_Research/csp/ 2004_Files/SCCSTabl5–8.pdf> (page 12 of PDF).

[55] National Center for State Courts, State Court Caseload Statistics, 2004, Table 1, available at <www.ncsconline.org/D_Research/csp/2004_Files/SCCSTables%201–4.pdf> (page 3 of PDF).

[56] Computed from ibid., Table 6, available at <www.ncsconline.org/D_Research/csp/2004_Files/ SCCSTabl5–8.pdf>.

[57] Federal Judicial Caseload Statistics, Table B-5, available at <www.uscourts.gov/caseload 2004/tables/B05Mar04.pdf>. For the number of unpublished opinions, see ibid. at Table S-3, available at <www.uscourts.gov/judbus2004/tables/s3.pdf>.

decision. This observation suggests that the focus of attention should shift toward these intermediate agents – and, prominent among them, to practicing lawyers advising their clients.

Another point is crucial: a great deal of legal work has little or nothing to do with disputes. Most law practice concerns transactions and compliance work (such as doing taxes or fulfilling bureaucratic reporting requirements), not litigation. It is important to understand why.

One often overlooked point on which Hart and Fuller agree concerns the nature of legal rules. Hart points out that in addition to the "thou shalt nots" of prohibitory rules – most people's dominant image of law – mature legal systems contain rules that empower rather than restrict human activity.[58] These include the procedures for getting married, forming a partnership, entering into a contract, creating a trust, and a host of other activities. Fuller took this point further, and insisted that the most fundamental and characteristic purpose of laws and legality consists in providing the architecture for social structures.[59] Private contracts form the paradigmatic examples of the architecture of social structure. Admittedly, the legal architect's work requires careful consideration of what happens when the edifice collapses and the shouting and suing begin. But Fuller insists that only bad lawyers focus their energy on drafting long, complex sets of risk terms in contracts, neglecting the performance terms. Laws are basically blueprints for getting things done, not for picking up the pieces when things go sour.

Hart would likely agree with Fuller that the most characteristic legal events are the meeting and the handshake, not the court order. Deals outnumber trials, and although parties hammer out deals in the shadow of past litigation, the Ghost of Trials Past need not cast a particularly dark or haunting shadow.

Not only do deals outnumber trials, but legal consultations outnumber deals. Every meeting between lawyers, clients, and their transactional counterparts will be prefaced by meetings between lawyers and clients. Furthermore, a great deal of legal work within the business world consists of routine compliance with regulatory requirements – SEC filings, tax preparation, environmental compliance, the formulation of sexual harassment or affirmative action policies. This takes us, as I have suggested earlier, to the

[58] Hart, CL, supra note 10, at 27–28.
[59] I discuss this aspect of Fuller's work in Chapter 3 of this book, and at greater length in *Rediscovering Fuller's Legal Ethics*, 11 Geo. J. Legal Ethics 801, 812–19 (1998), reprinted in Rediscovering Fuller: Essays on Implicit Law and Institutional Design (Willem J. Witteveen & Wibren van der Burg eds., Amsterdam University Press, 1999). Similar ideas about lawyers as architects of social structure appear in the classic textbook by Fuller's colleagues Henry Hart (not to be confused with H. L. A. Hart) and Albert Sacks. Henry M. Hart, Jr. & Albert M. Sacks, The Legal Process: Basic Problems in the Making and Application of Law (William Eskridge & Philip Frickey eds., 2001) (originally 1958).

most basic activity in the legal system: the consultation between lawyer and client, in which the client sketches out a problem and a lawyer tenders advice. This activity dominates the work lives of lawyers, and it represents the basic intellectual transaction defining the law – a transaction whereby the lawyer matches up an intellectual understanding of the legal system with a particular human problem. Whenever the client follows the lawyer's advice, or forms her own picture of the law based on that advice, lawyer and client together have laid down a tile in the social mosaic that makes up the law in action. The realist emphasis on the law in action, and the power relations that define it, should focus on the mosaic, not on the body of judicial opinions in the Westlaw data banks.

Judging and reason

Instead of focusing on judicial power, a second argument for judge-centered jurisprudence focuses on the fact that judges provide written opinions analyzing the meaning of the law – to borrow a phrase from the constitutional scholarship of the 1950s, "reasoned elaborations" of the law. That makes judges nearly unique within the legal system. Statutes, even statutes with preambles, do not explain themselves, and politicians talk in soundbites rather than arguments. They certainly do not defend one interpretation of law over others considering objections of injustice, inefficiency, or formal incoherence. Juries say "Guilty" or "Not guilty," "We find for the plaintiff" or "We find for the defendant," without stating why. Officials act, and give away as little as they possibly can about why they act as they do. Only judges work out disciplined arguments about law in a public setting. That is why their opinions are the focus of attention, and rightly so.

This argument might mean several things. One, plainly true but essentially trivial, is that published judicial opinions provide excellent exemplars of legal reasoning. But the fact that published opinions serve an indispensable pedagogic function implies nothing about whether jurisprudence should focus on them for reasons other than their ready availability. A second interpretation of the argument, plainly false, is that reasoning about the law can take place only in written, published form. A third, equally false, is that only judges analyze the law in writing. Lawyers in law firms and government agencies provide their clients or supervisors with written analyses of law all the time.

More plausible is the thought that someone writing an opinion for publication will reason more carefully than she would if the analysis were unwritten or confidential. Because judges, unlike lawyers, publish their analyses, their handiwork is likely to represent higher-quality elaborations of the law. However, there are significant problems with this view. First of all, many judicial decisions result in no written opinion. A trial judge, for example, makes dozens or even hundreds of legal rulings about objections to lawyers' questions, without providing written opinions. Second, as we have seen, even federal courts of appeal provide published opinions in fewer than one case in five. Most importantly, the "reasoned elaboration" view simply oversells the quality and wisdom of judicial opinions. Every serious reader of judicial opinions knows how frequently they fall short of the high ideals of "reasoned elaboration." They are often sloppy, illogical, or tendentious in their selection of facts. Indeed, the very fact that opinions are published encourages judges to legitimize their conclusions by writing what is, in effect, a brief supporting their result. Far too often, for example, readers learn the "bad facts" that undermine an otherwise persuasive appellate opinion only by reading the dissent – a clear indicator that the majority opinion's author is glossing over weaknesses to sell a result, rather than offering a balanced analysis of the case.

I do not wish to exaggerate this objection. Courts at every level contain superb judges. I recently saw an administrative law judge – by no means a lofty figure in the judicial hierarchy – craft a beautifully structured, gracefully written, logical, and artfully appeal-proofed opinion in ninety minutes between the end of a hearing and the moment she read the opinion aloud in court. But of course courts also contain less superb judges. Another, more experienced, judge in the same court took three months to write an opinion that was poorly reasoned and reached its result because the judge confused two pieces of evidence. Even US Supreme Court opinions contain solecisms and careless errors.[60]

Impartiality

However, one thing strongly differentiates judges from other lawyers, and that is their role in the adversary process itself. Parties offer reasoned arguments in an adversarial debate, and judges, informed by hearing the most powerful arguments for conflicting interpretations of the law, decide among them and offer reasons why they accepted some arguments and rejected others. The job of the judge is to render an impartial decision.

Impartiality is the key. It explains the privileged position of judges as expositors of the law. Advocates have a professional obligation to argue for whatever interpretation of the law most favors their clients. They are professional spinmeisters, and the formal rules of the profession permit them

---

[60] In a trivial example of carelessness, but one that an ethics teacher can hardly help but find galling, a 2002 decision refers to the legal ethics rules as "the Canons of Legal Ethics." Mickens v. Taylor, 535 US 162, 176 (2002). Apparently none of the nine justices or their numerous clerks knew that the ethics rules have not been called by this title for more than thirty years. Or maybe they just didn't care.

to argue any interpretation of law that passes the laugh test.[61] Indeed, adversarial ideology maintains that judges can do their interpretive job properly only if they hear the most forceful arguments on all sides, in an unvarnished form. Thus advocates may actually be duty bound to offer legal interpretations so one-sided that they defy good sense and good judgment (up to the brink of frivolity).

But lawyers are not always advocates. Equally important is the lawyer's role as advisor. Again we return to the paradigmatic legal moment, the consultation between lawyer and client in which the client explains a problem or asks for advice, and the lawyer explains the law. Here, the rules of ethics require lawyers to offer independent, candid advice, not advocacy for a position – advice about what the law permits and requires, even if the news frustrates or infuriates the client.[62] In other words, lawyers in the advisor's role lie under the same obligation of impartiality that judges do.

This stark contrast between the lawyer's role as advocate and as advisor makes sense once we understand the structural difference between the roles. In an open, adversary proceeding, the advocate makes the strongest arguments on behalf of the client's legal position because if she doesn't, no one will; and an advocate for the other side can counter the exaggerations. In a confidential conversation between lawyer and client, the same argument works in reverse: if the lawyer doesn't tell the client that what he plans is unlawful, in many instances nobody will.[63] Law enforcement is always spotty, and in innumerable areas of social and commercial interaction it is easy for clients to fly beneath enforcement's radar for years on end. Over a vast range of legal business, the conversation in the lawyer's office represents the last line of defense against client wrongdoing.

Often, clients come to lawyers because they want the lawyer to bless their endeavors – sometimes, with maximum cynicism, in order to create an advice-of-counsel defense for themselves – or to write an opinion letter stating that a dubious transaction is entirely proper. The temptation for the lawyer to play ball with the client is great: as Elihu Root said, "The client

---

[61] The ethics rules permit advocates to advance any argument "that is not frivolous, which includes a good faith argument for an extension, modification or reversal of existing law." ABA Model Rules of Professional Conduct, Rule 3.1. Rule 11 of the Federal Rules of Civil Procedure likewise requires only that claims are "warranted by existing law or by a non-frivolous argument for the extension, modification or reversal of existing law or the establishment of new law." FRCP Rule 11(b)(2).

[62] ABA Model Rule 2.1 states that a lawyer representing a client "shall exercise independent professional judgment and render candid advice," and comment [1] to the rule warns that "a lawyer should not be deterred from giving candid advice by the prospect that the advice will be unpalatable to the client."

[63] I borrow this argument from Lon L. Fuller & John D. Randall, *Professional Responsibility: Report of the Joint Conference of the ABA/AALS*, 44 ABAJ. 1159, 1161 (1958).

never wants to be told he can't do what he wants to do; he wants to be told how to do it, and it is the lawyer's business to tell him how."[64] As a general proposition, Root's adage is right: the lawyer's job is to help his client, not simply wag a censorious finger in the client's face. Nevertheless, there will be times when what the client wants to do is illegal and wrong. In such cases, lawyers must assume the (admittedly distasteful) gatekeeper's role. That is why the advisor's role requires the moral toughness to maintain independence and candor. Otherwise, there would be little social purpose behind creating confidentiality rules to encourage lawyer–client conversations. Without independence and candor, the rules would do little more than screen con-spiracies, or permit clients and lawyers to play responsibility games – the client insisting that the lawyer had approved his actions and the lawyer insisting that he was simply doing what the client asked.

To be sure, there are no reported cases of a lawyer disciplined for violating MR 2.1, the candid-advice rule.[65] But that has nothing to do with the merits of the rule. It has to do with the fact that the cases seldom come to light, and when they do, no one has an incentive to litigate them. Attorney–client advice is shrouded in confidentiality; clients are seldom in a position to know when their lawyer's advice has not been candid; aggrieved clients are more inter-ested in obtaining malpractice damages than in filing grievances; and in the rare case when a lawyer's bad advice becomes an issue – for example, when a receiver takes over a bankrupt corporation and goes after the lawyers who colluded with the old management – there are almost always easier-to-prove and more serious charges to file.

The lack of reported cases has perhaps led commentators to underrate the importance of the requirement of independent, candid advice. But, as my earlier observation about the confidentiality rules suggests, the independent, candid-advice requirement plays an often overlooked central role in con-ventional legal ethics. One of the major puzzles in legal ethics has always been how to justify the lawyer's duty of confidentiality. After all, on utili-tarian grounds it's a bad bet for society because it allows crooked clients to hide the evidence so frequently – as witness the forty-year history of Big Tobacco stonewalling the facts via their lawyers.[66] Given this embarrassing

---

[64] 1 Robert Swaine, The Cravath Firm and Its Predecessors, 1819–1947 667 (private printing, 1946).

[65] Here and in the ensuing paragraph, I am borrowing phrasing from my article *Liberalism, Torture, and the Ticking Bomb*, The Torture Debate in America 69–70 (Karen J. Greenberg ed., 2005).

[66] This point has been argued for more than a century, beginning with Jeremy Bentham's classic 5 Rationale of Judicial Evidence, Specially Applied to English Practice 302–11 (1827), and most recently and effectively in Daniel Fischel, *Lawyers and Confidentiality*, 65 U. Chi. L. Rev. 1 (1998). In a series of articles, Louis Kaplow and Steven Shavell have provided a nuanced analysis of the conditions under which confidentiality of legal advice is beneficial on utilitarian

fact, how does the profession justify its sacred norm of confidentiality? It does so by arguing that the lawyer needs confidential information

to advise the client to refrain from wrongful conduct. Almost without exception, clients come to lawyers in order to determine their rights and what is, in the complex of laws and regulations, deemed to be legal and correct. From experience, lawyers know that almost all clients follow the advice given, and the law is upheld.[67]

In other words: confidentiality is a good bet for society *only* because we can count on lawyers to give good advice on compliance (and on clients to take that advice).[68] If the lawyer doesn't give independent, candid advice, this entire argument, and indeed the whole edifice of confidentiality, comes tumbling down.

What about the fact that the lawyer is working for the client? The client retains her to solve problems, not to deliver impersonal pronouncements about law, client problems be damned. That is the point of Elihu Root's adage: the client wants to be told how to do what he wants to do, and it is the lawyer's job to tell him.

Well, not exactly. The lawyer's job is to tell the client lawful ways to get what he wants. If there are none, the lawyer will have to break the unwelcome news. If the lawyer believes that the law is unjust or immoral, she ought to explain why to the client. Official ethics rules forbid her from advising the client to break the law even when it is unjust, but ultimately the lawyer's own conscience must be the guide. Here we might think of the model of civil rights movement lawyers discussing with Martin Luther King, Jr., whether he ought to obey the injunction not to engage in the Birmingham civil rights march of 1963. Just as King's conscience led him to violate the injunction, his lawyers' consciences may well have led them to violate the professional rule against counseling disobedience. If the lawyer counsels disobedience, of course, she becomes morally and legally complicit with law-breaking and may well risk her license or even her liberty. Presumably,

---

grounds. Louis Kaplow & Steven M. Shavell, *Private Versus Socially Optimal Provision of Ex Ante Legal Advice*, 8 J. L. Econ. & Org. 306 (1992); Kaplow & Shavell, *Legal Advice About Acts Already Committed*, 10 Int. Rev. L. & Econ. 149 (1990); Kaplow & Shavell, *Legal Advice About Information to Present in Litigation: Its Effects and Social Desirability*, 102 Harv. L. Rev. 567 (1989); Shavell, *Legal Advice About Contemplated Acts: The Decision to Obtain Advice, Its Social Desirability, and the Protection of Confidentiality*, 17 J. Leg. Stud. 123 (1988).

[67] Comment [2] to Model Rule 1.6.

[68] There is a lot of wishful thinking built into this argument. If the client is a Holmesian bad man, who cares only about sanctions, and the lawyer informs the client that the size or likelihood of sanctions is lower than the client's expected gain, the advice will encourage the client to violate the law, even if doing so turns out to be socially harmful. Shavell, *Legal Advice About Contemplated Acts: The Decision to Obtain Advice, Its Social Desirability, and the Protection of Confidentiality*, supra note 66, at 131–36 (1988).

however, there are times when complicity with law-breaking is the right thing to do.[69] But acknowledging this point only serves to emphasize that when law-breaking and complicity with it are not a matter of conscience, lawyers must advise their clients against it, and rightfully deserve criticism, perhaps punishment, when instead their advice includes a wink at client wrongdoing or collusion with it.

Ultimately, then, the obligation of impartial legal judgment matters just as much for lawyer-advisors as it does for judges. It follows just as certainly from examining in functional terms the roles lawyers and judges play in the legal system. Nothing about the judge's impartial role should lead us to focus on judicial decisions rather than on the decisions lawyers make when advising clients about the law.

The ethics of advising

What should lawyers tell clients about the law when they advise them? Holmes offers one answer, which lies at the root of his judge-centrism. "People want to know under what circumstances and how far they will run the risk of coming against what is so much stronger than themselves ... the prediction of the incidence of the public force through the instrumentality of the courts."[70] We have already examined the deficiencies of this view. It nevertheless remains stubbornly embedded in the way lawyers conceive of their task. The 1969 ABA Code of Professional Responsibility – the predecessor to the current Rules of Professional Conduct – carefully and correctly distinguishes the roles of advocate and advisor, but then describes the role of advisor in Holmesian, court-predictive terms: "While serving as advocate, a lawyer should resolve in favor of his client doubts as to the bounds of the law. In serving a client as adviser, a lawyer ... should give his professional opinion as to what the ultimate decisions of the courts would likely be as to the applicable law."[71]

But why? Why not simply "his professional opinion as to what the applicable law actually requires"? The fact is that lawyers find it almost irresistible to turn the question of what the law means into the question of what courts would likely say it means. Answering law questions with

---

[69] I discuss these issues in Luban, *Conscientious Lawyers for Conscientious Lawbreakers*, 52 U. Pitt. L. Rev. 793 (1991). For present purposes I leave to one side the question of whether the lawyer must counsel open disobedience, or may instead suggest that a client disobey the law secretly and hope that neither of them gets caught. In my view, that depends on the overall justice of the law in question and how outrageous the consequences would be for lawyer or client. Presumably, a conscientious lawyer in Nazi Germany could help her Jewish client escape without defeating the escape by doing it openly.

[70] Holmes, *The Path of the Law*, supra note 2, at 457.

[71] ABA Model Code of Professional Responsibility, EC 7–3 (1969).

court-talk ("a court would probably say ... ") may be little more than a harmless, residual verbal tic induced by the prevailing judge-centrism of our legal culture. I suspect, however, that the temptation to court-talk comes from a more dangerous motivation than verbal habit. It is a means of ducking personal responsibility for a judgment, by fobbing it off on hypothetical "courts" and couching legal judgments as mere predictions.

Lawyers who do this when there is no litigation pending and no reason to suppose there ever will be – and that will be true most of the time – are in denial. They are in denial of the fact that their conversation with the client marks the end of the road. From the client's point of view, the lawyer's pronouncement is what the client takes the law to be.

The nightmare and the noble dream

The lawyer–client conversation is a morally fraught moment in which the legitimacy of the legal system is, at least in microcosm, up for grabs.[72] Some years ago, Austin Sarat and William Felstiner studied 155 taped conversations between divorce lawyers and their clients, and concluded that a great deal of legal advice consisted of more or less cynical realism about the large discrepancy between what the law says and what clients could really expect from the system.[73] They cautioned that "the law talk of the divorce lawyer's office may be partially responsible for the common finding that people who use legal processes tend, no matter how favorable the results of their encounter, to have a less positive view of the law than those with no direct experience."[74] Though the lawyers' cynicism is somewhat troubling, it is hard to fault them for warning their clients that the system might not deliver everything to which they are entitled. Perhaps the system doesn't deserve a better reputation than the lawyers convey.

The Nightmare vision of legal advice – to borrow Hart's image – is not one of cynical lawyers making their clients cynical. Rather, it is the suspicion that candid, independent advice is often, or always, an illusion. One version

---

[72] There is a large literature on the moral dimensions of counseling. See, e.g., Robert F. Cochran, Jr., Deborah L. Rhode, Paul R. Tremblay, & Thomas L. Shaffer, *Symposium: Client Counseling and Moral Responsibility*, 30 Pepp. L. Rev. 591 (2003); Stephen L. Pepper, *Counseling at the Limits of the Law: An Exercise in the Jurisprudence and Ethics of Lawyering*, 104 Yale L. J. 1545 (1995); Warren Lehman, *The Pursuit of a Client's Interest*, 77 Mich. L. Rev. 1078 (1979).

[73] Austin Sarat & William L. F. Felstiner, *Lawyers and Legal Consciousness: Law Talk in the Divorce Lawyer's Office*, 98 Yale L.J. 1663 (1989); see also Sarat & Felstiner, *Law and Strategy in the Divorce Lawyer's Office*, 20 Law & Soc'y Rev. 93 (1986); Sarat & Felstiner, *Law and Social Relations: Vocabularies of Motive in Lawyer–Client Interaction*, 22 Law & Soc'y Rev. 737 (1988).

[74] Sarat & Felstiner, *Lawyers and Legal Consciousness*, supra note 73, at 1687.

of the Nightmare is that lawyers dominate and manipulate clients, either to advance their own agenda or to line their own pockets.[75] More drastically, William Simon has suggested that the entire idea of client autonomy is an illusion, because the process of legal advising shapes an often inchoate ordering of client preferences.[76]

A second version of the Nightmare concerns lawyer complicity and capitulation to clients, rather than lawyer domination of clients. This is the concern I focused on earlier in this chapter, when I discussed Elihu Root's adage, and the fear that lawyers – economically dependent on their clients or in some cases ideologically aligned with them – will treat the advisor's role like that of an advocate, and spin the law to support whatever the client wishes to do.

Everyone who studies American business scandals is aware of how much this goes on. Rotten deals, dummy companies, and smoke-and-mirrors accounting rest on a slick foundation of legal opinions, giving new and unsavory meaning to Isaiah's prophecy that the crooked shall be made straight – or at least made to look straight. But the same thing goes on in government, a fact that emerged dramatically in summer 2004, when it was revealed that two years earlier the Department of Justice had written a spectacularly bizarre legal opinion to legitimize harsh interrogation techniques bordering on torture. In rapid succession, opinion after dubious opinion on the treatment of War on Terror detainees leaked out of the Departments of Defense and Justice, eventually suggesting that at the highest levels of government legal advice has been subsumed into advocacy for the party line. These memos, and the moral failure they represent among elite government lawyers, will form the subject of the next chapter.

What of the Noble Dream? Hart's phrase quite deliberately exploits both meanings of the word "dream," as ideal and as fantasy. For him, the Noble Dream of judge-centered jurisprudence is the ideal and fantasy of a judicial rationality that can eliminate all gaps in the law. Ultimately, Hart believed, both the nightmare and the noble dream in judge-centered jurisprudence are illusions.[77]

Is there a Noble Dream in a jurisprudence centered on the lawyer-advisor? Put most generally, it is the Parsonian vision of lawyers as independent intermediaries between private and public interests, translating client problems

---

[75] Classic expositions of this version of the Nightmare may be found in Douglas Rosenthal's study of personal injury lawyers, Lawyer and Client: Who's In Charge? (1974), and Abraham S. Blumberg's article *The Practice of Law as a Confidence Game: Cooptation of a Profession*, 1 Law & Soc'y Rev. 15 (1967).

[76] William H. Simon, *Lawyer Advice and Client Autonomy: Mrs. Jones's Case*, 50 Md. L. Rev. 213 (1991); Simon, *The Dark Secret of Progressive Lawyering: A Comment on Poverty Law Scholarship in the Post-Modern, Post-Reagan Era*, 48 U. Miami L. Rev. 1099 (1994).

[77] Hart, *American Jurisprudence Through English Eyes*, supra note 1, at 978, 989.

into the terms of the law, and presenting the law to the client in intelligible form. As the argument so far should make clear, however, my stance toward the Noble Dream differs from Hart's. I believe that it is no illusion. If the possibility of the independent legal advisor is an illusion, so is the possibility of law, understood as anything more than directives in a society of bad men and sheep.

But, though it is no illusion, in several obvious respects the Noble Dream falls short of reality and can serve as no more than a regulative ideal. First, as I suggested earlier, the great inequality of access to lawyers – nearly one in six Americans has no realistic access at all – skews and distorts the Noble Dream in nightmarish directions.[78] If only the well-off have legal advice, the law becomes hard to distinguish from a system of subordination like the mafia legal system. Second, the very feature that makes lawyers intermediaries between private and public interests, namely that they represent private parties, implies economic dependence on clients that undermines the incentive to give clients candid, independent legal advice. Third, well-understood psychological pressures are likely to push lawyers' views in the direction of their clients' interests, making genuine independence less likely.[79]

These are practical and institutional problems, and this is not the place to consider practical and institutional solutions to them. But they are also moral problems lawyers constantly confront. They are the everyday subject-matter of legal ethics, as (for that matter) the Nightmare scenarios of lawyers dominating clients and lawyers capitulating to them are as well. If my argument holds water, these, far more than the preoccupying problems of judicial decision-making, are fundamental to the legal system.

In his most systematic book, Dworkin refers to the rule of law as "Law's Empire," suggesting a vast system of governance with Judge Hercules on the imperial throne. A better metaphor than law's empire is law's landfill, the dregs of legal authority contained in the millions of lawyer–client conversations on which our actual legal civilization is erected.[80] Often, no doubt,

---

[78] I discuss this problem in chapters 11 and 12 of *Lawyers and Justice*, and more recently in Luban, *Taking Out the Adversary: The Assault on Progressive Public-Interest Lawyers*, 91 Calif. L. Rev. 209, 209–16, 245 (2003). By my calculation, the roughly 5,000 poor people's lawyers in the United States can handle at most 5 percent of the legal problems of the nearly 50 million people eligible for representation by a legal services lawyer – and that assumes, fancifully, that each problem takes only a single day to solve. Ibid. at 211–12.

[79] See, e.g., Paul R. Tremblay, *Moral Activism Manqué*, 44 S. Texas L. Rev. 127 (2002); Robert L. Nelson, *Ideology, Practice, and Professional Autonomy: Social Values and Client Relationships in the Large Law Firm*, 37 Stan. L. Rev. 503 (1985); and the articles by Donald Langevoort cited in chapter 8 of this book, note 3.

[80] David Luban, *The Art of Honesty*, 101 Colum. L. Rev. 1763, 1767 (2001).

the conversations are banal or conniving or both; in any case, they are largely invisible. But unlike Hercules' pronouncements, the advice of lawyers to clients involves genuine interaction, conferring the legitimacy necessary to make law out of the "gunman writ large." For better or for worse, their morality is the law's morality.[81]

---

[81] I am grateful for comments on an earlier draft by Barbara Fried, Tom Grey, Vicki Jackson, Mark Kelman, Carrie Menkel-Meadow, Scott Shapiro, and Norman Spaulding.

5

The torture lawyers of Washington

Revelations of torture and sexual humiliation at Abu Ghraib erupted into the news media at the end of April in 2004, when reporter Seymour Hersh exposed the scandal in *The New Yorker* magazine and CBS News broadcast the notorious photographs. Five weeks later, with the scandal still at the center of media attention, the *Wall Street Journal* and *Washington Post* broke the story of the Bybee Memorandum – the secret "torture memo," written by elite lawyers in the US Department of Justice's Office of Legal Counsel (OLC), which legitimized all but the most extreme techniques of torture, planned out possible criminal defenses to charges of torture, and argued that if the President orders torture it would be unconstitutional to enforce criminal prohibitions against the agents who carry out his commands. (The memo, written to then White House counsel Alberto Gonzales, went out over the signature of OLC head Jay S. Bybee, but apparently much of it was drafted by John Yoo, a law professor working in the OLC at the time. Before the Abu Ghraib revelations, Bybee left OLC to become a federal judge, and Yoo returned to the academy.)

Soon after, more documents about the treatment of War on Terror detainees were released or leaked – a stunning and suffocating cascade of paper that has not stopped, even after two years. When Cambridge University Press published *The Torture Papers* a scant six months after the exposure of the Bybee Memo, it included over 1,000 pages of documents.[1] Even so, *The Torture Papers* was already out of date when it was published. For that matter, so was a follow-up volume published a year later.[2] No doubt a

---

[1] The Torture Papers: The Road to Abu Ghraib (Karen J. Greenberg & Joshua L. Dratel, eds., Cambridge University Press, 2005). Hereafter: TP.

[2] The Torture Debate in America (Karen J. Greenberg, ed., Cambridge University Press, 2006). Hereafter: The Torture Debate. The second volume contains eight additional memoranda, but does not include such crucial documents as the Schmidt Report on interrogation techniques used in Guantánamo, US Attorney General Alberto Gonzales's written responses to US senators at his confirmation hearings about the legality of cruel, inhuman, or degrading treatment that

third volume, collected now (November 2006), would also be outdated by the time it was distributed. The reason is simple: the lawyers continue to lawyer away.

In the last chapter, I offered an argument about the jurisprudential and ethical importance of lawyers giving candid, independent advice about the law. This chapter will provide a case study of moral failure. The chapter will help us address some questions left over from the last – questions such as: (1) What does candid, independent advice entail? (2) Given a contentious legal issue, how much leeway does the candid advisor have to slant the law in the client's direction? (3) What is the difference between illicitly slanted advice and advice that is merely wrong?

But in setting out these questions, I don't mean to gloss over the most basic reason for writing about the torture lawyers in a book about legal ethics and human dignity. Torture is among the most fundamental affronts to human dignity, and hardly anything lawyers might do assaults human dignity more drastically than providing legal cover for torture and degradation. We would have to go back to the darkest days of World War II, when Hitler's lawyers laid the legal groundwork for the murder of Soviet POWs and the forced disappearance of political suspects, to find comparably heartless use of legal technicalities (and, as Scott Horton has demonstrated, the legal arguments turn out to be uncomfortably similar to those used by Bush Administration lawyers[3]). The most basic question, then, is whether the torture lawyers were simply doing what lawyers are supposed to do. If so, then so much for the idea that the lawyer's role has any inherent connection with human dignity.

If the law clearly and explicitly permitted or required torture, legal advisors would face a terrible crisis of conscience, forced to choose between resigning, lying to their client about the law, or candidly counseling that the law permits torture. But that was not the torture lawyers' dilemma. Faced with unequivocal legal prohibitions on torture, they had to loophole shamelessly to evade the prohibitions, and they evaded the prohibitions because that was the advice their clients wanted to receive. With only a few exceptions, the torture memos were disingenuous as legal analysis, and in places they were absurd. The fact that their authors include some of the finest intellects in the legal profession makes it worse, because their legal talent rules out any whiff of the "empty head, pure heart" defense. Possibly they believed that, confronted by terrorists, morality actually required them to evade the

---

falls short of torture, official correspondence surrounding these and other issues, or the responses offered by the US government to the UN's Committee Against Torture in May 2006. Nor does it contain major US legislation enacted while the book was in press, such as the Detainee Treatment Act of 2005; and the Military Commissions Act of 2006.

[3] Scott Horton, *Through a Mirror, Darkly: Applying the Geneva Conventions to "A New Kind of Warfare,"* in The Torture Debate, supra note 2, at 136–50.

prohibitions on torture, a position frankly defended by some commentators.[4] But the torture lawyers never admitted anything of the sort. Professor Yoo, for example, continues to maintain the pretense of lawyering as usual, and flatly denies that he was offering morally motivated advice.[5] The issue, then, is not whether lawyers may deceive their clients about the law in order to manipulate the clients into doing the right thing by the lawyer's lights. Although that is an interesting and important question, the torture memoranda raise a different one: whether lawyers may spin their legal advice because they know spun advice is what their clients want.[6]

To grasp just how spun the advice was, it will be necessary to dwell on legal details to a greater extent than in other chapters in this book,

---

[4] See, e.g., Charles Krauthammer, *It's Time to Be Honest About Doing Terrible Things*, The Weekly Standard, December 5, 2005; David Gelernter, *When Torture Is the Only Option*, L.A. Times, November 11, 2005; Jean Bethke Elshtain, *Reflections on the Problem of "Dirty Hands,"* in Torture: A Collection (Sanford Levinson ed., 2004), at 87–88. In Elshtain's words, "Far greater moral guilt falls on a person in authority who permits the deaths of hundreds of innocents rather than choosing to 'torture' one guilty or complicit person ... To condemn outright ... coercive interrogation, is to lapse into a legalistic version of pietistic rigorism in which one's own moral purity is ranked above other goods. This is also a form of moral laziness." Ibid.

[5] In an interview, Professor Yoo said: "At the Justice Department, I think it's very important not to put in an opinion interpreting a law on what you think the right thing to do is, because I think you don't want to bias the legal advice with these other considerations. Otherwise, I think people will question the validity of the legal advice. They'll say, 'Well, the reason they reached that result is that they had certain moral views or certain policy goals they wanted to achieve.' And actually I think at the Justice Department and this office, there's a long tradition of keeping the law and policy separate. The department is there to interpret the law so that people who make policy know the rules of the game, but you're not telling them what plays to call, essentially ... I don't feel like lawyers are put on the job to provide moral answers to people when they have to choose what policies to pursue." *Frontline Interview With John Yoo* (October 18, 2005), available at <www.pbs.org/wgbh/pages/frontline/torture/interviews/yoo. html>. "'The worst thing you could do, now that people are critical of your views, is to run and hide. I agree with the work I did. I have an obligation to explain it,' Yoo said from his Berkeley office. 'I'm one of the few people who is willing to defend decisions I made in government.'" Peter Slevin, *Scholar Stands By Earlier Writings Sanctioning Torture, Eavesdropping*, Wash. Post, December 26, 2005, A3. Discussing the torture memo, Yoo adds, "The lawyer's job is to say, 'This is what the law says, and this is what you can't do.'" Ibid. In other words, it is lawyering as usual, not unusual lawyering for moral purposes. (Oddly enough, however, when the US Supreme Court rejected Yoo's argument that the Geneva Conventions do not protect Al Qaeda captives, Professor Yoo complained that "What the court is doing is attempting to suppress creative thinking." Adam Liptak, *The Court Enters The War, Loudly*, N.Y. Times, July 2, 2006, section 4, at 1. Obviously, to call arguments "creative thinking" implies legal novelty, the antithesis of the straightforward "this is what the law says" that Yoo had previously used to describe his work.)

[6] This chapter therefore overlaps with another essay I wrote on torture and the torture lawyers: David Luban, *Liberalism, Torture, and the Ticking Bomb*, 91 Virginia L. Rev. 1425 (2005). The latter essay was reprinted in expanded form in The Torture Debate, supra note 2, 35–83. In a few parts of this chapter, I draw on the earlier paper.

even though the technicalities are of no lasting interest. The devil lies in the details, and without the details we cannot study the devil. Only the details permit us to discuss the difference between a memo that "gets the law wrong," but argues within acceptable legal parameters, and one that cannot be understood as anything more than providing political cover for a client's position. And that is the most fundamental distinction this chapter considers.

The background

To understand the work of the torture lawyers, it is crucial to understand two pieces of legal background: the worldwide criminalization of torture, and the overall movement of legal thought by the United States government in the wake of September 11, 2001.

Governments have tortured people, often with unimaginable cruelty, for as long as history has been recorded. By comparison with the millennia-long "festival of cruelty" (Nietzsche), efforts to ban torture are of recent vintage. The eighteenth-century penologist Beccaria (widely read and admired by Americans in the 18th century) was among the first to denounce torture, both as a form of punishment and as a method for extracting confessions; and European states legally abolished torture in the nineteenth century.[7] Legal abolition did not necessarily mean real abolition: Germany practiced torture throughout the Third Reich, France tortured terrorists and revolutionaries in Algeria during the 1950s and 1960s, and the United Kingdom engaged in "cruel and degrading" treatment of IRA suspects until the European Court of Human Rights ordered it to stop in 1977. The phenomenon is worldwide: states abolish and criminalize torture, but scores of states, including democracies, engage in it anyway. Nevertheless, the legal abolition of torture marked a crucial step toward whatever practical abolition has followed; and it drove underground whatever torture persists in a great many states.

The post-World War II human rights revolution contributed to the legal abolition of torture. The Nuremberg trials declared torture inflicted in attacks on civilian populations to be a crime against humanity, and the 1949 Geneva Conventions not only banned the torture of captives in international armed conflicts, they declared torture to be a "grave breach" of the Conventions, which parties are required to criminalize. Alongside Geneva's anti-torture rules for international armed conflicts, Article 3 of Geneva (called "common Article 3" because it appears in all four Geneva Conventions) prohibits mistreating captives in armed conflicts "not of an international character" – paradigmatically, civil wars, which throughout history have

---

[7] See the opening chapters of Michel Foucault, Discipline and Punish: The Birth of the Prison (Alan Sheridan trans., 1977).

provoked savage repressions.[8] Common Article 3 is particularly remarkable because prohibitions on what sovereign states can do within their own territory in times of crisis are few and far between. And US law classifies the torture and cruel treatment forbidden by common Article 3, along with grave breaches of Geneva, as war crimes carrying a potential death sentence.[9] In addition, the United States, together with almost 150 other states, has ratified the International Covenant on Civil and Political Rights, which flatly prohibits torture and inhumane treatment.[10]

[8] The Nuremberg Charter did not in those terms declare torture a crime against humanity; but torture fell under the rubric of "inhumane acts" in the list of crimes against humanity found in Article 6(c); furthermore, Allied Control Council Law No. 10, the occupying powers' domestic-law version of the Nuremberg Charter used in other postwar trials, did name torture (along with rape and imprisonment) as a crime against humanity. The Third and Fourth Geneva Conventions include "torture or inhuman treatment" among the so-called "grave breaches" that must be criminalized: see Geneva Convention III (on the rights of POWs), articles 129–30, and Geneva Convention IV (on the rights of civilians), articles 146–47. Article 3 common to all four Geneva Conventions prohibits "mutilation, cruel treatment and torture" as well as "outrages upon personal dignity, in particular humiliating and degrading treatment."

[9] 18 U.S.C. § 2441. Until the Military Commissions Act of 2006 (MCA), this section declared all violations of common Article 3 to be war crimes. The MCA decriminalized humiliating and degrading treatment, along with the practice of subjecting detainees to sentences and punishments resulting from unfair trials – both common Article 3 violations, but now no longer federal war crimes. Indeed, the MCA retroactively decriminalizes these violations back to 1997. The reason for decriminalizing these two Article 3 violations is, unfortunately, rather obvious. The MCA establishes military commissions to try detainees, and apparently its drafters wanted to insulate those who establish and serve on the commissions from potential criminal liability if a federal court ever finds the commissions unfair. (Decriminalizing the subjection of detainees to unfair trials is a noteworthy step, because the United States convicted and punished Japanese officers after World War II for illegitimately stripping downed US airmen of Geneva Convention status, trying them unfairly, and executing them. See *Trial of Lieutenant-General Shigeru Sawada and Three Others, United States Military Commission, Shanghai* (1946), in 5 United Nations War Crimes Commission, Law Reports of Trials of War Criminals 1 (1948).) And, as we shall see below, US interrogators employed humiliation tactics in interrogating Guantanamo detainees. After the US Supreme Court found that common Article 3 applies to detainees in the War on Terror, the awkward result was that, without retroactive decriminalization, all those who engaged in humiliation tactics, together with officials who authorized the use of such tactics, were federal war criminals.

[10] "No one shall be subjected to torture or to cruel, inhuman or degrading treatment or punishment." ICCPR, G.A. res. 2200A (XXI), 21 U.N. GAOR Supp. (No. 16) at 52, U.N. Doc. A/ 6316 (1966), 999 U.N.T.S. 171, *entered into force* Mar. 23, 1976, Article 7. The United States, however, does not believe that the ICCPR applies outside US jurisdiction, or during armed conflicts. For a careful argument defending this point of view, see Michael J. Dennis, *Application of Human Rights Treaties Extraterritorially During Times of Armed Conflict and Military Occupation*, 99 A.J.I.L. 119 (2005). For the alternative point of view, see United Nations Human Rights Committee, *General Comment No. 31 on Article 2 of the Covenant: The Nature of the General Legal Obligation Imposed on States Parties to the Covenant: 21 April 2004*, CCPR/C/74/CRP.4/Rev.6. (General Comments).

The most decisive step in the legal prohibition of torture took place in 1987, when the international Convention Against Torture (CAT) entered into force. Today, 144 states have joined CAT, and another 74 have signed. Several features of CAT turn out to be particularly important for understanding the work of the torture lawyers. First, CAT provides a legal definition of official torture as the intentional infliction of severe physical or mental pain or suffering on someone, under official auspices or instigation (Article 1). This was the definition that the Bybee Memo had to loophole its way around. CAT requires its parties to take effective steps to prevent torture on territories within their jurisdiction (Article 2(1)), and forbids them from extraditing, expelling, or returning people to countries where they are likely to face torture (Article 3). Parties must criminalize torture (Article 4), create jurisdiction to try foreign torturers in their custody (Article 5), and create the means for torture victims to obtain compensation (Article 14). A party must also "undertake to prevent in any territory under its jurisdiction other acts of cruel, inhuman or degrading treatment or punishment which do not amount to torture" (Article 16) – a requirement that the torture lawyers loopholed with tenacious ingenuity.

Strikingly, CAT holds that "no exceptional circumstances whatsoever, whether a state of war or a threat of war, internal political instability or any other public emergency, may be invoked as a justification of torture" (Article 2(2)). What makes this article striking, of course, is its rejection of the most common excuse states offer when they torture: dire emergency. Article 2(2) commits the parties to CAT to the understanding that the prohibition on torture is not merely a fair-weather prohibition. It holds in times of storm and stress, and by ratifying the Convention, states agree to forgo torture even in "new paradigm" wars.[11] With the worldwide adoption of CAT, torture became an international crime.

The United States signed CAT in 1988, and the Senate ratified it in 1994. However, the Senate attached declarations and reservations to CAT, including a declaration that none of its substantive articles is self-executing. That means the articles do not take effect within the United States until Congress

---

[11] Stunningly, however, in May 2006 the US State Department's legal advisor informed the United Nations Committee Against Torture that the United States has never understood CAT to apply during armed conflicts. *Opening Remarks by John B. Bellinger III, Legal Advisor, US Dep't. of State, Geneva, May 5, 2006,* available at <www.us-mission.ch/Press2006/0505BellingerOpenCAT.html>. He based this view on statements made by US representatives at the negotiations that created the CAT. The United States was apparently worried that CAT would displace international humanitarian law, including the Geneva Conventions. However, the Senate did not include this limitation among the reservations, declarations, and understandings it attached to CAT at ratification, so these isolated statements from the legislative history have no legal significance. This is particularly important given that US law currently maintains that international humanitarian law does not apply to the War on Terror, and so there is nothing for CAT to displace.

implements them with appropriate legislation. Congress did implement several of the articles. Most significantly, it passed a pair of criminal statutes, defining torture along the lines laid down by CAT and making torture outside the United States a serious federal felony.[12]

What about torture within the United States? Long before CAT, US domestic law outlawed torture, although not by name. The US Constitution forbids cruel and unusual punishment, and the Supreme Court held that official conduct that "shocks the conscience" violates the constitutional guarantee of due process of law.[13] Ordinary criminal prohibitions on assault and mayhem straightforwardly prohibit torture, and US military law contains parallel prohibitions. When foreign victims sued their home-state torturers in US courts, the courts found no difficulty in denouncing "the dastardly and totally inhuman act of torture."[14] If police investigators sometimes continue to give suspects the third degree in the back rooms of station houses, no one prior to the torture memos doubted that this broke the law; the 1997 torture of Abner Louima by New York City police officers led to a thirty-year sentence for the ringleader. If US agents abroad engaged in torture, nobody admitted it; and when federal agents allegedly tortured a criminal suspect while bringing him to the United States, the court held that he could not be tried if the allegations were true – a rare exception to the longstanding rule of the US courts that people brought for trial illegally can still stand trial.[15]

This is not to say that, when it comes to torture, the United States was squeaky clean. In 1996, the Pentagon admitted that the School of the Americas, in Fort Benning, Georgia – a US-run training school for Latin American military forces – had for years used instructional manuals that advocated torture; and there have been many allegations over the years of US "black ops" involving torture.[16] Nevertheless, until the torture lawyers began making the legal world safe for brutal interrogations, the United States was one of the leading campaigners in the worldwide effort to place torture beyond the pale of permissibility. Afterward, although the US government insists it has not backed down an iota in rejecting torture, the protestations ring hollow, and everyone understands that US officials can proclaim them only because the torture lawyers have twisted words like "torture," "cruel, inhuman, and degrading," and "humane" until they no longer mean what they say.[17]

---

[12] 18 U.S.C. §§ 2340–2340A.   [13] Rochin v. California, 345 U.S. 165, 172 (1952).

[14] Filartiga v. Pena-Irala, 630 F.2d 876, 883 (2d Cir. 1980).

[15] U.S. v. Toscanino, 500 F.2d 267 (2d Cir. 1974).

[16] See, e.g., Dana Priest, US Instructed Latins on Executions, Torture, Wash. Post, September 21, 1996; Alfred W. McCoy, A Question of Torture: CIA Interrogation, from the Cold War to the War on Terror (2006); Jennifer Harbury, Truth, Torture, and the American Way: The History and Consequences of US Involvement in Torture (2005).

[17] I discuss some of these redefinitions in David Luban, Torture, American-Style, Wash. Post, November 27, 2005, B1. At his confirmation hearing, Attorney General Gonzales redefined

The result

In the War on Terror, CIA techniques for interrogating high-value captives reportedly include waterboarding, a centuries-old torture technique of near-drowning. Tactics also include "Long Time Standing" ("Prisoners are forced to stand, handcuffed and with their feet shackled to an eye bolt in the floor for more than 40 hours"), and "The Cold Cell" ("The prisoner is left to stand naked in a cell kept near 50 degrees. Throughout the time in the cell the prisoner is doused with cold water.")[18] All these techniques surely induce the "severe suffering" that the law defines as torture. Consider Long Time Standing. In 1956, the CIA commissioned two Cornell Medical Center researchers to study Soviet interrogation techniques. They concluded: "The KGB simply made victims stand for eighteen to twenty-four hours – producing 'excruciating pain' as ankles double in size, skin becomes 'tense and intensely painful,' blisters erupt oozing 'watery serum,' heart rates soar, kidneys shut down, and delusions deepen."[19]

"cruel, inhuman, and degrading" treatment so that conduct outside US borders does not count. He also defined "humane" treatment as involving nothing more than providing detainees with food, clothing, shelter, and medical care; consistent with this view, the Army's Schmidt Report concluded that intensive sleep deprivation, blasting detainees with ear-splitting rock music, threatening them with dogs, and humiliating them sexually "did not rise to the level of being inhumane treatment." *Army Regulation 15–6 Final Report: Investigation of FBI Allegations of Detainee Abuse at Guantanamo Bay, Cuba Detention Facility* [hereafter: Schmidt Report], at 1, available at <www.defenselink.mil/news/Jul2005/d20050714report.pdf>. Legal obligations were defined so narrowly that US officials could truthfully say that the United States complies with its legal obligations, simply because it hardly has any to comply with.

[18] Brian Ross & Richard Esposito, *CIA's Harsh Interrogation Techniques Described*, ABC News, November 18, 2005, available at <http://abcnews.go.com/WNT/Investigation/story ?id=1322866&page=1>. At least one Afghani captive reportedly died of hypothermia in a CIA-run detention facility after being soaked with water and shackled to a wall overnight. Bob Drogin, *Abuse Brings Deaths of Captives Into Focus*, L.A. Times, May 16, 2004. The US government has never officially acknowledged which techniques it uses. However, in a September 2006 speech, President Bush for the first time admitted that the CIA held high-value detainees in secret sites, and interrogated them using "an alternative set of procedures," which he described as "tough ... and safe ... and lawful ... and necessary." Office of the Press Secretary, The White House, *President Discusses Creation of Military Commissions to Try Suspected Terrorists*, September 6, 2006, available at <www.whitehouse.gov/news/releases/2006/09/ 20060906-3.html>. Subsequently, the government argued that revelation of the techniques could cause "exceptionally grave damage" to national security – so much so, that detainees should not be permitted to tell their own civilian lawyers what was done to them. Declaration of Marilyn A. Dorn, Information Review Officer, CIA, in Majid Khan v. George W. Bush, U.S. Dist. Court, District of Columbia, Civil Action 06-CV-1690, October 26, 2006, available at <http://balkin.blogspot.com/khan.dorn.aff.pdf>; Respondents' Memorandum in Opposition to Petitioner's Motion for Emergency Access to Counsel and Entry of Amended, Protective Order, in Khan v. Bush, available at <http://balkin.blogspot.com/khan.doj.brief.pdf>.

[19] Quoted in Alfred W. McCoy, *Cruel Science: CIA Torture & US Foreign Policy*, 19 New England J. Pub. Pol. 209, 219 (2005).

More important, perhaps, than authorizations of specific tactics are open-ended, tough-sounding directives that incite abuse without explicitly approving it, such as a 2003 email from headquarters to interrogators in Iraq: "The gloves are coming off, gentlemen, regarding these detainees. Col. Boltz has made it clear we want these individuals broken."[20] In response, a military interrogator named Lewis Welshofer accidentally smothered an uncooperative Iraqi general to death in a sleeping bag – a technique that he claimed his commanding officer approved. Welshofer was convicted of negligent homicide, for which he received a slap on the wrist: a written reprimand, two months' restriction to base, and forfeiture of $6,000 in pay. The commanding officer who approved the sleeping-bag interrogation suffered no adverse consequences.[21] Similarly, Manadel Jamadi, a suspected bombmaker, whose ice-packed body was photographed at Abu Ghraib next to a grinning soldier, was seized and roughed up by Navy SEALS in Iraq, then turned over to the CIA for questioning. At some point, either the SEALS or the CIA interrogator broke Jamadi's ribs; then he was hooded and hung by his wrists twisted behind his back until he died. The CIA operative has still not been charged two years after Jamadi's death. And the SEAL leader was acquitted, exulting afterward that "what makes this country great is that there is a system in place and it works."[22] It worked as well in another notorious case of prisoner abuse, when two young Afghanis

were found dead within days of each other, hanging by their shackled wrists in isolation cells at the [US military] prison in Bagram, north of Kabul. An Army investigation showed they were treated harshly by interrogators, deprived of sleep for days, and struck so often in the legs by guards that a coroner compared the injuries to being run over by a bus.[23]

The investigation stalled because "officers and soldiers at Bagram differed over what specific guidelines, if any, applied," an ambiguity that "confounded the Army's criminal investigation for months and ... gave the accused soldiers a defense ..."[24]

In addition to harsh interrogations by its own personnel, the United States has engaged in so-called "extraordinary renditions," where detainees are sent to other countries for interrogation by local authorities of sinister reputation.

---

[20] CBS News, *Death of a General*, April 9, 2006, available at <www.cbsnews.com/stories/2006/04/06/60minutes/main1476781_page2.shtml>.

[21] Ibid. See also David R. Irvine, *The Demise of Military Accountability*, Salt Lake Tribune, January 29, 2006.

[22] Jane Mayer, *A Deadly Interrogation*, The New Yorker, November 14, 2005; John McChesney, *The Death of an Iraqi Prisoner*, NPR's All Things Considered, October 27, 2005, available at <www.npr.org/templates/story/story.php?storyId=4977986>; Seth Hettena, *Navy SEAL Acquitted of Abusing Iraqi Prisoner Who Later Died*, Associated Press, May 28, 2005, available at <www.sfgate.com/cgi-bin/article.cgi?file=/news/archive/2005/05/27/state/n171730D65.DTL>.

[23] Tim Golden, *Years After 2 Afghans Died, Abuse Case Falters*, N.Y. Times, February 13, 2006.

[24] Ibid. at A11.

The practice, nicknamed "outsourcing torture," has existed since the Clinton administration, but accelerated dramatically in the War on Terror.[25] Several detainees, seized by mistake, rendered, and later released, describe torture inflicted on them.[26] In May 2006, the State Department's legal advisor made explicit what observers had long surmised: that US lawyers believe the Torture Convention's ban on returning people to states where they face torture does not cover cases where the person is rendered from a country other than the United States.[27]

Thus, "We don't torture" comes with an asterisked proviso: "It depends who you mean by 'we,' and it depends what you mean by 'torture.' " Likewise, "The United States obeys its legal obligations" comes with the unspoken qualification " . . . which is easy because we hardly have any." The provisos are the torture lawyers' handiwork. They allow politicians to profess great respect for law and human rights, while operating without the fetters that their noble words suggest.

How did we get there?

---

[25] Jane Mayer, *Outsourcing Torture*, The New Yorker, February 5, 2004. See also an interview with Michael Scheuer, an ex-CIA officer who helped develop the program: *"Die CIA hat das Recht, jedes Gesetz zu brechen": Darf der US-Geheimdienst mutmassliche Terroristen entführen? Michael Scheuer, ein Hauptverantwortlicher, gibt erstmals Antworten*, Die Zeit (Hamburg), December 28, 2005, available at <www.zeit.de/2006/01/M__Scheuer?page=5>. An English translation is available at <www.counterpunch.org/kleine01072006.html>.

An investigation has revealed, perhaps unsurprisingly, that several European countries whose governments expressed shock at revelations that their bases and airports formed part of the secret CIA rendition network actually were colluding with the United States. Council of Europe Parliamentary Assembly, Committee on Legal Affairs and Human Rights, *Alleged Secret Detentions and Unlawful Inter-State Transfers Involving Council of Europe Member States*, Draft report by Dick Marty, June 7, 2006, available at <http://assembly.coe.int/Main. asp?Link=/CommitteeDocs/2006/20060606_Ejdoc162006PartII-FINAL.htm>.

[26] The best-known is Maher Arar. See Mayer, *Outsourcing Torture*, supra note 25; Katherine R. Hawkins, *The Promises of Torturers: Diplomatic Assurances and the Legality of "Rendition"*, 20 Georgetown Imm. L. J. 213 (2006). Another was Khaled El-Masri, a German cab driver seized while on holiday in Macedonia, turned over to US agents, and held for months in Afghanistan. See *Extraordinary Rendition*, Harper's Mag., February 2006, at 21–24 (excerpting El-Masri's statement). His was a case of mistaken identity, which created a sensation in Germany after he was released. US courts refused to hear lawsuits filed by Arar and El-Masri, on the astonishing basis that revealing "state secrets" about gross government misconduct could embarrass the United States and therefore be bad for national security. Arar v. Ashcroft, 414 F.Supp.2d 250, 281–83 (E.D.N.Y. 2006); El-Masri v. Tenet, E.D. Va., Case 1:05cv1417 (memorandum opinion of Ellis, J., May 12, 2006). Another rendition victim, Laid Saidi, claims that his US captors transported him to Afghanistan, hung him by his wrists for five days, and released him only after sixteen months, Craig S. Smith & Souad Mekhennet, *Algerian Tells of Dark Odyssey in US Hands*, N.Y. Times, July 7, 2006 available at <www. nytimes.com/2006/07/07world/africa/07algeria.html?_r=1&oref=slogin>.

[27] List of Issues to Be Considered During the Examination of the Second Periodic Report of the United States of America: Response of the United States of America 32–37 (2006), available at <www.us-mission.ch/Press2006/CAT-May5.pdf>.

The post-9/11 legal response

The torture lawyers went into overdrive in the wake of the September 11 attacks, producing a flood of documents in a remarkably short time. As an article in the *New York Times* explains,

The administration's legal approach to terrorism began to emerge in the first turbulent days after Sept. 11, as the officials in charge of key agencies exhorted their aides to confront Al Qaeda's threat with bold imagination.

"Legally, the watchword became 'forward-leaning,' " said a former associate White House counsel, Bradford Berenson, "by which everybody meant: 'We want to be aggressive. We want to take risks.' "

The challenge resounded among young lawyers who were settling into important posts at the White House, the Justice Department and other agencies.[28]

As an example of "forward-leaning" legal strategy, the article cites an OLC memorandum by John Yoo on how to overcome constitutional objections to the use of military force against terrorists within the US, for example "to raid or attack dwellings where terrorists were thought to be, despite risks that third parties could be killed or injured by exchanges of fire."[29] Yoo wrote the memo just ten days after September 11. The article explains that "lawyers in the administration took the same 'forward-leaning' approach to making plans for the terrorists they thought would be captured."[30]

Related to the "forward-leaning" strategy is what Ron Suskind refers to as "the Cheney Doctrine" or "the one percent doctrine," allegedly formulated by the US Vice-President in November 2001. In Suskind's words, "If there was even a one percent chance of terrorists getting a weapon of mass destruction ... the United States must now act as if it were a certainty."[31] "It's not about our analysis, or finding a preponderance of evidence," Suskind quotes Cheney as saying. "It's about our response."[32] Suskind asserts that the Cheney Doctrine formed the guiding principle in the War on Terror. It carries far-reaching implications for the interrogation of captives: if even a minute chance of catastrophe must be treated as a certainty, every interrogation becomes a ticking time-bomb case – and

---

[28] Tim Golden, *After Terror, a Secret Rewriting of Military Law*, N.Y. Times, October 24, 2004, A1, at A12. The lawyers were political conservatives, mostly veterans of the Federalist Society and clerkships with Justices Scalia and Thomas, and Judge Laurence Silberman. Some sources for the article stated that their "strategy was also shaped by longstanding political agendas that had relatively little to do with fighting terrorism," such as strengthening executive power and halting US submission to international law. Ibid.

[29] Ibid. This memo has not yet been released or leaked.   [30] Ibid.

[31] Ron Suskind, The One Percent Doctrine: Deep Inside America's Pursuit of Its Enemies Since 9/11 62 (2006).

[32] Ibid.

ticking time-bomb cases are the one situation where many people who otherwise balk at torture reluctantly accept that breaking the taboo is morally justified.

The most crucial portions of the "forward-leaning" strategy – which included not only interrogation issues but military tribunals and the applicability of the Geneva Conventions as well – were formulated in near-total secrecy by a small group of like-minded Administration lawyers, intentionally excluding anticipated dissenters in the State Department and the JAG Corps.[33] Indeed, when the chief JAG officers of the four military services learned of the Bybee Memo months after the fact, they responded with forceful criticism and barbed reminders that "OLC does not represent the services; thus, understandably, concern for servicemembers is not reflected in their opinion."[34] The chief Air Force JAG reminded the Secretary of the Air Force that "the use of the more extreme interrogation techniques simply is not how the US armed forces have operated in recent history. We have taken the legal and moral 'high road' in the conduct of our military operations regardless of how others may operate."[35] (This, by the way, is exactly the kind of moral reminder that a good lawyer ought to give clients.) Nevertheless, where in past administrations OLC weighed in only after relevant federal agencies had addressed legal questions, now the OLC "frequently had a first and final say."[36] The Bush Administration took pains to bypass legal advice it did not want to hear, and Vice President Dick Cheney's lead counsel, David Addington, was particularly suspicious that JAGs are too independent.[37] In 2006 it emerged that Defense Secretary Donald Rumsfeld had quietly signed off on a torture-permissive working group report without ever notifying officials who objected to it (and who were in the working group), including Navy general counsel Alberto Mora. Mora had argued for months against cruel or degrading interrogation techniques. He thought he had won his argument when Defense Department general counsel William Haynes wrote a US Senator that the military would not use abusive tactics. But Haynes, who had previously approved intimidation with dogs, forced

---

[33] Golden, *After Terror, a Secret Rewriting of Military Law*, supra note 28, at 12–13.

[34] Memorandum from Brigadier General Kevin M. Sankuhler (USMC) for the General Counsel of the Air Force, February 27, 2003, reprinted in The Torture Debate, supra note 2, at 383.

[35] Memorandum from Major General Jack L. Rives for the Secretary of the Air Force, February 5, 2003, reprinted in The Torture Debate, supra note 2, at 378.

[36] Golden, *After Terror, a Secret Rewriting of Military Law*, supra note 28, at 13.

[37] Chitra Ragavan, *Cheney's Guy*, US News & World Report, May 29, 2006, available at <www.usnews.com/usnews/news/articles/060529/29addington.htm>. According to Ragavan, Addington has been the most powerful and influential of the torture lawyers, a view confirmed by many sources in Jane Mayer's detailed article on Addington: Jane Mayer, *The Hidden Power*, The New Yorker, July 6, 2006, available at <www.newyorker.com/fact/content/articles/060703fa_fact 1>.

nudity, and sleep deprivation, outmaneuvered Mora.[38] In the words of reporter Jane Mayer, "Legal critics within the Administration had been allowed to think that they were engaged in a meaningful process; but their deliberations appeared to have been largely an academic exercise, or, worse, a charade."[39] Nor did Abu Ghraib change the Bush Administration's desire to keep politically independent JAG officers out of the advisory loop. In response to Abu Ghraib, the US Congress enacted legislation that prohibited Defense Department officials from interfering with JAG officers offering independent legal advice.[40] But although President Bush signed the legislation, his signing statement implied that the executive branch would not abide by these prohibitions.[41]

The post-9/11 OLC used the catastrophe to advance an extraordinarily militant version of executive supremacy – an agenda that, even before 9/11, had preoccupied Yoo, Cheney, and Addington.[42] Just two weeks after 9/11, a Yoo memorandum concluded "that the President has the plenary constitutional power to take such military actions as he deems necessary and appropriate to respond to the terrorist attacks upon the United States on September 11, 2001." No statute, he added, "can place any limits on the President's determinations as to any terrorist threat, the amount of military force to be used in response, or the method, timing, and nature of the response. These decisions, under our Constitution, are for the President alone to make."[43] This bold assertion prefigures the Bybee Memo, because it clearly implies that the decision whether to torture would be "for the President alone to make." The conclusion reappeared in one of the Bybee Memo's most controversial sections, which argued that the criminal laws

---

[38] Mora's battle is described in Jane Mayer, *Annals of the Pentagon: The Memo*, The New Yorker, February 27, 2006, available at <www.newyorker.com/fact/content/articles/060227fa_fact>. Haynes's approval is in TP, supra note 1, at 237; the list of techniques he recommended is in TP, at 227–28.

[39] Mayer, *The Memo*, supra note 38. The working group report is in TP, supra note 1, at 241–359.

[40] 10 U.S.C. §§ 3037, 5046, 5148, and 8037.

[41] Statement on signing the Ronald W. Reagan National Defense Authorization Act for Fiscal Year 2005, October 28, 2004, available at <www.highbeam.com/library/docfree.asp?DOCID=1G1:125646055&ctrlInfo=Round19%3AMode19b%3ADocG%3AResult&ao=>. On Bush's use of signing statements, see Charlie Savage, *Bush Challenges Hundreds of Laws*, Boston Globe, April 30, 2006, available at <www.boston.com/news/nation/articles/2006/04/30/bush_challenges_hundreds_of_laws/?>.

[42] In an article about Addington, Chitra Ragavan writes, "The 9/11 attacks became the crucible for the administration's commitment to restoring presidential power and prerogative." Ragavan, supra note 37. Mayer likewise emphasizes that Addington and his boss Dick Cheney both believe that the presidency had been wrongly weakened from the Nixon administration on. Mayer, *The Hidden Power*, supra note 37.

[43] Memorandum from John C. Yoo to Timothy Flanigan, Deputy Counsel to the President, September 25, 2001, reprinted in TP, supra note 1, at 24.

against torture could not be enforced against interrogators authorized by the President.[44]

One of the first steps the Administration took was to strip Geneva Convention protections from Al Qaeda and Taliban captives (a position eventually rejected by the Supreme Court in June 2006, when the Court held that common Article 3 of Geneva applies in the War on Terror and therefore protects even Al Qaeda captives).[45] In January 2002, OLC concluded that the President has unilateral authority to suspend the Geneva Conventions, and that customary international law (which incorporates Geneva protections) has no purchase on US domestic law – a deeply controversial position favored by some conservative academics but never accepted by mainstream lawyers or the Supreme Court.[46] In any event, two memos argued, the Geneva Conventions do not apply to Al Qaeda or the Taliban, because Al Qaeda is not a state and the Taliban were unlawful combatants. The President quickly adopted this position.[47] However, the President added, because "our Nation has been and will continue to be a strong supporter of Geneva and its principles ... the United States Armed Forces shall continue to treat detainees humanely and, to the extent appropriate and consistent with military necessity, in a manner consistent with the principles of Geneva."[48] Critics quickly noticed that this order applies only to the armed forces, not the CIA, and that the phrase "consistent with military necessity" creates a loophole for harsh interrogation. The carefully crafted phrasing, which makes the document superficially appear more protective of detainees than it actually is, was more handiwork of the White House torture lawyers. A few months later, Attorney General Gonzales qualified the protection even more dramatically when he stated that "humane" treatment of detainees need consist of nothing more than providing them food, clothing, shelter, and medical care.[49]

Stripping away Geneva protections from the detainees was crucial to all the further work of the torture lawyers. It was essential that as few

---

[44] Memorandum from Jay S. Bybee to Alberto R. Gonzales, August 1, 2002 [henceforth: Bybee Memo], reprinted in TP, supra note 1, at 204.

[45] Hamdan v. Rumsfeld, 2006 Lexis 5185 (June 29, 2006), at *124–9.

[46] Memorandum from Bybee to Gonzales, January 22, 2002, reprinted in TP, supra note 1, at 91, 93, 112–13.

[47] Ibid.; memorandum from Bybee to Gonzales, February 7, 2002, in TP, supra note 1, at 136; Memorandum from President Bush to the Vice-President and other officials, February 7, 2002, in TP, supra note 1, at 134–35.

[48] Ibid. at 135.

[49] "The President said – for example on March 31, 2003 – that he expects detainees to be treated humanely. As you know, the term 'humanely' has no precise legal definition. As a policy matter, I would define humane treatment as a basic level of decent treatment that includes such things as food, shelter, clothing, and medical care." Written response of Alberto R. Gonzales to questions posed by Senator Edward M. Kennedy, question #15, January 2005.

detainees as possible be classified as prisoners of war under the Third Geneva Convention, because POW status protects them not only from torture but from all forms of coercive questioning. Indeed, Article 17 provides that "prisoners of war who refuse to answer may not be threatened, insulted, or exposed to unpleasant or disadvantageous treatment of any kind." Stripping away common Article 3 protections against torture and humiliation was equally essential if harsh interrogators were to avoid war crimes charges: as we have seen, violations of common Article 3, like grave breaches of the Geneva Conventions, were war crimes under federal law. Bybee and Yoo argued that because the global war on terror (the "GWOT") is international, common Article 3 does not apply, because Article 3 is limited to armed conflicts "not of an international character."[50] (This is the interpretation the Supreme Court eventually rejected in June 2006.) These early opinions set the stage for the torture memos that followed.

The Bybee Torture Memo

Unquestionably, the Bybee Memo is the most notorious of the memos and advisory opinions dealing with abuse of detainees. According to John Yoo, the memo was written because the CIA wanted guidance on how far it could go interrogating high-value Al Qaeda detainees; the United States had already captured Abu Zubaydah, believed by some to be a top Al Qaeda leader.[51] Apparently, the CIA wanted to go quite far. Abu Zubaydah's captors reportedly withheld pain medication from him – he was wounded when he was captured – and the CIA wanted to know whether it would be illegal to waterboard him.[52] Evidently, eager as CIA interrogators might have been to

---

[50] Memorandum from Jay S. Bybee to Alberto Gonzales and William Haynes II, January 22, 2002, TP, supra note 1, at 85–89.

[51] Yoo interview on Frontline, supra note 5.

[52] Don Van Natta et al., Questioning Terror Suspects in a Dark and Surreal World, N.Y. Times, March 9, 2003, at A1; Douglas Jehl & David Johnston, White House Fought New Curbs on Interrogations, Officials Say, N.Y. Times, January 13, 2005, A1, A16. Suskind reports that Zubaydah received first-rate medical care, but quotes a CIA official who said, "He received the finest medical attention on the planet. We got him in very good health, so we could start to torture him." Suskind, supra note 31, at 100. Suskind also describes "[CIA Director George] Tenet's months of pressure on his legal team" to permit harsh interrogation. Ibid. at 100–1. See also Dana Priest, Covert CIA Program Withstands New Furor, Wash. Post, December 30, 2005, at A1 (describing aggressive positions taken by CIA lawyers). The Zubaydah interrogation, however, proved disappointing: Zubaydah proved not to be a big fish – an FBI specialist on Al Qaeda described him as a meet-and-greet guy, "Joe Louis in the lobby of Caesar's Palace, shaking hands." Suskind, at 100. Furthermore, he was insane. Ibid. at 95–96, 100. Eventually, he revealed the name of dirty-bomb suspect Jose Padilla – but only after harsh interrogation had stopped and interrogators switched to a different tactic, arguing religion with Zubaydah. Ibid. at 116–17. Suskind's account contradicts President Bush's assertion that

take the gloves off, they were unwilling to do so without a legal opinion to back them up. OLC did not disappoint. But it would be a mistake to suppose that OLC was acting on its own: lawyers and other officials in the White House, the Vice-President's office, and the National Security Council also vetted the torture memo.[53]

The Bybee Memo provided maximum reassurance of impunity to nervous interrogators. It concluded that inflicting physical pain does not count as torture until the pain reaches the level associated with organ failure or death; that inflicting mental pain is lawful unless the interrogator specifically intends it to last months or years beyond the interrogation; that utilizing techniques known to be painful is not torture unless the interrogator specifically intends the pain to be equivalent to the pain accompanying organ failure or death; that enforcing criminal laws against Presidentially authorized torturers would be unconstitutional; that self-defense includes torturing helpless detainees in the name of national defense; and that torture in the name of national security may be legally justifiable as the lesser evil, through the doctrine of necessity.

These conclusions range from the doubtful to the loony. Some can be supported by conventional, if debatable, legal arguments. These include the analysis of mental torture, which has some support in the language of the statute, and the discussion of specific intent, where OLC seizes on one of two standard readings of the doctrine but, quoting authorities quite selectively, ignores the other.

Others, however, have the mad logic of the Queen of Hearts' arguments with Alice. The analysis of self-defense, for example, inverts a doctrine permitting last-resort defensive violence against assailants into a rationale for waterboarding bound and helpless prisoners. OLC cites no conventional legal authority for this inversion, for the simple reason that there is none. Although OLC claimed to base its analysis on the teachings of "leading scholarly commentators" (again: "some commentators"), in fact there is only one such commentator, and OLC flatly misrepresents what he says.[54] Although

---

"alternative interrogation procedures" were "necessary" to break Zubaydah. Bush speech, supra note 18.

[53] Dana Priest, *CIA Puts Harsh Tactics on Hold*, Wash. Post, June 27, 2004, A1.

[54] The commentator is Michael S. Moore, *Torture and the Balance of Evils*, 23 Israel L. Rev. 280, 323 (1989). Here is what OLC says: "Leading scholarly commentators believe that interrogation of such individuals using methods that might violate [the anti-torture statute] would be justified under the doctrine of self-defense." TP, supra note 1, at 211, citing to Moore. And here is what Moore actually says on the page OLC cites: "*The literal law of self-defense is not available to justify their torture.* But the principle uncovered as the moral basis of the defense may be applicable" (emphasis added). OLC states that "the doctrine of self-defense" would justify torture, where Moore says, quite literally, the opposite. Note also the difference between OLC's assertive "would be justified" and Moore's cautious "may be applicable."

Professors Eric Posner and Adrian Vermeule quickly published a *Wall Street Journal* op-ed describing the Memo's arguments as "standard lawyerly fare, routine stuff,"[55] theirs was a distinctly minority view that seemed plainly to be an exercise in political damage control.[56] By ordinary lawyerly standards, the Bybee Memo was, in Peter Brooks's words, "textual interpretation run amok – less 'lawyering as usual' than the work of some bizarre literary deconstructionist."[57] Even the OLC – after Jack Goldsmith (a sometimes co-author of Professor Posner) took over from Jay Bybee – did not regard the Bybee Memo as standard lawyerly fare. In an unusual move, it publicly repudiated the Memo a few months after it was leaked.

This is not the place to offer a detailed analysis of the Bybee Memo (which I have done elsewhere).[58] To illustrate its eccentricity, I will pick just two examples: the organ-failure definition of "severe pain," and one curious portion of its discussion of the necessity defense.

The amazing fact about the organ-failure definition is that Yoo and his co-authors based it on a Medicare statute that has nothing whatsoever to do with torture. The statute defines an emergency medical condition as one in which someone experiences symptoms that "a prudent lay person ... could reasonably expect" might indicate "serious impairment to bodily functions, or serious dysfunction of any bodily organ or part." The statute specifies that severe pain is one such symptom. In an exquisite exercise of legal formalism run amok, the Memo infers that pain is severe only if it is at the level indicating an emergency medical condition. The authors solemnly cite a

---

[55] Eric Posner & Adrian Vermeule, *A "Torture" Memo and Its Tortuous Critics*, Wall St. J., July 6, 2004.

[56] The Bybee Memorandum provoked a flurry of commentary, almost entirely negative. Along with my own paper *Liberalism, Torture, and the Ticking Bomb*, in The Torture Debate, supra note 2, see, e.g., Julie Angell, *Ethics, Torture, and Marginal Memoranda at the DOJ Office of Legal Counsel*, 18 Geo. J. Legal Ethics 557 (2005); Richard B. Bilder & Detlev A. Vagts, *Speaking Law to Power: Lawyers and Torture*, 98 A.J.I.L. 689 (2004); Kathleen Clark, *Ethical Issues Raised by the OLC Torture Memorandum*, 1 J. Nat'l Security L. & Pol'y 455 (2005); Kathleen Clark & Julie Mertus, *Torturing the Law: The Justice Department's Legal Contortions on Interrogation*, Wash. Post, June 20, 2004, at B3; Christopher Kutz, *The Lawyers Know Sin: Complicity in Torture*, in The Torture Debate, supra note 2, at 241; Jesselyn Radack, *Tortured Legal Ethics: The Role of the Government Advisor in the War on Terrorism*, 77 U. Colo. L. Rev. 1 (2006); Michael D. Ramsey, *Torturing Executive Power*, 93 Geo. L. J. 1213 (2005); Robert K. Vischer, *Legal Advice as Moral Perspective*, 19 Geo. J. Legal Ethics 225 (2006); Jeremy Waldron, *Torture and the Common Law: Jurisprudence for the White House*, 105 Colum. L. Rev. 1681 (2005); Ruth Wedgwood & R. James Woolsey, *Law and Torture*, Wall St. J., June 28, 2004; W. Bradley Wendell, *Legal Ethics and the Separation of Law and Morals*, 91 Cornell L. Rev. 67 (2005).

[57] Peter Brooks, *The Plain Meaning of Torture?*, Slate, February 9, 2005, available at <www.slate.com/id/2113314>.

[58] I offer a detailed analysis of the Memo in *Liberalism, Torture, and the Ticking Bomb*, in The Torture Debate, supra note 2, at 55–68.

Supreme Court decision to show that Congress's use of a phrase in one statute should be used to interpret its meaning in another. Months later, when OLC withdrew the Bybee Memo and substituted the Levin Memo, the substitute memo rejected this argument and pointed out the obvious: that the Medicare statute was a definition of an emergency medical condition, not of severe pain, and the difference in context precludes treating it as an implicit definition of severe pain.[59] The organ-failure definition, perhaps more than any other portion of the Bybee Memo, involved lawyering that cannot be taken seriously. It seems obvious that OLC lawyers simply did an electronic search of the phrase "severe pain" in the United States Code and came up with the healthcare statutes (the only ones other than torture-related statutes in the entire Code to employ the phrase). Then they decided to see how clever they could get. The result is a parody of legal analysis.

The discussion of the necessity defense is bizarre for a different reason. Looked at dispassionately, necessity offers the strongest defense of torture on normative grounds. The necessity defense justifies otherwise criminal conduct undertaken to prevent a greater evil, and in extreme cases it is at least thinkable that torture might be the lesser evil.[60]

However, the Bybee Memo's authors were not content to argue for the possibility of the necessity defense. They also threw in an argument that even though the necessity defense is available to torturers, it would not necessarily be available in cases of abortion to save a woman's life.[61] At this point, the

---

[59] Levin Memo, in The Torture Debate, supra note 2, at 367–68, note 17.

[60] I should also note, however, that the claim that the necessity defense is available for the crime of torture runs flatly contrary to the official opinion of the United States government in its 1999 report to the UN Committee Against Torture, a fact that the Bybee Memo chooses not to mention: "US law contains no provision permitting otherwise prohibited acts of torture or other cruel, inhuman or degrading treatment or punishment to be employed on grounds of exigent circumstances (for example, during a 'state of public emergency') or on orders from a superior officer or public authority." Available at <www.state.gov/www/global/human_ rights/torture_intro.html>. The Memo also ignores a Supreme Court opinion decided just three months earlier asserting that it is an "open question" whether the necessity defense is ever available for a federal crime without the statute specifically making it available (and the Court's language suggests that the answer might turn out to be no). United States v. Oakland Cannabis Buyers' Coop, 532 U.S. 483, 490 (2001). I am grateful to Marty Lederman for calling these documents to my attention.

[61] Bybee Memo, in TP, supra note 1, at 209. In addition to its blatant political pandering, the argument is also garbled to the point of incoherence. When Congress enacted the US anti-torture statutes, it broadened CAT's definition of torture. Whereas CAT defines torture as the infliction of severe pain for reasons such as interrogation, intimidation, punishment, or discrimination, the US statute drops these reasons and bans torture regardless of why it is inflicted. Congress decided that all torture is criminal, not just torture for certain reasons. In other words, Congress evidently concluded that nothing can justify torture. OLC reads the Congressional emendation of CAT's language in the opposite way, concluding that "Congress has not explicitly made a determination of values vis-à-vis torture." This sentence is opaque

partisan political nature of the document becomes too obvious to ignore. It
is the moment when the clock strikes thirteen. Opposition to abortion was
an article of faith in the Ashcroft Justice Department, and apparently the
OLC lawyers decided to try for a "two-fer" – not only providing a
necessity defense for torture, but throwing in a clever hip-check to forestall
any possibility that their handiwork might be commandeered to justify life-
saving abortions if a legislature ever voted to outlaw them. Even abortion
opponents are likely to balk at the thought that torture might be a lesser evil
than abortion to save a mother's life. But this was the conclusion that the
OLC aimed to preserve.

The Levin Memo

But Bybee's is not the only torture memo that deserves similar judgments. On
the eve of Alberto Gonzales's confirmation hearing as Attorney General, the
Justice Department abruptly withdrew the Bybee Memo and replaced it with
another OLC opinion, the Levin Memo.[62] OLC lawyer Daniel Levin vehe-
mently denounced torture, retracted Bybee's specific intent analysis, rejected
the "organ failure" definition of severe pain, and no longer argued that it
would be unconstitutional to prosecute Presidentially authorized torturers. In
all these respects, the Levin Memo sounded more moderate than Bybee, and
perhaps restored a measure of credibility to the OLC. Furthermore, the Levin
Memo does not indulge in stretched, bizarre, or sophistical arguments – with
one striking exception I shall note shortly.

Read closely, however, the Levin Memo makes only minimum cosmetic
changes to the bits of Bybee that drew the worst publicity. Levin does not
point out the weaknesses in Bybee's criminal-defense arguments; he simply
never discusses possible defenses to criminal charges of torture.[63] The memo
likewise ducks the presidential-power question rather than changing Bybee's
answer. And, although Levin explicitly contradicts Bybee's conclusion that
pain must be excruciating to be severe, every one of the Memo's illustrations
of "severe pain" is, in fact, excruciating: "severe beatings to the genitals,
head, and other parts of the body with metal pipes, brass knuckles, batons, a
baseball bat, and various other items; removal of teeth with pliers ... cutting
off ... fingers, pulling out ... fingernails" and similar atrocities.[64] These

and clumsy; it is hard to speak clearly when you are fudging. The next sentence is even worse,
bordering on gibberish: "In fact, Congress explicitly removed efforts to remove torture from
the weighing of values permitted by the necessity defense."

[62] It is reproduced in The Torture Debate, supra note 2, at 361.

[63] He does say that "there is no exception under the statute permitting torture to be used for a
'good reason.'" Ibid. at 376. This might be read to suggest that the defenses of necessity and
self-defense are unavailable, but the context suggests otherwise.

[64] Ibid. at 369.

barbaric illustrations are the only operational guidance Levin has to offer on how to tell when pain is "severe," and they obviously suggest that milder techniques are not torture. While Levin's legal reasoning marks a return to normalcy, the opinion provides ample cover for interrogators who "merely" waterboard detainees or deprive them of sleep for weeks. Indeed, Levin specifically states that he has "reviewed this Office's prior opinions addressing issues involving treatment of detainees and do[es] not believe that any of their conclusions would be different under the standards set forth in this memorandum."[65] This includes another, still secret, August 2002 OLC opinion on specific interrogation techniques used by the CIA, believed to include waterboarding.[66]

Indeed, at one point the Levin Memo indulges in the kind of frivolous statutory interpretation that was the hallmark of the Bybee Memo it replaced – and that is a carefully crafted paragraph that reads a nonexistent word into the torture statute which would render it inapplicable to waterboarding.[67] Recall that the torture statutes define torture to include both severe physical pain and severe physical suffering. Waterboarding, by duplicating the experiences of drowning, would presumably fall under the "suffering" prong of this definition rather than the "pain" prong. And the suffering must indeed be severe: according to CIA sources, Khalid Sheikh Mohammed, the architect of 9/11, "won the admiration of interrogators when he was able to last between two and two-and-a-half minutes before begging to confess"; CIA agents who underwent waterboarding all broke in less than fifteen seconds.[68]

Enter the Levin Memo, which concludes that "to constitute torture, '*severe* physical suffering' would have to be a condition of some extended

[65] Ibid. at 362, note 8.

[66] See *Opening Statement of Senator Carl Levin at the Personnel Subcommittee Hearing on Military Commissions, Detainees and Interrogation Procedures*, July 14, 2005, available at <www.senate.gov/~levin/newsroom/release.cfm?id=240601> (referring to a second, still secret, Bybee memorandum). Bush Administration officials also stated that Michael Chertoff, then head of the Justice Department's Criminal Division, consulted on the second Bybee memorandum, which reportedly permitted waterboarding. David Johnston, Neil Lewis & Douglas Jehl, *Security Nominee Gave Advice to the C.I.A. on Torture Laws*, N.Y. Times, January 29, 2005, available at <www.nytimes.com/2005/01/29/politics/29home.html?page-wan-ted=1&ei=5090&en=8b261a9df1338e4a&ex=1264741200&partner=rssuserland>.

[67] I am grateful to Marty Lederman for pointing out the connection between this portion of the Levin Memo and waterboarding. See Lederman, *Yes, It's a No-Brainer: Waterboarding Is Torture*, Balkinization, October 28, 2006, available at <http://balkin.blogspot.com/2006/10/yes-its-no-brainer-waterboarding-is.html>.

[68] Brian Ross & Richard Esposito, *CIA's Harsh Interrogation Techniques Described*, ABC News, Nov. 18, 2005, available at <http://abcnews.go.com/WNT/Investigation/story?id=1322866&page=1>. On the treatment of KSM, see James Risen, State of War: The Secret History of the CIA and the Bush Administration 32–33 (2006). Risen asserts that CIA agents inflicted hundreds of abuses each week on KSM, and quotes one source who said that it was the accumulation of so many abuses that made the interrogation program torture.

duration or persistence as well as intensity."[69] That would exclude any technique that breaks victims in a matter of seconds or minutes, such as waterboarding. But in fact, the torture statute contains no mention whatever of "extended duration or persistence." This is especially striking because the statute does state that *mental* pain and suffering must be "prolonged" to count as torture – but it never says that physical pain or suffering must be prolonged. The authors of the Levin Memo simply made up the duration requirement out of whole cloth.

The Beaver Memo

Next consider the memorandum written for the Defense Department by LTC Diane Beaver (a JAG legal advisor at Guantánamo), on the legality of specific interrogation techniques. Like the Bybee Memo, Beaver's was written to respond to a specific request by interrogators who were having a hard time "breaking" a high-value Al Qaeda detainee; it was then forwarded to the Pentagon. In this case, the detainee was Mohammed Al-Kahtani (or Qahtani), one of the so-called "twentieth hijackers" who tried but failed to participate in 9/11. Kahtani was detained at Guantánamo, and in 2002 a series of requests went from Guantánamo to Washington for approval of harsh interrogation techniques.[70] Eventually, Kahtani was subjected to a wide variety of sexual humiliations, intensive sleep deprivation (20-hour-a-day interrogations for 48 out of 54 days, interrupted only when Kahtani's pulse-rate plummeted), and months of isolation. He was shot up with three-and-a-half bags of intravenous fluid and forced to urinate on himself; leashed and made to do dog tricks; threatened with working dogs (a technique specifically approved by Defense Secretary Donald Rumsfeld, who closely followed the interrogation of Kahtani[71]); straddled by a female interrogator who taunted him about the deaths of other Al Qaeda members; made to wear a thong on his head and a bra; stripped naked in front of women; and bombarded with ear-splitting "futility music" (the Army's term) by Metallica and Britney Spears.[72] A subsequent US Army report concluded that none of these

---

[69] The Torture Debate, supra note 2, at 371.   [70] TP, supra note 1, at 223–28.

[71] Michael Scherer & Mark Benjamin, *What Rumsfeld Knew*, Salon.com, April 14, 2006, available at <www.salon.com/news/feature/2006/04/14/rummy/index_np.html>. This article is based on an Army inspector-general's report Salon obtained through the Freedom of Information Act.

[72] These techniques (and the Army's judgment that they were approved) are described in the Army's own report, the so-called Schmidt Report, supra note 17. Most of this report remains classified, but a thirty-page summary has been released and is available at <www.defenselink.mil/news/Jul2005/d20050714report.pdf>. See also Adam Zagorin *et al.*, *Inside the Interrogation of Detainee 063*, and *Excerpts from an Interrogation Log*, both in Time Mag., June 20, 2005. The forced urination is described in the latter articles but not in the Schmidt Report.

techniques is "inhumane."[73] (Nor is "futility music" the most bizarre Guantánamo tactic: FBI agents have reported seeing interrogators force detainees to watch homosexual porn movies.[74])

Some of these techniques, including the dog threats, leading detainees around on a leash, placing women's underwear on detainees' heads and forced nudity, migrated to Abu Ghraib, where soldiers memorialized them in photos that soon became notorious throughout the world. In General Randall Schmidt's words, "Just for the lack of a camera, it would sure look like Abu Ghraib."[75] Compelling evidence suggests that the migration resulted when the Guantánamo commander, General Geoffrey Miller, was sent to Iraq to "Gitmoize" intelligence operations there (although Miller denies it).[76] If so, the implications are enormous: it would mean that Abu Ghraib does not represent merely the spontaneous crimes of low-level sadists, but rather the unauthorized spillover of techniques deliberately exported from Guantánamo to Iraq as a high-level policy decision.[77] That would imply a direct causal pathway connecting the advice of the torture lawyers to the Abu Ghraib abuses via General Miller. (A former State Department official traces the policy back to Cheney's then general counsel David Addington.[78])

Beaver labeled her memorandum a "legal brief" on counter-resistance strategies, and a brief rather than an impartial legal analysis is indeed what she wrote. Beaver rightly observes that interrogations must meet US constitutional standards under the Eighth Amendment. To identify these

---

[73] Schmidt Report, supra note 17.
[74] See documents obtained under the Freedom of Information Act by the ACLU, available at <www.aclu.org/torturefoia>.
[75] Quoted in Michael Scherer & Mark Benjamin, supra note 71.
[76] Janice Karpinski, the commander of the Military Police unit implicated in the Abu Ghraib abuses, claims that General Miller told her his job was to "GTMO-ize" or "Gitmoize" Abu Ghraib; Miller denies he ever used that phrase. Mark Benjamin, *Not So Fast, General*, Salon. com, March 7, 2006, available at <www.salon.com/news/feature/2006/03/07/major_general/index_np.html>. However, the mandate Miller received from Rumsfeld was to replicate his Gitmo intelligence successes in Iraq. John Barry *et al. The Roots of Torture*, Newsweek, May 24, 2004; see also Josh White, *Army General Advocated Using Dogs at Abu Ghraib, Officer Testifies*, Wash. Post, July 28, 2005, at A18 (testimony by top MP operations officer at Abu Ghraib that Miller "was sent over by the secretary of defense to take their interrogation techniques they used at Guantánamo Bay and incorporate them into Iraq"). The Fay-Jones Report on Abu Ghraib likewise concludes that it is possible that interrogation techniques had migrated from Guantánamo to Abu Ghraib. TP, supra note 1, at 1004. And Donald Rumsfeld briefed Miller on the Department of Defense's working group report on interrogation techniques. Mayer, *The Memo*, supra note 38. According to one released detainee, inmates received the worst treatment during Miller's command at Guantánamo. Michelle Norris, *Leaving Guantánamo: Enduring a Harsh Stay*, NPR's All Things Considered, May 22, 2006.
[77] For analysis along these lines, see Mark Danner, Torture and Truth (2004).
[78] *Former Powell Aide Links Cheney's Office to Abuse Directives*, Int'l Herald-Tribune, November 3, 2005.

standards, she analyzes the 1992 Supreme Court decision *Hudson v. McMillian*.[79] *Hudson* addressed the question whether mistreatment of prisoners must cause serious injury to violate the constitutional prohibition on cruel and unusual punishment, and its answer is no: even minor injuries can violate the Eighth Amendment if guards inflict them for no good reason. (A good reason would consist of subduing a violent inmate.) Beaver's analysis of the case virtually flips it upside down, and the message she draws from *Hudson* is that mistreatment is unconstitutional only if there is no "good faith legitimate governmental interest" at stake and the interrogator acted "maliciously or sadistically for the very purpose of causing harm."[80] Obviously, any interrogation technique, no matter how brutal, passes this test if the interrogator's sole purpose is to extract intelligence. Beaver inverted a Supreme Court decision designed to broaden the protections of prisoners and read it to narrow them dramatically.

And indeed, Beaver proceeded to legitimize every proposed technique, including "the use of a wet towel to induce the misperception of suffocation" – a version of waterboarding. Oddly, Beaver adds that "The use of physical contact with the detainee ... will technically constitute an assault," but immediately goes on to "recommend that the proposed methods of interrogation be approved."[81] In other words, her memo on the legality of interrogation techniques concludes by recommending government approval of a felony.

The Draft Article 49 Opinion

After Jay Bybee's departure, Jack Goldsmith, a distinguished University of Chicago law professor (now a Harvard law professor), took over the leadership of OLC. Goldsmith took several courageous stands against Administration hard-liners, stands for which he reportedly had to withstand the fury of David Addington, Cheney's volcanic general counsel, regarded by many as the hardest of hard-liners.[82] As early as December 2003, before the Abu Ghraib scandal and the leak of the Bybee Memo, Goldsmith advised the government not to rely on a March 2003 memo by John Yoo that had directly influenced the Defense Department's working group on interrogation.[83] And it was under Goldsmith's leadership that OLC

---

[79] 503 U.S. 1 (1992).   [80] TP, supra note 1, at 232.   [81] Ibid. at 235.

[82] Daniel Kleidman, Stuart Taylor, Jr., & Evan Thomas, *Palace Revolt*, Newsweek, Feb. 6, 2006. On David Addington's role, see Ragavan, supra note 37, and Mayer, *The Hidden Power*, supra note 37.

[83] In February 2005, OLC formally retracted this latter Yoo memorandum. OLC letter from Daniel Levin to William J. Haynes II, February 5, 2005, regarding the Yoo memorandum of March 14, 2003. So far as I know, this letter is unpublished, but I have a PDF of the signed letter; and a link to the PDF may be found in Marty Lederman's blog at http://balkin.blogspot.

repudiated the Bybee Memo. Some regard Goldsmith as an unsung hero in the torture debates.

Nevertheless, Goldsmith too drafted a memorandum that exemplifies the kind of loophole legalism I object to in the other memoranda. (Let me emphasize, however, that Goldsmith's draft was never given final approval, and that could indicate that Goldsmith thought better of it.) Written in March 2004, it concerned the question of whether detainees in Iraq could be temporarily sent out of the country for interrogation, despite plain language in Article 49 of the Fourth Geneva Convention stating:

Individual or mass forcible transfers, as well as deportations of protected persons from occupied territory to the territory of the Occupying Power or to that of any other country, occupied or not, are prohibited, regardless of their motive.[84]

Goldsmith divided the memo into two sections, one on whether Article 49 would prevent US authorities from deporting illegal aliens in Iraq "pursuant to local immigration law," and one on whether removing protected civilians from Iraq for interrogation violates Article 49.

In answer to the first question, Goldsmith contends that the drafters of Article 49 could not have meant to ban the removal of illegal aliens under an occupied state's immigration law. That conclusion sounds uncontroversial. But we shouldn't forget that during World War II, the removal of illegal aliens under an occupied state's immigration law included deporting stateless Jewish refugees from Vichy France to death camps in the East. The Vichy

com/2005/09/silver-linings-or-strange-but-true.html>, which also provides a useful chronology and analysis. The March 14, 2003 Yoo memorandum has not been released or leaked. Levin's letter mentions that twenty-four interrogation techniques are still approved; the implication is that the Yoo memorandum okayed techniques that OLC no longer approves.

[84] The *Washington Post* reports that Goldsmith had written an opinion five months earlier concluding that a ghost detainee named Rashul could not be removed from Iraq. By that time the CIA had already spirited Rashul away to Afghanistan, and after Goldsmith's opinion they quickly returned him to Iraq. According to an intelligence source, "That case started the CIA yammering to Justice to get a better memo." Dana Priest, *Memo Lets CIA Take Detainees Out of Iraq*, Wash. Post, October 24, 2004, A1, A21. However, Professor Goldsmith has informed me that this account is seriously defective: there was no previous memo on the topic, and he did not give in to any pressure. (Private e-mail communications, August 27 and 29, 2006.) The CIA's deputy inspector general "told others she was offended that the CIA's general counsel had worked to secure a secret Justice Department opinion in 2004 authorizing the agency's creation of 'ghost detainees' – prisoners removed from Iraq for secret interrogations without notice to the International Committee of the Red Cross – because the Geneva Conventions prohibit such practices." R. Jeffrey Smith, *Fired Officer Believed CIA Lied to Congress*, Wash. Post, May 14, 2006. Priest's article states that even though the draft was never released, the CIA relied on it to remove a dozen Iraqis from the country. However, other sources assert that the dozen detainees were not Iraqis. Douglas Jehl, *The Conflict in Iraq: Prisoners; U.S. Action Bars Rights of Some Captured in Iraq*, N.Y. Times, October 26, 2004.

government and the German occupation authorities made a point of beginning with stateless Jews, in order to fit the deportations under the rubrics of immigration law.[85] It's a little hard to believe that the drafters of Article 49 were oblivious to the Nazis' studied policy of using immigration law to facilitate the deportation of Jews to Auschwitz.[86] In this matter, a little historical sense would perhaps have given some moral clarity to the role of OLC in approving the removal of "illegal aliens" from Iraq. Goldsmith's argument would have legalized the deportation of Anne Frank.

For that matter, Goldsmith never questions whether forcible removal by US forces of foreign captives taken in Iraq actually *does* accord with Iraqi immigration law. It doesn't sound terribly likely, unless some conscientious American lawyer hastily rewrote Iraqi immigration law. Without the unarticulated premise that the US interest in Article 49 is nothing more than learning its implications for immigration enforcement, this portion of the memo has no point – unless, perhaps, "enforcement of immigration law" is the legal hook on which rendition of foreign insurgents hangs.

Goldsmith then turns to the question of whether Article 49 forbids sending Iraqi captives outside the country for interrogation, to which his answer is no. First he argues that "transfer" and "deportation" both imply permanent or at least long-term uprooting, not temporary removal for interrogation. To show this, he quotes authorities who indicate that uprooting and resettling people violates Article 49.[87] However, none of his sources suggests that resettlements are the *only* forcible transfers or deportations that violate Article 49, and so this argument by itself amounts to very little.

To show that Article 49 permits temporary transfers, Goldsmith argues that reading Article 49 to forbid all forcible transfers is inconsistent with Article 24, which says that occupiers must facilitate the reception of youthful war orphans in a neutral state.[88] If Article 24 permits occupiers to evacuate war orphans, he reasons, then Article 49 cannot possibly mean to forbid *all* forcible transfers, such as sending Iraqi nationals to Afghanistan for interrogation.

Unsurprisingly, no commentator before Goldsmith ever noticed an "inconsistency" between the duty to evacuate war orphans and the obligation not to deport or forcibly transfer captives. No one would reasonably describe

---

[85] This was the accord between Vichy and the Nazis of July 4, 1942, described in Michael R. Marrus & Robert O. Paxton, Vichy France and the Jews 249 (1981).

[86] Indeed, embedded in a footnote, Goldsmith quotes a Norwegian delegate "regarding the plight of 'ex-German Jews denationalized by the German Government who found themselves in territories subsequently occupied by the German Army'" TP, supra note 1, at 376 note 11. The trouble is that Goldsmith's sole point in including this quotation is to buttress his argument that deportation implies denationalization. He overlooks the more important point: the horrific history of using immigration law as a fig leaf for something far more sinister.

[87] TP, supra note, 1, at 376.   [88] TP, at 376–77.

parents sending their child to safety as a "forcible transfer" or "deportation." Nor, therefore, is it a forcible transfer or deportation when a child is moved out of harm's way by responsible adults acting *in loco parentis*. The authorities acting *in loco parentis*, not the child, are the responsible decision-maker, so long as they are aiming at the child's well-being. Goldsmith's analogy between captives sent to be interrogated and children sent to safety boggles the mind – and that analogy is the sole basis of his argument that if Geneva doesn't forbid the latter it doesn't forbid the former. Like the Bybee Memo's organ-failure definition of "severe pain," this is legal formalism divorced from sense.

A second argument dispenses more senseless formalism. Goldsmith turns to two other Geneva articles, one protecting impressed laborers and the other protecting people detained for crimes. Among their protections, both articles prohibit such people from being sent abroad. According to Goldsmith, if Article 49 really meant to forbid any and all temporary removals out of state, these two articles would become redundant, and therefore "meaningless and inoperative."[89]

The short response is: no, they wouldn't. The two articles say, in effect, that Article 49's protection against forcible removal applies even to persons detained for a crime or lawfully impressed into labor. The articles ward off potential misreadings of Article 49 that find implied exceptions to it for impressed laborers or accused criminals. In that way, the two articles strengthen and clarify Article 49 – and unsurprisingly, that is precisely how the Red Cross's official commentary to the Geneva Conventions explains the relationship among the three articles.[90]

Goldsmith rejects the commentary's explanation because Article 49 must not be read to make the other articles superfluous.[91] Evidently, he believes that the anti-redundancy canon articulated in a 1933 US Supreme Court opinion trumps all other rules of treaty interpretation. However, the canons of treaty interpretation explicitly recognized in the international law of treaties emphasize "good faith [interpretation] in accordance with the ordinary meaning to be given to the terms of the treaty in their context and in the light of its object and purpose"[92] – the very form of interpretation so conspicuously absent from Goldsmith's memo. The anti-redundancy canon

---

[89] TP, at 378–79. According to Article 51, impressed laborers can be compelled to work "only in the occupied territory where the persons whose services have been requisitioned are," and Article 76 requires that people accused or convicted of offenses can be detained only in the occupied country.

[90] 4 Jean S. Pictet, Commentary on the Geneva Conventions of 12 August 1949 279, 298, 363 (1958).

[91] He rejects the commentary's construction in TP, supra note 1, at 379 note 13.

[92] Vienna Convention on the Law of Treaties, Articles 31 and 32. Although the United States is not a party to the Vienna Convention, it accepts its sections on treaty interpretation as

he relies on appears nowhere in the Vienna Convention, not even its article on supplementary means of interpretation.

Finally, Goldsmith observes that a separate clause of Article 49 forbids occupying powers from deporting or transferring its own civilians *into* occupied territory. Presumably (he argues), that prohibition does not prevent the occupier from bringing civilian contractors or NGOs in for the short term. Hence, in this latter clause the words "transfer" and "deport" do not encompass short-term transfers and deportations. Thus, these words do not encompass short-term transfers of persons out of the country either, because "there is a strong presumption that the same words will bear the same meaning throughout the same treaty."[93]

Perhaps so, although the only legal authority Goldsmith cites for this "strong presumption" is a US Supreme Court dictum saying something different.[94] In opinions Goldsmith does not cite, the Court recognizes that in the interpretation of federal statutes, the same-words-same-meaning "presumption ... is not rigid and readily yields" to good reasons for distinguishing meanings in different contexts.[95] But even if there were a rigid same-words-same-meaning presumption, it hardly follows that words with the same meaning coincide in every respect. If a building code specifies safety requirements for "the cellar of a house" in one paragraph, obviously in that paragraph the word "house" refers only to houses with cellars. But it would be absurd to suppose that in other clauses of the code, dealing with other issues, the word "house" likewise refers only to houses with cellars. The word's core meaning covers both houses with cellars and houses with none. In precisely the same way, the fact that in one paragraph of the Fourth Geneva Convention the word "transfer" can refer only to long-term transfers implies nothing about its referent in a very different context. The word's core meaning – moving people from one place to another – covers both long-term and short-term transfers. Tellingly, Goldsmith fails to mention the Red Cross Commentary's observation that in the paragraph prohibiting occupiers from transferring or deporting their own civilians into occupied territory "the

customary international law. Restatement (Third) of the Foreign Relations Law of the United States, §325.

[93] TP, supra note 1, at 377.

[94] Air France v. Saks, 470 U.S. 392, 398 (1985). In the passage Goldsmith cites, the Court says that different words in a treaty presumptively refer to different things. That is the logical converse of Goldsmith's principle, and neither implies the other. For good reason, then, Goldsmith cites this case with a "cf." Presumably, if better authority existed, he would have cited it.

[95] General Dynamics Land Systems v. Cline, 540 U.S. 581, 595–98 (2004). For an even stronger statement to the same effect, see the unanimous opinion in Robinson v. Shell Oil Co., 519 U.S. 337, 343–44 (1997).

meaning of the words 'transfer' and 'deport' is rather different from that in which they are used in the other paragraphs of Article 49."[96]

I describe these admittedly arcane details of Goldsmith's memo because I have heard scholars who despise the Bybee Memo hold up Goldsmith's as the gold standard of what a pro-Administration OLC memo ought to look like. It is no such thing. Like the Bybee Memo, it reaches a preordained conclusion by kabbalistic textual manipulations. The basic recipe in both memos is the same: lean heavily on "structural" canons of construction, take unrelated bits of law having to do with very different problems, read them side by side as though a legislator had intended to link them, and spin out "consequences," "interpretations," and "contradictions." Where Bybee and Yoo interpret "severe" in the torture statute by looking at a Medicare statute, Goldsmith combines a treaty clause dealing with forcible transfer and a different clause dealing with war orphans to generate an imaginary contradiction. Neither memo writer asks the most basic interpretive question: *What is the point of this law?* To ask that question would have been fatal, because the object of both documents is to protect individuals in the clutches of their enemies, and here the captors – OLC's "client" – wanted to unprotect them. Unmooring a law from its point leaves only the formal techniques of textual manipulation to interpret it.

At one point, however, Goldsmith pushes back against detainee abuse. In a final footnote at the end of his draft, Goldsmith warns that some removals of prisoners might indeed violate Article 49 and constitute war crimes.[97] He also includes a reminder that a prisoner transferred out of Iraq for interrogation does not lose "protected person" benefits. These are important warnings, and they buttress reports of Goldsmith's admirably anodyne role in resisting "the program" (as executive branch officials chillingly refer to their detention, interrogation, and rendition policies).

But then why not say specifically that those benefits include those of Article 31: "No physical or moral coercion shall be exercised against protected persons, in particular to obtain information from them or from third parties"? Is it because a memo that explicitly said, "On the contrary, we believe he would ordinarily retain his Article 31 right against any form of coercive interrogation" would defeat the purpose of removing prisoners from Iraq? Why bury his vague warning in a footnote at the end of the memorandum? Why not quote Article 31 *in the text*, and point out that no form of coercive interrogation is permitted under Geneva IV?

---

[96] 4 Pictet, supra note 90, at 283. Pictet is pointing to the difference between transferring people into a country and transferring people out, but that does not matter, because the point is that the meaning of words (especially nontechnical terms like "transfer") can shift from context to context.

[97] TP, supra note 1, at 379–80, note 14.

It seems to me that the most charitable interpretation is that Goldsmith was working among hard-liners, and could subvert abusive interrogation only in a subtle and inconspicuous way. That may be the best an OLC lawyer could hope for. (Indeed, perhaps OLC never adopted his draft memo because even subtle and inconspicuous subversion was more than OLC's clients could stomach.) But a huge potential for self-deception exists in this strategy. To bury a warning risks its dismissal. And to say, in effect, "You can forcibly remove detainees from Iraq for interrogation, but it's up to you to make sure that the interrogation does not include coercion," comes awfully close to Tom Lehrer's Wernher von Braun (" 'Once the rockets are up, who cares where they come down? That's not my department,' says Wernher von Braun").

Cruel, inhuman, or degrading treament

Interrogation techniques such as sexual humiliation don't fall under the legal definition of torture, or under most people's informal understanding of what torture is. They do, however, constitute degrading treatment, one of the three subcategories of the "cruel, inhuman or degrading treatment" banned by CAT. (Jurists abbreviate the treaty phrase "cruel, inhuman or degrading treatment or punishment which does not amount to torture" by the acronym "CID.") So do many other forms of "torture lite." Arguably, the legality of CID matters more for US interrogation practices than the torture statutes do.

As we have seen, the torture convention obligates parties to "undertake to prevent" CID, but it does not require criminalizing CID, and the United States has never made CID a crime. To be sure, CID violates common Article 3 of the Geneva Conventions, and that made it a US war crime. But, in 2006 the US Congress decriminalized humiliating and degrading treatment of detainees.

The requirement to "undertake to prevent" CID nevertheless remains an international legal obligation of the United States; and, while the duties it entails are vague, the obligation surely rules out deliberately engaging in CID. However, at his confirmation hearing for Attorney General, Alberto Gonzales offered a startling legal theory about why that obligation does not apply. When the US Senate ratified the torture convention, Gonzales explained, it added the reservation that CID means the cruel, inhuman, or degrading treatment forbidden by the Constitution's Eighth Amendment ban on cruel and unusual punishments and Fifth Amendment ban on conduct that shocks the conscience. But the Eighth Amendment applies only to punishment, and the Supreme Court has held, in other unrelated contexts, that the Fifth Amendment does not protect aliens outside US territory. Therefore, in Gonzales's words, "the Department of Justice has concluded that ... there is no legal prohibition under the CAT of cruel, inhuman or degrading treatment with respect to aliens overseas." He reiterated the argument in written responses to senatorial questions.[98]

The argument is startling because it seems obvious that the Senate's reservation intended nothing of the sort. Before Gonzales's argument muddied the waters, it was perfectly clear that the Senate's reservation aimed to define CAT's concept of CID by using the substantive standards embodied in the constitutional rights, not to tie CAT to their jurisdictional reach. After Gonzales's testimony, three Democratic senators wrote an incredulous letter to the Justice Department requesting all legal opinions on the subject within three days. Justice ignored the request until two months later, after Gonzales was safely confirmed as Attorney General. Eventually the Department responded in a three-page letter, which refused to release OLC opinions but cited legal authority to back up Gonzales, most prominently some 1990 comments to the Senate by Abraham Sofaer, the State Department's legal advisor during debate over the ratification of CAT.[99] Like Gonzales, Sofaer had emphasized that "we would limit our obligations under this Convention to the proscriptions already covered in our own Constitution." If constitutional rights against CID do not apply to aliens abroad, then CAT's ban on CID cannot apply abroad.

But this was not at all what he or the Senate meant, according to Sofaer. In a letter to Senator Patrick Leahy disavowing the Gonzales interpretation, Sofaer explained that the purpose of the reservation was to ensure that the same standards for CID would apply outside the United States as apply inside – just the opposite of Gonzales's conclusion.[100] The point was to define CID, not to create a gaping geographical loophole.[101] Apparently, however, the Administration desperately wanted the geographical loophole. When Senator John McCain (a Vietnam torture victim) introduced legislation to close the loophole, the administration lobbied against it fiercely, threatening to veto major legislation rather than accede to banning CID by US forces abroad. When McCain's law nevertheless swept the Congress with veto-proof majorities, the Administration extracted a concession: federal

[98] Gonzales's oral response, quoted in a letter to John Ashcroft from Senators Patrick Leahy, Russell Feingold, and Dianne Feinstein, January 25, 2005. Written response to Senator Richard J. Durbin, question 1. PDF of both documents in my possession.

[99] Letter from William Moschella to Patrick Leahy, April 4, 2005, at 3. PDF in my possession.

[100] Letter from Abraham D. Sofaer to Patrick Leahy, January 21, 2005. PDF in my possession. Sofaer reiterated his views in an op-ed a few months later: Sofaer, *No Exceptions*, Wall St. J., November 26, 2005, at A11.

[101] It appears that the reservation was partly a response to the fact that some states declare corporal punishment to be CID, while the United States does not. It may also have been a response to a controversial European Court of Human Rights decision that had declared prolonged imprisonment in a US death row to be cruel and degrading. David P. Stewart, *The Torture Convention and the Reception of International Criminal Law within the United States*, 15 Nova L. Rev. 449, 461–62 (1991).

courts could no longer hear Guantánamo cases. CID might be illegal, but its Guantánamo victims would no longer have any recourse against it. And, as the final touch, President Bush attached a signing statement to McCain's CID ban implying a constitutional right to ignore it.

What's wrong with the torture memos?

Frivolity and indeterminacy

Kingman Brewster, asked what his years as a Harvard law professor had taught him, replied, "That every proposition is arguable."[102]

But not every proposition is arguable well, and not every argument is a good one. Law recognizes a category of frivolous arguments and positions, and it should. My claim is that arguments like the "organ-failure" definition of torture, Beaver's reading of *Hudson v. McMillian*, and Goldsmith's "contradiction" between Geneva's articles about war orphans and deportation are not just wrong but frivolous.

What makes an argument frivolous? Let me approach this question through what is, I hope, a straightforward example (unrelated to the torture memos), drawn from a 1989 case. Sue Vaccaro, a slightly built woman, attempted to use the first-class lavatory while traveling coach class with her husband on a cross-country flight. John Wellington Stephens, a large male first-class passenger, assaulted her. Stephens called her a "chink slut and a whore," told her she was too dirty to use the first-class washroom, and shoved her against a bulkhead. Vaccaro sued Stephens, and he counterclaimed, asserting that his ticket gave him a license to the first-class lavatory, and Vaccaro had trespassed on it. This harmed him, his counsel argued, because the donnybrook spoiled Stephens's flight. The judge punished his law firm for frivolous argument, and it may be hard to find a lawyer outside the firm who would disagree. The court of appeals wrote:

> To engage in a temper tantrum is not to suffer actual damage at the hands of a trespasser ... The federal district court is a very hospitable court but it is not yet hospitable to entertaining law suits against people who have the misfortune to engage in argument with irascible first class passengers ... The idea that if you sat in the wrong seat at a symphony, a play, a baseball game or a football game and did not get out instantly when the proper ticket holder appeared you could be sued in a federal court is not an attractive notion. It is not merely unattractive. It takes no account of the state of the law ... Rule 11 is not meant to discourage creative lawyering. It is meant to discourage pettifoggery. The state of the law, whether it is evolving or fixed in well-nigh permanent form, is important in making the distinction between the plausible and the silly.[103]

---

[102] Alex Beam, *Greed on Trial*, in Legal Ethics: Law Stories 291 (Deborah L. Rhode & David Luban eds., 2005).

[103] Vaccaro v. Stephens, 1989 U.S. App. LEXIS 5864; 14 Fed. R. Serv. 3d (Callaghan) 60, *9–12 (9th Cir. 1989).

No formula or algorithm exists for sorting out the plausible-but-wrong arguments from the silly, any more than an algorithm can distinguish jokes that are almost funny from jokes that aren't funny at all. But a theory of frivolity is unnecessary. As the philosopher Sidney Morgenbesser once wrote, to explain why a man slipped on a banana peel you do not need a general theory of slipping.[104] Legal plausibility is a matter for case-by-case judgment by the interpretive community, and the judgment will be grounded in specific arguments like those the court of appeals offered in *Vaccaro v. Stephens* and – more to the point – those I have offered here about the "analyses" contained in the torture memos.

Picture a bell curve representing the number of trained lawyers who find any given legal argument plausible. Some arguments are so recognizably mainstream that virtually all lawyers would agree that they are plausible. Those arguments lie under the fat part of the bell curve. Calling an argument plausible doesn't mean accepting it: readers of judicial opinions often find both the majority and the dissenting arguments plausible, and situate both within the fat part of the bell curve.

Moving further out on the bell curve, we find the kind of arguments that lawyers euphemistically call "creative" (or where one might say, "Nice try!"). Litigators resort to creative arguments when unfavorable law leaves them no better option than the brief-writer's equivalent of a Hail Mary pass. The argument is too much of a stretch to be genuinely credible, but it offers a novel way to think about the law, and someday the interpretive community might get there. At the moment, though, it lies outside the fat part of the bell curve, although not far out on the arms.

Frivolous arguments, on the other hand, *are* far out. Superficially, they make lawyer-like "moves," but they take such broad liberties with legal text, policy, and sense that only someone far removed from the mainstream would take them seriously. In the definition of federal judge Frank Easterbrook, "99 of 100 practicing lawyers would be 99% sure that the position is untenable, and the other 1% would be 60% sure it's untenable."[105] Easterbrook's numbers may be too high, and in any case the numerical imagery is only a figure of speech, because nobody is actually out there surveying lawyers.[106]

---

[104] Sidney Morgenbesser, *Scientific Explanation*, 14 Int'l. Encyclopedia Soc. Sci. 122 (David Sills ed., 1968).

[105] Quoted in Sanford Levinson, *Frivolous Cases: Do Lawyers Really Know Anything at All?* 24 Osgoode Hall L. Rev. 353, 375 (1987).

[106] Tax lawyers have long familiarity with numerical imagery to determine when a tax preparer can take an aggressive position without disclosing it. According to federal regulations, the preparer cannot do so unless "the position has approximately a one in three, or greater, likelihood of being sustained on its merits." 10 C.F.R. §10.34(d)(1). This regulation derives from a 1985 ABA ethics opinion replacing an earlier opinion according to which tax lawyers could take any position for which a reasonable basis could be found. "Doubtless there were some tax

But the idea should be clear: the legal mainstream defines the concept of plausibility.

It might be objected that legal arguments should be judged on their merits, not on how mainstream lawyers might vote about their merits. Judging arguments by their popularity seems like a category mistake.

That may be true in fields where truths are obscure and only the deep thinkers can discern them. But law is different. Law is not written for geniuses, and it is not written by geniuses. Legal texts are instruments of governance, and as such they must be as obvious and demotic as possible, capable of daily use by millions of people with no time or taste for riddles. Even when great judges with subtle, Promethean minds write opinions, their opinions had better contain no secret teachings, no buried allusions, no symbolism, no allegory, no thematic subtleties that need Harold Bloom or Leo Strauss to tease them out. Richard Posner once described legal texts as "essentially mediocre."[107] Both words are precisely right; but Posner forgot to add that when it comes to law, "essentially mediocre" is a compliment. Within a rule-of-law regime, rules must offer clear-cut guidance to average intelligences, and that makes essential mediocrity virtually a defining characteristic of law. Law does its job properly when it is all surface and no depth and what you see is exactly what you get.[108] That is why it makes no

practitioners who intended 'reasonable basis' to set a relatively high standard of tax reporting. Some have continued to apply such a standard. To more, however, if not most tax practitioners, the ethical standard set by 'reasonable basis' had become a low one. To many it had come to permit any colorable claim to be put forth; to permit almost any words that could be strung together to be used to support a tax return position. Such a standard has now been rejected by the ABA Committee ... A position having only a 5% or 10% likelihood of success, if litigated, should not meet the new standard. A position having a likelihood of success closely approaching one-third should meet the standard." *Report of the Special Task Force on Formal Opinion 85–352*, 39 Tax Law. 635 (1986). Because of the infrequency of tax audits, tax preparation is perhaps the paradigm case where the system depends on the honor of lawyers to give advice based on legal positions that are not frivolous. There are significant parallels between the tax advisor's role and the role of the equally unaccountable OLC.

[107] Richard A. Posner, Overcoming Law 91 (1995).

[108] Legal theorists might balk at this claim, pointing to the phenomenon of "acoustic separation" between the rules of conduct known by the hoi polloi and the more intricate rules of decision employed by officials. Meir Dan-Cohen, who introduced the concept of acoustic separation, pointed out that broad knowledge of available criminal defenses (for example, duress or necessity) would create perverse incentives for people to abuse those defenses. Hence it is better to keep decision rules and conduct rules acoustically separated, meaning that primary actors should not necessarily become aware of the more lenient decision rules officials actually use. Acoustic separation, with selective transmission of the law to different audiences, might actually be a useful strategy for lawmakers to adopt. Meir Dan-Cohen, *Decision Rules and Conduct Rules: On Acoustic Separation in Criminal Law*, 97 Harv. L. Rev. 625 (1984). The concept of acoustic separation is an interesting and useful one. In my opinion, however, legal theorists invoke the concept of acoustic separation more often than it warrants. Descriptively, the phenomenon of law intentionally tailored for acoustic separation seems like a marginal part

sense to suppose that the plausibility of legal arguments could deviate systematically from what the interpretive community thinks about their plausibility. What could it deviate to? In law, by design, there is no hidden there there.[109]

Although the interpretive community defines the bounds of the reasonable, there remains plenty of room for interpretive disagreement within those bounds.[110] Law, we must remember, emerges from political processes, and it

of the legal enterprise. Normatively, there is real danger behind the idea that some law is too dangerous for ordinary mortals to know and should be left to the experts. It presupposes the superior rectitude of experts, and therefore it underrates the perverse incentives for experts to shield their own abuses from accountability. Dan-Cohen, I should add, does not make this mistake: for him, "the option of selective transmission is not an attractive one, and the sight of law tainted by duplicity and concealment is not pretty." Ibid. at 673. Furthermore: by suggesting that society might be better off if people don't know the law too well, the doctrine of acoustic separation rationalizes a system where legal services are unaffordable by tens of millions of people, and only the wealthy can buy their way around acoustic separation.

[109] The thesis I am defending is that there are no truths about what law means or requires outside the range of views that the interpretive community finds plausible. This is a weak thesis, grounded in the specific functions of law, not a general metaphysical claim that interpretive communities constitute the meaning of the objects they concern themselves with. The latter is the view of relativists like Stanley Fish, *Anti-Professionalism*, 7 Cardozo L. Rev. 645 (1986). I've criticized his view in *Fish v. Fish or, Some Realism About Idealism*, 7 Cardozo L. Rev. 693 (1986), on two grounds: first, that interpretive communities could play the role Fish ascribes to them only if they meet internal political conditions of reciprocity and freedom; and second, that the vaporous concept of "constituting" meaning buys into a metaphysical contrast between idealism and realism that we would do well to abandon.

In the present chapter, I am fishing in shallower waters. Regardless of who is right about realist, idealist, and pragmatist conceptions of inquiry and truth *in general*, it seems to me we should all agree that law contains no truths hidden from the citizens it governs and the lawyers who help them understand it.

[110] To be sure, Ronald Dworkin has argued that legal questions have a single, unique right answer, namely that answer that displays the sources of law in the morally best light. Determining which answer that is may be something that only Judge Hercules (Dworkin's hypothetical über-jurist) can do. Ronald Dworkin, Law's Empire 52–53 (1986); Dworkin, *"Natural" Law Revisited,* 34 U. Fla. L. Rev. 165, 169–70 (1982); Ronald Dworkin, *Hard Cases,* in Taking Rights Seriously 81, 105–23 (1978); Dworkin, *No Right Answer?* in Law, Morality and Society: Essays in Honour of H. L. A. Hart 58 (P. M. S. Hacker & J. Raz eds., 1977). However, given the lack of a decision procedure or verification procedure about which people with conflicting good-faith moral views can agree (to say nothing of the unreality of Judge Hercules), it is hard to see why a Dworkinian "right answer" is anything more than a *Ding an sich*, an "as-if," that anchors a theory of objectivity without serving the basic function of law, namely governing a community. I discuss some of the perplexities raised by the possibility of a right answer that lacks a verification procedure in Luban, *The Coiled Serpent of Authority: Reason, Authority, and Law in a Talmudic Tale*, 79 Chi.-Kent L. Rev. 1253 (2004).

Lacking a decision procedure does not doom us to radical indeterminacy in which anything goes. Even if we cannot settle which of several competing answers is right, we can rule out answers that are obviously wrong. To illustrate with Fred Schauer's example, "That I am

typically represents the compromise, or vector sum, of competing social forces. Compromise whittles down sharp edges, and legal standards without sharp edges are bound to generate interpretive disagreements. It is worth taking a moment to see why.

Some ambiguity in law results because drafters finessed a ticklish political issue with strategic, diplomatic doublespeak. To take a famous and blatant example, the UN Security Council helped end the Six Days War with a resolution issued in two official languages, English and French. The French version requires the Israelis to withdraw from all the occupied territory, while the English requires them to withdraw only from some.[111] The reason for splitting the difference is obvious: it stopped the shooting and postponed the hardest question to another day. (Unsurprisingly, for forty years Israelis have cited the English version and Arabs the French.) Likewise, US Congressional staffers admit that ambiguity in statutes often results because "we know that if we answer a certain question, we will lose one side or the other."[112]

Although strategic ambiguity is the most obvious way that politics creates legal indeterminacy, it is not the only way. Other ambiguities enter through legislative log-rolling and mutual concessions. Political give-and-take generates statutes that qualify or soften requirements, attach escape clauses to bright-line rules, or balance clauses favoring one contending interest group with clauses favoring others. None of these provisions need be unclear in itself, but taken together they generate multiple interpretive possibilities. That is because jurists interpret statutory language in the light of its purpose, and when the statute itself reflects cross-purposes, its requirements can be viewed differently depending on which purpose the interpreter deems most vital. An interpreter who views the escape clauses and qualifications as important expressions of legislative purpose will stretch them to borderline or doubtful cases; another, who views the unqualified rules as the key, will interpret those rules strictly and find very few exceptions. Needless to say, judges' moral and political outlooks influence their understanding of legislative purpose: it's easier to grasp purposes you agree with than purposes you don't. Every

---

unsure whether rafts and floating motorized automobiles are 'boats' does not dispel my confidence that rowboats and dories most clearly are boats, and that steam locomotives, hamburgers, and elephants equally clearly are not." Frederick Schauer, *Easy Cases*, 58 S. Cal. L. Rev. 399, 422 (1985).

[111] UN Security Council Resolution 242 (1967). The English version calls for "withdrawal of Israeli forces from territories occupied in the recent conflict" ("territories," not "the territories," where "the" was dropped as the result of a US amendment to the British-proposed text), while the French version calls for "retrait des forces armées israéliennes des territoires occupés lors du récent conflit."

[112] Quoted in Victoria F. Nourse & Jane S. Schacter, *The Politics of Legislative Drafting: A Congressional Case Study*, 77 NYU L. Rev. 575, 596 (2002). On the deliberate use of ambiguity, see ibid. at 594–97, 614–19.

political fault line in a legal text automatically becomes an interpretive fault line as well.

Even judicially created doctrines reflect the push and pull of many outlooks. A court creates a legal doctrine that neatly resolves the case before it. Later, another court faces a case in which applying that doctrine would yield an obviously wrong outcome; so the court carves out an exception and identifies a counter-principle governing the exception. Subsequent courts decide whether the principle or counter-principle applies to a new case by judging whether the facts of the new case more closely resemble those of the original case or the exception – and typically, some facts in the new case will resemble each. Which analogy seems most compelling will depend on judges' varying senses of fairness. Over the course of centuries, lines of judicial authority elaborate both the principles and counter-principles into the architecture of the common law. As a result, legal doctrine resembles a multi-generational compromise, with principles and counter-principles that roughly track the political fault lines of different stages of evolving society.

The result is indeterminacy in legal doctrine, a familiar theme in the writings of the legal realists and critical legal studies. But it is indeterminacy of a special and limited sort – moderate, not global, indeterminacy. Indeterminacy attains its maximum along fault lines where the law most strongly reflects a political compromise. Where political conflict was unimportant to the shape a legal text assumed, indeterminacy may be minimal or non-existent. Brewster was wrong: *not* every proposition is arguable. Lawyers desperate for an argument will try to conjure up an indeterminacy where little or none exists, but they will have a hard time doing so honestly. The torture memos testify to that.

The ethics of legal opinions

Let me summarize. I have been suggesting that crucial arguments in the torture memos are frivolous. However, I have also insisted that no bright-line test of frivolity exists beyond whether an interpretive community accepts specific objections showing that the arguments are baseless or absurd. You know it when you see it.

In that case, why can't the torture lawyers simply reply that their interpretive community sees it differently from the interpretive community of liberal cosmopolitan lawyers? One answer, perhaps the strongest, is the moral certainty that they would have reached the opposite conclusion if the Administration wanted the opposite conclusion. The evidence shows that all these memos were written under pressure from officials determined to use harsh tactics – officials who consciously bypassed ordinary channels and looked to lawyers sharing their aims. An interpretive community that contours its interpretations to the party line is not engaged in good-faith interpretation.

In the case of the torture memos, the giveaway is the violation of craft values common to all legal interpretive communities. This is clearest in the Bybee Memo, but the preceding discussion reveals similar problems in the other documents. What makes the Bybee Memo frivolous by conventional legal standards is that in its most controversial sections, it barely goes through the motions of standard legal argument. Instead of addressing the obvious counter-arguments, it ignores them; its citation of conventional legal authority is, for obvious reasons, sparse; it fails to mention directly adverse authority; and when it does cite conventional sources of law, it employs them in unconventional ways, and not always honestly.

The other memos are less transparent about it, but they too discard the project of providing an analysis of the law as mainstream lawyers and judges understand it. Instead, they provide aggressive advocacy briefs to give those who order or engage in brutal interrogation legal cover.

One might ask what is wrong with writing advocacy briefs. Aren't lawyers supposed to spin the law to their clients' advantage? The traditional answer for courtroom advocates is yes. The aim is to persuade the judge or jury, not to write a treatise. To be sure, even courtroom advocates should not indulge in frivolous or dishonest argument. But, as Judge Easterbrook's formula indicated, the standards of frivolity leave plenty of room for pro-client spin.

But the torture memos are not briefs. They are legal advice, and in traditional legal ethics they answer to a different standard: not persuasiveness on the client's behalf but candor and independence.[113] As I suggested in the last chapter, perhaps the most fundamental rule of thumb for legal advice is that the lawyer's analysis of the law should be more or less the same as it would be if the client wanted the opposite result from the one the lawyer knows he wants.

Other rules of thumb follow from this. First, a legal opinion ought to lay out in terms intelligible to the client the chief legal arguments bearing on the issue, those contrary to the client's preferred outcome as well as those favoring it. Unlike a brief, which aims to minimize the opposing arguments and exaggerate the strength of its own, the opinion should evaluate the arguments as objectively as possible. Second, opinions must treat legal authority honestly. (Briefs should as well.) No funny stuff: if the lawyer cites a source, the reader should not have to double-check whether it really says what the lawyer says it says, or whether the lawyer has wrenched a quotation out of context to flip its meaning. And adverse sources may not simply be ignored. Just as litigation rules require lawyers to divulge directly adverse law to courts, an honest legal opinion does not simply sweep it under the rug and hope nobody notices.

---

[113] See ABA Model Rules of Professional Conduct 2.1: "In representing a client, a lawyer shall exercise independent professional judgment and render candid advice."

Finally, an honest opinion explains where its conclusion fits on the bell curve. While it is entirely proper for an opinion writer to favor a nonstandard view of the law, she must make clear that it *is* a nonstandard view of the law. She cannot write an opinion advancing a marginal view of the law with a brief-writer's swaggering self-confidence that the law will sustain no view other than hers.

An example might help. It is only fair to use an argument in one of John Yoo's OLC memos that fulfills these requirements. A memo of January 22, 2002 (which went out over Bybee's signature) argues, among other things, that common Article 3 of the Geneva Conventions does not apply to the US conflict with Al Qaeda. That is because Article 3 applies only to "armed conflicts not of an international character." By this phrase, Yoo argues, the framers of Geneva had in mind only civil wars, like the Spanish and Chinese civil wars.[114] That would plainly exclude the conflict with Al Qaeda.

There is nothing frivolous about this argument; indeed, it is quite forceful. But there is also a powerful reply to it. In legal terminology, "international" means "among nation-states," as in the phrase "international law." An international armed conflict is a conflict among nation-states, and therefore an armed conflict "not of an international character" would be *any* armed conflict not among nation-states, not only civil wars. (This, eventually, was the interpretation adopted by the US Supreme Court in its June 2006 *Hamdan* opinion.) In that case, the conflict with Al Qaeda would be classified as an armed conflict not of an international (i.e., state-against-state) character – and therefore common Article 3 would apply to it and protect even Al Qaeda captives. That conclusion would harmonize with the most obvious purpose of Article 3: protecting at least the most basic human rights of all captives, whether or not they qualify for the more extended protections Geneva offers to POWs and protected civilians in wars among nation-states. If, as a matter of policy, Article 3 aims to protect basic human rights in nonstandard wars, it would be irrational to protect human rights only in civil wars rather than all armed conflicts. Most international lawyers believe that human rights instruments should be interpreted in a broad, gap-filling way, precisely because of the importance of human rights.

The virtue of Yoo's opinion is that he explicitly discusses all this. He sketches the evolution of the law of armed conflict in the twentieth century, acknowledging that in recent years international law "gives central place to individual human rights" and "blurs the distinction between international and internal armed conflicts."[115] He cites one of the principal cases illustrating this view, the Yugoslav Tribunal's *Tadic* decision; and in a footnote he refers to other authorities taking the same view. In response, he emphasizes that the

---

[114] TP, supra note 1, at 86–87.
[115] Ibid. at 88.

Geneva framers were thinking principally about protecting rights in civil wars, and argues that to interpret Article 3 more broadly "is effectively to amend the Geneva Conventions without the approval of the State parties to the agreements."[116] In other words, where most international lawyers treat human rights instruments like a "living" constitution, Yoo treats them like contracts. I think this gives him the weaker side of the argument – and, obviously, the Supreme Court rejected his position – but that is not the point. The point is that he does a respectable job of sketching out the legal land-scape, making it clear that his own analysis runs contrary to that of most international lawyers, and representing their positions honestly.[117] That is the kind of candid advice a lawyer can legitimately provide the client, even if it deviates from mainstream views.[118]

The lawyer as absolver

But what happens when the client wants cover, not candid advice? – when the client comes to the lawyer and says, in effect, "Give me an opinion that lets me do what I want to do"?

Lawyers have a word for a legal opinion that does this. It is called a CYA memorandum – Cover Your Ass. Without the memorandum, the client who wants to push the legal envelope is on his own. But with a CYA memo in hand, he can insist that he cleared it with the lawyers first, and that way he can duck responsibility. That appears to be the project of the torture memos.

Notice that this diagnosis differs from Anthony Lewis's judgment that the Bybee Memo "read like the advice of a mob lawyer to a mafia don on how to skirt the law and stay out of prison."[119] The torture memos are not advice about how to stay out of prison; instead, they reassure their clients that they

---

[116] Ibid.

[117] Not entirely: he neglects to mention that the drafters of the Geneva Conventions explicitly *rejected* an Australian motion to limit Article 3 to civil wars. Special Committee Seventh Report at Vol. II B, p. 121. They also rejected other, similar efforts that would have had the same effect. See *Hamdan*, 2006 US Lexis 5185, *128.

[118] This portion of Yoo's opinion contrasts sharply with another section of the same opinion, arguing that the Geneva Conventions don't protect Taliban fighters because under the Taliban Afghanistan was a failed state. Here, Yoo was back in Bybee Memo form. His draft opinion drew an outraged response from the State Department's legal advisor, who pointed out that "failed state" is not a legal concept; that so many states are failed states that Yoo's no-treaties-with-failed-states argument would greatly complicate US foreign relations; that if the Taliban have no rights under Geneva they have no obligations either, and therefore don't have to apply Geneva to any Americans they capture; and that Yoo's argument would annul every treaty with Afghanistan on every subject. Memo from William Howard Taft IV to John Yoo, January 11, 2002, available at <www.cartoonbank.com/newyorker/slideshows/01TaftMemo.pdf>. The "failed-state" argument quietly disappeared.

[119] Anthony Lewis, *Making Torture Legal*, N.Y. Review of Books, July 15, 2004.

are not going to prison. They are opinion letters blessing or koshering conduct for the twin purposes of all CYA memos: reassuring cautious lower-level employees that they can follow orders without getting into trouble, and allowing wrongdoers to duck responsibility. The fact that they emerge from the Justice Department – the prosecutor of federal crime – makes the reassurance nearly perfect.

When they write CYA memos, lawyers cross the fatal line from legal advisor to moral or legal accomplice. Obviously, it happens all the time. Journalist Martin Mayer, writing about the 1980s savings-and-loan collapse, quoted a source who said that for half a million dollars you could buy a legal opinion saying anything you wanted from any big law firm in Manhattan.[120] In the Enron case, we saw lawyers writing opinion letters that approved the creation of illegal Special Purpose Entities, even though they knew that they were skating on thin ice. I am arguing that this is unethical. In white-collar criminal cases, some courts in some contexts will accept a defense of good-faith reliance on the advice of counsel, and presumably that defense is the prize the client seeks from the lawyer. But when the client tells the lawyer what advice he wants, the good faith vanishes, and under the criminal law of accomplice liability, both lawyer and client should go down.[121]

Giving the client skewed advice because the client wants it is a different role from either advocate or advisor. I call it the Lawyer As Absolver, or, less nicely, the Lawyer As Indulgence Seller. Luther began the Reformation in part because the popes were selling papal dispensations to violate law, along with indulgences sparing sinners the flames of hell or a few years of purgatory. Rodrigo Borgia once brokered a papal dispensation for a French count to sleep with his own sister. It was a good career move: Rodrigo later became Pope Alexander VI.[122] Jay Bybee had to settle for the Ninth Circuit Court of Appeals.

It is important to see why the role of Absolver, unlike the roles of Advocate and Advisor, is illegitimate. The courtroom advocate's biased presentation will be countered by the adversary in a public hearing. The advisor's presentation will not. In the courtroom, the adversary is supposed to check the advocate's excesses. In the lawyer's office, advising the client, the lawyer is supposed to check the client's excesses. Conflating the two roles moves the lawyer out of the limited role-based immunity that advocates enjoy into the world of the indulgence seller.

---

[120] Martin Mayer, The Greatest-Ever Bank Robbery: The Collapse of the Savings and Loan Industry 20 (Collier Books 1992).

[121] The lawyer who okays unlawful conduct by the client has also harmed the client, and therefore been a bad fiduciary of the client. But, both as a matter of law and morality, that is a distinct ethical violation from becoming the client's accomplice.

[122] Ivan Cloulas, The Borgias 38 (Gilda Roberts trans., 1989).

In short: if you are writing a brief, call it a brief, not an opinion. If it is an opinion, it must not be a brief. If you write a brief but call it an opinion, you have done wrong.

Government lawyers

Some might reply that in the real world outside the academy, legal opinions by government offices *are* briefs. When the State Department issues an opinion vindicating a military action by the US government, everyone understands that this is a public statement of the government's position, not an independent legal assessment. To suppose otherwise is naive.

In that case, however, why keep up the charade? Consider, for example, a pair of documents authored by the British Attorney General, Lord Peter Goldsmith. The first was a confidential legal memorandum to Tony Blair on the legality of the Iraq war, dated March 7, 2003, less than two weeks before the war began. The memo consisted of thirteen densely packed pages, and in my view it is a model of what such an opinion should be. It carefully and judiciously dissects all the pro and con arguments, which were closely balanced, consisting largely of interpretive debates over the meaning of characteristically soapy UN Security Council resolutions. Goldsmith concluded that, while in his opinion obtaining a second Security Council resolution authorizing the use of force "is the safest legal course," a reasonable argument can be made that existing resolutions would suffice to justify the war.[123] It was a cautious go-ahead to Blair, larded with substantial misgivings and caveats. If Blair's request to Goldsmith was to give him the strongest argument available for the legality of the war, Goldsmith replied in the best way he could: he articulated the argument Blair wanted, advised him that it was reasonable, but also made it clear that the argument did not represent his own view of how the law should best be read. This represents the limit to which an honest legal advisor can tailor his opinion to the wishes of his client. Goldsmith's office wrote a sophisticated, honest document.

Ten days later – three days before the bombing began – Lord Goldsmith presented the same issue to Parliament, and now all the misgivings were gone. In place of thirty-one subtle paragraphs of analysis, the "opinion" to Parliament consists of nine terse, conclusory paragraphs with no nuance and no hint of doubt.[124] In place of the confidential memorandum's conclusion that the meaning of a Security Council resolution was "unclear," Goldsmith's public statement expressed no doubts whatever. It was pure vindication of the course of action to which Blair was irrevocably committed.

---

[123] Goldsmith memo, paragraphs 27–28. Available at <www.comw.org/warreport/fulltext/0303goldsmith.html>.

[124] Hansard, 17 March 2003, column 515W.

Two years later, Goldsmith told the House of Lords that his public statement was "my own genuinely held, independent view," and that allegations "that I was leant on to give that view ... are wholly unfounded."[125] Unfortunately for Lord Goldsmith, the confidential memorandum leaked a few weeks later, and readers could see for themselves what his genuinely held, independent view actually had been. The kerfluffle that followed fanned public suspicion about the decision to go to war, and weakened Blair in the next election.

It is obvious why Lord Goldsmith gave Parliament the unqualified opinion he did. The war was about to begin, the government was committed to it, and it was deeply controversial. An opinion laden with doubts would have had devastating repercussions for the government's policy and its relationship with the United States. Knowing this, Goldsmith wrote a brief, just as the realists think he should. But realists should notice that when he had to defend it two years later, Goldsmith continued to pretend that it was something else – a backhanded acknowledgment of the principle I am proposing: *If you write a brief but call it an opinion, you have done wrong.* In his second, brief-like opinion, he did wrong.

This is doubly true for the OLC, because in modern practice its opinions bind the executive branch.[126] That makes them quasi-judicial in character. In the preceding chapter, I argued that legal advice from lawyers to clients is always "jurisgenerative" and quasi-judicial, but obviously, written opinions binding entire departments of the government are judicial in a more direct way. As such, the obligation of impartiality built into the legal advisor's ethical role is reinforced by the obligation of impartiality incumbent on a judge. Two additional factors make the obligation more weighty still. First, some of the opinions were secret. Insulated from outside criticism and alternative points of view, written under pressure from powerful officials and, perhaps, from hair-raising intelligence about Al Qaeda's intentions, they were memos from the bunker. Recognizing a professional obligation to provide impartial analysis represented an essential tether to reality. Finally, the OLC is charged by statute with helping the executive discharge its constitutional obligation to "take care that the laws be faithfully executed." Fidelity to the law, not to the Administration, requires impartiality.

---

[125] Hansard, 1 March 2005, column 112, available at <www.publications.parliament.uk/pa/ld199697/ldhansrd/pdvn/lds05/text/50301-03.htm>.

[126] Randolph D. Moss, *Executive Branch Legal Interpretation: A Perspective from the Office of Legal Counsel*, 52 Admin. L. Rev. 1303, 1318–20 (2000). I am grateful to Dawn Johnsen, Marty Lederman, and Nina Pillard for illuminating email discussions of OLC's role and ethics. For Lederman's view, see *Chalk on the Spikes: What is the Proper Role of Executive Branch Lawyers, Anyway?*, available at <http://balkin.blogspot.com/2006/07/chalk-on-spikes-what-is-proper-role-of.html>.

In December, 2004, nineteen former lawyers in the OLC drafted a set of principles for the office reaffirming its commitment to this standard conception of the independent legal advisor. Apparently, this is not how the Bush Adminstration's OLC conceives of its job, for none of its lawyers was willing to sign.[127]

Conclusion

I drafted this chapter before the United States Supreme Court rebuffed the Bush administration's detainee policies in *Hamdan v. Rumsfeld*. Among other significant holdings, *Hamdan* found that common Article 3 of the Geneva Conventions applies to detainees in the war on terror. Article 3 forbids torture and humiliating or degrading treatment – an awkward holding, because, as we have seen, high-level officials, including the Secretary of Defense and possibly the Vice-President or even the President, had authorized such treatment for high-value detainees. Worse, federal law declared violations of common Article 3 to be war crimes. *Hamdan* pushed administration lawyers into overdrive, and they produced a bill, the Military Commissions Act of 2006, to respond to the Court. After intense negotiations with moderate Republican Senators, the final bill was approved by Congress and signed into law in October 2006.

The bill responded to *Hamdan*'s challenge in a drastic way. It stripped federal courts of habeas corpus jurisdiction over Guantánamo, defined "unlawful enemy combatants" broadly, prohibited detainees from arguing for Geneva Convention rights, retroactively decriminalized humiliating and degrading treatment, declared that federal courts could not use international law to interpret war crimes provisions, vested interpretive authority over Geneva in the President, allowed coerced evidence to be admitted, gave the government the power to shut down revelation of exactly what techniques were used to obtain such coerced evidence, and defined criminally cruel treatment in a deeply convoluted way. For example, the bill distinguishes between "severe pain," the hallmark of torture, and merely "serious" pain, the hallmark of cruel treatment short of torture – but it then defines "serious" pain as "extreme" pain. Such bizarre legalisms call the Bybee Memo to mind, of course, and they should. This bill (the worst piece of legislation I can recall from my own lifetime) was clearly inspired by the style of legal thinking perfected by the torture lawyers. In effect, the torture lawyers helped to define a "new normal," without which the Military Commissions Act would not exist.

---

[127] The statement of principles was published as *Guidelines for the President's Legal Advisors*, 81 Ind. L. J. 1345 (2006).

This chapter chronicles a legal train wreck. The lawyers did not cause it, but they facilitated it. As a consequence, enmity toward the United States has undoubtedly increased in much of the world. Sadly and ironically, the net effect on US intelligence gathering may be just the opposite of what the lawyers hoped, as potential sources who might have come willingly to the Americans turn away out of anger or fear that they might find themselves in Guantánamo or Bagram facing pitiless interrogators.

This is also a chapter on the legal ethics of opinion-writing. I have focused on what Fuller might have called the procedural side of the subject: the requirements of honesty, objectivity, and non-frivolous argument, regardless of the subject-matter on which lawyers tender their advice. But that does not mean the subject-matter is irrelevant. It is one thing for boy-wonder lawyers to loophole tax laws and write opinions legitimizing financial shenanigans. It is another thing entirely to loophole laws against torture and cruelty. Lawyers should approach laws defending basic human dignity with fear and trembling.[128]

To be sure, honest opinion-writing will only get you so far. Law can be cruel, and then an honest legal opinion will reflect its cruelty. In the centuries when the evidence law required torture, no lawyer could honestly have advised that the law prohibited it. Honest opinion-writing by no means guarantees that lawyers will be on the side of human dignity.

The fact remains, however, that rule-of-law societies generally prohibit torture and CID, practices that fit more comfortably with despotism and absolutism. For that reason, lawyers in rule-of-law societies will seldom find it easy to craft an honest legal argument for cruelty. Like the torture lawyers of Washington, they will find themselves compelled to betray their craft. Of course, they may think of it as creative lawyering or cleverness, not betrayal. I have little doubt that only intelligent, well-educated lawyers could write these memos, larded as they are with sophisticated-looking tricks of statutory interpretation. But there is such a thing as being too clever for your own good.[129]

---

[128] I thank Christopher Kutz for emphasizing this point to me. Jeremy Waldron makes the same point in *Torture and the Common Law*, supra note 56.

[129] I owe special thanks to Lynne Henderson and Marty Lederman for comments and suggestions on this chapter. I do not wish to attribute any of my views or errors to them, however. (In particular, I know that Lederman disagrees with my discussion of the OLC draft memo on Article 49 of the Fourth Geneva Convention.) In addition, Jack Goldsmith raised important objections to my analysis of his Article 49 draft memo – fewer than he would have wished to raise, because his confidentiality obligations made it impossible for him to go into details. I have made some revisions based on these objections. I am grateful to him for his generosity, fairness, and objectivity in responding to my polemical comments. Obviously, remaining mistakes in my analysis are mine alone, not his – nor those of Sandy Levinson, who also offered helpful comments on an earlier draft.

III

Moral complications and moral psychology

6

Contrived ignorance

The sad fact is that honest lawyers sometimes have crooked clients. In a notorious 1980 case of client fraud, a pair of businessmen used the services of an unsuspecting law firm to close hundreds of millions of dollars worth of crooked loans for their computer leasing company. The businessmen created forged leases to inflate the value of their company's contracts, which they used as collateral for the loans. In the evenings, the pair would turn the lights off in their office. Goodman would crouch beneath a glass table shining a flashlight upward so that Weissman could trace signatures from genuine leases on to the forgeries. New loans serviced previous loans in a decade-long pyramid scheme.

After nearly ten years, Goodman and Weissman's accountant stumbled across their frauds. He wrote a detailed warning to the swindlers' law firm, which the accountant's lawyer tried to hand-deliver to Joseph Hutner, the law firm's lead partner.

But Hutner didn't want to see it. In fact, he wanted the accountant to take the letter back. Above all, Hutner seemed to want to preserve his own oblivion. As the accountant's lawyer later recounted, "I had visions of him clamping his hands over his ears and running out of the office."[1]

Well, wouldn't you? Hutner had been used. He had mouths to feed in his firm, and the computer crooks represented more than half the firm's annual billings. His flight reaction probably came straight from the gut. It may also have been the result of a calculation, however. Legal ethics rules forbid lawyers from knowingly participating in fraud, and Hutner may have reasoned that if he didn't know about any fraud, his firm would not have to part ways with its bread-and-butter client. At the very least, maintaining deniability might buy some time to figure out the next move.

The fact is that ignorance can be vital. A white-collar defense attorney offers the following recollection: "I can remember years ago when I represented a

---

[1] Stuart Taylor, Jr., *Ethics and the Law: A Case History*, N.Y. Times Mag., Jan. 9, 1983, at 33.

fellow in a massive case of political corruption. I was very young, and I asked him, 'Would you please tell me everything that happened.' And he said, 'What, are you out of your mind?' "[2]

The man had a point. Because lawyers are forbidden from lying or knowingly putting on perjured testimony, knowing too much can tie a lawyer's hands.[3] The lawyer is foreclosed from using the strongest arguments on the client's behalf because, unfortunately, the strongest arguments are false.

Lawyers often complain that it's hard to get clients to tell them the unvarnished truth. But it can be an equal challenge to avoid facts that the lawyer really doesn't want to know. Criminal defense lawyers rarely ask their clients, "Did you do it?" Instead, they ask the client what evidence he thinks the police or prosecution have against him – whom he spoke with, who the witnesses are, what documents or physical evidence he knows about. If the client seems too eager to spill his guts, the lawyer will quickly cut him off, admonishing him that time is short and that it will be best if the client answers *only* the questions his lawyer asks him. The lawyer will pose the questions carefully and frame them narrowly. "Don't ask, don't tell" is the strategy, and the preservation of deniability is its goal.[4]

Lawyers may be exceptional in the self-conscious casuistry they bring to their quest for deniability, but they are in no way exceptional in the quest itself. The very word "deniability," which originated after the Bay of Pigs debacle, gained currency in the Watergate era to describe something that Richard Nixon's subordinates wanted to preserve for him at all costs. The Iran-Contra principals turned out to be veritable Balanchines when it came to choreographing Ronald Reagan's deniability. They knew very well that deniability is a politician's best friend. Business managers also understand the value of deniability. Analyzing the authority system in large American corporations, sociologist Robert Jackall writes that "pushing down details relieves superiors of the burden of too much knowledge, particularly guilty knowledge."[5] In the familiar corporate adage, bad news doesn't flow upstream.

A superior will say to a subordinate ... "Give me your best thinking on the problem ... " When the subordinate makes his report, he is often told: "I think you can do better than that," until the subordinate has worked out all the details of the boss's predetermined solution, without the boss being specifically aware of "all the eggs that have to be broken."[6]

[2] Kenneth Mann, Defending White-collar Crime: A Portrait of Attorneys at Work 104–5 (1985).
[3] ABA Model Rule of Professional Conduct 3.3(a)(3) states that "A lawyer shall not knowingly offer evidence that the lawyer knows to be false"; Rule 8.4(c) forbids a lawyer from engaging in "conduct involving dishonesty, fraud, deceit or misrepresentation."
[4] See Lincoln Caplan, *Don't Ask, Don't Tell*, Newsweek, August 1, 1994, at 22.
[5] Robert Jackall, Moral Mazes: the World of Corporate Managers 20 (1988).   [6] Ibid.

Deniability refers to one's capacity to deny guilty knowledge truthfully. Clearly, deniability is a state of affairs desirable almost beyond price, and not only for lawyers, politicians, and executives. Deniability is the key to succeeding at the world's work, which is often dirty, while keeping a clean conscience – or at least a serviceable facsimile of a clean conscience. Perhaps the truth will set us free, but sometimes ignorance of the truth leaves us freer still.

Virtually all of us prefer not to know things, if knowing them will require us to take unwelcome action. Why does our conscience work that way? The reason, I suspect, is that the quest for deniability seems not as bad as dishonesty. A dishonest person learns the truth and then simply lies about it. Evading truth is an expedient for *avoiding* lies. It's a stratagem for tarnished angels like you and me, not for unrepentant scoundrels. It's the homage that vice pays to virtue.

And yet avoiding lies cannot be as simple as shutting one's eyes. Hungry lions don't go away when the ostrich in the legend sticks her head in the sand – that is one reason we know that the story must be a legend. Guilty knowledge is a hungry lion, and it can't be ignored out of existence. Or can it? This is the question I propose to investigate. Soon it will lead us into complications, but for the moment we can pose the question itself in three simple words: Does deniability work?

Willful ignorance in the criminal law

Let us start by asking what light the law sheds on our question. To lawyers in the common-law tradition, deniability brings to mind a familiar criminal law doctrine called *willful ignorance* – or, as it is sometimes called, "willful blindness" or "conscious avoidance."[7] In essence, the doctrine states that willful ignorance is equivalent to knowledge. Self-generated deniability doesn't work: you can be convicted of knowingly committing a crime even if you don't commit it knowingly – provided that you contrived your own ignorance.

The doctrine seems intuitively just. But why? It is Biblical wisdom that we forgive those who know not what they do. Culpability presupposes a guilty mind. But ignorance is nothing more than an empty mind, and for that reason there is a profound puzzle in explaining exactly why ignorance, willed or not, should support criminal convictions. The Orwellian-sounding identity IGNORANCE = KNOWLEDGE is, to put it mildly, an equation crying out for a theory. Criminal lawyers take two approaches to this problem, neither of which turns out to be entirely satisfactory.

---

[7] One writer identifies fourteen different terms for the concept in the criminal law. See Robin Charlow, *Willful Ignorance and Criminal Culpability*, 70 Tex. L. Rev. 1351, 1352 n. 1 (1992).

The negligence approach

The first approach is to argue that even if the wrongdoer didn't know, he should have known. But the phrase "should have known" triggers a familiar line of legal reasoning. "Should have known" implies a legal duty to know, and failure to know amounts to negligence.

In other words, "he should have known, but he didn't" means in the common law that he was negligent. This familiar point of doctrine leads to two problems. The first is explaining why we have a duty to know. The law is generally reluctant to impose affirmative duties on people, unless they occupy posts of special responsibility. And a duty to know looks especially dubious. It cannot really be that we have a duty to inform ourselves about everything that might affect our obligations – that duty would know no outer bound, and fulfilling it would take up all of our time for the rest of our lives. It also raises moral problems of its own. Is it a duty *not* to mind our own business? A duty to meddle? A duty to pry? A duty to snoop? A duty to mistrust and double-check every suspicious fact someone else tells us? Common sense tells us that we have no such duty. But then where is the negligence?

The second problem is that even if we agree that willful ignorance is a kind of negligence, doing something negligently is less culpable than doing it knowingly. The usual hierarchy of blame in the criminal law moves in ordered steps. The Model Penal Code, for example, distinguishes four levels of culpability. The worst is acting *willfully* or *purposely*, by making the misdeed our conscious object.[8] Next is acting *knowingly*, by acting in full awareness of our misdeed, although not necessarily with the misdeed as our object. Next comes acting *recklessly*, by consciously disregarding a substantial and unjustifiable risk that we are doing wrong. Last comes acting *negligently*, by acting when we should be aware of a substantial and unjustifiable risk of misdeed, even if we are not actually aware.[9]

In other words, negligence isn't as bad as knowledge; in the Model Penal Code scheme, it is two levels removed from knowledge. Suppose that a statute forbids *knowingly* transporting a controlled substance across state lines. If I transport a controlled substance negligently – *merely* negligently, as my lawyer will insist – I cannot be convicted under this statute. The prosecutor must prove that I did it knowingly. Under the negligence analysis of willful ignorance, willful ignorance *cannot* be equivalent to knowledge, and the common law equation collapses.

Nor is this a purely theoretical problem. Every good criminal lawyer understands how it might play out in practice. The most frequent complaint

[8] See Model Penal Code §2.02(2)(a) (Proposed Official Draft 1962).
[9] See ibid. §2.02(2)(b).

about willful-blindness instructions to a jury is that such instructions illicitly convert crimes requiring knowledge to crimes of mere negligence. As the Seventh Circuit Court of Appeals admonished while reversing a willful-blindness conviction, ostriches "are not merely *careless* birds."[10]

The Model Penal Code approach

The alternative to treating willful blindness as negligence is to find an actual, occurrent mental state to which willful blindness corresponds. The drafters of the Model Penal Code simply abandoned the doctrine that willful blindness can substitute for knowledge. In its place, they proposed that awareness of the high probability of a fact is tantamount to knowledge of that fact.[11] In this way, they preserved the root intuition that criminal guilt requires some guilty mental state. Here, the guilty mental state is awareness of the high probability of a fact, presumably whatever fact the willfully blind person has arranged not to know.

Unfortunately, this proposal raises more problems than it solves. First of all, being aware that something is highly probable simply isn't the same as actually knowing it. I don't mean that knowledge implies certainty rather than probability. Knowledge claims need not be infallible. But knowledge does require belief – I can hardly be said to know something if I don't even believe it – whereas awareness that something is highly probable may stop short of the inferential leap into belief. We can see this by comparing the two statements "I know X but I don't believe X" and "I'm aware that X is highly probable, but I don't believe X." The first of these verges on performative self-contradiction – an observation that philosophers call Moore's Paradox – while the second does not.

This difference between awareness of high probability and knowledge has not passed unnoticed by commentators, who draw various conclusions from it. One recommends cutting the Gordian knot by *defining* knowledge of a fact as awareness that it is highly probable.[12] That solves the problem, but only by converting the word "knowledge" into a legal term of art. Departing from the everyday meaning of words is seldom a good idea in law, and never more so than in criminal law, in which substituting eccentric meanings for words risks punishing us without fair notice. Other commentators go in the opposite

---

[10] United States v. Giovannetti, 919 F.2d 1223, 1228 (7th Cir. 1990).

[11] See Model Penal Code §2.02(7) (Proposed Official Draft 1962) ("When knowledge of the existence of a particular fact is an element of an offense, such knowledge is established if a person is aware of a high probability of its existence, unless he actually believes that it does not exist").

[12] See Jonathan L. Marcus, Note, *Model Penal Code Section 2.02(7) and Willful Blindness*, 102 Yale L.J. 2231, 2233, 2253 (1993).

direction, and conclude that the Model Penal Code awareness-of-high-probability formula can really support convictions only for crimes requiring some mental state less than knowledge.[13]

The trouble with all these proposals is that they are not really about willful ignorance at all. Instead, they change the subject. The focus in a willful-ignorance case is on whether the actor deliberately avoided guilty knowledge. The inquiry is about whatever steps the actor took to ward off knowledge prior to the misdeed. By contrast, the Model Penal Code focuses on how certain the actor was about a fact. The inquiry is about the actor's subjective state at the moment of the misdeed. These are completely different issues. An actor can be aware of the high probability of a fact whether or not she took steps to avoid knowing it, and an actor can screen herself from knowledge of facts regardless of whether their probability is high or low.[14]

In practice, to be sure, the Model Penal Code standard provides a serviceable substitute for willful ignorance. That is because in most cases of willful ignorance the defendant will be aware of the high probability of the fact that he has hidden from himself, so that the Model Penal Code doctrine succeeds in convicting most of the miscreants who deserve it. It convicts the drug mule who deliberately refrains from looking in the satchel he's delivering. It convicts the corporate manager who doesn't ask why his overseas salesman needs a million in cash for "commissions." And it just may convict

---

[13] One, for example, argues that the Model Penal Code standard defines not knowledge but recklessness, which (you will recall) means consciously disregarding a substantial risk of wrongdoing. See Ira. P. Robbins, *The Ostrich Instruction: Deliberate Ignorance as a Criminal Mens Rea*, 81 J. Crim. L. & Criminology 191, 223–27 (1990). Another thinks that the Code standard, which requires awareness of *high* risk rather than mere *substantial* risk, has thereby defined something between recklessness and knowledge. See Charlow, supra note 7, at 1394–97. Both conclude that Code-based willful ignorance should support convictions only for crimes requiring mental states less culpable than knowledge.

[14] Douglas Husak and Craig Callender illustrate the latter with a nice pair of examples. Suppose that a dope distributor tells each of his three couriers never to look in the suitcase he gives to each one, adding that it isn't necessary for them to know what the suitcases contain. If the suitcases contain dope, the case is plainly one of willful ignorance. But now suppose that the distributor adds that two of the three suitcases contain nothing but clothing, that he is truthful, and that the distributors know he is truthful. If the couriers deliver the suitcases without looking inside and without asking any questions, the case seems indistinguishable from the first case. It is still willful ignorance. But in the second case, the courier with dope in his suitcase lacks awareness of the high probability that it contains dope. Indeed, he knows that the probability is only one-third. He may even believe that his suitcase contains nothing but clothes. Thus, in the language of the Model Penal Code §2.02(7), he not only lacks awareness of a high probability of the fact's existence, "he actually believes that it does not exist." See Douglas N. Husak & Craig A. Callender, *Willful Ignorance, Knowledge, and the "Equal Culpability" Thesis: A Study of the Deeper Significance of the Principle of Legality*, 1994 Wis. L. Rev. 29, 37–38.

the lawyer who clamps his hands over his ears and runs out of the office because he doesn't want to stop closing loans for crooked clients.[15]

Unfortunately, it does *not* convict the high-ranking executive who deliberately, skillfully, and self-consciously fashions an entire structure of deniability, a reporting system in which for years at a time guilty knowledge never flows upstream. Once that system is in place, business goes on as usual – most of it proper, but some of it perhaps improper. But the executive has no awareness of the probability of the improper stuff, maybe not even awareness of its possibility, because when he contrived the reporting system, he had no specific crimes in mind.

How does a structure of deniability work? It goes like this. The CEO lets everyone know that he hates to micro-manage. He is interested only in the big picture of *whether* goals are met, not in details about *how* they are met. It goes without saying (and I do mean without saying) that the CEO is to be sheltered from bad news, especially knowledge that anyone in the organization has cut legal corners. Like ambitious subordinates everywhere, his management team tries to anticipate his wishes and, in the familiar corporate adage, "follow them in advance" so they won't actually have to be spoken aloud. Managers too obtuse to understand this are said to lack initiative, and their careers are short. Prominent among the unspoken directives is the first commandment: Thou shalt maintain thy boss's deniability.[16]

For public consumption, the organization sets up an elaborate accountability mechanism, requiring employees to report in writing anything they observe that is illegal, unethical, or unsafe. In practice, however, employees who follow these instructions find themselves reassigned to the company's North Dakota Wind Chill Test Facility. Old-timers explain to newcomers that the purpose of the reporting mechanism is *not* to be utilized, thereby ensuring that only the lowest-level employees – those who fail to file their written reports – will bear the blame if anything goes wrong. In fact, management sees little advantage in an accurate system for tracking responsibility within the corporation. Too many managers advance by getting promoted to new divisions before the chickens come home to roost at the old divisions. This is called "outrunning your mistakes."[17] The last thing they want is a paper trail.

---

[15] In fact, Hutner was never indicted for aiding and abetting the computer crooks. But, for a case in which a lawyer went to jail for writing his client's lies into an opinion letter without investigating them, see United States v. Benjamin, 328 F.2d 854, 863–64 (2nd Cir. 1964).

[16] See John M. Darley, *How Organizations Socialize Individuals into Evildoing*, in Codes of Conduct: Behavioral Research in Business Ethics 13, 24–25 (David M. Messick & Ann E. Tenbrunsel eds., 1996). See also Jackall, supra note 5, at 18–19.

[17] See Jackall, supra note 5, at 90–95. Jackall details the ways in which managers exploit the absence of responsibility tracking mechanisms to "milk" their businesses, get promoted up the corporate ladder as a reward for cost-cutting, and stick their successors with the aftermath.

Few subjects are as fascinating, important, or hard to conceptualize as the many and subtle ways in which organizations screen individuals within them from liability and dissolve employees' sense of personal accountability. In my view, concepts of collective or corporate responsibility are poor substitutes for individual responsibility. For one thing, blaming the collective may let individuals off the hook too easily. It's not for nothing that the Nuremberg Charter made individual criminal liability the linchpin of its approach to state-sponsored crime. At the same time, collectivizing guilt may blame innocent employees. Last but not least, collective responsibility concepts teeter on the brink of quack metaphysics or mystical science fiction, treating groups of people as single minds. No better illustration of this can be found than the collective knowledge doctrine in federal criminal law.[18] According to this doctrine, a corporation "knows" the sum of what all of its employees know, whether they communicate with each other or not. The doctrine treats employees as synapses in the nonexistent brain of a legal fiction.

How, then, can the law apportion individual responsibility within the organizational context, where too many involved individuals act at a distance and each knows too little? In my view, the most promising approach is through the concept of complicity – aiding and abetting – and the concept of willful ignorance. Supervisors implicitly or explicitly encourage their subordinates to meet their targets by any means necessary. That's abetting. Supervisors provide assistance and resources. That's aiding. And supervisors structure the organization to preserve their own deniability. That's willful ignorance. Willful ignorance is a concept that applies almost uniquely to crimes committed by group enterprises. Of course, a good whodunit author can devise clever scenarios in which a lone gunman contrives his own ignorance at the moment he pulls the trigger. But, in real life, I can contrive ignorance only when I work with others who know the facts that I don't.

Together, the concepts of aiding, abetting, and willful ignorance enable us to understand the dimensions of supervisory wrongdoing – the wrongdoing C. S. Lewis had in mind when he wrote about evils committed by "quiet men with white collars and cut fingernails and smooth-shaven cheeks who do not need to raise their voice."[19] In that case, however, the Model Penal Code substitute for the willful ignorance doctrine should be rejected because it is simply too narrow for the task at hand.

In sum, the common law's equation of willful ignorance with knowledge leaves us in a dilemma: is willful ignorance a guilty mental state, or the violation of a duty to know? The Model Penal Code employs a knowledge concept (awareness of a high probability) rather than mere negligence. But

---

[18] See, e.g., United States v. Bank of New England, 821 F.2d 844, 856 (1st Cir. 1987).

[19] C. S. Lewis, The Screwtape Letters and Screwtape Proposes a Toast, at x (Collier, 1962).

not only is the Model Penal Code standard quite distinct from willful ignorance, it is also too weak for organizational settings. The negligence theory succeeds in explaining how mere ignorance can be culpable, as the Model Penal Code does not. But the negligence theory employs a duty-to-know concept less stringent than knowledge, and too demanding for real life.

A nasty example

Let me propose a diagnosis. The two theories fail because willful ignorance is neither knowledge nor negligence. Consider an example – a sinister example, but one that I find particularly thought-provoking.

In the early days of the Third Reich, Albert Speer was Hitler's official architect. Later, he moved into more essential posts, and eventually he became the minister of armaments during the war, responsible for, among other things, producing war materials through slave labor in concentration camps. Unsurprisingly, the Allies put Speer on trial in the first tier of Nuremberg defendants, as a member of the leadership of the Third Reich.

Speer stood out at the trial, because he was the only defendant who insisted on taking full responsibility for the crimes of the Reich. He accepted responsibility, he explained, in order to ensure that the German people would not suffer any more than they already had for the sins of their leaders. Probably because of his confession, Speer received a twenty-year sentence, where others no guiltier were hanged. After his release from Spandau Prison, Speer published a best-selling memoir, *Inside the Third Reich*, and followed it up with two more volumes of recollections. In the books, he once again took full responsibility for the crimes of the Third Reich, and cemented his reputation as, in the sarcastic title of a recent biography, "the good Nazi."[20]

Let me be a bit more specific about what Speer did and did not confess to. Four points stand out:

1. He accepted full responsibility for the crimes of the Reich.
2. He denied, however, that he actually knew anything about the Final Solution.
3. He also acknowledged that he could have known, but he chose not to know in order to keep his conscience clear.
4. He insisted that his willful ignorance was just as bad as knowledge, and thus he refused to let himself off the hook.

For example, Speer recalls that in 1944 a friend of his warned him "never to accept an invitation to inspect a concentration camp in Upper Silesia.

---

[20] Dan Van Der Vat, The Good Nazi: The Life and Lies of Albert Speer (1997).

Never under any circumstances."[21] Speer described his thought processes as follows:

I did not query him, I did not query Himmler, I did not query Hitler, I did not speak with personal friends. I did not investigate – for I did not want to know what was happening there ... From that moment on, I was inescapably contaminated morally; from fear of discovering something which might have made me turn from my course, I had closed my eyes ... Because I failed at that time, I still feel, to this day, responsibility for Auschwitz in a wholly personal sense.[22]

For Auschwitz was the very camp Speer's friend was warning him to avoid.

The interesting thing about Speer is that he was almost certainly lying about how little he knew. Indeed, journalists and historians have made a minor cottage industry of smoking out Albert Speer's lies.[23] Speer's response, to the end of his life, was to insist that he really didn't know.

What makes this interesting, of course, is that Speer also insisted that whether he knew or not is irrelevant, because his guilt was the same whether he knew or not. Then why insist on ignorance? The legal theorist Leo Katz suggests that Speer "was being coy, was playing Marc Anthony by saying he was not seeking to excuse himself while going to such extraordinary pains to establish his willful ignorance. He really did think it mitigated his guilt."[24]

I am sure that Katz is right about Speer being coy. I am less certain that Speer really thought willful ignorance mitigated his guilt. Albert Speer was a master of public relations. From Nuremberg on, he instinctively understood that the best way to dodge responsibility is to assume it – but not to assume responsibility for any particular heinous deeds. Whether or not he himself believed that willful ignorance mitigated his guilt, I am sure Speer understood that the world at large believes it.

Or rather, he understood that the world at large can't make up its mind. The paradox is that we seem to accept his subtext, "I'm not as guilty as if I really knew!," but only because his text insists that he *is* as guilty as if he really knew. We nod yes when Albert Speer writes, "I was inescapably contaminated morally," and then we forgive him, at least in part.

---

[21] Albert Speer, Inside the Third Reich: Memoirs 375–76 (Richard & Clara Winston trans., 1970).

[22] Ibid. at 376.

[23] See, e.g., Henry T. King, Jr., with Bettina Elles, The Two Worlds of Albert Speer: Reflections of a Nuremberg Prosecutor 97–106 (1997); Matthias Schmidt, Albert Speer: The End of a Myth (Joachim Neugroschel trans., 1982); Albert Speer: Kontroversen um ein Deutsches Phänomen (Adelbert Reif ed., 1978); Van Der Vat, supra note 20. It should be noted that the evidence of the extent of Speer's knowledge is entirely circumstantial.

[24] Leo Katz, Ill-Gotten Gains: Evasion, Blackmail, Fraud, and Kindred Puzzles of the Law 41 (1996).

I think that Leo Katz draws the wrong conclusion from this example. He argues that the forgiveness, the subtext, reflects our deepest moral understanding, and thus he concludes that willful ignorance really is a proper moral excuse. But why assume that we actually believe the subtext, when we nod yes to the text? Perhaps we do absolve Albert Speer, at least in part. But we also convict criminals on willful-blindness instructions. Curiously, Katz overlooks this fact. He writes that willful ignorance excuses "often work at a legal level ... The law here as so often is a good gauge of our moral intuitions. So I rather think the ruses work at a moral level as well."[25] Katz relies on an example to demonstrate that willful-ignorance excuses work at a legal level – the criminal defense lawyer who uses a "Don't ask, don't tell" strategy for circumventing the ethics rule against knowingly helping a client commit perjury. This is an example we have seen before. It's an apt example, for this is one place in the law where the "ostrich excuse" does work. The bar's legal ethics rules do not require a lawyer to investigate the client's story, nor do they incorporate the doctrine that willful ignorance equals knowledge.[26] But of course the criminal law does incorporate that doctrine, and that makes the legal ethics rules exceptional within the law. For some reason, Katz overlooks the fact that in the criminal law, willful ignorance is ground for conviction, rather than for acquittal.

The proper conclusion is that the law speaks with a divided voice about willful-ignorance excuses. If Katz is correct that the law is a good gauge of our moral intuitions, it would follow that morality speaks with a divided voice as well. The question is why.[27]

---

[25] Ibid. at 44.

[26] ABA Model Rule 1.0(f) carefully defines the words "knowingly," "known," and "knows" to denote "actual knowledge of the fact in question."

[27] This puzzle exists in theological discussions as well. Christian moralists developed an elaborate theory about when ignorance excuses wrongdoing and when it does not. The key variables in the theory concern how cognizant of his own ignorance the wrongdoer is, whether he lies under a duty to dispel it, and whether he did anything, either by omission or commission, to foster his ignorance. The moralists distinguished ignorance arising from mere neglect to inform oneself – so-called "crass" or "supine" ignorance – from ignorance deliberately cultivated – "affected ignorance" (*ignorantia affectata*). Affected ignorance corresponds closely with the common law's willful blindness. According to one writer, "an act done through ignorance, even if that ignorance be crass or supine, is less culpable than an act done with clear knowledge; for it is less fully voluntary, and, therefore, less imputable. As regards the ignorance which is deliberately fostered, there is a divergence of opinion among moralists." G. H. Joyce, *Invincible Ignorance*, in 7 Encyclopedia of Religion & Ethics 404 (James Hastings ed., 1915). This "divergence of opinion among moralists" seems appropriate, given the divided voice in the law and in our moral intuitions.

Judaism places less emphasis than Christianity does on interior states of soul and more on external behavior. As befits a faith based on thousands of years of fidelity to a divinely authored text, Judaism also emphasizes the letter of the law over the spirit. Some of the most ingenious reasoning in Jewish law has been loophole lawyering designed to mitigate the rigors

The ostrich and the fox

Let's go back to something Albert Speer said in his *mea culpa* about his responsibility for Auschwitz. "From fear of discovering something which might have made me turn from my course, I had closed my eyes."[28] Speer's formulation gets close to the heart of our problem. Suppose for the sake of argument that Speer was *not* lying. Suppose that he really didn't know about Auschwitz, because he had closed his eyes. In that case, we confront the question of what Speer would have done had he *not* closed his eyes. He might have turned from his course, he tells us, but would he have? If the answer is yes, then we mitigate our judgment of him, at least a little bit.[29] If the answer is no, then we blame him *more*. Not only did he knowingly participate in genocide, but he prepared a coverup, a clever willful-ignorance defense, as well.

That's one reason why we can't make up our minds about willful-ignorance excuses. They amount to counterfactual assertions that if the person had known, he would have changed his course. To which the response must be: Maybe so, maybe not. Maybe the person offering the excuse really is an ostrich, a moral weakling in self-inflicted denial that a terrible moral choice confronts him. In that case, willful ignorance seems not as bad as actual knowledge. But maybe the would-be ostrich is actually a fox – a grand schemer who fully intends to follow the path of wrongdoing, and who contrived his ignorance only as a liability-screening precaution, like a good getaway car. In that case, willful ignorance seems *more* culpable than knowledge, because it adds to knowledge an element of unrepentant calculation.

Ostrich or Fox? We may never know. Nor can we ever be sure whether the Ostrich would have turned from wrongdoing if she had only taken her head out of the sand to learn that it was wrongdoing. Would she or wouldn't she? The excuse of willful ignorance functions precisely to make that question unanswerable.

of the commandments in the face of life on the edge of constant menace. A rigid textualism sometimes turns out to be the compassionate rabbi's best tool for blunting the law's harsh edges. As one contemporary rabbi explains, "God made no mistakes ... If he left a loophole, he put it there to be used." Clyde Haberman, *Alon Shevut Journal: Thank the Lord for Loopholes: Sabbath Is Safe*, N.Y. Times, December 19, 1994, at A4. Unsurprisingly, then, Jewish ethics do not condemn willful blindness. In fact, in some cases Jewish ethics encourage it. The law treats bastard children harshly, and so a good Jew should remain willfully blind to the circumstances of birth of a suspected bastard. Likewise, compassion suggests willfully blinding ourselves to circumstances that would void a contract on which an innocent person relies. (I owe these examples to my colleague, Professor Sherman Cohn.)

[28] Speer, supra note 21, at 375–76.

[29] We no longer hold him fully accountable for knowingly participating in genocide, just for knowingly participating in the murder of Hitler's opponents, the planning of World War II, and twelve years of violent racism! If you're Albert Speer, you take your mitigation where you can find it.

The question may be unanswerable even by the Ostrich herself. Speer says only that knowledge *might* have made him turn from his course, and in this observation he is keenly perceptive. Many of us who close our eyes actually have no idea what we would do if we had dared to leave them open. We like to think that if we really knew that our course was wrongful we would turn from it; but perhaps we lack the guts. Willful ignorance is a moral strategy for postponing the moment of truth, for sparing ourselves the test of our resolve. St. Augustine famously prayed to God to give him the strength to resist temptation, only not yet.[30] The Ostrich hopes to God that she has the strength to resist temptation – only she doesn't want to find out yet. It's Augustine Lite, Augustine in a slightly more infantile form.

The Fox, on the other hand, is a premeditating crook, a grand schemer who guards himself from knowledge only to prepare a defense of ignorance.[31] Our ambivalence about the willful-ignorance excuse reflects, at least in part, our inability to resolve a fuzzy stereoscopic image, the portrait of an Ostrich superimposed on the portrait of a Fox. Our intuitions run very differently depending on which image we have in mind, and, without thinking about matters carefully, we probably have both images in mind.

In fact, we have *three* images superimposed on each other, not just two. Alongside the Fox, we can imagine the weak-willed, unrighteous Ostrich who would have continued to do wrong even if she knew that that was what she was doing, *and* the stronger-willed, half-righteous Ostrich who shields herself from guilty knowledge, but would actually do the right thing if the shield were to fail.

At this point, let me venture a diagnosis of why we have so much difficulty deciding how blameworthy willful ignorance really is. The grand-scheming Fox, who aims to do wrong and structures his own ignorance merely to prepare a defense, has the same level of culpability as any other willful wrongdoer – the highest level, in the Model Penal Code schema. The Unrighteous Ostrich, who doesn't want to know she is doing wrong, but would do it even if she knew, seems precisely fitted for the common-law equation of willful ignorance with knowledge. By definition, her guilt is unchanged whether she knows or not, because her behavior would be unchanged. And the Half-Righteous Ostrich, who won't do wrong if she

---

[30] "I had prayed to you for chastity and said 'Give me chastity and continence, but not yet.' For I was afraid that you would answer my prayer at once and cure me too soon of the disease of lust, which I wanted satisfied, not quelled." St. Augustine, Book VIII, in Confessions 169 (S. Pine-Coffin trans., 1961).

[31] In conversation, David Wasserman has pointed out another possible motivation for the Fox to choose willful ignorance. The Fox may fear that he is too squeamish to carry out his misdeed if he knows at the time what he is doing – but he nevertheless wants to carry it out, and therefore contrives to be ignorant. This alternative motivation still makes the actor a Fox, not an Ostrich, because the ignorance is willed only as a stratagem to facilitate the misdeed.

knows, but would prefer not to know, is in a state of conscious avoidance of a substantial and unjustifiable risk of wrongdoing – precisely the Model Penal Code's definition of recklessness.

In short, motivation makes a difference. Three different motivations correspond with three levels of blame. One is less blameworthy than knowledge, one is precisely as blameworthy as knowledge, and one is more blameworthy. Our moral intuitions aren't contradictory after all. Instead, our puzzles arise because when we evaluate willful ignorance we have three distinct moral intuitions, depending on which inhabitant of the bestiary we call to mind.

The structure of contrived ignorance

At this point, I want to look more carefully at the structure of contrived ignorance. The crucial point is that it involves not one set of actions, but two. The first consists of the actions or omissions by which an actor shields herself from unwanted knowledge. For convenience, let me call them the *screening* actions. When the lawyer interviewing her client breaks off a dangerous line of questioning, when the drug courier refrains from looking in the suitcase, when the executive rewards subordinates who maintain his deniability, they have performed screening actions. The second set of actions consists of whatever misdeeds the actor subsequently commits that would be innocent if, but only if, she was legitimately ignorant. Call these the *unwitting misdeeds*.[32]

Once we draw this distinction, several interesting points emerge. The first is that screening actions, like unwitting misdeeds, can be performed with various degrees of *mens rea*. If we use words carefully, the word "willful" modifying "ignorance" should describe the *mens rea* with which an actor contrives her own ignorance. That leaves open the possibility that ignorance can be contrived at other levels of culpability. A political leader or corporate executive who intentionally sets up an organizational structure designed to maintain his deniability is willfully ignorant. His partner, who didn't set up the structure but is perfectly happy to benefit from it, may not be *willfully* ignorant, but is nonetheless *knowingly* ignorant. Their successor, who decides to run the risk of keeping the structure in place, may well be *recklessly* ignorant. And Reckless's dimwitted partner Feckless, who never even wonders why their predecessors are taking unpaid leave at Club Fed, is negligently ignorant. None of these levels of culpability, except willful ignorance, is a category recognized by the law, even though the hierarchy of mental

---

[32] I am borrowing the term from Holly Smith, who speaks of "unwitting wrongful acts." Holly Smith, *Culpable Ignorance*, 92 Phil. Rev. 543, 547 (1983). Smith uses the nice term "benighting acts" for what I call "screening actions." I depart from her terminology with regret, and only because I've encountered too many people unfamiliar with the word "benighting."

states (willful, knowing, reckless, negligent) is entirely familiar. Contrived ignorance turns out to be a genus, and each of these mental states a distinct species.

Ignoring the distinction between screening actions and unwitting misdeeds can lead to an overly simple theory of contrived ignorance. The Model Penal Code approach, which we examined earlier, is a perfect example. It focuses entirely on the level of awareness accompanying the unwitting misdeed, and completely ignores the screening actions. This leads to particularly troublesome results when the screening actions succeed completely in shielding the actor from guilty knowledge, as in our corporate cases. The actor lacks awareness of the high probability of guilty facts, so by the lights of the Model Penal Code she is off the hook – precisely because her contrived ignorance succeeded so well!

Ignoring the distinctions among the different species of contrived ignorance is a more subtle error, but an error nonetheless. A good example is what might be called the *waiver theory* of willful ignorance. According to the waiver theory, willful blindness waives the defense of ignorance. The waiver theory packs intuitive appeal, and it actually explains the mysterious equation IGNORANCE = KNOWLEDGE. The idea is that when ignorance is self-imposed, the plea of ignorance is nothing but *chutzpah*. The standard example of *chutzpah* is the young man who murders his parents and then pleads for mercy because he is an orphan. Now, of course, murdering one's parents is intrinsically evil, while screening actions may be as innocent as simply not looking in a suitcase. But the example nevertheless has much in common with willful ignorance. In both, the wrongdoer has intentionally caused the condition of his own defense, and thereby waived that defense.[33]

The problem with the waiver theory is that it is too harsh. It seems appropriate when the accused is our grand-scheming Fox, craftily contriving his own defense. But what if the accused has been only recklessly ignorant, or negligently ignorant? In that case it seems unjust to waive the defense of ignorance, and convict him of performing the misdeed knowingly. He did nothing knowingly. He has been, at most, reckless in his screening actions, and his misdeeds were unwitting. Recklessness plus ignorance doesn't add up to knowledge.[34]

The Model Penal Code standard and the waiver theory demonstrate the perils of focusing completely on the unwitting misdeeds while ignoring the screening actions. I now want to argue that it is equally wrong to focus entirely on the screening actions and ignore the unwitting misdeeds.

---

[33] See generally Paul H. Robinson, *Causing the Conditions of One's Own Defense: A Study in the Limits of Theory in Criminal Law Doctrine*, 71 Va. L. Rev. 1 (1985).
[34] See ibid. at 8–15.

The locus of wrongdoing

A natural question arises as to whether the blameworthiness of willful ignorance comes from the screening actions or from the unwitting misdeeds. In the criminal law, the answer is simple. The actor will be convicted for knowingly committing the unwitting misdeed, not for willfully blinding himself. He could hardly be convicted for the screening actions, which most likely are perfectly lawful. There is nothing criminal about not looking in a suitcase.

Outside the criminal law, matters are not so straightforward. Screening oneself from knowledge can be viewed on analogy with drinking oneself into oblivion. If a driver injures someone while he is too drunk to know what he is doing, it may be unfair to blame him for driving poorly. His pickled synapses don't permit him to drive better, or even to realize that he is too drunk to drive. But it seems perfectly appropriate to blame him for drinking himself into oblivion. By the same token, one might argue that if an executive who screens herself from guilty knowledge then unwittingly sets performance goals that her subordinates cannot achieve lawfully, she shouldn't really be blamed for instigating their crimes. She should be blamed for discouraging them from telling her the truth. She wrongfully screened herself from guilty knowledge. As people sometimes say to one another in everyday life, "I don't blame you for what you did, but I do blame you for getting into the situation in the first place." This is a theory of willful blindness as a form of *culpable ignorance* – very literally, ignorance that is itself blameworthy.

On a culpable-ignorance theory, the screening actions bear the primary blame. What about the unwitting misdeeds? According to Holly Smith, who has published an admirable analysis of culpable ignorance, they should be regarded as mere consequences ensuing from the screening acts, consequences over which the actor has ceded control. He has done this by screening himself from the knowledge that would give him a reason to avoid an otherwise blameless action, the unwitting misdeed.

Smith suggests that whether we blame him for the unwitting misdeed as well as for the screening action depends entirely on whether we blame people for bad consequences of their actions, even when they have no control over those consequences.[35] The law is inconsistent on this issue. We do punish completed crimes more severely than failed attempts, even if the difference between success and failure was out of the criminal's control, but we don't typically punish criminals for the remote consequences of their crimes. Indeed, this is a well-known paradox in criminal law. Generations of theorists

---

[35] See Smith, supra note 32, at 569.

have labored to little avail trying to devise a theory to explain why bad consequences, not merely bad intentions, matter.[36]

Fortunately, we need not enter this debate, because Smith is mistaken in treating unwitting misdeeds as brute consequences caused by the screening actions. In effect, Smith treats the actor at the time of the unwitting misdeeds as if he were a different person from the actor at the time of the screening actions.[37] The "screener" becomes something akin to a manipulative criminal who causes an innocent agent – his own later self – to commit a crime. In such cases, the principal rightly gets all the blame, and the innocent agent gets none.[38]

But this analysis overlooks the important fact that the later self is not *entirely* innocent. The later self at least knows that he performed the screening actions at an earlier time. He is on notice that the sword of potential wrongdoing dangles over his head. The later self has an opportunity to reconsider and abandon a course of action that might turn out to be an unwitting misdeed. If he persists in acting, he shares in the blame. The more probable he believes the misdeed is, the more he shares in the blame. Thus, the right analogue is not that of a guilty principal (the earlier self) and an innocent agent (the later self) whose unwitting misdeed is a causal consequence of the earlier self's screening actions. The right analogue is that of a guilty principal and an agent who is at least reckless. The analogy, in other words, is to complicity, not causation – remembering, of course, that the complicitous principal and agent are the same person at two different times.

---

[36] George Fletcher has noted: "The relevance of the victim's suffering in the criminal law poses a serious hurdle to the struggle for reasoned principles in the law. Generations of theorists have sought to explain why we punish actual homicide more severely than attempted homicide, the real spilling of blood more severely than the unrealized intent to do so. Our combined philosophical work has yet to generate a satisfactory account of why the realization of harm aggravates the penalty. Yet the practice persists in every legal system of the Western world. We cannot adequately explain why harm matters, but matter it does." George P. Fletcher, A Crime of Self-Defense: Bernard Goetz and the Law on Trial 82–83 (1988). Fletcher explains the dimensions of the debate between "traditionalists," who focus on the consequences of criminal actions, which may be outside the actor's control, and "modernists," who focus on whatever is within the actor's control. Ibid. at 67–83.

[37] See Smith, supra note 32, at 565–66.

[38] To be precise, the analogy is not quite to a principal causing an innocent agent to act, because the innocent-agent doctrine applies only in cases where the principal intends the agent's action. The Fox intends his later self to perform the unwitting misdeed, but the Ostrich may not. In the Ostrich's case, the analogy is not to innocent agency, but to a different causation analysis: A is held liable for B's crime if B is innocent, and A unintentionally causes B to commit it. See Sanford H. Kadish, *Complicity, Cause and Blame: A Study in the Interpretation of Doctrine*, 73 Cal. L. Rev. 323, 392 (1985). My argument and terminology in this and the succeeding paragraphs has been heavily influenced by Kadish's article. Kadish revisits the requirement of intention in a later article. See Sanford H. Kadish, *Reckless Complicity*, 87 J. Crim. L. & Criminology 369 (1997).

Just as the Model Penal Code and the waiver theory err by focusing attention entirely on the unwitting misdeed (performed by the later self), the culpable-ignorance theory errs by focusing attention entirely on the screening actions (performed by the earlier self). To do full justice to cases of contrived ignorance, we need some way of combining the two. Here, unfortunately, the analogy to a guilty principal and a reckless agent doesn't help. There is no formula for combining the guilt of a principal with that of an agent to determine the guilt of both together, and thus there is no formula for assessing an actor's guilt by combining the guilt of the earlier and later selves. We need some alternative approach.

A proposal

The very statement of the problem suggests its solution. If it is a mistake to treat the screening actions and the wrongful misdeeds in isolation from each other, we must reunite them into a single complex. In essence, this amounts to broadening the time-frame in which we consider the unwitting misdeed, by regarding it as a unitary action *that begins when the actor commits the screening actions*.[39] Thus, the current suggestion avoids the errors of both the Model Penal Code and the culpable ignorance theory. On this proposal, the relevant question is "What was the actor's state of mind toward the unwitting misdeed at the moment she opted for ignorance?"[40] As support for this suggestion, we can return to the analogy of principal and agent. The agent, the self at the moment of the unwitting misdeed, in effect ratifies the earlier self's decision to screen off potentially guilty knowledge. This seems like a good reason for making the earlier self's attitude toward the unwitting misdeed the focus of inquiry – for that is the attitude that the later self is ratifying.[41]

---

[39] See Mark Kelman, *Interpretive Construction in the Substantive Criminal Law*, 33 Stan. L. Rev. 591 (1981) (distinguishing broad and narrow time-frames in constructing criminal liability).

[40] This proposal is Paul H. Robinson's suggested analysis of causing the conditions of one's own defense, although Robinson does not apply it to willful ignorance. See Robinson, supra note 33, at 28–31. David Wasserman suggested to me the possibility of applying Robinson's idea in the context of willful ignorance, and sketched the idea in a paper we co-authored with Alan Strudler. See David Luban, Alan Strudler, & David Wasserman, *Moral Responsibility in the Age of Bureaucracy*, 90 Mich. L. Rev. 2348, 2387–88 (1992). I now believe that my co-authors and I erred by coupling this analysis of willful ignorance with the kind of negligence analysis that I criticized earlier.

[41] A word of explanation about what I mean by "the earlier self's attitude toward the unwitting misdeed." Readers may object that if the earlier self has an attitude toward the misdeed, it is not unwitting. If a business executive sets up a structure of deniability so that he never learns that his employees must break laws to accomplish the goals he sets them, then he never knows that his instructions unwittingly abet crimes. Thus, he has no attitude toward *specific* acts of aiding and abetting crime.

This sounds too abstract. To see the point of the proposal, let us revisit our old friends the Fox and the Ostrich. The grand-scheming Fox has mischief in his heart from the get-go, and his foray into contrived ignorance is nothing more than an exercise in liability-screening. What was his state of mind toward the unwitting misdeed at the moment he opted for ignorance? That's easy. Like Alfred P. Doolittle in *My Fair Lady*, he's wishing to commit mischief, he's wanting to commit mischief, he's waiting to commit mischief. And what is the judgment of him? It is a judgment that he *has* committed mischief *and* willfully so.

The case of the Ostrich is a bit more complicated, because, at the moment she pops her head in the sand, she herself may not know what her attitude is toward the unwitting misdeeds she prefers not to think about. So, when the Ostrich successfully contrives not to have any mental attitude toward a possible future misdeed, it may seem impossible, or even contradictory, to evaluate her blameworthiness by investigating the very mental attitude that, by assumption, does not exist.

However, matters are not as hopeless as this way of putting things suggests. The Ostrich contrives to block certain thoughts, but a mental state such as intention is not the same thing as an occurrent thought. As Wittgenstein pointed out, "intention is neither an emotion, a mood, nor yet a sensation or image. It is not a state of consciousness. It does not have a genuine duration."[42] For example, the fact that I intend to go away tomorrow does not entail that some kind of thought about going away hovers in my consciousness from now until I leave.[43] Rather, the intention consists of a

---

However, even if he has no specific act of aiding and abetting in mind, he may still have *a generic* action in mind when he sets up the structure of deniability. That is, he may set up the structure with the intention of establishing his own deniability for whatever future crimes he expects his employees to commit on his orders, in which case his attitude toward those crimes is one of willfulness. Or he may set up the structure in conscious disregard of the substantial and unjustifiable risk that it will result in his giving orders that can be followed only by unlawful means. In that case, his attitude is recklessness. His attitude is toward the general act-type of aiding and abetting wrongdoing, not the particular instances – what philosophers call "tokens" of that type – the wrongful character of which he has concealed from himself.

[42] Ludwig Wittgenstein, Zettel, §45, at 10 (G. E. M. Anscombe trans., G. E. M. Anscombe & G. H. von Wright eds., 1970).

[43] " 'I have the intention of going away tomorrow.' – When have you that intention? The whole time; or intermittently?" Ibid. §46, at 10. Wittgenstein presumably means us to doubt both answers – but if we must choose one, it is "the whole time," even though the conscious thought of going away tomorrow is intermittent: hence the conclusion that the intention is distinct from the thought. Wittgenstein elaborates on this idea: "Really one hardly ever says that one has believed, understood or intended something 'uninterruptedly' since yesterday. An interruption of belief would be a period of unbelief, not the withdrawal of attention from what one believes – e.g. sleep." Ibid. §85, at 17.

disposition to plan my activities around going away tomorrow.[44] In the same way, we answer our question about the Ostrich's mental state toward the misdeed by answering a counterfactual question about her disposition to commit it: "What would the Ostrich have done had she not contrived her own ignorance?" There is no reason to doubt that often we know what the answer to this question is.

Indeed, outside observers may be able to answer the question even when the Ostrich herself cannot. In everyday life, our friends and relatives often are able to predict what we are going to do in a major life-choice even while we ourselves twist in an agony of indecision. Self-knowledge has never been humankind's strong suit, and none of us is as unpredictable as we like to think. Even though we can't answer the counterfactual question "What would she have done had she not contrived her own ignorance?" by scrutinizing the Ostrich's psyche at the moment she performed the screening actions, other, less subjective evidence may allow us to answer with reasonable confidence. We never have direct access to another person's psyche in any event, and so every inquiry into subjective states infers them from external evidence. The counterfactual question is no harder to answer from external evidence than other questions about subjective states, and juries answer those every day, precisely by using external evidence to infer dispositions. Evidence about the Ostrich's way of life may shed light on how she would act if her contrived ignorance were stripped away. Remember Albert Speer, our prototypical ostrich. We know quite enough about him to predict that no revelation of horrors, not even a trip to Auschwitz, was likely to make Hitler's minister of slave labor resign in protest. Even in cases where the objective evidence is too scanty to judge confidently what the Ostrich would have done had she known all the facts, there is no reason in principle to doubt that the question has an answer.

So we can still say this: If she *would* do the right thing had she not screened herself from knowledge, then her attitude toward the misdeed at the time she opted for ignorance is recklessness. For at that moment she consciously elected to run the risk of unwitting wrongdoing. But, if she actually would persist in ways of wickedness whether she had full knowledge or not, it seems fair to attribute that willingness to her at the moment she performed the screening actions. Even if she is in denial about it, hindsight reveals that she is, very literally, the moral equivalent of a knowing performer of misdeeds.

In other words, the proposal to examine states of mind toward the misdeed at the time the actor opts for ignorance yields exactly the same judgments as our earlier intuitions about the Fox and the Ostrich. That is no coincidence, of

---

[44] This view is defended in Michael E. Bratman, Intention, Plan, and Practical Reason 1–5 (1987).

course. The question we answer to determine the Ostrich's mental state – "What would the Ostrich have done had she not contrived her own ignorance?" – is exactly the same question that in our earlier discussion we used to grade her culpability. That is at least one reason to think that the proposal gets it right: it leads us to ask the same question that underlies our moral intuitions about the culpability of the Ostrich and the Fox.

Lawyers behaving badly: a reprise

To conclude, I want to return to the cases I began with – cases of contrived ignorance by lawyers. As a law teacher, and in particular a teacher of legal ethics, these cases seem particularly pressing to me. In this final section, I consider two questions: first, whether the conclusion that willful ignorance is morally equivalent to culpable *mens rea* for the unwitting misdeeds should be embodied in the formal rules of legal ethics – to which my answer is a tentative no – and second, whether it nonetheless should figure in lawyers' moral deliberations – to which the answer is yes. To say that it should figure in lawyers' moral deliberations does not, however, mean that lawyers should never engage in contrived ignorance. Like most moral principles, the importance of avoiding contrived ignorance can be outweighed by other morally relevant factors in specific cases. I illustrate this point with an extended example in which – or so it seems to me – contrived ignorance is the lawyer's best choice.

Should the law penalize willful ignorance by lawyers of their clients' deceits?

We've seen that the formal rules of legal ethics, unlike criminal law, contain no willful-blindness doctrine. Except in certain specialized circumstances, a lawyer is under no obligation to press her client for knowledge or to corroborate what her client tells her.[45] If she uses a "Don't ask, don't tell" interviewing strategy, and her client subsequently commits perjury, the lawyer will not be charged with knowingly putting on perjurious testimony. Here, willful blindness does not equal knowledge. The question is whether it should.

The approach developed in this chapter would ask about our lawyer's mental state toward possible client perjury at that moment in the interview

---

[45] One special circumstance is imposed by Rule 11 of the Federal Rules of Civil Procedure, which requires lawyers to certify that the assertions they file in court papers are warranted in fact. Fed. R. Civ. P. 11(b)(3). Another is the issuing of opinion letters containing assertions about a client's financial position. See Greycas v. Proud, 826 F.2d 1560 (7th Cir. 1987) (holding lawyer liable for damages resulting when lawyer relied upon fraudulent client assertions when writing an opinion letter to lender).

when she orders her client not to tell her too much. In my experience, many lawyers expect clients to perjure themselves when the stakes are high, suggesting that the "Don't ask, don't tell" lawyer is at least reckless toward future perjury, and, perhaps, willful. This intuition suggests that "Don't ask, don't tell" is an ethically dubious way for lawyers to proceed.

Perhaps, then, legal ethics rules should be modified so that willful and knowing ignorance count as knowledge. Doctrinally, adding a willful-blindness doctrine to legal ethics would involve nothing more than a minor change in the terminology section of the Model Rules of Professional Conduct. Where the Model Rules now state that " 'knowingly,' 'known,' or 'knows' denotes actual knowledge of the fact in question," the amended terminology would add: "or conscious avoidance of actual knowledge of the fact in question."

Minor as the change appears on the printed page, it has the potential to transform the nature of the client–lawyer relationship, and thus of legal practice, if it were honestly enforced. Most obviously, adding the willful-blindness doctrine to ethics rules leaves great uncertainty about how much inquiry into a client's case a lawyer must undertake to avoid disciplinary action. Perhaps the doctrine would be read narrowly, so that "conscious avoidance of knowledge" means only that the lawyer consciously refrained from asking questions that, but for the fear of discovering guilty knowledge, she would obviously have asked in order to help prepare the case. But even then it is unclear what questions this obligation encompasses. For example, does the doctrine require a criminal defense lawyer to ask every client if he did the acts alleged? Faced with uncertainties, the fear of liability might provoke lawyers to ratchet up the level of inquiry, which carries enormous potential for damaging the elements of trust essential to a successful client–lawyer relationship. Moreover, to determine how much due diligence a lawyer actually did undertake, or whether the lawyer employed impermissible "Don't ask, don't tell" interview techniques, disciplinary authorities would have to scrutinize privileged and confidential conversations between attorney and client – perhaps all their conversations. If these worries are genuine, the willful-blindness doctrine threatens to leave the client–lawyer relationship in a shambles.

Sophisticated clients with something to hide would have reason to actively frustrate their own lawyers' factual investigation of their case, because they would know that their lawyer is ethically required to ferret out guilty information that under some circumstances she might be ethically required to disclose. The worried client may frustrate the lawyer's investigation even of innocent facts that the lawyer needs, because the client does not know that the facts are innocent. For the lawyer's part, a lawyer who fears liability for consciously avoiding knowledge, and who in any case needs information to represent her clients competently, may be forced to play a cat-and-mouse game of sleuthing against her own evasive clients. Adding to the tension is the fact that in many cases the client is paying by the hour for his lawyer to investigate him – and the more the client tries to frustrate the investigation, the more time-consuming and costly it becomes. The client retains the lawyer because he must, while viewing the lawyer askance, with a certain measure of dread and resentment. The client fears, sometimes rightly, that he would be better off with no lawyer at all.

All of these concerns have a familiar ring to them: they sound very much like the bar's standard objections to proposals that would weaken confidentiality in the name of truth. Invariably, the bar springs to the defense of confidentiality and trots out a parade of horribles if confidentiality is weakened – damage done to the client–lawyer relationship, clients evading their lawyers' questions for fear that the lawyer could be compelled to disclose damaging information, lawyers being left out of the loop in business decisions, clients hiding innocent information from their lawyers because they don't know that the facts are innocent. As William Simon has recently argued, none of these objections is very persuasive, for two fundamental reasons. First, they all focus exclusively on the costs to clients of enhanced disclosure, without considering the social benefits of hampering dishonest clients. Second, they all make behavioral assumptions about lawyers and clients that are at best unconfirmed and at worst implausible.[46] Do Simon's arguments apply here?

They may. The willful-blindness doctrine, which requires lawyers to ask clients hard questions that they would otherwise leave unasked because they prefer not to know the answers, will elicit evasive tactics only from clients who believe they have something to hide. If the aim is to diminish the amount of client crime and fraud by making it harder for dishonest clients to enlist lawyers in their efforts, that may be all to the good.

On the other hand, the number of clients who believe they have something to hide may be very large, and they are not all crooks. When disputes lead to litigation, all parties may have done something discreditable or embarrassing; and when clients enter into business transactions, all sides may be concealing weaknesses or defects in their wares. None of them will appreciate a doctrine that they fear will require their own lawyers to ferret out their dishonesties and then resign or report them. This result is much more alarming than rules weakening confidentiality, under which the client with a secret blemish at least has the option of withholding information from the lawyer, who can remain passive and do the best she can with whatever information the client gives her. Under the willful-blindness doctrine, the lawyer cannot remain passive. Her license is in jeopardy unless she actively investigates the client.

[46] See William H. Simon, The Practice of Justice: A Theory of Lawyer's Ethics 54–62 (1998).

The behavioral assumptions of this scenario are few and harmless. It assumes only that clients whose lawyers are investigating their embarrassments will try to hide the ball, that lawyers who face professional discipline if they avoid knowledge will feel impelled to investigate their clients, and that neither lawyers nor clients will like each other very well while all this is going on.

No doubt some of these problems could be solved. And perhaps the gain in preventing lawyers from assisting client fraud is worth disrupting the client–lawyer relationship as we now understand it. At the very least, however, we should be extremely cautious about affixing a willful-blindness doctrine to legal ethics. The Law of Unintended Consequences looms large.

Miriam's case, or, the messy morality of "Don't ask, don't tell"

Suppose, then, that formal legal ethics doctrine remains as it is today. The argument developed in this chapter tells us that willful blindness is morally equivalent to recklessness, or knowledge, or even willfulness, depending upon the lawyer's motive in avoiding knowledge. In that case, should the good lawyer avoid "Don't ask, don't tell" strategies even without a legal doctrine telling her to do so?

That is the conclusion toward which the argument points us. If, for example, a client commits perjury, most states' ethics rules require lawyers to disclose it to the court if the client insists on standing pat. In most cases, I believe, that is the morally right result.[47] If the lawyer avoids her disclosure obligation by arranging not to know that the client's story is false – the "Don't ask, don't tell" strategy – that is morally equivalent to knowingly (or recklessly, or willfully) failing to disclose known perjury.

There might, nevertheless, be exceptional cases in which the morally troubling consequences of knowing too much outweigh the duty to avoid "Don't ask, don't tell" strategies. An imaginary example will illustrate the point.[48] Consider a political asylum case involving a political activist – let's call her Miriam – who fled to the United States from a dictatorship. Miriam's asylum application is denied, which means that to avoid deportation she must prove her case in an immigration court. She hires a lawyer, and tells him her story. She had been imprisoned for two months by the political police in her home country because of her dissident activities. While in prison, she was raped and beaten. After her release, the police continued to threaten and harass her, until finally, following a credible death threat, she fled the country.

Miriam's lawyer sets about documenting the case, because he must prove to the judge that she truly was persecuted at home. He quickly confirms the

---

[47] So I argue in *Lawyers and Justice*, at 197–201.

[48] The example is hypothetical, but I have drawn bits of it from real cases.

essential details. Fortunately, Miriam brought a birth certificate proving her identity, and she saved newspaper clippings from her home country that identify her as a political activist. Furthermore, Amnesty International reported on her arrest and imprisonment at the time. She even has a dated document showing when she was released from prison; and the Amnesty report gives the date she went in. A friend of Miriam's who moved to the United States a year before her will testify that Miriam phoned him from her home country when she received the death threat. So far, so good. Miriam has a powerful case for political asylum. A psychiatric examination finds symptoms of post-traumatic stress disorder in her, consistent with her terrible experiences in prison.

In the initial interview, Miriam mentioned that her brother, who has already won asylum, lives nearby. The lawyer asks her to arrange an interview with the brother, who can corroborate her story. Suddenly, however, Miriam becomes evasive. Her brother is very busy, Miriam tells the lawyer; he is studying for his college exams. In any case, she hardly ever speaks with her brother. And she is sure that her brother will not want to talk with the lawyer. As she says these things, Miriam seems flustered and alarmed; she won't look the lawyer in the face. He notices tears in her eyes; then she gets angry. What is going on?

Many things are possible. Maybe her PTSD is causing her strange reaction. Maybe she had a fight with her brother. Maybe her brother fears that if he testifies, the government will vindictively try to reopen his own asylum case. Or maybe he doesn't really have asylum, but is undocumented. Maybe, just maybe, he really is studying for his college exams.

But there is a worse possibility. Could it be that Miriam doesn't want the lawyer to speak with her brother because the brother won't corroborate Miriam's story? The lawyer has already documented the essentials. But perhaps she exaggerated some things. What if, despite her friend's testimony, the police never threatened her with death? Or what if she was never raped or beaten in prison, but said she was because someone (wrongly) told her that otherwise she wouldn't get asylum? The lawyer has seen it happen: refugees often get bad legal advice from other refugees. If so, her lie was understandable. She comes from a country where it doesn't pay to tell the truth to the government; her persecution was genuine; and everything her lawyer has learned convinces him that her peril if she is sent home is all too real.

What should the lawyer do? Immigration judges have discretionary power to turn down asylum applications if they doubt the credibility of the asylum-seeker; and this particular judge is less sympathetic to asylum-seekers than most. To insist on interviewing Miriam's brother, or even pressing Miriam on the issue, runs the risk of learning that parts of her story are untrue. In that case, the lawyer is ethically bound to retract court filings containing the false details. Doing so, however, would dynamite Miriam's credibility, even though the details aren't essential to proving her case; and a case that Miriam deserves to win is lost, perhaps at the cost of her life.

The alternative? Willful blindness – break off the investigation, elect not to interview the brother, go with the story that's already in the application and is well documented. It's almost certainly enough to win her case. I suspect that most lawyers would choose this alternative with scarcely a second thought, and the rules of legal ethics clearly permit it. But the theory that I have been elaborating counsels that such willful blindness is morally indistinguishable from knowingly (or recklessly) going along with Miriam's deception – if deception is what it is.

I know of no easy way out of the lawyer's dilemma, but in Miriam's case I accept the willful-blindness alternative. The reason is that in Miriam's case, in which telling the truth might defeat justice, and the stakes are enormous, even a lie might be morally excusable. It is a good principle to require candor to the court from lawyers, but even good principles have exceptions.[49] If a lie to save Miriam's life would be morally excusable, then why not avail oneself of willful blindness, which doesn't force the lawyer to lie and doesn't violate any rules?

Of course, this is moral loopholing, but here I think that there is a sound reason to indulge in it. In part, no doubt, lawyers choose willful blindness over morally excusable (but unlawful) lying to spare themselves the possibility of professional discipline. But even when there is no realistic chance of being caught, they still prefer willful blindness over morally excusable lying. That is because it matters to them that in legal ethics willful blindness is permissible and lying is not. Abiding by their rules of professional ethics is important to most lawyers' sense of professional identity. A lawyer who knew that Miriam's asylum application contains falsehoods might well withdraw it, even where going along with the false submission is morally preferable to the truth. Paradoxically, in Miriam's case, the lawyer should prefer willful blindness to knowledge *because willful blindness might spare him the temptation of wrongfully making her tell the truth.* Earlier, we observed that people engage in willful blindness to spare themselves moral dilemmas. Exactly that dynamic is at work here – only in this case sparing oneself a dilemma is the right thing to do, not because one might give in to the temptation to break a formal ethics rule, but because one might give in to the temptation to obey it. Breaking a rule of professional misconduct is a Rubicon many lawyers refuse to cross, even when it is the right thing to do. Availing themselves of the loophole that contrived ignorance provides enables them to do the right thing without crossing the Rubicon.

---

[49] Here I agree with William H. Simon, *Virtuous Lying: A Critique of Quasi-Categorical Moralism*, 12 Georgetown J. Legal Ethics 433 (1999), which criticizes an exceptionless prohibition on lying.

Just call me an ostrich. But on this issue I am an unrepentant ostrich, because I don't think that the misdeed of putting on a fundamentally truthful case that may have a few unimportant false details – which the lawyer does not know are false – really is a misdeed. And that allows me to retain the conclusion that *as a general rule*, lawyers should avoid willful ignorance of inconvenient knowledge, just as everyone should, although this general rule has exceptions in extreme cases like Miriam's.

The fact that the general rule has exceptions should not deflect us from the moral importance of the rule, which takes away an excuse lawyers contrive for themselves when they have no reason more exalted than not wishing to have awkward confrontations with paying clients. In my view, the most inexcusable form of lawyer willful ignorance occurs when lawyers paper questionable deals for questionable clients because the price is right. A banker recollects that in the Roaring Eighties "for half a million dollars you could buy any legal opinion you wanted from any law firm in New York."[50] The ethics rules prohibit lawyers from knowingly counseling or assisting a client in fraud, but if there's no "due diligence" duty to investigate the client and no willful-blindness doctrine, it becomes too easy for lawyers to evade the rule by evading the facts. Surely, a good lawyer should regard it as her duty to learn the facts before closing a deal.

That leads us back to Joseph Hutner and the computer crooks. We left Mr. Hutner figuratively clamping his hands over his ears and running out of the office. What happened next?

Hutner's law firm retained a pair of legal ethics experts, and made it clear that the firm hoped it wouldn't have to fire or blow the whistle on its wayward client. The ethics experts were only too happy to oblige. They advised that the law firm *could not* reveal the client's past frauds, and *could* continue to close deals for the computer company, provided that steps were taken to detect dishonesty. In fact, the experts cautioned, if the firm *stopped* representing the computer company it would signal that something was amiss, and that would violate client confidentiality.

Unfortunately, willful ignorance seems to be habit-forming, and the law firm's monitoring of the loans was timid and easy for the resourceful criminals to evade. Some evidence suggests that the firm wanted to know as little as possible about the uprightness of the loans it was closing, because it didn't want to part ways with the client. As a result, the firm closed another $60 million in crooked loans for the computer company. When the lawyers discovered the new frauds, an ethics farce ensued. Their ethics experts advised that these new frauds had now become past frauds protected by the confidentiality rule. At this point, Hutner's firm decided that it was finally time

[50] Martin Mayer, The Greatest-Ever Bank Robbery: The Collapse of the Savings and Loan Industry 20 (1990).

to resign. The ethics experts sternly admonished that the firm should keep strict confidentiality while it turned the client over to another law firm. As a result, the new law firm proceeded in honest ignorance to close $15 million in fraudulent loans for the crooks before the plot finally unraveled. First farce, then tragedy. Hutner's law firm paid $10 million to defrauded lenders to settle lawsuits.

It's not a happy ending, but perhaps it's an edifying one. The law firm had two experts' opinions attesting that it had done what the ethics rules required, but it was nevertheless prepared to pay millions of dollars *not* to have its willful blindness put before a jury. Perhaps that tells us something about what we really think of contrived ignorance as a moral excuse.

7

The ethics of wrongful obedience

A century ago the legal realists declared that the real law is the law in action, not just the law in books. They urged us to think things, not words, and placed their faith in the power of the still youthful social sciences to think legal things accurately and rigorously. In legal ethics, I think most scholars would agree on the single biggest discrepancy between the law in books – the profession's ethics codes – and the law in action. The ethics codes are almost entirely *individualist* in their focus. They treat lawyers (clients, too, for that matter) largely as self-contained decision-makers flying solo. In fact, however, lawyers increasingly work in and for organizations. While most lawyers continue to practice in small firms, and sole practitioners still form the largest single demographic slice of the profession, the trend is toward organizational practice. The largest law firms and corporate legal departments have more than a thousand lawyers, and the biggest firms in the country three decades ago would not make this year's top hundred.

The importance of these trends for legal ethics can hardly be exaggerated. Psychologists, organization theorists, and economists all know that the dynamics of individual decision-making change dramatically when the individual works in an organizational setting. Loyalties become tangled, and personal responsibility diffused. Bucks are passed, and guilty knowledge bypassed. Chains of command not only tie people's hands, they fetter their minds and consciences as well. Reinhold Niebuhr titled one of his books *Moral Man, Immoral Society*, and for students of ethics no topic is more important than understanding whatever truth this title contains.

My own students, I might add, think about it without any prompting. No dilemma in the ethics class causes them more anxiety than the prospect of being pressured by their boss to do something wrong. Not only do they worry about losing their jobs if they defy the boss to do the right thing, they also fear that the pressures of the situation might undermine their ability to know what the right thing is.

An example: the Berkey–Kodak case

One of the best-known and most painful examples of this phenomenon was the Berkey–Kodak antitrust litigation in 1977, a bitterly contested private antitrust action brought by Berkey Photo against the giant of the industry. In the heat of adversarial combat, Mahlon Perkins, an admired senior litigator for the large New York law firm representing Kodak, snapped. For no apparent reason, he lied to his opponent to conceal documents from discovery, then perjured himself before a federal judge to cover up the lie. Eventually he owned up, resigned from his firm, and served a month in prison. Perhaps this sounds like an instance of chickens coming home to roost for a Rambo litigator. But by all accounts, Perkins was an upright and courtly man, the diametrical opposite of a Rambo litigator.[1]

Joseph Fortenberry, the associate working for him, knew that Perkins was perjuring himself and whispered a warning to him; but when Perkins ignored the warning, Fortenberry did nothing further to correct his misstatements. "What happened," recalls another associate, "was that he saw Perkins lie and really couldn't believe it. And he just had no idea what to do. I mean, he ... kept thinking there must be a reason. Besides, what do you do? The guy was his boss and a great guy!"[2]

Notice the range of explanations here. *First*, the appeal to hierarchy: the guy was his boss. *Second*, to personal loyalty: the guy was a great guy. *Third*, to helplessness: Fortenberry had no idea what to do. *Fourth*, Fortenberry couldn't believe it. He kept thinking there must be a reason. The last is an explanation of a different sort, suggesting that Fortenberry's own ethical judgment was undermined by the situation he found himself in.

As a matter of fact, the same may be said of Perkins. He wasn't the lead partner in the litigation; he belonged to a team headed by a newcomer to the firm, an intense, driven, focused, and controlling lawyer, who (though he was entirely ethical) put pressure on himself and pressure on those around him.[3] In a situation of supreme stress, Perkins's judgment simply failed him.

In Berkey–Kodak, neither Perkins nor Fortenberry received an explicit order to break the rules, but sometimes lawyers do. (And in Berkey–Kodak, Perkins's behavior, ignoring Fortenberry's whispered warnings, amounts to a tacit instruction to Fortenberry to say nothing.) What guidance do the ethics rules give when this happens? ABA Model Rule 5.2(a) denies the defense of superior orders to a subordinate lawyer ordered to behave unethically, but

---

[1] For an extended account, see James B. Stewart, The Partners: Inside America's Most Powerful Law Firms 327–65 (1983).

[2] Steven Brill, *When a Lawyer Lies*, Esquire 23–24 (December 19, 1979).

[3] Stewart, The Partners, supra note 1, at 338.

Rule 5.2(b) states that a subordinate may defer to "a supervisory lawyer's reasonable resolution of an arguable question of professional duty." The problem is that the pressures on subordinate lawyers may lead them to misjudge when a question of professional duty is arguable and when the supervisor's resolution of it is reasonable. Remember that Fortenberry "kept thinking there must be a reason" when he heard Perkins perjure himself before a federal judge. This was not even close to an arguable question, and there is nothing reasonable about perjury – but the very fact that it was Fortenberry's respected supervisor who committed it undermined his own confidence that he understood what was reasonable and what was not. When that happens, Rule 5.2(b) will seem more salient to an associate than the bright-line prohibition on wrongful obedience that the first half of the rule articulates.[4]

The Milgram obedience experiments

I want to see what we can learn about wrongful obedience from the most celebrated effort to study it empirically, Stanley Milgram's experiments conducted at Yale thirty-five years ago. Even though these experiments are very well known, it is useful to review the details of what Milgram did and what he discovered.[5]

Imagine, then, that you answer Milgram's newspaper advertisement, offering \$20 if you volunteer for a one-hour psychology experiment.[6] When you enter the room, you meet the experimenter, dressed in a gray lab coat, and a second volunteer, a pleasant, bespectacled middle-aged man. What you don't know is that the second volunteer is in reality a confederate of the experimenter.

The experimenter explains that the two volunteers will be participating in a study of the effect of punishment on memory and learning. One of you, the learner, will memorize word-pairs; the other, the teacher, will punish the learner with steadily increasing electrical shocks each time he makes a mistake. A volunteer, rather than the experimenter, must administer the shocks because one aim of the experiment is to investigate punishments administered by very different kinds of people. The experimenter leads you to the shock-generator, a formidable-looking machine with thirty switches,

---

[4] See Carol M. Rice, *The Superior Orders Defense in Legal Ethics: Sending the Wrong Message to Young Lawyers*, 32 Wake Forest L. Rev. 887 (1997).

[5] I draw all my descriptions of the Milgram experiments and their variations from Stanley Milgram, Obedience to Authority: An Experimental View (1974).

[6] Milgram actually offered \$4, but this was in 1960 dollars, which I have scaled up for purposes of this example.

marked from 15 volts to 450. Above the voltages, labels are printed. These range from "Slight Shock" (15–60 volts) through "Danger: Severe Shock" (375–420 volts); they culminate in an ominous-looking red label reading "XXX" above 435 and 450 volts. Both volunteers experience a 45-volt shock. Then they draw lots to determine their role. The drawing is rigged so that you become the teacher. The learner mentions that he has a mild heart problem, and the experimenter replies rather nonresponsively that the shocks will cause no permanent tissue damage. The learner is strapped into the hot seat, and the experiment gets under way.

The learner begins making mistakes, and as you escalate the shocks he grunts in pain. Eventually he complains about the pain, and at 150 volts he announces in some agitation that he wishes to stop the experiment. You look inquiringly at the man in the gray coat, but he says only, "The experiment requires that you continue." As you turn up the juice, the learner begins screaming. Finally, he shouts out that he will answer no more questions. Unflapped, the experimenter instructs you to treat silences as wrong answers. You ask him who will take responsibility if the learner is injured, and he states that he will. You continue.

As the experiment proceeds, the agitated learner announces that his heart is starting to bother him. Again, you protest, and again the man in the lab coat replies, "The experiment requires that you continue." At 330 volts, the screams stop. The learner falls ominously silent, and remains silent until the bitter end.

But it never actually gets to the bitter end, does it? You may be excused for thinking so. In a follow-up study, groups of people heard the Milgram experiment described without being told the results. They were asked to guess how many people would comply all the way to 450 volts, and to predict whether they themselves would. People typically guessed that at most one teacher out of a thousand would comply – and no one believed that they themselves would.[7]

In reality, 63 percent of subjects complied all the way to 450 volts. Moreover, this is a robust result: it holds in groups of women as well as men, and experimenters obtained comparable results in Holland, Spain, Italy, Australia, South Africa, Germany, and Jordan; indeed, the Jordanian experimenters replicated the 65 percent result not only among adults but among seven-year-olds. Originally, Milgram had intended to run his experiments in Germany, to *try* to understand how so many Germans could participate in the Holocaust; his American experiments were merely for the purpose of perfecting his procedures. After the American dry run, however,

---

[7] Arthur G. Miller, The Obedience Experiments: A Case Study of Controversy in Social Science 13, 21 (1986).

Milgram remarked: "I found so much obedience, I hardly saw the need of taking the experiment to Germany."[8]

In my view, we should regard the radical underestimates of subjects' willingness to inflict excruciating shocks on an innocent person as a finding just as important and interesting as the 65 percent compliance rate itself.[9] The Milgram experiments demonstrate not only that in the right circumstances we are quite prone to destructive obedience, but also that we don't believe this about ourselves, or about our neighbors – nor do we condone it.[10] Corroborating this final conclusion, subjects in another experiment had the Milgram set-up described to them, and were shown the photograph of a college student who had supposedly participated in the experiment as a "teacher." They were asked to rate the student in the photograph (weak-strong, warm-cold, likable-not likable), based on appearance. Unsurprisingly, the ratings varied drastically depending on what level of shock the student had supposedly proceeded to – the higher the shock, the weaker, colder, and

---

[8] Quoted in Robert B. Cialdini, Influence: Science and Practice 176 n. 2 (3rd edn., 1993). In 1970, David Mantell repeated some of the Milgram experiments in Munich, obtaining an 85 percent compliance rate in the basic experiment. David Mantell, *The Potential for Violence in Germany*, 27 J. Social Issues 101 (1971). So perhaps destructive obedience is a German pathology after all! – except that a similar 85 percent compliance rate appeared in an American replication as well (17 compliant subjects out of 20 – David Rosenhan, *Some Origins of Concern for Others*, in Trends and Issues in Developmental Psychology 143 [P. Mussen, J. Langer, & M. Covington eds., 1969]). Interestingly, Mantell introduced still another variation, in which the subject would see a prior "teacher" – a confederate of the experimenter – refuse to proceed with the experiment and indignantly confront the experimenter. At that point, the experimenter revealed that he was actually an unsupervised undergraduate, and not a member of the institute where the experiment was conducted. In this version, more than half the subjects nevertheless complied, even after having observed the melodramatic scenario just described; and in subsequent interviews many of them criticized the previous teacher who had broken off the series of shocks. In his American replication, Rosenhan also obtained a compliance rate over 50 percent when it was revealed the experimenter was an unsupervised undergraduate.

[9] The fact that those who hear the experiments described vastly underestimate compliance may result in part from the "false consensus effect," the well-confirmed tendency to exaggerate the extent to which others share our beliefs. Lee Ross & Richard E. Nisbett, The Person and the Situation: Perspectives of Social Psychology 83–85 (1991). That is, once a subject in the follow-up surveys has concluded that she would defy the experimenter in Milgram's set-up, she is also likely to conclude that most people would. A sophisticated subject aware of the false consensus effect should compensate for it by upping her initial estimate of how many people would comply, say from 1 percent to 5 percent. Yet even this 500 percent compensation would drastically underestimate what Milgram actually found. Something more than false consensus is evidently at work here. Moreover, the follow-up subjects' belief that they would defy the Milgram experimenter is itself an unwarranted prediction, since we know that in the basic experiment two-thirds of them would comply to the 450-volt maximum. That is, the very premise for their false consensus – their prediction of their own behavior – is itself most likely false.

[10] Miller, The Obedience Experiments, supra note 7, at 28–29.

less likable the subject. The natural explanation of the "likability" finding is that subjects found the teacher unattractive to the degree that they found her behavior unattractive – from which it follows that they disapproved of her compliance.

In short, Milgram demonstrates that each of us ought to believe three things about ourselves: that we strongly disapprove of destructive obedience; that we think we would never engage in it; and that the odds are almost two to one that we are fooling ourselves to think we would never engage in it.

Milgram was flabbergasted by his findings. He and other researchers ran dozens of variations on the experiment, which I won't describe, although I'll mention some of them shortly. His battery of experiments, which lasted for years and ultimately involved more than 1,000 subjects, stands even today as the most imaginative, ambitious, and controversial research effort ever undertaken by social psychologists.

The Milgram experiments place moral norms in conflict. One is what I will call the *performance principle*: the norm of doing your job properly, which in hierarchical work-settings includes the norm of following instructions. The other is the *no-harm principle*: the prohibition on torturing, harming, and killing innocent people. In the abstract, we might think, only a sadist or a fascist would subordinate the no-harm principle to the performance principle. But the Milgram experiments seem to show that what we think in the abstract is dead wrong. Two out of three people you pass in the street would electrocute you if a laboratory technician ordered them to.

The question is why. At this point, I am going to run through several explanations of the Milgram results. None of them fully satisfies me. After exploring their weaknesses, I turn to the explanation that seems to me most fruitful.

The Agentic Personality

Each of the explanations I will discuss focuses on a different aspect of human personality, and I will label them accordingly. There is, first, Milgram's own explanation. He describes the mentality of compliant subjects as an *agentic* state – a state in which we view ourselves as mere agents or instruments of the man giving the orders. The terminology is entirely familiar to lawyers, of course, because it is agency principles that govern the relationship between lawyer and client.

The problem with this explanation is that it merely relabels the question rather than answering it. Why do we turn off our consciences and "go agentic" when an authority figure starts giving us orders? Saying "Because we enter an agentic state" is no answer; it's reminiscent of Molière's physician, who explains that morphine makes us sleepy because it possesses a "dormative virtue."

Admittedly, Milgram's subjects usually offered the agentic explanation in their debriefing. But as we all know, "I was just following orders" is often an insincere rationalization. Remember that no one who heard the Milgram experiment described stated that they would comply, and that is another way of saying that none of them accept "just following orders" as a valid reason for complying. Even if the subjects offered the agentic explanation sincerely, we should never accept it at face value, because we human beings are not very gifted at explaining our own behavior.

The Libertarian Personality

Indeed, one of Milgram's experiments dramatizes this fact. Many of Milgram's subjects insisted that they went along with the experiment only because the learner had consented. Their response is, of course, quite different from the agentic explanation. Here, subjects claim to be impressed by the learner's consent, not the experimenter's orders. Their consent-centered explanation of why they complied is in line with classical-liberal or libertarian political philosophy – the learner has consented to participate, therefore it is not wrong to subject him to what he consented to, even if he regretted it. Perhaps being impressed by the learner's consent is the basic explanation of Milgram compliance. If so, the theory must be that compliers represent "Libertarian Personalities" – if, that is, their understanding of why they complied is correct.

To test this libertarian explanation, Milgram ran a variation in which the nervous learner expressly reserved the right to back out of the experiment whenever he wanted. He did this out loud, in the presence of the teacher and the experimenter. But even so, 40 percent of the subjects followed the experimenter's instructions to the bitter end despite the learner's protests; and three-fourths of the subjects proceeded long past the point where the learner withdrew his consent. Apparently, whether the learner consented or not is actually not especially relevant to whether subjects are willing to administer high-level shocks to him regardless of his subsequent protests. We simply can't take subjects' own explanations for their obedience at face value.

The Authoritarian Personality

If the Agentic Personality and the Libertarian Personality cannot explain Milgram's results, how about the *Authoritarian Personality?* A group of researchers in the early 1950s devised a famous questionnaire to measure the cluster of personality traits that they believed characterized supporters of fascist regimes – traits that include an emotional need to submit to authority, but also an exaggerated and punitive interest in other people's sexuality, and a propensity to superstition and irrationalism. They called this measure the *F-scale* – "F" for fascist.[11]

Interestingly, Milgram's compliant subjects had higher F-scores than his defiant subjects.[12] Indeed, isn't it mere common sense that authoritarians are more obedient to authority?

Unfortunately, the answer is no. For one thing, subsequent research has largely discredited the authoritarian personality studies. The F-scale turns out to be a good predictor of racism, but a bad predictor of everything else politically interesting about authoritarianism (such as left-right political orientation).[13] For another, people who volunteer for social psychology experiments are generally low-F, which makes Milgram's subjects at best atypical authoritarians.[14] For a third, high-F individuals typically mistrust science, so it rather begs the question to assume that they regard the experimenter as an authority to be deferred to. Finally, remember that the F-scale measures other things besides emotional attachment to hierarchy. We might as well call high-F something other than the Authoritarian Personality: we might call it the Superstitious Personality, or even the Perverted Prude Personality. In that case, the explanation only raises new questions. Why should Perverted Prudes or believers in alien abduction be specially prone to obedience?

The Sadistic Personality

Some researchers, perhaps with the Perverted Prude in mind, argued that the true explanation for Milgram's results is the *Sadistic Personality*: the experimenter's orders remove our inhibitions, and permit us to act out our repressed urge to hurt other people for pleasure.

The problem is that there is no evidence that we *have* such an urge. None of Milgram's compliant subjects seemed to take even the slightest pleasure in administering punishment, and many of them seemed downright agonized. They protested, they bit their lips until they bled, they broke into sweat or hysterical giggles. One went into convulsions. Milgram writes, "I observed a

---

[11] Theodor W. Adorno, Else Frenkel-Brunswik, & Daniel J. Levinson, The Authoritarian Personality (1950).

[12] Alan C. Elms & Stanley Milgram, *Personality Characteristics Associated With Obedience and Defiance Toward Authoritative Command*, 1 J. Experimental Res. in Personality 282 (1966).

[13] John J. Ray, *Why the F Scale Predicts Racism: A Critical Review*, 9 Political Psychology 671 (1988).

[14] Indeed, it is unclear whether the compliant Milgram subjects were high-F compared with the population at large, or only compared with the defiant subjects. The latter alternative is fully compatible with the compliant subjects being normal, or even low-F, compared with the population at large.

mature and initially poised businessman enter the laboratory smiling and confident. Within twenty minutes he was reduced to a twitching, stuttering wreck, who was rapidly approaching a point of nervous collapse ... At one point he pushed his fist into his forehead and muttered: 'Oh God, let's stop it.' And yet he continued to respond to every word of the experimenter, and obeyed to the end."[15] This hardly describes a sadist at work.

And, as it happens, the researchers who proposed the Sadistic Personality had an ax to grind.[16] They claimed, based on Rorschach tests done on the Nuremberg defendants and Adolf Eichmann, that every last one of the top Nazis was a psychopath. Like Professor Goldhagen today, they wanted to show that there was nothing ordinary about Hitler's executioners, nothing banal about Nazi evil. Their interest in Milgram seemed largely a competitive interest in shoring up their own theory of Nazism.

But their studies were flawed and their argument fallacious. Without interviews and other evidence of clinical pathology, Rorschach diagnoses are quack psychiatry; in any case, the researchers used a discredited method to analyze their Nazi Rorschachs. More basically, Rorschach diagnoses are based on deviations from statistical norms – and Milgram compliance is the statistical norm! To say on the basis of Rorschachs that two-thirds of adults are sadists is arithmetically impossible, like saying that all the children are above average.[17]

The Deferential Personality

A very different kind of explanation grows out of the cognitive psychology of the past three decades. Much of this research has revolved around the claim that we all rely on heuristics – rules of thumb – to make everyday judgments. Life is too short for us to be Cartesian rationalists, thinking everything through to the bottom, and natural selection is not kind to Cartesian rationalists. Instead, evolution statistically favors creatures who make snap judgments by applying largely reliable heuristics – even though, in atypical situations, the heuristic gets things badly wrong.

One of these is what might be called the *Trust Authority* heuristic. And this suggests that what drives Milgram's compliant subjects is not the Agentic

[15] Stanley Milgram, *Behavioral Study of Obedience*, 67 J. Abnormal & Social Psych. 371, 375–77 (1963).

[16] Florence Miale & Michael Selzer, The Nuremberg Mind: The Psychology of the Nazi Leaders (1975); Michael Selzer, *The Murderous Mind*, N. Y. Times Mag., November 27, 1977, 35–40.

[17] See, e.g., Stephen W. Hurt *et al.*, *The Rorschach*, in Integrative Assessment of Adult Personality 202 (Larry E. Beutler & Michael R. Berren eds., 1995); Eric A. Zillmer *et al.*, The Quest for the Nazi Personality: A Psychological Investigation of Nazi War Criminals 73–76, 94 (1995); 1 John E. Exner, Jr., The Rorschach: A Comprehensive System – Basic Foundations 330 (1993).

Personality, nor the Authoritarian Personality, nor the Sadistic Personality, but the *Deferential Personality*. Indeed, some of Milgram's subjects said in their debriefings that they went along with the experimenter because they were sure he knew what he was doing. Remember the Berkey–Kodak associate, who "kept thinking there must be a reason" for Perkins to lie. Ordinarily, we do well to follow the Trust Authority heuristic, because in many common situations authorities know better than lay people. At times, though, even the best heuristic fails – and Milgram devised one such situation.[18]

This is a sophisticated explanation, but I think that Milgram's own findings cast serious doubt on it. In one experiment, Milgram places the naive subject who draws the role of teacher with two experimenters instead of one. Before the session begins, one experimenter announces that a second volunteer has unexpectedly canceled his appointment. After some discussion of how they are going to meet their experimental quota, one of the experimenters decides that he himself will take the learner's place. Like the learner in the basic set-up, he soon begins complaining about the pain, and at 150 volts he demands to be released. Indeed, he follows the entire schedule of complaints, screams, and ominous silence.

Surely, if subjects were relying on the Trust Authority heuristic, the fact that one of the authorities was demanding that the experiment stop should have brought about diminished compliance. Indeed, in another version of the experiment, in which two experimenters disagree in the subject's presence about whether the subject should go on shocking the learner after the learner begins protesting, all of the subjects broke off the experiment immediately. Here, however, the usual two-thirds of the subjects complied to 450 volts. Apparently, it isn't deference to the experimenters' superior knowledge that promotes obedience.

Another variant of Milgram's experiment reinforces this conclusion. In this version, the experimenter gives his orders from another room, in a situation where it is clear that he cannot see what level of shock the teacher is actually administering. Unsurprisingly, compliance drops drastically; and yet the experimenter's superior knowledge is no different than if he was standing directly behind the teacher. Again, it appears that whatever causes the teacher to obey, it is not the experimenter's perceived expertise.

The situationist alternative

Perhaps the most radical suggestion is that *nothing* in the subjects' personalities accounts for their compliance. The so-called situationist view holds

---

[18] Alan Strudler & Danielle Warren, *Authority, Wrongdoing, and Heuristics*, in Social Influence on Ethical Behavior in Organizations (David Messick, John Darley & Tom Tyler eds., 2001).

that situational pressures, not personalities, account for human behavior.[19] Indeed, situationists argue that attributing behavior to personality is one of the fundamental delusions to which human beings are prey – it is, in their terminology, the "fundamental attribution error." Situationists point out that small manipulations of Milgram's experimental set-up are able to evoke huge swings in compliance behavior. For example, in some experiments Milgram placed the teacher on a team with other "teachers," who were actually actors working for Milgram. When the fellow teachers defied the experimenter, compliance plunged to 10 percent, but when they uncomplainingly delivered the shocks, compliance shot up to 90 percent. Obviously, variation like this arises from the situation, not from the subjects' personalities. As a consequence, situationists argue that the only reliable predictor of how any given person will behave in a situation is the baseline rate for the entire population. The person's observable character traits are by and large irrelevant.

Situationism offers an important reminder that human character and will do not operate in a vacuum. The Achilles' heel of situationism is explaining why anyone deviates from the majority behavior. If individual personality and idiosyncrasy are largely irrelevant to subjects' responses, we should find more or less uniform compliance behavior. In the Milgram experiments, situationists must explain why one-third of the subjects defy the experimenter. Remember that when audiences were asked whether they would comply in the Milgram experiment, 100 percent said no. What, if not individual personality and idiosyncrasy, causes a one-third/two-thirds split when the situation changes from being an audience member filling out a questionnaire to performing in the actual experiment?

The situationists' explanation is that even though people respond similarly to similar situations, different individuals perceive situations differently from one another. Idiosyncrasy operates at the level of perception and not at the level of behavior.

On this theory, the defiant minority simply don't perceive the experiment in the same way as the compliant majority.[20] Yet I find this explanation a little too convenient, particularly because there is no evidence to back it up – no independent study of how Milgram's subjects perceived the experiment, and no attempt to correlate perception with response. Just what did the defiant subjects perceive in the experiment that their compliant brethren perceived differently? Without an answer to this question, and evidence to support it, it seems to me that the situationist explanation of individual differences fails, and with it the situationist explanation of Milgram compliance.[21]

---

[19] A clear and forceful statement of situationism may be found in Ross & Nisbett, The Person and the Situation, supra note 9.

[20] Ibid., at 11–13.   [21] I develop this argument further in the next chapter.

A proposal: the corruption of judgment

And yet I agree that the key to understanding Milgram compliance lies in features of the experimental situation. The feature I wish to focus on is the slippery-slope character of the electrical shocks. The teacher moves up the scale of shocks by 15-volt increments, and reaches the 450-volt level only at the thirtieth shock. Among other things, this means that the subjects never directly confront the question "Should I administer a 330-volt shock to the learner?" The question is "Should I administer a 330-volt shock to the learner *given that I've just administered a 315-volt shock?*" It seems clear that the latter question is much harder to answer. As Milgram himself points out, to conclude that administering the 330-volt shock would be wrong is to admit that the 315-volt shock was probably wrong, and perhaps *all* the shocks were wrong.[22]

Cognitive dissonance theory teaches that when our actions conflict with our self-concept, our beliefs and attitudes change until the conflict is removed.[23] We are all pro se defense lawyers in the court of conscience.[24] Cognitive dissonance theory suggests that when I have given the learner a series of electrical shocks, I simply won't view giving the next shock as a wrongful act, because I won't admit to myself that the previous shocks were wrong.

Let me examine this line of thought in more detail. Moral decision-making requires more than adhering to sound principles, such as the no-harm principle. It also requires good judgment, by which I mean knowing which actions violate a moral principle and which do not. Every lawyer understands the difference between good principles and good judgment – it is the difference between knowing a rule of law and being able to apply it to particular cases. As Kant first pointed out, you can't teach good judgment through general rules, because we already need judgment to know how rules apply. Judgment is always and irredeemably particular.

Let's assume that most of Milgram's subjects do accept the no-harm principle, and agree in the abstract that it outweighs the performance principle – again, the responses of audiences hearing the Milgram experiments described strongly suggest that this is so. *The subjects still need good judgment to know at what point the electrical shocks violate the no-harm principle.* Virtually no one thinks that the slight tingle of a 15-volt shock violates the no-harm principle: if

---

[22] Milgram, Obedience to Authority, supra note 5, at 149.

[23] This formulation of dissonance theory – a refinement of Lionel Festinger's original hypothesis of cognitive dissonance – comes from Elliot Aronson, The Social Animal 230–33 (7th edn., 1995).

[24] I take the lawyer metaphor from Roderick M. Kramer & David M. Messick, *Ethical Cognition and the Framing of Organizational Dilemmas: Decision Makers as Intuitive Lawyers,* in Codes of Conduct: Behavioral Research Into Business Ethics 59 (David M. Messick & Ann E. Tenbrunsel eds., New York: Russell Sage, 1996).

it did, medical researchers would violate the no-harm principle every time they take blood samples from volunteers. Unsurprisingly, only two of Milgram's thousand subjects refused to give any shocks at all.

But how can 30 volts violate the no-harm principle if 15 volts didn't? And if a 30-volt shock doesn't violate the no-harm principle, neither does a shock of 45 volts.

Of course we know that slippery-slope arguments like this are unsound. At some point, the single grains of sand really do add up to a heap, and at some point shocking the learner really should shock the conscience as well. But it takes good judgment to know where that point lies. Unfortunately, cognitive dissonance generates enormous psychic pressure to deny that our previous obedience may have violated a fundamental moral principle. That denial requires us to gerrymander the boundaries of the no-harm principle so that the shocks we have already delivered don't violate it. However, once we knead and pummel the no-harm principle, it becomes virtually impossible to judge that the next shock, only imperceptibly more intense, crosses the border from the permissible to the forbidden. By luring us into higher and higher level shocks, one micro-step at a time, the Milgram experiments gradually and subtly disarm our ability to distinguish right from wrong. Milgram's subjects never need to lose, even for a second, their faith in the no-harm principle. Instead, they lose their capacity to recognize that administering an agonizing electrical shock violates it.

What I am offering here is a *corruption of judgment* explanation of the Milgram experiments. The road to hell turns out to be a slippery slope, and the travelers on it really do have good intentions – they "merely" suffer from bad judgment.

The corruption-of-judgment theory fits in well with one of the other classic experiments of social psychology, Freedman and Fraser's 1966 demonstration of the so-called foot-in-the-door effect. In this experiment, a researcher posing as a volunteer asks homeowners for permission to erect a large, ugly "Drive Carefully!" sign in their front yards. The researcher shows the homeowners a photo of a pleasant-looking home completely obscured by the sign. Unsurprisingly, most homeowners refuse the request – indeed, the only real surprise is that 17 percent agree to take the sign. (Who *are* these people?)

Within one subset of homeowners, however, 75 percent agree to take the sign. What makes these homeowners different? Just one thing: two weeks previously, they had agreed to place a small, inconspicuous "Be a Safe Driver" sticker in their windows. Apparently, once the public-service foot insinuates itself in the door, the entire leg follows.[25] Perhaps what is

---

[25] Jonathan L. Freedman & Scott C. Fraser, *Compliance Without Pressure: The Foot-in-the-Door Technique*, 4 J. Personality C'r Social Psych. 195 (1966).

surprising is only that such a small foot could provide an opening for such a large and unattractive leg. The slippery slope from sound judgment to skewed judgment is a lot steeper than we may have suspected.

According to this explanation of the Milgram experiments, it is our own previous actions of shocking the learner that corrupt our moral judgment and lead us to continue shocking him long past the limits of human decency. In a sense, then, we "do it to ourselves" – Milgram compliance turns out to be the result of cognitive dissonance and our need for self-vindication, rather than of obedience to authority. In that case, what role does the man giving the orders play in this explanation?

The answer, I believe, is twofold. First, his repeated instruction – "The experiment requires that you continue!" – prompts us to view the shocks as morally indistinguishable, to downplay the fact that the shocks are gradually escalating. After all, his demeanor never changes, and his instructions never vary. The authority of the superior lies in his power to shape our perceptions, by making us regard everything he asks us to do as business as usual. The experimenter's unflappable demeanor communicates a message: "This experiment is as worthwhile now as it was at the outset. Nothing has changed." Good judgment lies in drawing distinctions among near-indiscernables, whereas authoritative instructions reinforce the theme that indiscernables are identical. The experimenter undermines our judgment, rather than over-mastering our will. Second, his orders pressure us to make our decisions quickly, without taking adequate time to reflect. Together, these two effects of orders subtly erode the conditions for good judgment, and contribute to judgment's self-corruption.

The idea that obedience to evil may result from corrupted judgment rather than evil values or sadism is central to the most famous philosophical study of wrongful obedience in our time, Hannah Arendt's *Eichmann in Jerusalem*.[26] Adolf Eichmann, on Arendt's account, was neither a monster nor an ideologue, neither an antisemite nor a sadist. He was a careerist – an organization man through and through, who could never understand why doing a responsible job well might be regarded as a crime against humanity.

Arendt was struck by the many statements Eichmann made that showed that he never perceived anything at all extraordinary about mass murder. Eichmann would relate the "hard luck story" of his failure to win promotion in the SS to an Israeli policeman whose parents he knew had been murdered by the Nazis; or describe the "normal, human" conversation he had had with an inmate of Auschwitz, who was actually begging for his life.[27] He was utterly oblivious to the way that his listeners would regard these war stories. For Arendt, who understood that thinking is the inner dialogue by which we

---

[26] Hannah Arendt, Eichmann in Jerusalem: A Report on the Banality of Evil (rev. edn. 1963).
[27] Ibid. at 49–51.

examine our situation from various perspectives, Eichmann's inability to think from another person's point of view meant that he could not think at all. Instead, he fell back on the slogans and party euphemisms that had structured his experience throughout his career. Eichmann insulated himself from reality with an impenetrable wall of routines, habits, and clichés.

The result was a man who was incapable of judging reality for what it was; he could experience the world only through the arid, Newspeak categories of a functionary. Eichmann's inability to think from another's point of view deprived him of the ability to think from his own point of view, perhaps even the capacity to *have* a point of view of his own. As in the Milgram experiments, Eichmann allowed his superiors to define the situation he was in; and that is why Eichmann, "an average, 'normal' person, neither feeble-minded nor indoctrinated nor cynical, could be perfectly incapable of telling right from wrong."[28]

The parallels between Arendt's account and the corruption-of-judgment theory offered here are straightforward. To begin with, consider the slippery slope that led Eichmann to the dock in Jerusalem. Eichmann "knew" that his conscience was clear about his casual decision to follow a friend's advice and join the Nazi Party, about which he knew very little at the time. As for his subsequent decision to transfer into the SS, that was a simple mistake: he thought he was joining a different service with a similar name. He regarded his early work in Jewish affairs as something close to benevolent, as he expedited the deportation of Jews from Austria by making it easier for them to obtain their exit papers (in return for all their property). When the mission changed from expelling Jews to concentrating them in camps in the East, Eichmann persuaded himself that this was the best way to fulfill the Zionist ambition of "putting firm ground under the feet of the Jews."[29] As for the Final Solution, all the glitterati in the Nazi hierarchy embraced it enthusiastically; so after six weeks of bad conscience, Eichmann came to see things their way. In his own eyes, each step on Eichmann's road to damnation seemed innocent, sanctioned, almost inevitable. There was no sticking-point, no clear moment of demarcation that his judgment, accustomed to functioning solely in terms of conformism and career advancement, could grab ahold of. The ordinary incentives of career-making colluded with his sense of dutifulness (the performance principle) to launch Eichmann on his slippery slope. His own thoughtlessness and *amour propre* prevented him from seeing it for what it was; as a result, his judgment became entirely corrupt without Eichmann ever ceasing to believe in his own rectitude.

For Arendt, the case of Adolf Eichmann posed profound questions in moral psychology, questions she wrestled with for the rest of her life. What is thinking? What is judgment? How can thought, which is not the same as

---

[28] Ibid. at 26.   [29] Ibid. at 76.

judgment, insulate us, at least in part, from bad judgment?[30] These are ultimate questions that I shall not even try to answer here. But the corruption-of-judgment account presented here can at least provide us with a point of connection between Arendt's philosophizing and the empirical phenomena revealed in social psychology experiments such as Milgram's.

To many readers, the idea of analogizing issues of legal and organizational ethics to the Eichmann case will be preposterous and even offensive. On the one side, the analogy demonizes the Joseph Fortenberrys of the American workplace; on the other, it trivializes the Holocaust. But this objection misses the point. Obviously, I am not suggesting that wrongfully obedient law-firm associates are the moral equivalent of Eichmann, nor that genocide is just one more form of wrongful obedience in the workplace. Rather, the point for both Arendt and Milgram is that if an ordinary person's moral judgment can be corrupted to the point of failure even about something as momentous as mass murder – or shocking an innocent experimental volunteer to death! – it is entirely plausible to think that the same organizational and psychological forces can corrupt our judgment in lesser situations. The extreme situations illuminate their ordinary counterparts even if, in the most obvious ways, they are utterly unlike them.

Explaining Berkey–Kodak through corruption-of-judgment theory

With these thoughts in mind, let me return to the Berkey–Kodak case and see what light the corruption-of-judgment theory may shed on it. The theory suggests that we should find the partner's and associate's misdeeds at the end of a slippery slope, beginning with lawful adversarial deception and culminating with lies, perjury, and wrongful obedience. Following this lead, one fact leaps out at us: the misdeeds occurred during a high-stakes discovery process.

Every litigator knows that discovery is one of the most contentious parts of civil litigation. Civil discovery is like a game of Battleship. One side calls out its shots – it files discovery requests – and the other side must announce when a shot scores a hit. It makes that announcement by turning over a document. There are two big differences. First, unlike Battleship, it isn't always clear when a shot has scored a hit. Lawyers get to argue about whether their document really falls within the scope of the request. They can argue that the request was too broad, or too narrow, or that the document is privileged, or is attorney work-product. Second, unlike Battleship, lawyers don't always get to peek at the opponent's card after the game. When the opponent concludes that a shot missed her battleship, she makes the decision ex parte – she doesn't have to announce it to her adversary, who may never learn that a

---

[30] See Arendt's paper *Thinking and Moral Considerations: A Lecture*, 38 Social Research 417 (1971), reprinted in Responsibility and Judgment (Jerome Kohn ed., 2003).

smoking-gun document (the battleship) was withheld based on an eminently debatable legal judgment.[31]

Every litigation associate goes through a rite of passage: she finds a document that seemingly lies squarely within the scope of a legitimate discovery request, but her supervisor tells her to devise an argument for excluding it. As long as the argument isn't frivolous there is nothing improper about this, but it marks the first step on to the slippery slope. For better or for worse, a certain kind of innocence is lost. It is the moment when withholding information despite an adversary's legitimate request starts to feel like zealous advocacy rather than deception. It is the moment when the no-deception principle encoded in Model Rule 8.4(c) – "It is professional misconduct for a lawyer to engage in conduct involving dishonesty, fraud, deceit or misrepresentation" – gets gerrymandered away from its plain meaning. But, like any other piece of elastic, the no-deception principle loses its grip if it is stretched too often. Soon, if the lawyer isn't very careful, every damaging request seems too broad or too narrow; every smoking-gun document is either work-product or privileged; no adversary ever has a right to "our" documents. At that point the fatal question is not far away: *Is lying really so bad when it is the only way to protect "our" documents from an adversary who has no right to them?* If legitimate advocacy marks the beginning of this particular slippery slope, Berkey–Kodak lies at its end.

Are compliant subjects morally blameworthy?

The Milgram experiments lead quite naturally to the depressing reflection that human nature is much more readily disposed to wrongful obedience than we might have expected or hoped. Milgram seems to have established that in situations where obedience struggles with decency, decency typically loses. What does this conclusion imply about moral responsibility for wrongful obedience? Let us consider two possible lines of thought, which, for reasons that will become clear, I shall call the *Inculpating View* and the *Exculpating View*.

The Inculpating View holds that no matter how widespread wrongful obedience is, and no matter how deep its roots within human nature, wickedness remains wickedness; the fact that wickedness is the rule rather than the exception excuses no one. Suppose that experimenters were to demonstrate that two out of three people will walk off with someone else's $100 bill if they are sure they can get away with it. The experiment suggests that greed has roots deep within human nature, but that creates no excuse for theft. The temptation to obey is like greed or any other temptation. It is perfectly natural

---

[31] On the game-playing aspects of discovery, see William J. Talbott & Alvin I. Goldman, *Legal Discovery and Social Epistemology*, 4 Legal Theory 93, 109–22 (1998).

to give in to it – that's why they call it temptation! – but being perfectly natural excuses nothing.[32]

It might be objected that the analogy between Milgram obedience and greed is a bad one. No matter what his rationalizations, the thief knows that theft is wrong, or so we may suppose. He simply allowed his baser drives to override his moral judgment, and that is why we don't allow his greed to excuse him. If our earlier corruption-of-judgment explanation of Milgram obedience is correct, however, the drive to obey operates at a deeper level, undermining our very capacity to distinguish right from wrong.

But this objection overlooks the fact that we generally do *not* excuse wrongful behavior because it resulted from bad judgment – if anything, the fact that the wrongful choice was the product of judgment rather than of passion or pathology condemns it even more. So the corruption-of-judgment explanation supports rather than undermines the Inculpating View.

Or does it? Try a thought experiment. Suppose a group of high-school seniors is given a test of judgment, such as the familiar multiple-choice analogies test. And suppose that the test's difficulty is calibrated so that every student in a control group passes it. This time, however, the test is administered under extraordinary conditions: throughout the test, a large-screen television in the testing room broadcasts a video of a good-looking couple making enthusiastic, noisy, and improbably athletic love. Under these conditions, we will suppose, two-thirds of the students fail the test.

Clearly, we should conclude that passing the test under such distracting conditions is really hard. The numbers prove it.[33] We would be foolish to blame the students for failing; and we would be cruel to punish those who failed, for example by refusing to admit them to college because of their bad

---

[32] On this point, see Ferdinand Schoeman, *Statistical Norms and Moral Responsibility*, in Responsibility, Character, and the Emotions 296, 305 (Ferdinand Schoeman ed., 1987). Schoeman's important paper is, so far as I know, the first to address explicitly the question of whether Milgram's experimental demonstration of two-to-one odds against subjects defying the experimenter implies that we must revise our moral expectations to reflect the difficulty of defiance – whether, that is, moral norms should reflect statistical norms. One might well refer to this as the *Schoeman problem*.

[33] "The mere fact that most people fail in a given environment suggests that succeeding in that environment is difficult." Ibid. at 304. Schoeman takes this idea from Fritz Heider, The Psychology of Interpersonal Relations 89 (1958). Heider was one of the founders of attribution theory, the psychological study of how we make judgments attributing causal responsibility for the actions of others as well as to ourselves.

Doing the right thing in the Milgram set-up is emotionally as well as cognitively difficult. In an Austrian replication of the Milgram experiment, the pulse rates of defiant subjects went up at the moment they broke off the experiment, signaling that defiance (and not only compliance) generates physiological stress. Thomas Blass, *Understanding Behavior in the Milgram Obedience Experiment: The Role of Personality, Situations, and Their Interactions*, 60 J. Personality & Soc. Psych. 404 (1991).

scores. Surely we would blame the situation, which obviously undermined their capacity to judge.

The analogy to Milgram is straightforward. When people had the Milgram experiments described to them, they all passed the "test" of moral judgment: without exception, they predicted that they would break off the experiment well before the 450-volt maximum (and it should be clear that their prediction is in reality a moral judgment that complying to 450 volts would be wrong). But in the actual experiment, two out of three failed their test. Pursuing the parallel, we would be foolish to blame them for failing, and cruel for punishing them. The situation excuses their compliance. This is the Exculpating View.

In short, the Inculpating View holds people responsible for their wrongful obedience, regardless of how common wrongful obedience is, or how deeply rooted it may be in human nature. The Exculpating View excuses wrongful obedience whenever it is the statistical norm, because that fact shows how unreasonably difficult it must be to disobey under such circumstances. One view accuses, the other excuses.

How are we to decide between the Inculpating and the Exculpating Views? I propose approaching the problem indirectly, by looking at parallel puzzles in the treatment of psychologically based defenses in the criminal law. Admittedly, criminal responsibility raises different issues from moral responsibility, and the psychological defenses the law recognizes do not include the deep-seated propensity to obey. Despite these obstacles, there are enough suggestive parallels that examining the criminal law issues will allow us to triangulate toward our own question.

Consider the "heat of passion" or "extreme emotional disturbance" defense in homicide cases, which reduces murder to manslaughter.[34] In its formulation in the Model Penal Code, the defense is available whenever a "homicide which would otherwise be murder is committed under the influence of extreme mental or emotional disturbance for which there is reasonable explanation or excuse."[35] The canonical situation is a husband murdering his wife and her lover when he finds them in bed.

Surprisingly, however, this clichéd bit of melodrama is *not* the typical situation in which the defense actually arises. Victoria Nourse examined every reported heat-of-passion decision in US courts between 1980 and 1995, and discovered a disturbing pattern. The paradigm case for heat of passion turns out to be men angry at women for exiting a relationship: boyfriends upset that their girlfriends have left them; long-separated husbands whose

---

[34] In the ensuing discussion, I closely follow the brilliant treatment of the emotional-disturbance defense in Victoria Nourse, *Passion's Progress: Modern Law Reform and the Provocation Defense*, 106 Yale L. J. 1331 (1997).

[35] Model Penal Code, §210.3(1)(b).

wives finally file for divorce; long-divorced husbands who learn that their ex-wives are remarrying; and men served with protective orders forbidding them from approaching wives or girlfriends they have battered. In other words, the typical heat-of-passion "provocation" turns out not to be infidelity, but a woman's attempt to lead her own life free from her killer's dominion; and the killer's "passion" seems not to be sexual jealousy so much as the over-whelming desire to control and own a woman.[36]

The Model Penal Code aimed to reform the criminal law by taking a scientific approach to human psychology. It treats passion and irrationality as demonstrable facts of human existence that must be acknowledged rather than denounced. In this respect, it holds what Dan Kahan and Martha Nussbaum label the "mechanistic conception" of emotion – the idea "that emotions ... are energies that impel the person to action, without embodying ways of thinking about or perceiving objects or situations in the world."[37] From a clinical point of view, it hardly matters what circumstances provoke an emotional disturbance. All that matters is whether the emotional dis-turbance undermines the defendant's self-control. The MPC embodies the idea that psychological drives are causes, not reasons, for human behavior, and that it is senseless to moralise about nonrational causes. For that reason, juries in MPC jurisdictions are asked to determine whether, *from the killer's "subjective" point of view*, a woman's declaration of independence is a reasonable explanation of murderous anger.[38] Sadly enough, from the killer's point of view, it often is.

Nourse is critical of the Model Penal Code's approach, and I am as well. Her findings about the circumstances under which the heat-of-passion defense gets invoked provide a virtual *reductio ad absurdum* of the mechanistic treatment of provocation. Mitigations reflect judicial and legis-lative compassion for wrongdoers who have committed crimes under un-usually trying circumstances. Does a man who flies into a murderous rage because his wife dates someone else three years after they separated really deserve our compassion?[39] Surely not; and surely it is appropriate to moralize about whether his murderous rage was justified.

---

[36] Nourse, supra note 34, at 1342–68.

[37] Dan M. Kahan & Martha C. Nussbaum, *Two Conceptions of Emotion in Criminal Law*, 96 Colum. L. Rev. 269, 278 (1996).

[38] Even though the MPC requires a reasonable explanation or excuse for the emotional dis-turbance, it insists that "The reasonableness of such explanation or excuse shall be determined from the viewpoint of a person in the actor's situation under the circumstances as he believes them to be" – a subjective, rather than an objective, test of reasonableness. Model Penal Code, §210.3(1)(b).

[39] Nourse, supra note 34, at 1360, discussing State v. Rivera, 612 A.2d 749 (Conn. 1992) (common-law husband kills his wife's lover three years after he and the wife separated).

In line with this thought, Nourse proposes a different approach to extreme emotional disturbance, based on the concept of a *warranted excuse*.[40] Begin with the philosophically attractive idea that emotions can be appropriate or inappropriate – that they embody (or at least correspond with) evaluative judgments of objects and situations that can be true or false, warranted or not warranted.[41] If a man flies into a murderous rage because his wife has been raped, his emotion reflects a warranted evaluative judgment about the rape – that rape is wicked and horrible. If the enraged man kills his wife's rapist, his extreme emotional disturbance provides a warranted excuse that rightly mitigates the murder to a manslaughter.[42]

If, on the other hand, the killer has become enraged because his wife is leaving him, his emotion corresponds with the evaluative judgment that she is not entitled to leave him – perhaps even that wives are never entitled to leave their husbands. This evaluative judgment deserves no endorsement from the law. Even assuming that he was in the grip of extreme emotional disturbance when he killed her, the heat-of-passion excuse should be unavailable to him, because the emotion is unjustified. In line with this reasoning, Nourse proposes a legal test to distinguish warranted from unwarranted extreme-emotional-disturbance excuses for homicide. If the killer's emotional disturbance is provoked by an act, like rape, which the law condemns, the excuse is warranted; if it is provoked by an act that the law protects, like leaving a relationship, the excuse is unwarranted.

There is one way in which the "warranted excuse" terminology can be misleading. It is important to realize that what makes the excuse unwarranted is not just that the actor's emotion corresponds with a *false* evaluative judgment. The excuse is unwarranted because the actor's emotion corresponds with an *evil* evaluative judgment – one that reflects badly on the actor's character. The excuse fails not because its underlying evaluative judgment is epistemologically unwarranted; the excuse fails because its underlying evaluation is morally detestable.

Admittedly, it runs deeply against the modern temper to moralize about psychological forces over which we arguably have no control. That is what the warranted-excuse approach does, inasmuch as it relies on moral judgments to distinguish causal explanations for behavior that mitigate liability from causal explanations that do not.

---

[40] In the present essay I follow Nourse's examples and terminology. But the same approach was proposed several years earlier in Andrew von Hirsch & Nils Jareborg, *Provocation and Culpability*, in Schoeman, Responsibility, Character, and the Emotions, supra note 32, at 241–55.

[41] Kahan and Nussbaum refer to this as the "evaluative conception" of emotion. See supra note 37.

[42] To avoid confusion, notice that this does not say that killing the rapist is justified. Justified emotions can lead to unjustifiable actions. That is why the appeal to heat of passion is only a partial excuse, reducing murder to manslaughter, and not a full excuse or a justification.

Yet assigning responsibility in a world of causal explanations is what compatibilism (the approach to the free-will problem that insists that moral responsibility is *compatible* with determinism) is all about – and the criminal law is compatibilist through and through. Criminal lawyers are rightly agnostic about the possibility that all behavior can be causally explained, but they will insist that even so the law must ascribe responsibility to some people but not others for their actions. Given that we inevitably make such judgments, it seems plausible to make them on moral grounds – in effect, blaming agents for their susceptibility to morally obnoxious causes.

Viewed abstractly, then, the strategy for separating warranted from unwarranted heat-of-passion excuses amounts to this. First, we make explicit the underlying judgment that the emotion reflects. Second, we ask whether the judgment is warranted. Third, if the judgment underlying the emotion is unwarranted, we ask whether in addition it is morally condemnable. If so, the excuse is unwarranted.

How can we apply these ideas to Milgram obedience? Notice first that the propensity to obey is not an emotion. It is more like a hankering, like wanting to smoke a cigarette or scratch an itch. But even though the urge to obey is not an emotion, we can treat it along the same lines as the heat-of-passion defense: first, by making explicit whatever underlying judgments it corresponds with; second, by asking if they are justified; and third, if they are unjustified, by asking whether they are in addition morally condemnable.

What underlying judgments correspond with Milgram obedience? That depends on what the explanation of Milgram obedience is. Here, I will assume that the corruption-of-judgment explanation I defended earlier is the right explanation. Subjects obey, according to the corruption-of-judgment account, because the experiment manipulates them into misjudging the point at which an electric shock violates the no-harm principle. The experiment begins innocuously, and each incremental step implicates the teacher a bit further in the project of shocking the learner. The experimenter's repeated instruction – "The experiment requires that you continue" – reinforces the idea that every shock level is morally indistinguishable from those that went before. As a result, breaking off the experiment for moral reasons generates cognitive dissonance, because it suggests that the teacher has willingly participated in wrongdoing. The teacher cannot eliminate the dissonance by undoing what he's already done. Instead, he eliminates the dissonance by gerrymandering the scope of the no-harm principle so that participating in the experiment does not appear to violate it. As one psychologist puts it, "Dissonance-reducing behavior is ego-defensive behavior; by reducing dissonance, we maintain a positive image of ourselves – an image that depicts us as good."[43] In other words, our judgment gets corrupted because only by

---

[43] Aronson, The Social Animal, supra note 23, at 185.

corrupting our judgment can we continue to think well of ourselves. Conscience must be seduced into flattering our self-image.

On this analysis, the propensity to obey corresponds with the following line of (unconscious) reasoning: "If the next shock is wrong, the one I just administered was wrong as well. If so, I would have to believe that I had done something morally wrong; I would have to think badly of myself. That's unacceptable. So the next shock can't be wrong."

That this line of reasoning is unsound goes without saying. It takes one's own inevitable moral uprightness as a given, and our inevitable moral uprightness is never a given. But the reasoning is more than merely unsound. It reflects badly on our character. It reveals us as so childishly resistant to moral self-criticism that we will distort our sense of right and wrong to avoid admitting that we have done wrong. We are willing to electrocute the learner if the alternative is feeling a little bad about ourselves. *Amour propre über alles*!

The Milgram experiments demonstrate that two-thirds of us are fatally susceptible to this kind of unconscious reasoning, from which it follows that avoiding it must be rather difficult. On the Exculpating View, the difficulty of avoiding it mitigates our moral culpability. But the argument I have been elaborating leads to the opposite conclusion. Compliance originates in corruption of judgment, and corruption of judgment in this case corresponds with the line of reasoning that I have summarized as *amour propre über alles* – a line of reasoning that is not only unsound but morally repugnant. A traditional theologian like St. Augustine would have labeled it, far more simply, as the sin of pride. Our susceptibility to self-corrupted judgment reflects badly on us, and no mitigation is warranted. In this case, at any rate, the Inculpating View seems closer to the truth.

It is important to understand what I am *not* arguing. I am not arguing that whenever a bad choice arises from fallacious unconscious reasoning that corrupts our judgment we bear full responsibility for making the bad choice. We bear full responsibility only when the unconscious reasoning is not only fallacious but morally reprehensible. Sometimes, fallacious unconscious reasoning casts no discredit on us, and in those cases the difficulty of avoiding it *does* mitigate our blame.

For example, cognitive psychologists have discovered that when we face risk-decisions we unconsciously employ quick-and-dirty heuristics that in trick cases can lead us to faulty probability-judgments. Presumably, natural selection bred these heuristics into us because they make up in ease and speed what they sacrifice in reliability. They are useful rules of thumb, and Mother Nature is a rule-utilitarian. The principle is the same as in optical illusions: our brain learns quick-and-dirty optical heuristics like "Small is far and big is near," which can be exploited by illusionists to fool the eye. The rule "Small is far and big is near" is fallacious; but it does not reflect badly on us that we unconsciously follow it. Even if following it leads us to a fatal mistake, we aren't to blame. In the same way, we aren't to blame for mistakes arising from our quick-and-dirty cognitive heuristics, because it doesn't reflect badly on us that we employ them. Finite creatures like us must and should employ them.[44]

Milgram compliance is different, because the unconscious reasoning compliant teachers follow *does* reflect badly on them. What follows from these observations is that neither the Inculpating View nor the Exculpating View is entirely right, because each holds sway in some cases but not in others. Suppose psychologists discover that under some experimental condition C most people suffer a failure of judgment. The Inculpating View says that the large number of people suffering the failure doesn't excuse the failure, while the Exculpating View says that it does. What we have discovered instead is that when susceptibility to C reflects badly on our character, the Inculpating View is true; when susceptibility to C does not reflect badly on our character, the Exculpating View is true. In Milgram, the Inculpating View is true; compliant subjects are to blame for their wrongful obedience, even though it resulted from bad judgment, and their judgment was corrupted by dynamics they were unaware of. That is because their susceptibility to corruption of judgment, arising from the sin of pride, reflects badly on them.

Warranted excuses and free will

Those who hold the Exculpating View are likely to find this analysis question-begging. If it is extraordinarily difficult to avoid fallacious unconscious reasoning based on excessive self-regard, as the two-thirds Milgram compliance rate suggests, giving in to it should not reflect badly on us. That, recall, was the argument behind the Exculpating View, and the analysis offered here seems to assume at the outset that it fails. Hence the concern that the analysis begs the question.

The point of the objection is that we should be held responsible only for choices that are ours to make, and if we cannot help reasoning as we do – it is, remember, *unconscious* reasoning – it follows that the choice is not really ours. Let's use the term "moral self" to describe those aspects of a person that engage in moral choice. Unconscious reasoning that we can't easily avoid seems to come from outside the moral self, and for that reason it does not reflect badly on the moral self.

Take an extreme illustration. Suppose that a Milgram subject believes he is morally infallible, but he believes it only because a brain tumor has given him delusions of grandeur. And suppose that because of this belief he

---

[44] On this point, see Christopher Cherniak, Minimal Rationality (1992).

becomes a Milgram complier in just the way that the corruption-of-judgment theory suggests. He is, in other words, a typical Milgram complier, with the one difference that excessive self-regard (the sin of pride) has become part of his make-up only because of the misfortune of the brain tumor. Surely, we should hold him blameless, because his judgment has been corrupted by something foreign to his moral self.

If that is right, however, we must consider the possibility that even in less extreme cases – everyday cases where we can't point to an obvious cause like a brain tumor – susceptibility to excessive self-regard also derives from causal factors foreign to the moral self (brain chemistry, psychological laws, upbringing). According to psychologist Melvin Lerner, "as any reasonable psychologist will tell you, all behavior is 'caused' by a combination of antecedent events and the genetic endowment of the individual."[45]

Clearly, we are here treading in the vicinity of the general question whether moral responsibility and determinism are compatible – an aspect of the Problem of Free Will, which one writer has aptly described as the most difficult problem in philosophy.[46] I have no reason to believe myself equipped to solve that problem. A distinguished philosopher once warned that "it is impossible to say anything significant about this ancient problem that has not been said before."[47] He wrote these words in 1964; if they were true then, they obviously remain true now. Instead, I will simply lay out, with a minimum of argument, the views about free will and compatibilism that underlie the argument of this chapter. More importantly, though, I will show how these views respond to the objection I have just rehearsed.

Melvin Lerner's deterministic line of argument suggests a blanket disclaimer of responsibility for all bad acts, and – as legal theorist Michael Moore rightly argues – this implication amounts to a *reductio ad absurdum* of the theory that caused action is blameless action.[48] Not that everyone would regard the implication as a *reductio*. Lerner believes "that (a) the way people act is determined by their past experience and their biological inheritance, and (b) this perspective neutralizes the condemning or blaming reaction to what people do."[49]

Yet Lerner finds that he himself blames members of his family for actions of which he disapproves. His explanation: "I want to, must, believe that people have 'effective' control over important things that happen, and I will hang on to this belief, even when it requires that I resort to rather primitive,

[45] Melvin J. Lerner, The Belief in a Just World: A Fundamental Delusion 120 (1980).

[46] Susan Wolf, Freedom Within Reason vii (1990).

[47] Roderick M. Chisholm, *Human Freedom and the Self*, reprinted in Free Will 24 (Gary Watson ed., Oxford University Press, 1982).

[48] Michael Moore, Placing Blame: A General Theory of the Criminal Law 504–5 (1997).

[49] Lerner, supra note 45, at 121.

magical thinking."[50] A few moments' reflection will reveal that to abandon this "primitive, magical thinking" is to abandon all the reactive attitudes such as gratitude, resentment, forgiveness, and indignation – that is, to abandon the cement of the social universe.[51] That is one reason Moore calls the argument a *reductio ad absurdum*.[52] Before accepting its drastic conclusion, we should explore the possibility that praising and blaming do not require primitive, magical thinking, even in a deterministic universe.

Moore's preferred alternative is to insist that we are morally responsible for our choices, whether or not determinism is true. To avoid the counter-intuitive argument that his position blames people for acting even though they could not do otherwise, he adopts G. E. Moore's analysis of the phrase "could have done otherwise": it means "could have if the actor had chosen to do otherwise."[53] According to this analysis, even an actor whose behavior is determined could have done otherwise, as long as the causal laws that link choosing with doing remain valid. For then, the actor could have done otherwise if only he had chosen to.

I cannot accept this alternative, however, because it falls prey to the well-known objection that "He could have done otherwise if he had chosen to do otherwise" can be true even of someone who could not have chosen to do otherwise. As Susan Wolf illustrates the objection, "the fact that a person attacked on the street would have screamed if she had chosen cannot possibly support a positive evaluation of her responsibility in the case if she was too paralyzed by fear to consider, much less choose, whether to scream."[54] Indeed, "she could have screamed if she had chosen to" may be true (in a hypothetical sort of way) even if the victim had fainted – hardly a condition under which it is reasonable to insist that she could have screamed!

Wolf suggests a better characterization of the ability to do something, namely that one possesses the necessary skills, talents, and knowledge to do it, and nothing interferes with their exercise.[55] And indeed, this may come close to another of Michael Moore's ideas, namely that one can do something if one has the capability and opportunity to do it.[56] If this characterization of freedom is right, atom-by-atom physical determinism seems pretty much beside the point.[57]

---

[50] Ibid. at 122.

[51] See Peter Strawson, *Freedom and Resentment*, 48 Proceedings of the British Academy 125 (1962), reprinted in Watson, Free Will, supra note 47, at 59–80.

[52] Moore, Placing Blame, supra note 48, at 542–43.

[53] Ibid. at 540–41; again at 553. The analysis comes from G. E. Moore, Ethics 84–95 (1912).

[54] Wolf, supra note 46, at 99. This objection originally comes from Chisholm, supra note 47, at 26–27.

[55] Wolf, supra note 46, at 101.   [56] Moore, Placing Blame, supra note 48, at 525.

[57] Wolf skillfully argues this point in Freedom Within Reason, supra note 46, at 103–16.

A worry nevertheless arises about whether Wolf's alternative will help us understand the Milgram experiment or similar cases where psychological forces distort our judgment at the unconscious level. Moore rightly maintains that "the freedom essential to responsibility is the freedom to reason practically without the kind of disturbances true [psychological] compulsions represent";[58] and Wolf likewise insists that "agents *not be psychologically determined* to make the particular choices or perform the particular actions they do."[59] But what if we aren't free in that way? In that case, even Wolf's definition of ability will lead to the conclusion that Milgram's compliers were unable to act differently. After all, in social psychology the determinist argument is not that agents are unfree because the motions of every particle in the Universe are determined by the laws of physics. The argument is that psychological forces distort the judgment even of sane, healthy people.

However, the numbers in the Milgram experiments suggest that such distortion does not rise to the level of determination. If every last one of Milgram's thousand subjects had complied with the experimenter, we would undoubtedly conclude that some powerful psychological force, as irresistible as the brain tumor in our earlier example, compels our obedient behavior and excuses otherwise wrongful compliance. Our only remaining puzzles would be isolating and identifying the force, and explaining why naive observers don't predict the result. Furthermore, if only one or two of the thousand subjects complied, we would likewise suspect that pathology had something to do with it, precisely because the experimenter's orders prove so easy for normal people to resist.

In the actual experiment, the numbers fall in between. The two-thirds compliance rate provides strong evidence that some previously unsuspected psychological force distorts the judgment of otherwise normal people. But, because a third of the subjects did not comply, the evidence hardly supports the hypothesis of an irresistible compulsion.

The corruption-of-judgment theory I have defended here grounds the urge to comply in cognitive dissonance, a dynamic that all people share. But it links the subjects' susceptibility to the urge to excessive self-regard, which two-thirds of us (apparently) have despite our conscious beliefs to the contrary, and the rest do not. This difference, no doubt, results from differences in how we are put together and brought up.

What makes the warranted-excuse theory distinctive is its insistence that such differences are not morally neutral brute facts about us that excuse bad judgment. When distorted moral judgment arises from bad values like excessive self-regard, it seems wrongheaded to release the actor from blame for his actions. That, at any rate, is the idea underlying the warranted-excuse strategy defended here. Because susceptibility to corruption of judgment

---

[58] Moore, Placing Blame, supra note 48, at 525.   [59] Wolf, supra note 46, at 101.

reflects badly on the agent, corruption of judgment provides no excuse for wrongdoing. A person's character flaw, or so I am assuming, provides a basis for criticism, not a basis for excuse.

Notice that on this approach, we blame people only for their chosen actions, not for their characters; the warranted-excuses approach should not be confused with the theory that actions are wrong only because they manifest bad character. Michael Moore criticizes this "character theory" because it implies that people of bad character deserve to be punished even if they do nothing blameworthy.[60] It is important to understand why his objection does not apply to the warranted-excuses approach. On our approach, the ground for criticizing Milgram compliers is not that they have bad characters. It is that they knowingly administered lethal electrical shocks to an innocent person pleading with them to stop. The character trait that renders them susceptible to authoritarian pressure is a moral fault, but that fact functions only to rob them of an excuse, not to explain why shocking the learner is wrong.

The warranted-excuses approach does share features with the character theory. First, as Moore observes, it recognizes two very different sorts of moral judgments we make about persons – judgments that they are blameworthy because of their wrongful actions, and judgments that their characters are bad.[61] Second, it accepts Moore's point that the latter judgments are "a kind of aesthetic morality"[62] which in effect judges people by how well formed their souls are. But, unlike Moore, it rejects any implication that "aesthetic morality" is illegitimate. What should we judge people (as distinguished from their actions) by except the content of their characters?

Moore confuses matters when he marks the distinction between the two sorts of moral judgments by describing them as judgments holding people responsible for their chosen actions and judgments holding them responsible "for being the sort of people that *they* are."[63] To be sure, this description makes character-based moral judgment sound irrational, because holding people responsible for being who they are sounds irrational. But that is only because Moore has inadvertently collapsed two very different meanings of the word "responsibility" – responsibility as authorship, and responsibility as blameworthiness (or, for that matter, praiseworthiness). He is right that a person is not the author of her character, but that does not mean she can't be morally judged according to her character. She is praised or blamed for her character not because she created it, but because in an important sense she is her character – there is no moral self beneath or beyond it. The distinction between judgments of deeds and judgments of character does not rest on extravagant Romantic ideas about self-creating selves.

---

[60] Moore, Placing Blame, supra note 48, at 584–87.   [61] Ibid. at 571.   [62] Ibid.   [63] Ibid.

Both kinds of moral judgments are legitimate, and the warranted-excuse approach utilizes both. It assigns blame by judging actions, and accepts or rejects excuses by judging character. This procedure is fair, because it grounds blameworthiness solely in what we do, and withholds deterministic excuses only when the bad acts result from judgment corrupted by bad character. Deterministic excuses remain available whenever our judgment is corrupted by forces beyond our moral selves – forces outside of us in the way that bad character in not outside of us. But doubts surely remain, unless there is something we can do to guard against corrupted judgment and wrongful obedience.

Conclusion

There is no reason to believe that corruption of judgment is inevitable in organizations or in the adversary system. But neither do I have a failsafe remedy to protect lawyers or anyone else from the optical illusions of the spirit that authority and cognitive dissonance engender. (I take up this subject in more detail in chapter 8.) A first step, no doubt, is understanding the illusions themselves, their pervasiveness, the insidious way they work on us. Understanding these illusions warns us against them, and perhaps forewarned is forearmed, at least in contexts similar enough to call the warning to mind. I have argued here that to understand all is *not* to forgive all. But in some situations, to understand all may put us on our guard against doing the unforgivable.

Unfortunately, the experimental evidence suggests that small differences in situations can generate large differences in behavior, which strongly suggests that we have a very weak capacity to generalize the lessons of one situation to another, even if the latter situation resembles the former in ways that should be apparent but turn out not to be.

But perhaps understanding the power of situations to corrupt our judgment can put us on our guard in a more indirect fashion. One of Milgram's compliant subjects wrote him years later to say that his participation in the experiment subsequently led him to refuse military service in the Vietnam war. This is an instructive example. The subject's experience in the Milgram experiment did not necessarily immunize him from wrongful obedience, and indeed there is no reason to suppose that anything can immunize us. Instead, it caused him to take a dramatic step to steer clear of a situation where destructive obedience was a genuine and ever-present possibility. In other words, by participating in Milgram's experiments he may have learned the power of situations to distort judgment; and, rather than indulging in the wishful thought that he would do better next time, he tried to insulate himself from the very possibility of there being a next time. Of course, so long as wars continue to be fought, someone will have to serve in the military, and so this man's personal solution is not available to everyone. More generally, it is sheer illusion to suppose that society can be organized to eliminate hierarchies of command and obedience; and so long as command and obedience exist, destructive obedience remains an ever-present possibility. A disquieting conclusion, no doubt: we may find ourselves engaged in destructive obedience, responding to pressures that we cannot insulate ourselves from or even be aware of; and we may nevertheless still be blameworthy for giving in to those pressures. St. Augustine, who argued that predestination does not relieve us of the burden of sin, would not have been surprised.

There is still one hopeful finding of the Milgram experiments. Recall that when subjects were paired with a fellow teacher who refused to go along with the experimenter's commands, compliance plunged to 10 percent – just as, when the second teacher enthusiastically went along with the experiment, compliance ballooned to 90 percent. Our moral compass seems tremendously susceptible to the responses of the people around us. That fact creates the problem of wrongful obedience, but it also implies that noncompliers can influence their compliant fellows. The social psychologist Serge Moscovici has argued for many years that even a small minority of virtuous noncompliers can sometimes exert enough influence to break the corrupting spell of situations.[64] Human nature seems malleable more than overtly wicked – and that means susceptibility can be toward the good as well as the bad. The thought that a small number of righteous dissenters can sometimes sway the judgment of a larger majority is a profoundly hopeful one.

---

[64] See, e.g., Moscovici, Psychologie des minorités actives (1979); Moscovici et al., *Influences of a Consistent Minority on the Responses of a Majority in a Colour Perception Task*, 32 Sociometry 365 (1969).

8

Integrity: its causes and cures

Integrity is a good thing, isn't it? In ordinary parlance, we sometimes use it as a near synonym for honesty, but the word means much more than honesty alone. It means wholeness or unity of person, an inner consistency between deed and principle. "Integrity" shares etymology with other unity-words – integer, integral, integrate, integration. All derive from the Latin *integrare,* to make whole. And the person of integrity is the person whose conduct and principles operate in happy harmony.

Our psyches always seek that happy harmony. When our conduct and our principles clash with each other, the result, social psychology teaches us, is *cognitive dissonance.* And dissonance theory hypothesizes that one of our fundamental psychic mechanisms is the drive to reduce dissonance.

You can reduce dissonance between conduct and principles in two ways. The high road, if you choose to take it, requires you to conform your conduct to your principles. That occasionally demands agonizing, sacrificial choices: to resign your job, for example, when continuing to do what your client asks requires you to cheat and shred and cover up. Think of the Enron lawyers. This is a lot to ask of people, particularly when those around you send the message that the actions you object to are nothing more than what the grown-ups do to keep a competitive edge in a dog-eat-dog world.[1] In the business

---

[1] Robert Jackall, in his superb study of moral line-drawing in corporate settings, tells the story of an accountant who got himself fired from a big company for making waves about an internal slush fund. The accountant told Jackall that he was "frightened of losing ... my self-respect ... a fear of falling down in a place where you have stuck a flag in the ground and said: 'This is where I stand.'" Robert Jackall, Moral Mazes: The World of Corporate Managers 109 (1988). But his colleagues had no pity for him. In their opinion, he broke the rules of corporate life and ignored good excuses for not acting. To them, the slush fund was simply business as usual, and the accountant's moralism was abstract and maybe even hypocritical, because nobody rises as high in a corporation as the accountant had without having dirtied his hands. Worst of all, the accountant's moral code made everyone else uncomfortable. "The guy's an evangelist." Ibid. at 109–11.

world, gaining a competitive edge is universally recognized as good rather than bad, and if it conflicts with Sunday-school morality, those around you will send artfully mixed signals about which you're supposed to obey. They will say "Both," deny the conflict, and leave you to draw your own conclusions about what their denial is supposed to mean. It's hard to maintain the courage of your convictions when your convictions are at war with one another, and those around you say they back one side, but behave as though they back the other.

Taking the high road to integrity may prove unappealing as an intellectual matter as well, because we recognize that hanging on to principles regardless of situations often bespeaks a kind of rigid inflexibility rather than a virtuous soul. Training in the common law teaches lawyers that the meaning of principles gets determined only in their application to specific cases, so that someone who insists on taking general principles literally can be fairly accused of misunderstanding the basic realist insight that rules have no existence apart from cases. For this reason, some leading legal ethicists argue for contextualism, the view that ethical judgment must be sensitive to situational differences that cannot be captured in abstract principles.[2] Contextualists will not necessarily endorse rigid moralism – and the high road to integrity seems nothing if not rigidly moralistic.

The low road is so much simpler – that, of course, is what makes it the low road. If your conduct conflicts with your principles, modify your principles. This is the path of least resistance; so much so that apparently we follow it unconsciously all the time. That, at any rate, is what fifty years of research in social psychology teaches us. In situation after situation, literally hundreds of experiments reveal that when our conduct clashes with our prior beliefs – when, in the jargon of social science, we act "counterattitudinally"– our beliefs swing into conformity with our conduct, without our ever noticing.[3]

[2] E.g., William H. Simon, The Practice of Justice: A Theory of Lawyers' Ethics 9–10, 69–74, 138–39 (1998) (defining and defending a "Contextual View" of legal ethics, which rejects categorical norms in favor of context-sensitive norms); David B. Wilkins, *Making Context Count: Regulating Lawyers After Kaye, Scholer*, 66 S. Cal. L. Rev. 1147 (1993) (arguing that different contexts of legal practice demand different norms of professional conduct); Geoffrey C. Hazard, Jr., *Context in Ethics*, 2 APA Newsletters No. 2, Spring 2003, at 163 (arguing that philosophers' overreliance on categorical norms wrongly neglects the context-sensitive aspects of moral judgment).

[3] Both here and in the remainder of this chapter, my discussion of the impact of social-psychological forces on lawyer behavior draws instruction and inspiration from work of my colleague Donald Langevoort. See Donald C. Langevoort, *Behavioral Theories of Judgment and Decision Making in Legal Scholarship: A Literature Review*, 51 Vand. L. Rev. 1499 (1998); Langevoort, *Ego, Human Behavior, and Law*, 51 Va. L. Rev. 853 (1995); Langevoort, *The Epistemology of Corporate-Securities Lawyering: Beliefs, Biases and Organizational Behavior*, 63 Brook. L. Rev. 629 (1997); Langevoort, *Where Were the Lawyers? A Behavioral Inquiry into Lawyers' Responsibility for Clients' Fraud*, 46 Vand. L. Rev. 75 (1993) (hereinafter Langevoort, *Where*

Integrity as dissonance reduction

Counterattitudinal advocacy

In one classic dissonance experiment, subjects were asked to perform a boring, repetitive task – rotating screws in holes of a pegboard – and afterwards were paid to tell the next student waiting to perform the same task that it was really very interesting. This is "counterattitudinal advocacy," known more colloquially as "lawyering." The reigning behaviorist paradigm in social psychology of the day hypothesized that higher rewards would reinforce the task more strongly, and therefore predicted that the higher the pay, the more likely the subjects were to evince belief in what they were advocating. But dissonance theory yields the opposite prediction. Deceiving one's fellows for little or no benefit to oneself creates dissonance, and so the "pro bono" advocates should be more likely to internalize the belief they were advocating. And so the experiments proved, to the dismay of behaviorists and the delight of dissonance theorists. Apparently, when my behavior makes me, as St. Augustine says, a great riddle to myself, I solve the riddle in the simplest way: *if I said it, I must believe it, at least a bit; if I did it, I must think it's right.*[4] All this, I emphasize, goes on unconsciously. But the net effect is a happy harmony between what I do and what I believe – the textbook definition of integrity. It is, however, a kind of integrity in which my beliefs always rationalize my actions after the fact, and in which I therefore automatically inhabit the best of all possible moral worlds: the world of my own inevitable righteousness.

Subsequent research has refined the dissonance idea. Experiments reveal that we don't always resolve dissonance between cognitions by changing our beliefs. Rather, we do so when the dissonant cognitions threaten to undermine our own self-concept – paradigmatically, when it occurs to us that we may have done something wrong.[5] Apparently, we are all highly resistant to the thought of our own wrongdoing, and the result is that we will bend our moral beliefs and even our perceptions to fight off the harsh judgment of our own

---

Were the Lawyers?). I am in overall agreement with Langevoort; and the principal addition to his work in the present chapter lies in two observations at the heart of my argument: first, that as a matter of psychological theory, cognitive dissonance theory has a kind of primacy, because it organizes a great deal of the subsequent research into disparate topics; and secondly, that dissonance reduction bears an uncomfortable resemblance to the quest for integrity.

[4] See Leon Festinger & James M. Carlsmith, *Cognitive Consequences of Forced Compliance*, 58 J. Abnormal & Soc. Psych. 203 (1959). See also the discussion in Lee Ross & Richard E. Nisbett, The Person and the Situation: Perspectives of Social Psychology 66 (1991), and additional sources cited therein.

[5] See Elliot Aronson, The Social Animal 230–33 (7th edn., 1995), on this refinement of the dissonance idea.

behavior. As some psychologists say, we are *intuitive lawyers.*[6] Nietzsche had a similar insight. "'I have done that,' says my memory. 'I cannot have done that,' says my pride, and remains inexorable. Eventually – memory yields."[7]

Of course, a little niggling voice might call this self-deception. Some might find it less than entirely admirable. If so, lawyers for pay can perhaps take comfort from the counterattitudinal advocacy experiment: it suggests that the higher they bill, the less likely they are to deceive themselves into believing what they say on behalf of clients. But they shouldn't take too much comfort, because the difference between them and their pro bono peers is only a matter of degree. Other experiments have shown that counterattitudinal advocacy, whether it be cheap or dear, typically nudges beliefs in the direction of the advocacy. Furthermore, bystanders aren't immune to the same effect. Observers hearing someone give a speech supporting or opposing Fidel Castro will believe that the speaker's own attitude is either pro- or anti-Castro *even if they know that someone else has picked which side the speaker should argue.*[8] Indeed, observers will draw conclusions about the speaker's belief even knowing that the speaker is merely reading out loud an essay written by someone else.[9] More bizarrely, subjects told that a person being described to them had been assigned to write a pro- or anti-abortion essay will believe that the person favors the conclusion supported in the essay, *without reading the essay.*[10] Our tendency to infer attitudes from advocacy-behavior apparently leads us to discount almost entirely information about external constraints on what others are advocating.[11] Add to this finding the fact – about which more later – that what those around us believe influences what we believe, and it should scarcely be surprising that the very process of advocacy tends to swing our beliefs into line with the positions we advocate.

More importantly, well-paid lawyers have people around them, called clients, who may believe strongly in what they tell their lawyer to say – and our beliefs have a tendency to fall in line with those of the people around us. In the famous experiments of Solomon Asch, many people identified a short line-segment as longer than a long line-segment, after having heard other

[6] See Roderick M. Kramer & David M. Messick, *Ethical Cognition and the Framing of Organizational Dilemmas: Decision Makers as Intuitive Lawyers,* in Codes of Conduct: Behavioral Research Into Business Ethics 59 (David M. Messick & Ann E. Tenbrunsel eds., 1996); see generally Aronson, supra note 5, at 175–245.

[7] Friederich Nietzsche, Beyond Good and Evil §68 (Walter Kaufmann trans., 1966).

[8] Edward E. Jones & Victor A. Harris, *The Attribution of Attitudes,* 3 J. Experimental Soc. Psych. 1 (1967).

[9] Arthur G. Miller, *Constraint and Target Effects in the Attribution of Attitudes,* 12 J. Experimental Soc. Psych. 325, 330–33 (1976).

[10] Icek Ajzen et al., *Consistency and Bias in the Attribution of Attitudes,* 37 J. Personality and Soc. Psych. 1871, 1874 (1979).

[11] See generally Edward E. Jones, Interpersonal Perception 138–66 (1990); Edward E. Jones, *The Rocky Road from Acts to Dispositions,* 34 Am. Psychologist 107 (1979).

people (who in reality were confederates of the experimenter) say that the shorter line was longer. Asch's results have been duplicated in numerous settings, both in and out of the laboratory, and the startling conclusion that bare-bones sense perception can be influenced by the company we keep is robustly supported by the evidence.[12]

Lon Fuller noticed the phenomenon in the work lives of lawyers. He puts the observation in the form of a hypothetical story about a young lawyer, five or six years out of law school,

> working in an office with at least, let us say, six other lawyers – perhaps with as many as a hundred or more ... When he was in law school he used to worry that he might be called upon by his office to advocate causes in which he did not personally believe. He finds that this is not a real problem ... In those instances where he had some doubts about the client's case at the beginning, these doubts evaporate after he has worked on the case for a few days; his client's cause then comes to seem at once logical and just. He worries a little that he might have experienced the same conversion had he been working on the other side, but this slight concern does not detract from his zeal or his desire to advance his client's interests.[13]

In Fuller's shrewdly perceptive fable, we see dissonance reduction in the direction of advocacy and the socially induced perception of the justness of the client's cause as two sides of a single phenomenon.

Diffusion of responsibility and social cognition

The socially influenced character of perception also helps to explain so-called "diffusion of responsibility," the well-known fact that groups of people are often less likely to respond helpfully in emergency situations than are individuals. (The relevance of diffusion of responsibility to the behavior of organizational lawyers who do nothing about client wrongdoing should be clear.[14]) When a college student has an apparent epileptic seizure in the company of five bystanders, he receives help only a third of the time. Does this show heartless indifference? Not necessarily: when the student has a seizure in front of a single bystander, he receives help 85 percent of the time.[15] In a classic set of experiments by Darley and Latané, subjects either

---

[12] See, e.g., Solomon E. Asch, *Effects of Group Pressures Upon the Modification and Distortion of Judgments*, in Groups, Leadership, and Men 177 (Harold Guetzkow ed., 1951). See Ross & Nisbett, supra note 4, at 30–35.

[13] Lon L. Fuller, *Philosophy for the Practicing Lawyer*, in Principles of Social Order 287–88 (Kenneth I. Winston ed., 1981).

[14] See Langevoort, *Where Were the Lawyers?*, supra note 3.

[15] John M. Darley & Bibb Latané, *Bystander Intervention in Emergencies: Diffusion of Responsbility*, 8 J. Personality & Soc. Psych. 377 (1968).

heard a crash of glass and a woman screaming from the next room, or witnessed smoke coming through the vent into their own room. When the subjects were alone, most responded to the apparent emergency; but when another person sat next to them and failed to respond, most subjects mimicked the other person and did not respond themselves.[16] Evidently, we respond to situations by checking to see how other people respond, and their response in large measure determines how we perceive the situation and therefore how we ourselves will respond. And of course the phenomenon is reciprocal: as we watch the other, the other watches us. We reinforce each other, in wrong beliefs as well as accurate ones (a phenomenon psychologists call *pluralistic ignorance*). The shaping and reciprocal reinforcement of perception by seeing how others perceive the same thing constitutes the basic phenomenon of socially influenced cognition, or, for short, *social cognition.* Pedestrians stepping around the body of a homeless man collapsed in the street may simply be taking their cues from one another; the evidence suggests that they would stop to help if they were alone. Our moral compass may point north when we are by ourselves, but place us next to a few dozen other compasses pointing east, and our needle will fall into alignment with theirs – and, in doing so, influence the needles of others' compasses.

It may appear that social cognition theory and cognitive dissonance theory represent two distinct ideas: one, that we conform our beliefs to the perceived beliefs of the people around us, and the other, that we conform our beliefs to our own prior actions. In fact, however, some psychological theorists regard them as two aspects of the same theory. Here, the significant idea came from a 1967 paper by Daryl Bem.[17] Recall that dissonance theory and behaviorism originally seemed to be rival theories. Bem provided a behaviorist reinterpretation of dissonance. The Achilles' heel of classical dissonance theory consisted of its need to postulate a felt inner tension – the irritating psychological experience of dissonance – that we need to resolve. The problem was that subjects did not report an inner experience of tension, and the theory therefore had to stipulate that the felt tension was unconscious. The unconscious experience of tension thus turned out to be a postulate founded not on observed data but on the needs of the theory, always an embarrassment in a supposedly experimental science.[18]

---

[16] See generally Bibb Latané & John M. Darley, The Unresponsive Bystander: Why Doesn't He Help? (1970); for a literature review, see Bibb Latané & Steve Nida, *Ten Years of Research on Group Size and Helping*, 89 Psych. Bull. 308 (1981).

[17] Daryl J. Bem, *Self-Perception: An Alternative Interpretation of Cognitive Dissonance Phenomena*, 74 Psych. Rev. 183 (1967).

[18] But cf. Aronson, supra note 5, at 235–37 (arguing that dissonance does cause actual psychological arousal). However, the experiments Aronson cites infer the existence of psychological arousal rather than measuring it directly. I suspect that this issue can only be settled by experiments in which subjects are tested for physiological indicators of arousal.

Bem suggested a simpler mechanism than unconscious experiences (unexperienced experiences) to explain the alteration of belief after counterattitudinal action. According to Bem, we have no direct introspective access to our own beliefs. Man, remember, is a great riddle to himself. Instead, we infer our own beliefs in exactly the same way we infer other people's beliefs: by observing our behavior and its context, and reasoning from outward manifestation to inner belief.

In effect, Bem invites us to regard our own self as a sequence of different selves, each one a time-slice of the four-dimensional space-time worm called "me." Inferring my own beliefs from the observed behavior of the society of my own past selves seems, on this interpretation, no different from inferring my own beliefs about the length of a line-segment or the urgency of a scream in the next room from the observed behavior of those around me. Dissonance reduction turns out to be a special case of social cognition.

Recursively reinforcing commitment and the road to perdition

One consequence of dissonance theory is that once I act, my beliefs will rationalize the action and therefore impel me to further action of the same sort – which, in turn, calls for renewed rationalization, and further action. Action, we might say, breeds *commitment,* and commitment breeds further action in an ever steeper slippery slope. The pattern

action $\rightarrow$ rationalization $\rightarrow$ commitment $\rightarrow$ further action

has a recursive character. Psychologists call this the foot-in-the-door effect. In 1966, Freedman and Fraser dramatically demonstrated that persuading someone to place a one-inch-square pro-driving-safety sticker in their window quadruples their willingness to consent two weeks later to having a ferociously ugly, large pro-driving-safety sign in their yard.[19]

To moralists, the step-by-step road to perdition forms a familiar trope. "Let me tell you how you will start acting unethically," Patrick Schiltz writes in a well-known article on life in large law firms. It starts with the time sheets, Schiltz tells us – with the moment when you first pad a time sheet just a little bit, intending to pay back the "loan" from the client with a little unbilled time next month. Soon the loans become more frequent, and after a while you lose the desire to pay them back. Then come the lies – first, the white lie about why you missed a deadline, then the darker lie that you carefully proofread the prospectus that you didn't, then the misleading answer to a deposition that you prep your client to give, then the smoking-gun document that you don't turn

---

[19] Jonathan L. Freedman & Scott C. Fraser, *Compliance Without Pressure: The Foot-in-the-Door Technique,* 4 J. Personality & Soc. Psych. 195 (1966).

over in discovery. In every case, you will have a rationalization. Speaking, he tells us, from personal experience, Schiltz ruefully observes that "after a couple years of this, you won't even notice that you are lying and cheating and stealing every day that you practice law."[20]

C. S. Lewis concurs. According to Lewis, "To nine out of ten of you the choice which could lead to scoundrelism will come, when it does come, in no very dramatic colours. Obviously bad men, obviously threatening or bribing, will almost certainly not appear."[21] According to Lewis, the fatal first step on the road to perdition comes simply because you want oh so much to belong to the Inner Ring, or the inner circle or in-crowd. A member of the in-crowd offers you a hint of friendship and a glimpse of life on the inside, and tempts you to do something that "we always do" – "and at the word 'we' you try not to blush for mere pleasure"[22] – that isn't quite kosher. Once you have been tempted, "next week it will be something a little further from the rules, and next year something further still, but all in the jolliest, friendliest spirit. It may end in a crash, a scandal, and penal servitude: it may end in millions, a peerage and giving the prizes at your old school. But you will be a scoundrel."[23]

The trope, I have said, is familiar – but what strikes me as less familiar is that this pattern, the very picture of lost integrity, exemplifies to social psychologists something close to the opposite – the self's incessant *pursuit* of integrity, of harmony between belief and action. That first small departure from the straight and narrow is like the one-inch-square sticker in Freedman and Fraser's experiments.[24] Agreeing to place it in our window leads us to reformulate our self-concept in a way that rationalizes the action, and the new self-concept impels us toward further action of the same sort as its own vindication. What Lewis implies, and Schiltz says outright, is that all the while that you're giving the Devil his due, a little bit more each day, you're also persuading yourself that the Devil is a misunderstood fellow whose hidden virtues are only now becoming transparent to you.

Perhaps the most famous example of the slippery slope to fatal commitment is the Milgram experiments, in which subjects are ordered to administer escalating electrical shocks to another subject in an experiment on the effects of pain on learning. The victim, of course, is a confederate of the experimenter, and the shocks are fake; the real goal of the experiment is to study subjects' responses to destructive orders. Milgram's astonishing discovery, replicated many times in several countries, is that almost two-thirds of the

---

[20] Patrick J. Schiltz, *On Being a Happy, Healthy, and Ethical Member of an Unhappy, Unhealthy, and Unethical Profession*, 52 Vand. L. Rev. 871, 917–18 (1999).

[21] C. S. Lewis, *The Inner Ring*, in They Asked for a Paper: Papers and Addresses 139, 146 (London, Geoffrey Bles 1962).

[22] Ibid. at 146–47.   [23] Ibid. at 147.   [24] Freedman & Fraser, supra note 19.

subjects prove willing to go all the way to the end of the sequence of shocks, despite the fact that the victim spends much of the time screaming for the experiment to stop, and eventually falls ominously silent, while the label on the shock-generator reads "Danger: Severe Shock."[25] The literature on these famous and alarming experiments is large, and many explanations have been offered for the depressingly high rate of compliance. The explanation I defended in the preceding chapter focuses on the gradually escalating character of the shocks. The shock-generator has thirty switches, beginning at 15 volts and going up in 15-volt increments to 450. The result is that Milgram's subjects never confronted the pure question, "Should I administer this 330-volt shock?" Instead, the question was, "Should I administer this 330-volt shock given that a minute ago I administered a 315-volt shock – and I did that after administering twenty previous shocks?" To think, "That would be wrong!" virtually requires a subject to conclude that the previous shock, only insignificantly less severe, was also wrong – and cognitive dissonance makes that a very difficult conclusion to accept. It's not that Milgram's subjects became committed sadists. Rather, each shock they administered committed them to the belief that the next shock is neither sadistic nor even wrong (because the prior shocks were not sadistic or wrong). The dissonance-induced commitment leads the subjects unconsciously to gerrymander the boundary between right and wrong. Commitment breeds commitment, and leads to overshooting the bounds of reasonableness as outside observers perceive those bounds, but as the subject clearly does not. The subject is keeping faith with his own commitments, and the shock-victim must suffer at the hands of the subject's pursuit of integrity.

Advocacy to excess

These reflections on the self-reinforcing character of commitment may help us explain puzzling cases in which lawyers whom one would have expected to dislike a particular cause or client, and to do the bare minimum that competent advocacy requires, instead go the extra mile on behalf of a cause they presumably detest. A celebrated example is Francis Bacon, who at one point in his career found himself prosecuting his own friend and patron, the Earl of Essex. As Macaulay reports, Bacon

did not confine himself to what would have been amply sufficient to procure a verdict. He employed all his wit, his rhetoric, and his learning, not to ensure a conviction, – for the circumstances were such that a conviction was inevitable, – but to deprive the

---

[25] See generally Stanley Milgram, Obedience to Authority: An Experimental View (1974); Arthur A. Miller, The Obedience Experiments: A Case Study of Controversy in Social Science (1986).

unhappy prisoner of all those excuses which, though legally of no value, yet tended to diminish the moral guilt of the crime, and which, therefore, though they could not justify the peers in pronouncing an acquittal, might incline the Queen to grant a pardon.[26]

Then, after the execution of Essex, Bacon published a pamphlet to traduce his memory.[27] It was this miserable last straw that led Macaulay to his often quoted rhetorical question about lawyers, "whether it be right that a man should, with a wig on his head, and a band round his neck, do for a guinea what, without those appendages, he would think it wicked and infamous to do for an empire."[28] But those who quote this celebrated epigram sometimes forget that Macaulay did *not* criticize Bacon for following the role-morality of lawyers – the separation of the personal and the professional. Macaulay had no wish to question the prevailing professional rules. "If ... Bacon did no more than these rules required of him, we shall readily admit that he was blameless, or, at least, excusable."[29] The problem was that Bacon went so much further than the rules required, as Macaulay goes to great and entertaining rhetorical lengths to emphasize. Bacon did everything in his power to ensure that no mercy would or could be shown to Essex. Why? Macaulay thinks he knows the reason. "The real explanation of all this is perfectly obvious ... The moral qualities of Bacon were not of a high order."[30] According to Macaulay's diagnosis, Bacon's "desires were set on things below."[31] Bacon was simply too enamored of "wealth, precedence, titles, patronage, the mace, the seals, the coronet, large houses, fair gardens, rich manors, massy services of plate, gay hangings, curious cabinets."[32]

Perhaps so; Bacon would hardly be the first or last lawyer to succumb to such temptations. But before accepting this diagnosis, let us consider a more contemporary example. In 1993, a black lawyer named Anthony Griffin made headlines by representing the grand dragon of the Texas Knights of the Ku Klux Klan as an American Civil Liberties Union (ACLU) volunteer. The KKK had engaged in a campaign to terrorize black residents who wished to move into an all-white housing project, and the State of Texas attempted to obtain the Klan's membership lists in an effort to prosecute them. The ACLU agreed to represent the Klan's grand dragon, and steered him to Griffin – who, as it happens, not only worked with the ACLU, but was also General Counsel for the Port Arthur Branch of the National Association for the

---

[26] Thomas Babington Macaulay, *Francis Bacon*, in 2 Critical and Historical Essays 290, 314 (1926).

[27] "The faithless friend who had assisted in taking the Earl's life was now employed to murder the Earl's fame." Ibid. at 315.

[28] Ibid. at 317.   [29] Ibid.   [30] Ibid. at 319–20.   [31] Ibid. at 320.   [32] Ibid.

Advancement of colored people (NAACP), which soon fired Griffin because he was representing the Klan.[33]

No great mystery exists about why the ACLU – or even a black ACLU lawyer – might wish to defend the Klan's right to keep its membership lists secret. During the civil rights movement, the state of Alabama harassed the NAACP by demanding membership lists, and the Supreme Court's decision in *NAACP v. Alabama* that the lists need not be given to the state stands as a landmark First Amendment protection of political association.[34] The puzzle is that Griffin went much further than defending *NAACP v. Alabama* by representing the Klan. Apparently, Griffin couldn't stop. He went on to represent the Klan in its attempt to "adopt a highway" next to the housing project, a transparent effort to evade a restraining order to keep away from the project.[35] The integrity of the First Amendment hardly required this further representation, any more than Bacon's persecution and assassination of the Earl of Essex had anything to do with the requirements of the prosecutor's role. Yet no one would suggest that Griffin had fallen under the sway of curious cabinets or massy services of plate.

David Wilkins, who has analyzed the ethics of Griffin's representation of the Klan in great detail, gets closer to the truth than Macaulay in explaining the puzzle of counterattitudinal advocacy that goes above and beyond the call of duty in its zeal:

It is virtually impossible for someone in an adversarial role to keep their clients, and more importantly their client's view of the world, at arms [*sic*] length. It is a familiar truth in social science that those who are called upon to support positions that they initially find morally abhorrent will search for ways to reduce the distance between their beliefs and their practices.[36]

In short, cognitive dissonance strikes again. If Wilkins is right, Griffin – and, I am speculating, Bacon – went the extra mile in their advocacy to keep faith with their initial decision to undertake the advocacy in the first place. Apparently, their integrity called for nothing less.

Group polarization in adversary systems

I have suggested, in the spirit of Bem's version of dissonance theory, a structural similarity between social cognition (the way our beliefs adapt to the beliefs of others) and individual belief modification (the way our beliefs

---

[33] David B. Wilkins, *Race, Ethics, and the First Amendment: Should a Black Lawyer Represent the Ku Klux Klan?*, 63 Geo. Wash. L. Rev. 1030, 1030 (1995).
[34] NAACP v. Alabama, 357 US 449 (1958). [35] Wilkins, supra note 33, at 1051–53.
[36] Ibid. at 1055–56.

adapt to our own prior actions). The similarity runs in both directions. Not only do we become committed to our own courses of action – out of solidarity, one might say, with the company of our prior selves – but we become equally committed to other members of our own "team" in social competitions. Here, too, the relevance of the research to lawyer behavior should be obvious: the adversary system sets up a social competition in litigation, and the free-enterprise system sets up a social competition in transactional practice. Henri Tajfel told subjects that a test of their aesthetic tastes showed that they prefer Klee to Kandinsky – and that bit of misinformation proved sufficient for them to discriminate in favor of others who supposedly prefer Klee, and against those who supposedly prefer Kandinsky.[37] Similarly, thirty-two young boys were told, after an experiment in visual perception, that they belonged to a group that systematically overestimates (or underestimates) the number of dots flashed on a screen. They were then given the task of dividing money among the group. They systematically discriminated in favor of those supposedly in the same perceptual group and against those in the other group – the phenomenon of in-group favoritism resulting from *group polarization,* intimately familiar to participants in adversarial proceedings.[38] Remember that advocacy makes others think that we believe what we are advocating, even when they ought to know better – and, through a combination of commitment and taking cues from those others, we are likely to believe it ourselves. Group polarization and belief-change in the direction of one's group reinforce each other.

Blaming the victim

In a 1973 experiment, subjects were assigned tasks in pairs, in which a "worker" would carry out the task for pay while the "supervisor" would give instructions. They then watched an event in which a supervisor bungled the task, ruining a highly successful effort by the worker. Knowing the results of the other group polarization experiments, it should not surprise us that those who expected to be workers themselves blamed the supervisor, while those who expected to be supervisors blamed the equipment or circumstances, but did *not* blame the supervisor. More surprisingly, however, when it became clear that the mishap would cost the worker the money he had earned, the other "supervisors" went one step further, and severely disparaged the personal qualities of the worker.[39]

[37] See Henri Tajfel et al., Social Categorization and Intergroup Behaviour, 1 Eur. J. Soc. Psych. 149 (1971); see also Social Identity and Intergroup Relations (Henri Tajfel ed., 1982).
[38] Harvey A. Hornstein, Out of the Wilderness?, 29 Contemp. Psych. 11, 11 (1984).
[39] Alan L. Chaikin & John M. Darley, Victim or Perpetrator?: Defensive Attribution of Responsibility and the Need for Order and Justice, 25 J. Personality & Soc. Psych. 268 (1973).

This last phenomenon – blaming the victim – occurs even in settings where us-and-them polarization is not the issue. In an ingenious series of experiments, Melvin Lerner confirmed repeatedly that the worse someone is treated, the more likely observers are to regard the victim as an unattractive, flawed person.[40] Lerner explains this phenomenon as an unconscious attempt to ward off the scary thought that if unfair treatment can happen to the victim, it can happen to me. We disparage the victim in order to find a distinction, some distinction, between her and us in order to reassure ourselves that we won't be victimized next.[41]

Lerner's explanation of blaming the victim has the ring of truth, but I think that it may work in tandem with another phenomenon, more akin to the dissonance-based effects discussed above. Strikingly, out of over 1,000 subjects in Lerner's experiments, not a single one tried to help the victim or walked out of the experiment in protest.[42] Why not? One explanation, in the spirit of Darley and Latane's diffusion-of-responsibility research, is that the subjects witnessed the scene of victimization in groups – and groups don't act as readily as individuals do.[43] Whether or not that explanation is right, the fact that no subject protested the injustice done to the victim suggests, according to dissonance theory, that these subjects will justify their own inaction to themselves by minimizing the injustice – and the simplest way to minimize the injustice is to denigrate the victim. This, too, is familiar common sense about lawyers: even if lawyers dislike the side they are representing, they often wind up disliking the other side even more, and they relieve their own discomfort at what representing their client requires them to do by the consoling thought that at least the party they are harming is a bad person who has it coming.

The scripted self: playing roles

Another important feature of the worker–supervisor experiment is that the subjects conformed their own pro and con attitudes to the role they themselves anticipated playing. When placed in the role of worker before witnessing a scene in which a supervisor's mistake costs the worker his pay, one faults the supervisor. When placed in the role of supervisor, one blames the equipment or circumstances and denigrates the worker. Along with the other

---

[40] Melvin J. Lerner, The Belief in a Just World: A Fundamental Delusion 89–103 (1980).

[41] Ibid. at 21.   [42] Ibid. at 51–52.

[43] The diffusion-of-responsibility phenomenon should not be confused with the well-known economic result, based in the free-rider problem, that groups typically underprovide collective goods. What Darley and Latané discovered was not the logic of collective action, but the illogic of collective action – that is, they discovered not the rational decision to free-ride on others, leading to mutual inactivity, but an irrational overreliance on our perception of what others think, leading to mutual inactivity because nobody wants to make the first move.

dissonance-based phenomena discussed above – belief modification, social cognition, diffusion of responsibility, commitment escalation, the foot-in-the door effect, group polarization, and blaming the victim – conformity to social role plays a prominent part in our psychic make-up.

Undoubtedly the most famous of all experiments in the power of roles to shape cognitions is the Stanford Prison Experiment ("SPE"), conducted by Philip Zimbardo, Craig Haney, and their associates. Volunteer undergraduate subjects were divided randomly into "guards" and "inmates" in a mock prison. In less than a day, guards began bullying and brutalizing the inmates, while the inmates began to exhibit the pathologies of real-life prisoners, so much so that five had to be released very soon because of "extreme emotional depression, crying, rage and acute anxiety."[44] By the second day, the prisoners revolted and the guards put down the rebellion by blasting them with fire extinguishers.[45]

The transformation of the subjects almost defies belief. One guard wrote in his diary before the experiment, "As I am a pacifist and nonaggressive individual, I cannot see a time when I might maltreat other living things."[46] By day five of the experiment, this same student wrote the following in his diary:

This new prisoner, 416, refuses to eat. That is a violation of Rule Two: "Prisoners must eat at mealtimes," and we are not going to have any of that kind of shit . . . Obviously we have a troublemaker on our hands. If that's the way he wants it, that's the way he gets it. We throw him into the Hole ordering him to hold greasy sausages in each hand. After an hour, he still refuses . . . I decide to force feed him, but he won't eat. I let the food slide down his face. I don't believe it is me doing it. I just hate him more for not eating.[47]

Part way through the experiment, some of the inmates' parents came to visit them, and were horrified by the degraded state their sons had been reduced to. But after a little tough talk from Warden Zimbardo, the parents simply backed down.[48] Later, the inmates were visited by a prison priest and

[44] Craig Haney et al., Interpersonal Dynamics of a Simulated Prison, 1 Int'l. J. Criminology & Penology 69, 81 (1973).
[45] Philip Zimbardo et al., The Mind Is a Formidable Jailer: A Pirandellian Prison, N.Y. Times, April 8, 1973, §6 (Magazine), at 41.
[46] Craig Haney & Philip Zimbardo, The Socialization into Criminality: On Becoming a Prisoner and a Guard, in Law, Justice, and the Individual in Society: Psychological and Legal Issues 198, 207 (June L. Tapp & Felice J. Levine eds., 1977).
[47] Ibid. at 209.
[48] Philip G. Zimbardo, Stanford Prison Experiment: A Simulation Study of the Psychology of Imprisonment Conducted at Stanford University (1999), at <www.prisonexp.org/slide-24. htm>. "Some of the parents got upset when they saw how fatigued and distressed their sons were. But their reaction was to work within the system to appeal privately to the superintendent

a lawyer. Like the parents, neither of these professionals had been instructed to act in a role, or had agreed to do so – but both of them did. For example, it simply never occurred to the lawyer (or parents, or priests) to tell the students that they were not inmates, but rather volunteers in an experiment that they could leave at any time. Astoundingly, the prison script seemed to induce everyone to act in role.

Taking stock of situationism

The Stanford Prison Experiment seems to portray a world in which the very idea of personal integrity seems absent – a Goffmanesque world where there are no selves, only selves-in-roles, selves who slide frictionlessly from role to role, in each case conforming to the expectations of the role and whatever principles of right behavior come attached to its script. Behind the mask, another mask; behind all the masks, a vacuum; beneath the vacuum, a mask once again. Indeed, some theorists have drawn conclusions very close to the claim that when it comes to character, there's no there there. John Doris, in his recent book *Lack of Character,* concludes from a careful examination of the experimental literature that human character, defined as a fixed set of dispositions toward certain behavior, is largely a myth.[49] Gilbert Harman, drawing on the same experimental literature, agrees.[50] Both draw on an interpretation of the experiments I have been reviewing called *situationism,* defended most cogently by Lee Ross and Richard Nisbett. At this point, I want to detour briefly to discuss the merits of situationism, in order to distinguish the argument I am offering from a version of situationism that I think is wrong.

The thesis of situationism is, quite simply, that differences in situations account for much more of the observed variation in human behavior than do differences in personality. Our tendency to believe otherwise, that is, to ascribe people's behavior to their personality or character – or, for that matter, their voluntary choices – rather than the situation they are in, is what situationists criticize as the "fundamental attribution error."[51] Situationists

---

to make conditions better for their boys. When one mother told me she had never seen her son looking *so* bad, I responded by shifting the blame from the situation to her son. 'What's the matter with your boy? Doesn't he sleep well?' Then I asked the father, 'Don't you think your boy can handle this?' He bristled, 'Of course he can – he's a real tough kid, a leader.' Turning to the mother, he said, 'Come on, Honey, we've wasted enough time already.' And to me, 'See *you* again at the next visiting time.'" Ibid.

[49] See generally John M. Doris, Lack of Character: Personality and Moral Behavior (2002).

[50] Gilbert Harman, *Moral Philosophy Meets Social Psychology: Virtue Ethics and the Fundamental Attribution Error,* 99 Proc. Aristotelian Soc'y 315 (1999).

[51] Ross & Nisbett, supra note 4, at 29–89.

point, for example, to some of Milgram's findings.[52] In one variant of his shock experiment, Milgram placed the subject on a team with another subject – actually, of course, a confederate of Milgram. When the confederate uncomplainingly obeyed orders to continue the shocks, 90 percent of the subjects went along, but when the confederate refused to administer high-level shocks and walked away from the experiment, compliance by subjects plummeted to 10 percent. Clearly, it would be implausible to assume that the subject population in one variant differs radically in propensity to comply from the subject population in the other. Instead, the conclusion must be that situational differences generate this dramatic swing from near-universal compliance to near-universal rebellion. Similarly, Doris points to experiments by Isen and Levin that showed that people who find a dime in the coin return of a pay telephone were vastly more likely to help a stranger pick up papers she has dropped than people who find no dime.[53] Again, the power of the situation appears to dominate or even dwarf the power of personality and character in determining behavior. The lesson of situationism, drawn by Harman and Doris, seems to be that we have *no* character that disposes us to behave consistently across situations.[54] The disconcerting picture seems to be a near-determinism of situations, in which minuscule differences in the situation – a dime or no dime, the presence or absence of other people in the room – turn into major differences in behavior, and individual idiosyncracy

---

[52] Doris, supra note 49, at 46; Milgram, supra note 25, at 116–22.

[53] Doris, supra note 49, at 30–31 (discussing A. M. Isen & P. F. Levin, *Effect of Feeling Good on Helping: Cookies and Kindness*, 21 J. Personality & Soc. Psychol. 384 [1972]). Fourteen of sixteen subjects who found the dime helped pick up the stranger's fallen papers, while only one out of twenty-five subjects who found no dime stopped to help. Ibid. at 387.

[54] Doris puts the idea nicely in a chapter entitled "The Fragmentation of Character": "It's not crazy to think that someone could be courageous in physical but not moral extremity, or be moderate with food but not sex, or be honest with spouses but not with taxes. If we take such thoughts seriously, we'll qualify our attributions: 'physical courage' or 'moral courage,' instead of 'courage,' and so on. Would things were so simple. With a bit of effort, we can imagine someone showing physical courage on the battlefield, but cowering in the face of storms, heights, or wild animals. Here we go again: 'battlefield physical courage,' 'storms physical courage,' 'heights physical courage,' and 'wild animals physical courage.' Things can get still trickier: Someone might exhibit battlefield courage in the face of rifle fire but not in the face of artillery fire. If we didn't grow sick of it, we could play this little game all day." Doris, supra note 49, at 62 (internal citation omitted). Doris's point is that the quest to explain experiments by reference to personality traits should simply be abandoned.

The salience to legal ethics of this critique of character should be clear, but nowhere clearer than in the bar admissions process, with its requirement of screening applicants on the basis of character. In the leading article on the subject, Deborah Rhode points to the lack of empirical support for belief in character traits that are consistent across situations, and the lack of predictive power of behavior in one situation for behavior in another. She argues, in a fashion similar to Doris, that the experimental findings undermine the entire enterprise of character assessment, which she believes that the bar should abandon. Deborah L. Rhode, *Moral Character as a Professional Credential,* 94 Yale L. J. 491, 555–62 (1985).

explains very little of the differences. (It is a near-determinism, not a strict determinism, because individual idiosyncrasy still plays some explanatory role.[55])

I believe that caution is in order about what conclusions to draw from these observations, however. There's no denying the situationists' point that minute changes in situation can dramatically affect the proportion of people exhibiting a given behavior. But the situationists have a hard time explaining why different people behave differently in the *same* situation. In Milgram's basic experiment, two-thirds of the subjects complied, but one-third did not. The point is more general. Throughout the experimental literature of social psychology we find striking and statistically significant correlations between experimental variables and subjects' responses – but, significant as they may be, the correlation coefficients seldom exceed 0.5, which by the standards of physics is a low correlation, signifying that the manipulated variable accounts for only one-fourth of the variance in behavior. People differ, and the question for situationism is how these differences should be explained.

The answer, Ross and Nisbett tell us, lies in the fact that people construe situations differently, that "it is the situation as construed by the subject that is the true stimulus."[56] Thus, the differences in response arise not from differences in human character but rather from differences in perception and construal.

Perhaps. Yet I find this explanation, according to which the one-third noncompliance rate in the Milgram experiment is explained by arguing that the noncompliant third perceived the situation differently from the two-thirds of compliers, to be both too convenient and too *ad hoc*, given that we don't actually know anything about how Milgram's subjects construed the situation. In Ross and Nisbett's view, what I have called a near-determinism of situations becomes more like a true determinism. Ross and Nisbett localize

---

[55] One must be careful about this question, however. Psychologists sometimes write as though what I am calling "individual idiosyncrasy" is itself a set of deterministic factors – personality traits, perhaps biological in origin, that cause whatever component of behavior the situations do not cause. See, e.g., Lerner, supra note 40, at 120 ("As any reasonable psychologist will tell you, all behavior is 'caused' by a combination of antecedent events and the genetic endowment of the individual"). We leave the framework of determinism only when we insist that "individual idiosyncrasy" includes a component of individual choice. Thinking in this way of course lands one squarely in the midst of the problem of free will; but when were we ever out of that problem? Here I agree with John Doris, who argues that situationism pretty much leaves the problem of free will, with its unsettled and unsettling debates between hard and soft determinism, compatibilism and incompatibilism, untouched. Doris, supra note 49, at 132–33. But cf. ibid. at 133–46 (Doris's ensuing arguments about ways in which situationism complicates some approaches to the free-will problem). In the preceding chapter, I tried to lay out the assumptions necessary for a compatibilist analysis of the Milgram experiments.

[56] Ross & Nisbett, supra note 4, at 11; see generally ibid. at ch. 3.

individual idiosyncracy in the capacity for perception and construal, while accepting a version of stimulus–response determinism according to which the stimulus (the situation-as-construed) leads subjects to uniform responses. But why? Why parse the individual this way, into a perception/construal capacity that exhibits idiosyncrasy and a responsive capacity that exhibits little or none? To do so seems arbitrary, and borders on downright inconsistency. After all, construing a situation is itself a kind of action, and one would suppose that a consistent situationist should posit that situations account for most of the variation in construals as well as in responses. In that case, however, the situationist is left with *no* explanation for variation among individuals placed in the same situation. Moreover, even if the situationist is right about individual variability in construing situations, one can reply that personality lies in large part in our habits of perception and construal, so at least some form of personality theory survives the situationist objection.

I prefer to think of situations – the independent variables that experimenters manipulate – as sources of pressure or of temptation. Quite simply, the experiments demonstrate how difficult – but not impossible – swimming against the situational tide is. It's so difficult that in the basic Milgram experiment only a third of the subjects are able to bring it off. Adding a compliant team-mate makes it more difficult still, so that only one subject out of ten was able to resist; while adding a noncompliant team-mate makes resistance easy enough that nine out of ten subjects were able to succeed at resisting the orders to continue administering shocks. In the terms of our initial metaphor, situational changes alter the relative gradient of both the high road and the low road. What the experiments do show, quite graphically, is that seemingly minor manipulations of the environment can cause astonishingly large changes in the ease or difficulty of action, the angle of incidence between the two roads.

Putting the situationists' point in these terms – that is, that situations transform the ease or difficulty of certain courses of action – avoids the implication of determinism. The situation sets conditions under which we choose, but the numbers strongly imply that these conditions do not render choice impossible. Notice that if every subject complied with Milgram's experiment, it would provide evidence that the experiment had uncovered a mechanism akin to a physical reflex, over which we have no choice or control. And if only a few subjects out of the thousand complied, we might regard them as pathological cases, and excuse them from blame on the grounds that they have a screw loose somewhere. The actual two-thirds/one-third split precludes us from drawing either of these deterministic conclusions about the compliers.

Because I resist situational determinism, I resist as well the radical suggestion that our deep-seated propensity to fall into predetermined roles (as in the SPE) means that we have no core self whose integrity matters, only a collection of selves-in-roles, each seeking its own harmony between behavior and principle, but without any larger unity of self. The experiments do show that we lack robust consistency across situations. This should not surprise us, however. After all, if some of my roles impose inconsistent moral demands – if, for example, with a wig on my head and a band round my neck I will be asked to do for a guinea what I would otherwise think it wicked and infamous to do for an empire – and my daily life leads me to occupy all these roles, and if, further, the actions I take in each role lead me to adopt beliefs that vindicate those actions, then dissonance theory predicts that I will preserve my conception of myself as a morally upright individual in the only way left: by abandoning the belief that my other beliefs should be consistent.[57] We purchase integrity, what Gerald Postema calls the "unity of practical consciousness," at the price of logic, the unity of theoretical consciousness.[58] The experimental demonstration that we lack robust consistency across situations shows that integrity consists of a complex unity, stitched together with a great deal of self-deception that allows us to deny inconsistencies and the dissonance they induce. Integrity remains something that we seek. The problem, then, remains the one we began with: that the quest for integrity, manifested in all the psychological phenomena we have been reviewing, can drive us to behavior as disconcerting and morally repellent as that shown in the Stanford Prison Experiment or in Milgram's demonstration.

The difference between integrity and dissonance reduction

I do not suppose that I am reporting anything novel or recondite. All of these experiments are widely known, and the Milgram and Stanford experiments are famous, almost legendary. My argument, which is perhaps less familiar, is that these are not simply an array of discrete, unrelated psychological curiosities. Rather, they are aspects of cognitive dissonance, in its social and individual guises. They emerge, therefore, from our drive toward inner harmony – our drive toward integrity. The quest for integrity kills, and in killing it leaves the survivors with their own sense of rectitude intact, like a tattered flag flapping in the wind over the fallen.

To all this there is a simple reply: *You are not talking about genuine integrity.* Integrity does not consist of molding and adapting one's principles to whatever behaviors we and those around us find convenient. Integrity consists of taking the high road, the road of conforming our behavior to our principles. I mentioned earlier that the word 'integrity', like 'integer',

---

[57] The philosopher Sidney Morgenbesser, asked if he believes in the law of noncontradiction, replied, "Yes and no."

[58] Gerald J. Postema, *Self-Image, Integrity, and Professional Responsibility*, in The Good Lawyer: Lawyers' Roles and Lawyers' Ethics 286, 296 (David Luban ed., 1983).

'integral', and 'integrate', comes from the Latin *integrare*, to make whole. That word, in turn, derives from *in-*, "not", plus *tangere*, "touch." An entity is whole if it is untouched, unsullied; the Latin *integer vitae* meant innocent, pure, blameless in life. And thus the person of integrity is not merely the person whose principles and behavior harmonize, regardless of how that harmony gets achieved, but rather the person who has kept her principles intact ("intact" is another word whose Latin root means "untouched"). We think of the person of integrity in the terms C. S. Lewis uses in *Perelandra* to describe Ransom, his protagonist: "even if the whole universe were crazy and hostile, Ransom was sane and wholesome and honest."[59] His moral compass never turns from north, no matter how many other compasses point elsewhere.

Of course, as an analysis of the concept of integrity this must be right. When we are done in by situational forces that distort our moral judgment, we are hardly "untouched." Just the opposite: we are all too touched. The low road to integrity is simply not the same as the high road, and bending your principles to rationalize your actions is not the same as bringing your actions into conformity with your principles.

The problem, however, lies in telling them apart *from the inside.* As I noted above, merely asserting categorical principles and refusing to deviate from them regardless of the situation we find ourselves in may be Ransom-like integrity, but it may also be an inability to learn from experience, a kind of fatal priggishness and narrow-minded inflexibility. Every normal life contains episodes of learning from experience, during which principles are reinterpreted, contexts are distinguished, and precommitments modified, along with episodes of sticking to your guns, drawing lines in the sand that you will not cross, and keeping faith with your ideals. This implies that a life of integrity – the high-road, genuine kind of integrity, not the low-road, ersatz kind – will normally contain episodes in which preexisting moral judgments get discarded in the face of experience. Ransom may always have been sane and wholesome and honest, but his judgment of what particular behaviors are sane, wholesome, and honest may well have changed between the ages of fifteen and fifty. One supposes and hopes that they did. His fifteen-year-old self might view some of the fifty-year-old's beliefs as sold-out ideals, where the fifty-year-old Ransom sees a story of growing wiser (and maybe sadder). From the agent's point of view – from the inside – how do you tell which is which?

One plausible answer is that genuine integrity consists not simply of adherence to principles, but adherence to the right principles, or at any rate to reasonable principles. As Deborah Rhode puts it:

[59] C. S. Lewis, Perelandra 6 (Collier, 1944).

At a minimum, persons of integrity are individuals whose practices are consistent with their principles, even in the face of strong countervailing pressures. Yet the term also implies something more than steadfastness. Fanatics may be loyal to their values, but we do not praise them for integrity. What earns our praise is a willingness to adhere to values that reflect some reasoned deliberation, based on logical assessment of relevant evidence and competing views. Some theorists would add a requirement that the values themselves must satisfy certain minimum demands of consistency, generalizability, and respect for others.[60]

That may be true in a formal sense, but from the agent's point of view the formula won't help. For one thing, many of the psychological forces discussed here leave our principles untouched, instead affecting our judgment of whether or not a case falls under a principle. It seems likely, for example, that Milgram's compliant subjects believed before, during, and after the experiment that it is wrong to inflict undeserved suffering on the innocent. What changed was their perception of whether the 330-volt shock they were administering was an instance of inflicting undeserved suffering on the innocent. Even when cognitive dissonance reduction causes a change in values, it will not help the agent to be told that integrity consists in adherence to values that are right and reasonable, because the agent knows only what is right and reasonable to her, and what seems right and reasonable to her may have been corrupted by the psychological forces we have been examining.

But perhaps matters are not as hopeless as they appear. Many of the phenomena revealed by experimentalists are short-lived aberrations, recognized as such even by the subjects once the spell wears off. As Doris puts it, the motives induced by the experiments "are not readily enmeshed in ... biographies; they look like psychological tics or glitches."[61] Asch's subjects did not continue to perceive shorter lines as longer after they left the experiment. Nor did most of Milgram's compliant subjects continue to believe that compliance was the right thing to do once the experiment ended and they talked it over with the experimenter and the man they had supposedly been shocking. In fact, they probably *never* believed that compliance was the right thing to do. When Milgram described his experimental set-up to audiences and asked them to guess the rate of total compliance, and whether they themselves would comply, most guessed around 1 percent (as compared with the 65 percent compliance rate in the actual experiment); and no one believed that they themselves would comply – an unmistakable sign that normal people believe compliance would be wrong. We have no reason to suppose that Milgram's compliant subjects would have responded any

---

[60] Deborah L. Rhode, *If Integrity Is the Answer, What Is the Question?*, 72 Fordham L. Rev. 333, 335–36 (2003).

[61] Doris, supra note 49, at 143 (internal citation omitted).

differently to the question. Instead, as I suggested earlier, the experiment seemed to corrupt their judgment temporarily, disabling their capacity to apply their principles correctly to the situation they found themselves in.

Perhaps the most dramatic evidence that dissonance-induced belief-change is an ephemeral thing comes from Zimbardo's personal recollections of the SPE. At one point, Prisoner #819 became ill and broke down emotionally. Zimbardo found him "sobbing uncontrollably while in the background his fellow prisoners were yelling that he was a bad prisoner" because the guards had ordered them to do so. Remarkably, when Zimbardo tried to lead him away he refused, because he had to show his fellow-inmates that he was *not* a bad prisoner.

Zimbardo said to him, "Listen, you are not #819. You are [his name], and my name is Dr. Zimbardo. I am a psychologist, not a prison superintendent, and this is not a real prison. This is just an experiment, and those are students, not prisoners, just like you. Let's go." He stopped crying suddenly, looked up at me like a small child awakened from a nightmare, and replied, "Okay, let's go."[62]

The suggestion, then, is that dissonance-induced belief-change does not resemble genuine integrity, even from within, because outside the experimental situation it fades and vanishes, unlike our genuine long-term moral and personal commitments.

Unfortunately, there is one crucial state of affairs in which this will not be true: the state of affairs in which the agent returns again and again to the situation that caused the belief-change. Recall the earlier argument that the pattern

action → rationalization → commitment → further action

has a recursive character. Put the same subject in the belief-altering situation day after day – better yet, have the subject put herself in the situation day after day – and it seems overwhelmingly likely that the transitory will become permanent.

For example, suppose that the belief-altering situation is *your job,* and that each day you voluntarily go to the office and put yourself back in the situation – for, let us say, 2,400 billable hours a year, year in and year out. And each night you take yourself out of the situation. By day, with a wig on your head and a band round your neck, you occasionally have to do things for a guinea that at night you would think it wicked and infamous to do for an empire. It seems very likely that before too long you will find yourself believing that a special professional morality, distinct from the morality of your extra-professional

---

[62] Zimbardo, supra note 48, at <www.prisonexp.org/slide-31.htm>.

life, justifies what you do – and this belief will be no transitory thing, but rather a fixed part of your moral personality. Nor will this dualistic view of morality bother you. You will effortlessly negotiate the transition from one form of life to the other, with no sense of tension or contradiction.

Let me give two literary examples. One comes from *Lawyerland,* Lawrence Joseph's fictionalized account of a dozen or so southern Manhattan lawyers. In a chapter entitled "Something Split," a corporate dealmaker named Wylie relates a story about his partner, Jack, who is in psychoanalysis.

So what does the mind doctor say? He tells Jack that, as a lawyer, he has to be capable of deep moral compromise ... Well, you can't argue with that. We all know there are times when you're working on some deal that, if you were to think it through, you'd realize that it was going to ruin the lives of thousands of people and their families. We all do it in one size, shape, form, or other.[63]

But Wylie and Jack think the psychoanalyst is a sanctimonious fool – and Wylie finds Jack's reply to the soul doctor hilarious: "Well, yes, doctor, that is what I do ... Yes, I am a lawyer. That is how I make my living, doctor. I make my living by committing acts of violence against myself and acts of violence against others."[64] Jack baits the psychoanalyst until he flees his own office – and Wylie and Jack laugh about it later.

My guess is that most lawyers would respond to the psychoanalyst the same way, and I must admit that it is hard not to sympathize with Jack. But Wylie agrees with the substance of the shrink's accusation ("We all do it," that is, "ruin the lives of thousands"), and the point of the story seems to be that lawyers like Wylie and Jack have no difficulty living with that diagnosis. Where one would expect to find "something split," eerily enough the protagonists experience no split at all.

The second example comes from a very different quarter, Montaigne's essay "Of Husbanding Your Will."[65] The essay praises those who remain aloof and emotionally detached from causes and enterprises, and in part it is a reflection on Montaigne's own tenure as mayor of Bordeaux. At one point he writes:

The mayor and Montaigne have always been two, with a very clear separation. For all of being a lawyer or a financier, we must not ignore the knavery there is in such callings. An honest man is not accountable for the vice or stupidity of his trade, and should not therefore refuse to practice it: it is the custom of his country, and there is profit in it.[66]

---

[63] Lawrence Joseph, Lawyerland 41 (1997).   [64] Ibid. at 43.

[65] Michel de Montaigne, *Of Husbanding Your Will,* in The Complete Works of Montaigne 766 (Donald M. Frame trans., 1943).

[66] Ibid. at 774.

A few paragraphs earlier, Montaigne wrote, "I have been able to take part in public office without departing one nail's breadth from myself, and to give myself to others without taking myself from myself."[67]

These boasts bear the telltale signs of dissonance reduction at work, especially striking in a self-observer and psychologist as acute as Montaigne. As Gerald Postema points out, Montaigne seemed to be making two different claims: first, that "the mayor and Montaigne have always been two people, clearly separated," suggesting that the professional self and the personal self are two distinct selves; and second, perhaps inconsistently, that because Montaigne served as mayor "without moving the length of my nail from myself," there is only one true self, and Montaigne (but not the mayor) is the true self.[68] In Postema's terminology, the first claim is a "schizophrenic" strategy for proving that an honest man "is not accountable for the vices or stupidity of his calling"; the second is a "restricted identification" strategy.[69] Both strategies seem like self-deception, convenient ruses for denying that a person should be held responsible for the "knavery" of his calling. On the schizophrenic strategy, Montaigne is not responsible because the other fellow – "the mayor" – should bear the blame. On the restricted identification strategy, *no one* bears the blame, because Montaigne's true self is not invested in the mayoralty. Apparently, the mayoralty itself bears the blame – a rhetorical strategy similar to lawyers' frequent recourse to the excuse that "the adversary system did it."[70] Both arguments neglect the fact that Montaigne *is* the mayor, and regardless of whether Montaigne is invested in the mayoralty, it is he who performs the mayor's duties.

Strikingly, Montaigne resorts to these psychological fictions of schizophrenia and restricted identification in order to argue that one need not abandon professions that are customary and profitable, regardless of their knavery. If I am right that schizophrenia and restricted identification *are* fictions, and that Montaigne's arguments for nonaccountability fail, we are left with the situation of someone whose practice of a customary, profitable profession drives him to stable, self-justifying belief-changes whose only drawback is that they happen to be lies. Montaigne claims that he has kept his

---

[67] Ibid. at 770.

[68] Postema, supra note 58, at 292 (quoting Charles P. Curtis, *The Ethics of Advocacy,* 4 Stan. L. Rev. 3, 20 [1951–52]).

[69] Ibid.

[70] To cite one example, Charles Fried distinguishes between a lawyer's personal wrongs and institutional wrongs in which the lawyer is merely the occasion, the person who pulls the legal levers enabling the system to operate. Charles Fried, *The Lawyer as Friend: The Moral Foundations of the Lawyer–Client Relation,* 85 Yale L.J. 1060, 1084–85 (1976). For criticism of the idea that the adversary system provides robust moral excuses for otherwise objectionable acts performed by lawyers and for criticism of Fried's views, see chapter 1 of this book.

integrity – he has not departed one nail's breadth from himself. But he has kept it, it appears, by fooling himself. This is a significant point for legal ethics, because one of the first modern articles on the subject quotes these sentences from Montaigne and takes them as a model of Stoic morality to justify the ethics of advocacy.[71] As Trollope, another shrewd literary psychologist, observed, "Men will not be talked out of the convictions of their lives. No living orator would convince a grocer that coffee should be sold without chicory; and no amount of eloquence will make an English lawyer think that loyalty to truth should come before loyalty to his client."[72]

The problem, in the end, comes to this: the ethical value of integrity is experienced from the inside as a kind of harmony or equilibrium between values and actions, whereby one does what one does without departing a nail's breadth from oneself. But the experiments show that integrity has a kind of evil twin, induced by our need to see ourselves as ethically righteous people regardless of the knavery of our calling. From the inside, the quest for integrity and the process of rationalizing our actions prove nearly impossible to distinguish. We would like our moral compass to point north, but our only instrument for detecting north is our moral compass. And so, even though integrity and its evil twin may differ, the *quest* for integrity can drive us to the high road or the low road, without any landmarks to alert us about which path we have taken.

Is there a cure for integrity?

The truth cure

I fear that no cure for integrity exists. The problem is, quite simply, that the dissonance-based phenomena we have been examining, our urgent desire as intuitive lawyers to arrange our world so that we remain upstanding citizens in it regardless of what we do, all operate unconsciously.

One comforting idea is that the truth will set us free – or, more precisely, that understanding the dynamics of self-corruption (integrity's sturdy twin) can help us fend it off. Robert Cialdini has written an admirable textbook on the power of social psychological forces to influence us in directions we don't want.[73] At the end of each chapter, Cialdini offers a section entitled "Defense," which distills from the experimental literature recommendations on how not to be taken in by the fundamental forces of reciprocation, commitment and consistency, social proof, liking, authority, and scarcity – the "weapons of influence." Cialdini's basic defensive recommendation is

---

[71] See Charles P. Curtis, *The Ethics of Advocacy,* 4 Stan. L. Rev. 3, 20 (1951–52).
[72] Anthony Trollope, Orley Farm 130 (1951).
[73] Robert B. Cialdini, Influence: Science and Practice (3rd edn., 1993).

enhanced awareness.[74] Yet he understands that enhanced awareness of unconscious forces may be impossible precisely because the forces are unconscious.[75] His recommendations may well be the best we can do, but I have doubts that the best we can do will often be good enough.[76]

A personal recollection. A few years ago, I was walking across a park in Dublin with my wife and in-laws. It was a nice summer day, and I noticed a man napping on the grass. As we drew nearer, I observed that he was lying on his stomach, not his back. Then, as we walked by, I saw that his head was not turned to one side like someone asleep. His face was pressed directly into the ground. His limbs were splayed at awkward angles, and he was completely motionless. I had what I can only describe as a moment of listless recognition that he seemed to be dead – listless, because although I recall the thought that he was dead passing through my mind, I kept walking. The listlessness was not too surprising, as we had taken a red-eye from America and spent the whole day touring: all four of us had been awake more than twenty-four hours. It just seemed so natural to keep walking.

At that time, I had been a consumer of experimental social psychology for more than five years, and had discussed the Darley–Latané experiments on bystander passivity in my classes at least three times. It wasn't until we were past the motionless man that I suddenly recognized why none of us were doing anything. It had nothing to do with the red-eye. It had everything to do with diffusion of responsibility. I said, "That guy looks dead! We should do something." We all turned back to look at him, and saw a Good Samaritan with a cell phone standing next to the fallen man, excitedly phoning for help. Just as the experiments predicted, the Good Samaritan was all by himself. Score one for Darley and Latané.

Of course, one explanation for my passivity is that Luban is a weak vessel, who talks the talk of morality and compassion but won't walk the walk – or

---

[74] For example: "The only effective defense I know against the weapons of influence embodied in the combined principles of commitment and consistency is an awareness that, although consistency is generally good, even vital, there is a foolish, rigid variety to be shunned." Ibid. at 90. "If we can become sensitive to situations where the social proof automatic pilot is working with inaccurate information, we can disengage the mechanism and grasp the controls when we need to." Ibid. at 134. "A better understanding of the workings of authority influence should help us resist it." Ibid. at 196.

[75] "Here's our predicament, then: Knowing the causes and workings of scarcity pressures may not be sufficient to protect us from them because knowing is a cognitive act, and cognitive processes are suppressed by our emotional reaction." Ibid. at 228.

[76] In saying this, I take issue not only with Cialdini, but also with Doris, supra note 49, at 153 (expressing cautious optimism that knowing situationist results can help us lead better lives) – and also with myself, for in the preceding chapter I argued that "perhaps a first step is understanding the illusions themselves, their pervasiveness, the insidious way they work on us. Understanding these illusions warns us against them, and forewarned truly is forearmed, at least in contexts similar enough to call the warning to mind."

rather, who walks the walk right past collapsed strangers in a park. Perhaps that's it. But another example might persuade you that the case is not simply one man's fecklessness and hypocrisy. The example comes from Philip Zimbardo's recollections of his Stanford Prison Experiment. Zimbardo recalls a critical moment several days into the experiment:

One of the guards overheard the prisoners talking about an escape that would take place immediately after visiting hours. The rumor went as follows: Prisoner #8612, whom we had released the night before, was going to round up a bunch of his friends and break in to free the prisoners.

How do you think we reacted to this rumor? Do you think we recorded the pattern of rumor transmission and prepared to observe the impending escape? That was what we should have done, of course, if we were acting like experimental social psychologists. Instead, we reacted with concern over the security of our prison. What we did was to hold a strategy session with the Warden, the Superintendent, and one of the chief lieutenants, Craig Haney, to plan how to foil the escape.

Haney was one of the psychologists conducting the experiment. Zimbardo continues:

After our meeting ... I went back to the Palo Alto Police Department and asked the sergeant if we could have our prisoners transferred to their old jail. My request was turned down ... I left angry and disgusted at this lack of cooperation between our correctional facilities (I was now totally into my role).

It only got worse:

I was sitting there all alone, waiting anxiously for the intruders to break in, when who should happen along but a colleague and former Yale graduate student roommate, Gordon Bower. Gordon had heard we were doing an experiment, and he came to see what was going on. I briefly described what we were up to, and Gordon asked me a very simple question: "Say, what's the independent variable in this study?"

To my surprise, I got really angry at him. Here I had a prison break on my hands. The security of my men and the stability of my prison was [*sic*] at stake, and now, I had to deal with this bleeding-heart, liberal, academic, effete dingdong who was concerned about the independent variable! It wasn't until much later that I realized how far into my prison role I was at that point – that I was thinking like a prison superintendent rather than a research psychologist.[77]

When I first described the Stanford Prison Experiment, I noted that the "prisoners" and "guards" were not the only ones to become captives of their roles. Their parents, the priest who visited them, and even the lawyer

---

[77] Zimbardo, supra note 48, at <www.prisonexp.org/slide-25.htm>, slide-26, and slide-27.

who came in to consult with them about their "parole hearings" all did as
well. Why not? None of these people were trained to recognize psychological
mechanisms of influence at work. But Haney and Zimbardo were. If anyone
should have recognized the "Pirandellian prison" of the mind, it is psychologists who devote their careers to mapping its gates and cell blocks.
Apparently, it isn't so. Nor should that surprise us: if cognitive dissonance
and social cognition truly represent universal psychological forces, it is a
little much to expect that scientific expertise can free us from them.
Understanding how Snell's Law explains the bent-stick effect does not make
the partially submerged stick look any less bent to the physicist.

The canary in the mineshaft

I have said that there is no real cure for integrity – the low-road kind of
integrity, that is, the unconscious gerrymandering of principles to rationalize
commitments and actions that are too inconvenient to forgo. I do have a few
suggestions, however. If you really fear the gradual unconscious corruption
that performing in role induces, you must decide in advance what line you
won't cross – and then, when you find yourself standing at that line, or,
worse, when you find yourself having just crossed it, you will know that
it's time to quit. The inspiration for this suggestion comes from David
Heilbroner, a former New York City prosecutor who wrote a fascinating
memoir of his time in the District Attorney's office – a story of inexperience
and naivete gradually replaced by competence and cynicism. Heilbroner
underwent a deep immersion in the seamy side of life where the good guys
and the bad guys all lie sometimes, and where even doing good often leaves a
bad taste. Heilbroner writes:

Before joining the DA's office I had promised myself that above all, I would never
take a case to trial if I had any doubt about the defendant's guilt. At the time it seemed
an easy enough standard to abide by. But during the past few weeks I realized that the
Quintana case would probably force me to put my personal ethics to the test.[78]

Heilbroner was prosecuting Quintana for theft, and had just learned that
his star witness, the clean-cut, appealing, young victim, was really a drug
dealer, bail jumper, and liar. Heilbroner's supervisor was unimpressed by the
revelations about the witness, and insisted that Heilbroner take the case to
trial. He did so, and Quintana was acquitted. Soon after, Heilbroner quit his
job. "To stay on much longer meant maintaining a blindered belief in the
rectitude of our work, wanting to punish defendants, believing that our
policies were all to the good: becoming the very sort of prosecutor I had

---

[78] David Heilbroner, Rough Justice: Days and Nights of a Young D. A. 261–62 (1990).

always disliked and distrusted. It was time to leave."[79] Heilbroner admits that he was temperamentally unsuited to the prosecutor's job, and that some Assistant District Attorneys "loved prosecuting in an unquestioning way that I never could."[80] Perhaps, then, Heilbroner's resignation was inevitable and overdetermined. Nevertheless, I like the way he set himself a mental tripwire, or, switching metaphors, a single action that would serve as his canary in the mineshaft. The moment the canary died, he knew that it was time to evacuate. Heilbroner's canary was taking a case to trial when he wasn't convinced that the defendant was guilty. Other lawyers, in other practices, must choose their own canaries. The formula is simple: "Whatever else I do, and however else my views change, I will never, ever ..." You name it. Cover up someone else's crime. Lie about money. Falsify a document. Let a colleague suffer the consequences for my own screw-up. Do something where I couldn't look my father in the eye if I told him about it.

My advice is to choose your canary carefully, understanding that before you enter a role your ideas about what ethical demands it entails may well be naive. But, once you've selected the canary, never ignore it. If necessary, write down the "I will never, ever" formula. Put it in an envelope, keep it in a drawer, and pull it out sometimes to remind yourself what it says. And, the moment the canary dies, get out of the mineshaft.

Noticing when you are deflecting blame to someone else

A second recommendation takes its inspiration from Milgram's research. When he debriefed subjects after the electric-shock experiment, Milgram asked them to apportion responsibility for shocking the victim among the three protagonists – the subject himself, the "scientist" giving him orders to proceed, and the victim repeatedly earning electric shocks by giving wrong answers. As one might expect, compliant subjects seldom attributed the horrible outcome of the experiment to themselves. Characteristically, they blamed it on the scientist, and often on the victim. Taking a cue from this, my recommendation is the following: whenever you find yourself doing things but denying (to yourself or to others) that you are responsible for doing them, treat it as a sign that you have succumbed to the unconscious psychological drive toward intuitive lawyering.

This recommendation may sound peculiar, given the situationists' warning that assigning responsibility for behavior to personality, not to situational pressures, amounts to a "fundamental attribution error." Am I now suggesting that you must *not* blame the situation for what you have done, that you must take personal responsibility – in short, that you must commit the fundamental attribution error? Well, yes, in a way. Recall my earlier critique

[79] Ibid. at 279.   [80] Ibid. at 283, 284.

of situational determinism, where I argued that situations do not determine behavior, but merely alter the difficulty gradient, making it easier or harder to behave in certain ways. This, I suggested, is compatible with a view that emphasizes the responsibility of agents in dealing with situations. To blame others – one's boss, one's co-workers, one's situation – amounts (to borrow Sartre's term) to a kind of bad faith.[81] Regardless of whether or not it is bad faith, however, my suggestion at the moment is simply that whenever you find yourself blaming others for your actions, treat that as an alarm bell, signaling that you may well be in the grips of the psychological forces of rationalization.

Socratic skepticism

My third and final suggestion is less specific, but perhaps more important. Throughout this discussion I have been emphasizing the dangers of our innate tendency to falsify facts and abandon principles in order to avoid the belief that we are doing wrong. Apparently, the need to believe in our own righteousness runs deep. One possible antidote to the drive toward self-righteousness is a stance toward the world that might be labeled "Socratic skepticism."

In Plato's *Apology,* Socrates tells the Athenian jury at his trial that throughout his life he has listened to an inner voice, a *daimon.* The voice tells him when he is in danger of doing wrong. It never speaks when he is doing right – only when he is doing wrong.[82] To give an example, Socrates mentions a period in which Athens was ruled by the Thirty Tyrants. These rulers wished to implicate as many Athenians as possible in their crimes. At one point, they called Socrates and some others in and ordered them to arrest Leon the Salaminian so that he might be executed. The others went off to fulfill the command, but (Socrates tells his hearers), his *daimon* spoke up, and, at risk of forfeiting his own life, he simply went home. Socrates adds that his own life was spared only because the Tyrants were overthrown very soon after.[83]

Socrates goes on to explain that throughout his life he has made it his mission to seek out those who claim to know, and test them with probing questions, hoping (in vain, he informs us) to find someone whose high opinion of his own wisdom stood the test. He insists that he himself knows only that he does *not* know.[84] Although Socrates does not draw the connection

---

[81] See Jean-Paul Sartre, Being and Nothingness 71–79 (Hazel E. Barnes trans., 1956). I would make an exception in genuine cases of duress – for example, the situation of soldiers who are told that unless they do something wrong they will themselves be shot. In such cases, it does not seem like bad faith to blame their commander.

[82] Plato, Apology *31d.   [83] Ibid. at *32c–d.   [84] Ibid. at *23a–b.

between his *daimon* and his skeptical stance toward his own knowledge and that of others, it seems straightforward enough: the *daimon* tells him when his action has no justification, and his skepticism leads him to test every justification that he hears.

This stance toward the world – a stance of perpetual doubt toward one's own pretensions as well as the pretensions of others – is what I am calling Socratic skepticism. It aims to combat our basic drive to believe in our own righteousness in the most straightforward way possible: by trying to make a habit of doubting one's own righteousness, of questioning one's own moral beliefs, of scrutinizing one's own behavior – "Know thyself!" – with a certain ruthless irony.

This advice will no doubt seem strange and disagreeable to many. Americans admire confident, can-do leaders who never second-guess their own decisions, and who avoid skepticism and self-doubt, the telltale signs of neurotics and losers. In the world of business and government, feelings of guilt or regret are career-destroyers, best cabined to ceremonial occasions like Bible breakfasts and sentencing hearings. Nevertheless, I suggest chronic skepticism and discomfort with oneself as a possible antidote for integrity – if, that is, any antidote for integrity can be found.

IV

Moral messiness in professional life

9

A midrash on Rabbi Shaffer
and Rabbi Trollope

In this *Propter Honoris Respectum*, I want to begin by quoting from a review that I had the pleasure of writing some years ago of one of Tom Shaffer's books:

Thomas Shaffer is the most unusual, and in many ways the most interesting, contemporary writer on American legal ethics. A lawyer impatient with legalisms and hostile to rights-talk, a moral philosopher who despises moral philosophy, a Christian theologian who refers more often to the rabbis than to the Church Fathers, a former law school dean who is convinced that law schools have failed their students by teaching too much law and too little literature, a traditionalist who wholeheartedly embraces feminism, an apologist for the conservative nineteenth-century gentleman who describes his own politics as "left of center," Shaffer is a complex thinker who, I suspect, takes more than a little pleasure in the contradictions he bestraddles. In any event, Shaffer has produced a series of books and articles on professional ethics written with profundity, gentility, and polemical passion.[1]

All of Shaffer's work that I know (and that is only a small fraction of his dozen books and 300 articles) could bear the title of one of his most famous books: *On Being a Christian and a Lawyer*.[2] As Shaffer has written elsewhere, "People show what their morals are by claiming where they come from," and, more briefly, "Belonging explains reality."[3] Where Shaffer comes from is the "community of the faithful" to which he belongs.[4] Christianity deeply conditions Shaffer's views of law, lawyers, morals, adversary representation, truth, and community.

---

[1] David Luban, *The Legal Ethics of Radical Communitarianism*, 60 Tenn. L. Rev. 589, 589 (1993).

[2] Thomas L. Shaffer, On Being a Christian and a Lawyer: Law for the Innocent (1981).

[3] Thomas L. Shaffer with Mary L. Shaffer, American Lawyers and Their Communities: Ethics in the Legal Profession 25, 28 (1991).

[4] Ibid. at 201.

To proceed in the spirit of Shaffer's own dictum, a response to his work should begin by claiming where its author comes from. "An ethic that is not found in a community is not an ethic; it is only somebody's idea."[5] The place I begin, therefore, is my membership in an American Jewish community, and my response will be a Jewish approach to some of Shaffer's themes. I want to challenge Shaffer's reading of Anthony Trollope's novel *Orley Farm*, along with the views of law and lawyers he finds in the novel, and challenge it from a specifically Jewish perspective.[6]

Saying that I speak from within an American Jewish community is not specific enough, however, because there are many Jewish communities, and all of them are famously fractious.[7] A story gives the idea. A religious Jew is cast away on an island and rescued ten years later. His rescuers notice that he has fashioned two splendid buildings, lovingly assembled of driftwood and stone and bamboo, and elaborately decorated with stones and shells of many colors. They ask him what the buildings are. "Oh, they're synagogues," he replies. "But why are there two of them?" He points at the nearer of the two. "That one I pray in." Then he points at the other. "And that one I wouldn't go near." Or, in the words of an old saying: two Jews, three opinions.

Very well, then. I begin from the community of Jews who have departed from orthodoxy, but who persevere in the hard upstream swim to the ancestral identity, which we would be devastated to lose; of Jews who consider ourselves political progressives and ethical cosmopolitans; and of Jews who dislike the narrow parochialism and downright jingoism of some Jewish communities, but who secretly fear that without these traits the Jews might disappear (one Jew, two opinions). I suspect that we are not a small community.

Trollope's *Orley Farm*

Why *Orley Farm*? Quite simply, it is a great novel about legal ethics, and Shaffer has drawn large conclusions from it about his themes of law, lawyers, morals, adversary representation, truth, and community. I begin by quoting Shaffer's own summary of its plot:

Orley Farm is the story of a guilty woman, Lady Mary Mason, who has forged what appears to be a codicil to the will of her dying husband, Sir Joseph Mason. She has

---

[5] Ibid. at 130 n. 4.

[6] Shaffer analyzes *Orley Farm* in On Being a Christian and a Lawyer, supra note 2, at 45–57, 81–91, and again in American Lawyers and Their Communities, supra note 3, 88–93.

[7] Rabbi Arthur Hertzberg believes that fractiousness is one of the defining characteristics of the Jews as a people. See Arthur Hertzberg & Aron Hirt-Manheimer, Jews: The Essence and Character of a People 33–40 (1998). On the fractiousness of contemporary American Jews, and the struggle over Jewish identity, see Samuel G. Freedman, Jew vs. Jew: The Struggle for the Soul of American Jewry (2000).

done this twenty years before the novel begins. The codicil has been proved, in litigation, through Lady Mason's testimony. As a result, her son Lucius is in possession of the devise at issue, Orley Farm. Sir Joseph's eldest son, Joseph Mason, has been cheated out of the farm. He is a child of Sir Joseph by a former marriage; Lucius is Lady Mason's only child. Her forgery is like the misdeed of the biblical Rebekah; she has acted dishonestly to benefit her child.

A scheming and vengeful solicitor named Dockwrath has, as he believes, been mistreated by Lucius. Dockwrath sets out to prove the forgery from old documents which will show how Lady Mason got through the will contest. What she did was this: On the day the codicil was supposedly executed the witnesses to it signed another document for Sir Joseph – a partnership deed. Lady Mason gave the codicil that same date; the witnesses to the deed thought (and testified) that what they signed was the codicil. Dockwrath produces the partnership deed and the aging witnesses, and the witnesses are prepared to say that they signed only one paper. Dockwrath succeeds in getting Joseph Mason and his respectable London lawyers to agree to prosecute Lady Mason for perjury, based on her testimony in the will contest. That is the suspense in the story. Trollope thought it was his best plot in forty-seven novels.[8]

So far, so good. However, Shaffer's lucid plot summary is incomplete. He omits one important feature of the plot, without which I think we cannot understand the moral situation in its richness. That feature is the circumstance that led Lady Mason to her crime.

Sir Joseph Mason was a very wealthy man, and Orley Farm – "a small country house"[9] – is only a small portion of Sir Joseph's estate. Sir Joseph's actual will provided small incomes for Lady Mason and Lucius, but he left everything else, including Orley Farm and a far larger estate at Groby Park, to his eldest son Joseph, Lucius's half brother (*OF* I.1–2). The codicil that Lady Mason forged made just one change in these devises. Lady Mason was a clever forger – she knew enough not to be too greedy, and her codicil awarded Lucius only one additional prize, namely the modest farm (Orley Farm) on which she and Lucius were already living (*OF* I.2–4). The insignificant amount of the loss does not mollify Joseph Mason, however. For twenty years, he has seethed with bitter resentment that he did not get everything. When we first meet him, Trollope describes him as "a bad man in that he could never forget and never forgive ... He was a man who considered that it behoved him as a man to resent all injuries, and to have his pound of flesh in all cases" (*OF* I.49). As Trollope reminds us several times, Mason's only regret at the prospect of seeing Lady Mason imprisoned for perjury is that he would prefer to see her hanged (*OF* I.61). As the novel progresses, we watch his hatred of Lady Mason grow and devour him, and by the time it ends, nothing remains

---

[8] On Being a Christian and a Lawyer, *supra* note 2, at 45–46.
[9] 1 Anthony Trollope, Orley Farm 2 (Dover Publ'ns, Inc. 1981) (1862). Hereafter, I give references to *Orley Farm* parenthetically in the text, giving volume number and then page.

of Joseph Mason except his hatred, tempered by a small, redeeming smidgen of rational self-interest. Shaffer does not mention any of this; later, we will see why this omission is important.

The story of the litigation is not all there is to the plot, of course. Trollope also provides a large cast of supporting characters with designs of their own, no fewer than six love triangles, and a number of set-piece genre scenes – over 600 vastly entertaining pages. I will bring in other bits of the plot as we need them.

Orley Farm has plenty of lawyers in its cast in addition to the vindictive Dockwrath. Most significant among them is Thomas Furnival, Lady Mason's attorney in the earlier litigation over the authenticity of the will, and her principal legal advisor in the perjury litigation. As Furnival becomes increasingly convinced that Lady Mason is in serious trouble, he brings in two skilled gutter-fighter criminal defense lawyers, the barrister Chaffanbrass and the attorney Solomon Aram. To this legal team Furnival adds Felix Graham, a young barrister who is also the romantic lead in the novel. On the other side we meet the respected London firm of Round and Crook, with its elder partner Round, who opposed Furnival in the will litigation twenty years past, and his son Matt Round, who handles the prosecution case for Joseph Mason against Lady Mason. There are other lawyers as well, but these are the most important.

The legal ethics problem in *Orley Farm*

A legal ethics problem lies at the heart of *Orley Farm*. The main legal protagonist is Lady Mason's lawyer Furnival, and his difficulty is this. When Lady Mason first learns that Dockwrath is trying to revive the old litigation against her, she turns to Furnival for advice (*OF* I.89–96). Much as he would like to believe that Lady Mason is innocent, Furnival suspects immediately that she is not, and that the victory he won twenty years earlier on her behalf was achieved through falsehood – a thought he entertained at that time, but then repressed (*OF* I.93). Yet Furnival does not want to believe Lady Mason's guilt – in part because (without admitting it to himself) he is infatuated with Lady Mason, but also because he fears that he will not be able to muster adequate professional zeal on her behalf unless he thinks her innocent. Trollope is at his keenest unfolding the delicate games with belief and truth that Furnival plays against himself, holding at arm's length his steadily growing certainty that Lady Mason is guilty, and masking from himself the understanding that that is what he is doing.

Throughout the novel, Furnival never doubts that Lady Mason will be acquitted of criminal charges, because he knows that jurors will find her appealing and will perceive that her persecutors are revolting. The ticklish issue is what should be done about the ill-gotten Orley Farm. Even if she is acquitted, should not the farm be returned to Joseph Mason, its rightful owner? Lucius Mason poses an obstacle to any effort to return Orley Farm. Furnival knows that Lucius has no suspicion that his mother is really the forger that her enemies say she is. Control of the farm passed to him when he turned twenty-one, and if it is to be returned to Joseph Mason, Lucius is the one who will have to sign it over. An even more important obstacle is that returning the farm before the trial would be damning evidence of Lady Mason's guilt. Furnival realizes that if he ever tells Lady Mason that he thinks she is guilty, she will very likely confess to him – and if she confesses, he will have no alternative except to instruct her to return the farm regardless of whether that leads to her perjury conviction. So Furnival has to enter into a conspiracy of silence with Lady Mason. Even when he becomes certain of her guilt, he never tells her what he believes; and even when she becomes certain that he thinks her guilty, she never lets him know that she has guessed his mind.[10]

Furnival is an extremely good lawyer – good enough to understand (as every good white-collar defender understands today) that legal victory by itself will not save his client unless he also acquits her in the eyes of her community. His conclusion is straightforward: the only successful outcome for Lady Mason is acquittal on the perjury charge *and* keeping her guilty secret from everyone, including Lucius. The result for Furnival is an intricate slalom around the truth, a struggle to know the truth while not knowing it – a struggle of a kind that every successful criminal lawyer will recognize instantly.

Shaffer rightly notes that Trollope carefully situates Furnival between two lawyerly extremes.[11] On the one side is young Felix Graham, who holds the unusual view that lawyers should never disserve the truth, and, therefore, should represent only the truthful side in a case. (Not surprisingly, Graham's fledgling career as a barrister is going nowhere.) On the other side are the hardened Old Bailey warriors Aram and Chaffanbrass, who never need to ask whether their clients are guilty, because they assume that if their services are required the client must be guilty.[12] Furnival is neither self-righteous like Graham (equal parts self-absorbed and righteous) nor, like Chaffanbrass, a "Pharisee" (Shaffer's word, and, I will shortly suggest, a word fraught with significance).[13] Instead, Furnival is – as Shaffer elaborately argues in *American Lawyers and Their Communities* – a gentleman.[14] As a gentleman, he wants to defend the weak (for that is how Furnival wrongly perceives Lady Mason). He also wants to do so with honor. The outcome Furnival

---

[10] *OF* I.101 ("And then – for the first time – she felt sure that Mr. Furnival had guessed her secret. He also knew it, but it would not suit him that any one should know that he knew it!").

[11] On Being a Christian and a Lawyer, supra note 2, at 48–49.   [12] Ibid. at 49.   [13] Ibid.

[14] American Lawyers and Their Communities, supra note 3, at 88–94.

desires – acquitting Lady Mason and restoring her to her community, which as a practical matter requires her to keep Orley Farm and perpetuate her twenty-year-old lie – dictates that he, Furnival, play hide-and-seek with the truth. He hides, and he hopes that the truth will not seek him out. He understands all too well that the alternative to perpetuating the lie is disaster – Lady Mason disgraced, exiled, turned out of her home, and perhaps jailed; her son, disinherited and very likely estranged from his own mother. And for what? So that a very rich, very hateful man, Joseph Mason, who inherited almost all of his father's estate, will now have the last piece of it, along with his vengeance against Lady Mason.

Let me repeat the conclusion: because Furnival is a gentleman, he desires above all to save Lady Mason from a great deal of suffering. Because he is a man of honor, he hides, from himself and from others, for as long as he can, the lie that he is perpetuating. He perpetuates the lie to avert the far greater wrong of Lady Mason's destruction at the hands of Dockwrath and Joseph Mason.

Shaffer's legal ethics: the advocate on the cross

So far, I have largely followed Shaffer's reading of *Orley Farm*, in particular his keen understanding of Furnival's dilemma and his penetrating insight that Furnival's dilemma arises out of the ethics of the gentleman-lawyer. Shaffer draws far more from *Orley Farm* than this, however. For him, the significant counterpoint to Furnival is neither Graham nor Chaffanbrass and Aram. Rather, it is Lady Mason's friend Edith Orme.[15] Although she is not a lawyer, Mrs. Orme ministers to Lady Mason in a way that Furnival cannot bring himself to do, and that makes her a better lawyer than Furnival. The reason takes us into the deepest portion of Shaffer's vision of what it is to be a Christian and a lawyer. It is to be like Mrs. Orme.

For Shaffer, the Christian answer to the commonly asked question of how a lawyer can serve the guilty is that Jesus served the guilty.[16] Christ's ministry brought him into the company of disreputable people and despised people – into the company of sinners, prostitutes, tax-collectors, publicans, and thieves. It had to: a physician practices among the sick, not among the healthy.

But it must not be supposed that Shaffer is offering an easy excuse to the criminal lawyer, the facile reply that if representing the guilty is good enough for Jesus, it is good enough for me. That would be a short and sweet way out of moral accountability for lawyers' decisions about whom to represent. Nothing could be further from Shaffer's intentions, because what Shaffer is talking about is not legal representation but ministry, and ministry is a

---

[15] Ibid. at 88–89.   [16] See On Being a Christian and a Lawyer, supra note 2, at 55–56.

perilous profession that offers no shield against moral accountability. Quite the contrary. "When Jesus touched the leper, Jesus became a leper."[17] Ministry requires a kind of faithfulness to the other person that knows no circumscription, no limit-point. Ministry may, in the end, bring you to Calvary. Shaffer could hardly be more blunt, or more terrifying:

> The scene to superimpose on the jail cells where we talk to the guilty is Jesus and the tax-gatherers. The scene to superimpose on the frightful image of my client receiving his punishment is Dismas on the cross, Dismas with an advocate and a companion hanging by his side.[18]

The advocate hanging on the cross beside the thief is, to say the least, a far cry from the old trial lawyer's cynical advice to make sure you are on the outside when the jail door closes on your client.

Shaffer raises the stakes in legal ethics to an almost unimaginable degree. In his hands, it becomes a different subject, "a turn away from analysis of duty and consequence, of critical moments and 'ethical dilemmas' and *statements* and dry rationality."[19] The moral requirements of faithful ministry replace the entire dispiriting casuistry of the Model Rules of Professional Conduct and "public policy" that make up so much of our legal ethics discourse. Gone, too, is the liberal–secular discourse about the public interest and justified rule-breaking. For Shaffer, rules and policy have nothing to do with what matters, the I–Thou relationship between lawyer and client.[20] I read Shaffer's language about the thief on the cross with his advocate hanging by his side quite seriously and literally. It means, I think, that if ministering to the client requires a lawyer to break a Model Rule, or a law, and undergo punishment for it, then the Christian who is a lawyer will break the Model Rule and the law – not because doing so is in the larger public interest, but because doing so is what faithful ministry demands. Rejecting arguments based on "the Constitution or the adversary function" about how a lawyer should treat client perjury, Shaffer comments, "A moral person cannot allow either the government or the profession to decide what is truth and what is not."[21] Sometimes, good people and good lawyers tell lies.[22]

Of course, Shaffer is not presenting a "win at all costs" ethic – far from it. In the authentic I–Thou relationship, the lawyer "may have to refuse to go further with the client,"[23] and refusing to go further might itself violate rules and laws under some circumstances – for example, if the lawyer finds himself

---

[17] Ibid. at 52.   [18] Ibid. at 79.

[19] Thomas L. Shaffer, *On Lying for Clients*, 71 Notre Dame L. Rev. 195, 195 (1996).

[20] See On Being a Christian and a Lawyer, supra note 2, at 28–32.   [21] Ibid. at 102.

[22] Shaffer, *On Lying for Clients*, supra note 19, at 205.

[23] On Being a Christian and a Lawyer, supra note 2, at 29; see also ibid. at 104.

morally compelled to reveal privileged information. Shaffer distinguishes between loyalty to the client, which is what the win-at-all-costs ethic demands, and fidelity, which is deeper and riskier, and which may take both the lawyer and the client to places where they would prefer not to go.[24]

Edith Orme's ministry

Edith Orme takes Lady Mason to places where she would prefer not to go. The crucial scenes in *Orley Farm* are Mrs. Orme's conversations with Lady Mason after she learns the truth about Lady Mason's crime, the scenes in which "they sat together for hours and hours, they spoke and argued, and lived together as though they were equal" (*OF* II.178). Mrs. Orme's concern is, above all else, with the state of Lady Mason's soul. She herself forgives Lady Mason (*OF* II.41), and she hopes that Lady Mason will be acquitted at her trial – but forgiving her and hoping for legal acquittal do not mean accepting her crime. Mrs. Orme never wavers from her purpose: to support Lady Mason through her travails, but also to bring her to repent her sin. Mrs. Orme is a true Christian – in Trollope's typical wry understatement, "a good church-woman but not strong, individually, in points of doctrine. All that she left mainly to the woman's conscience and her own dealings with her Saviour" (*OF* II.41).

Mrs. Orme believes that repentance requires renouncing the crime, and that will include giving Orley Farm back to Joseph Mason. Lady Mason will have to confess everything to Lucius, for the farm belongs to Lucius now, and the law makes him the one who will have to renounce it. For her own part, Lady Mason can bear any pain except the pain of confessing to Lucius. Through hour after excruciating hour, Mrs. Orme gently insists that Lady Mason must place herself in the hands of her Savior, for the sake of her soul (*OF* II.153–60). Above all, she must tell Lucius the truth and have faith that Lucius will forgive her. The more Mrs. Orme insists, the more the increasingly distraught Lady Mason resists. Better death than the scorn of her son, the first creature she had ever loved, and still the creature she loves the best. The contest between the two friends is remarkable. "Lady Mason was greater than [Mrs. Orme] in force of character, – a stronger woman in every way, endowed with more force of will, with more power of mind, with greater energy, and a swifter flow of words" (*OF* II.155). But in the end, Mrs. Orme – "the weaker, softer, and better woman" (*OF* II.153) – prevails.

The outcome is not what Mrs. Orme had hoped. The stunned Lucius does give back Orley Farm, but he never forgives his mother, and eventually he emigrates to Australia and abandons her in exile in Germany (*OF* II.320). At the end of the novel, Trollope expresses pious hopes that God will someday

---

[24] See ibid. at 87–91.

allow life to smile on Lady Mason again, "for no lesson is truer than that which teaches us to believe that God does temper the wind to the shorn lamb" (*OF* II.312). But his show of piety is surely ironic, even disingenuous, because he deliberately offers the reader nothing beyond it. If Lady Mason's life ended better than the bleak desolation in which we leave her, it was within Trollope's power to tell his readers about it, which he refuses to do. At the point where Trollope breaks off Lady Mason's story, she remains in unalloyed misery.

But to Shaffer, none of this implies that Mrs. Orme made a mistake. Christians know that it is impossible "to make things come out right, without suffering."[25] That is how Mrs. Orme, representing Christianity, contrasts with Mr. Furnival, representing only the ethic of the gentleman:

The gentleman had become merely optimistic ... where the faithful Jew or Christian was hopeful: Hope is optimism that is truthful. It rejoices in the truth. When it comes to the gentleman's ethic, the virtue of hope can come to terms with and deal truthfully with the certainty that the moral life will cause others to suffer. Hope, which says that the Ruler of the Universe is in charge, that fate is finally benign, also says that the harm that may come to others is not an argument against taking a moral direction. It was hope that caused Mrs. Orme to advise Lady Mason to tell the truth, as it was mere optimism that led Thomas Furnival to use his lawyer's skill to keep her from telling the truth ... He wants too much for things to come out right.[26]

Introducing Rebekah

I have presented Shaffer's approach to *Orley Farm* in what I hope is a sympathetic and accurate way. But there is much about its moral position that troubles me and much about his reading of the novel that does not ring true.

Let me return to Shaffer's summary of *Orley Farm's* plot, quoted above. I want to take issue with its very first phrase, "*Orley Farm* is the story of a guilty woman."[27] A few pages later he echoes and expands this judgment: "The guilty are repulsive. Lady Mason, as pretty and respectable as she is, comes to be repulsive to everyone in the story, even to herself."[28] These ideas form the theme of a chapter in *On Being a Christian and a Lawyer*, entitled "The Problem of Revulsion," which uses *Orley Farm* to raise the question of how lawyers should come to terms with the revulsion they feel for their guilty clients.

The trouble with Shaffer's reading is that Lady Mason is *not a* repulsive figure. On the contrary, she is from start to finish the most attractive character

---

[25] American Lawyers and Their Communities, supra note 3, at 90.   [26] Ibid. at 90–91.
[27] On Being a Christian and a Lawyer, supra note 2, at 45.   [28] Ibid. at 49.

in the novel, and I for one have no doubt that Trollope fully intended her to be. As Trollope writes at the end of the book,

I may, perhaps, be thought to owe an apology to my readers in that I have asked their sympathy for a woman who had so sinned as to have placed her beyond the general sympathy of the world at large. If so, I tender my apology, and perhaps feel that I should confess a fault. But as I have told her story that sympathy has grown upon myself till I have learned to forgive her, and to feel that I too could have regarded her as a friend (*OF* II.312).

The final sentence is ironic Trollopean understatement. Trollope knows full well that he has given us a great fictional heroine and made her sympathetic from the very first page. He lets us know it at the outset, in further ironic understatement: "Persistent novel readers ... will probably be aware that she is not intended to be the heroine. The heroine, so called, must by a certain fixed law be young and marriageable" (*OF* I.10). Which is to say: *Of course* Lady Mason is the heroine. (None of the three young and marriageable ladies in *Orley Farm* comes within hailing distance of being a heroine.) Lady Mason is "the chief interest of our tale" (*OF* II.312).

From the moment we meet her, Trollope dwells on Lady Mason's attractions, and I think that Shaffer trivializes them when he describes her only as "pretty and respectable" (*OF* I.14). She is, to be sure, "tall and comely," and her widowed life before the novel begins was "successful ... prudent and well conducted" (*OF* I.14). But, in addition, she is "a woman of no ordinary power," with "considerable mental faculties" (*OF* I.14) – and much more than that.

The quietness and repose of her manner suited her years and her position; age had given fulness to her tall form; and the habitual sadness of her countenance was in fair accordance with her condition and character. And yet she was not really sad, – at least so said those who knew her. The melancholy was in her face rather than in her character, which was full of energy, if energy may be quiet as well as assured and constant (*OF* I.15).

At the moment of Lady Mason's greatest travail, Trollope describes her thus: "She was a woman who with a good cause might have dared anything. With the worst cause that a woman could well have, she had dared and endured very much" (*OF* II.35). And later: "There was much that was wonderful about this woman" (*OF* II.179).

When we first get to know her, Lady Mason has become aware that trouble is brewing, and Trollope shows her thinking her way through her problems. He makes it a pleasure for us to watch her in action, for her intelligence, her judgment of other people, and her sense of strategy are nearly infallible.

(Indeed, one of the key elements of the plot – her estrangement from her son Lucius – arises because Lady Mason rightly senses that Lucius's own judgment was too poor for her to confide in him.) She takes steps to make allies of the local gentry, Sir Peregrine Orme and his daughter-in-law Edith. First, strategically, she approaches Sir Peregrine for advice about a different, lesser matter – the bad judgment of her son – and then circles around to what is really on her mind, the legal troubles that Dockwrath is contriving for her. She asks Sir Peregrine's advice about whether to see a lawyer; even though he advises her not to do so, she does anyway. Lady Mason understands that Sir Peregrine is an innocent, who naively assumes that when you are in the right the courts will inevitably vindicate you.[29] We quickly come to understand that Lady Mason was not really after Sir Peregrine's advice. She solicited it in order to win him over to her cause. Next, very deliberately, she campaigns to enlist Thomas Furnival, her lawyer of twenty years ago, as an ally. This she accomplishes by a show of feminine weakness that stops properly short of flirtation, but that (as she well knows) Furnival finds irresistible. Step by masterful step, Lady Mason does everything in her power to recruit allies and avert the catastrophe. She holds only a few good cards in her hand, but she plays them flawlessly.

All this makes Lady Mason sound ruthlessly manipulative, but throughout the novel Trollope takes great pains to show us otherwise. She is never *merely* strategic; and, while she has ulterior motives for all her moves, she never uses her friends merely as means to an end. She genuinely loves them, and she never abuses their trust.[30] In fact, the great crisis of the novel occurs when Sir Peregrine falls in love with Lady Mason and asks her to marry him. Lady Mason realizes that in order to save him from a disgraceful marriage to a woman who may well be doomed, she has to confess her crime to the hitherto unsuspecting Sir Peregrine. She does so, knowing that by doing so she is unraveling all her plans and bringing inescapable ruin on herself. Trollope's chapter title – "Showing How Lady Mason Could Be Very Noble" – is clearly *not* ironic. Shaffer thinks that as the novel proceeds she "comes to be repulsive,"[31] but I do not see it. Even at the end, Sir Peregrine loves her and wants to marry her, and I imagine that most readers are rooting for a storybook ending in which they marry and live happily ever after.

---

[29] "An English judge and an English jury were to him the Palladium of discerning truth. In an English court of law such a matter could not remain dark" (*OF* II.122). "Poor Sir Peregrine! His innocence in this respect was perhaps beautiful, but it was very simple" (*OF* II.125). Lady Mason understands that "Sir Peregrine's friendship was more valuable to her than that of Mr. Furnival, but a word of advice from Mr. Furnival was worth all the spoken wisdom of the baronet, ten times over" (*OF* I.91).

[30] Trollope writes, for example, that "could she have shown her love by any great deed, there was nothing which Lady Mason would not have done for Mrs. Orme" (*OF* II.178).

[31] On Being a Christian and a Lawyer, supra note 2, at 49.

Trollope could easily have written a novel in which, to cover up her crime, Lady Mason had to commit new misdeeds and betrayals, and make herself – in Shaffer's word – repulsive. But that is not the book Trollope wrote. Nothing blemishes Lady Mason except the twenty-year-old crime she committed before the book begins.

Even that crime she committed for the sake of Lucius, not for herself. In one of the crucial chapters of the book, "What Rebekah Did For Her Son," Lady Mason debates her crime with Mrs. Orme:

"What did Rebekah do, Mrs. Orme? Did she not do worse; and did it not all go well with her? Why should my boy be an Ishmael? Why should I be treated as the bondwoman, and see my little one perish of thirst in this world's wilderness?"

"No Saviour had lived and died for the world in those days," said Mrs. Orme.

"And no Saviour had lived and died for me," said the wretched woman, almost shrieking in her despair (*OF* II.158).

Actually, Lady Mason has performed a double self-identification, as Rebekah but also as Sarah – for it was Sarah who caused her bondwoman Hagar to be driven into the wilderness with her son Ishmael.

Twice more, Trollope repeats the identification of Lady Mason with Rebekah: "She remembered Rebekah, and with the cunning of a second Rebekah she filched a world's blessing for her baby" (*OF* II.311). And, more elaborately:

As Rebekah had deceived her lord and robbed Esau, the first-born, of his birthright, so had she robbed him who was as Esau to her. How often had she thought of that, while her conscience was pleading hard against her! Had it been imputed as a crime to Rebekah that she had loved her own son well, and loving him had put a crown upon his head by means of her matchless guile? Did she love Lucius, her babe, less than Rebekah had loved Jacob? And had she not striven with the old man, struggling that she might do this just thing without injustice, till in his anger he had thrust her from him. "I will not break my promise for the brat," the old man had said; – and then she did the deed (*OF* II.275).

On my reading, these scenes and identifications are the keys that unlock *Orley Farm*. To see why, we will have to do some Biblical delving.

How the Hebrew Bible undermines primogeniture

Rebekah, remember, wants her favorite son Jacob, rather than his elder brother Esau, to get Isaac's paternal blessing. So she tricks the blind Isaac into thinking that Jacob is really Esau, by placing kid skin on his hands and neck so that the smooth-skinned Jacob would feel like his hairy brother (Gen. 27). Jacob has already talked Esau into selling his birthright (Gen. 25:29–34), and, assisted by Rebekah's matchless guile (to use Trollope's words), Jacob completely supplants Esau (Gen. 27:19–37).

What attitude should a Jewish reader have toward Jacob and Rebekah – or, for that matter, toward Sarah, who drives Ishmael and Hagar into the desert, to suffer a terrible death, for all she knows, so that Ishmael's younger half-brother Isaac can inherit the legacy of Abraham?[32] Both are stories in which mothers defeat the law of primogeniture to capture an inheritance for their sons – precisely Lady Mason's crime. The Torah tells both Rebekah's and Sarah's tales without any comment or any redeeming narrative to moralize and sugarcoat them. Yet to a Jewish reader, Rebekah, Jacob, and Sarah cannot be mere criminals. These are the patriarchs and the matriarchs, and God endorses their actions. Their story is the story of Jewish origin, the explanation of how God's covenant and God's Torah passed to the children of Israel. Their story is *our* story.

Nothing is more central to Jewish identity than the connection to history, the braiding of what I do today into the many-stranded cable of Jewish deeds and observance running unbroken back into time. Jewish ritual takes care to bind us to the Biblical stories in the most powerful and immediate way possible. At the Passover Seder, we are told to regard ourselves as though we had been personally rescued from slavery in Egypt. Then is now.

The stories of the patriarchs and matriarchs stand, mythically at least, at the beginning of the cable. The centerpiece and core of every Jewish service is a silent meditation called the Eighteen Blessings (Shemoneh Esrei). It is almost 2,000 years old, and the Talmud calls it simply Tefilah, "the prayer."[33] The worshiper stands up, takes three steps forward – symbolically walking into the divine presence – and, bowing, begins the first blessing, the *avot*, the invocation of the ancestors. "Blessed are You, Hashem our God and the God of our forefathers, God of Abraham, God of Isaac, and God of Jacob." The gender-egalitarian Conservative and Reform liturgies add the *imahot*, the invocation of the mothers –"God of Sarah, God of Rebekah, God of Rachel, and God of Leah." Repeated three times a day by observant Jews, the *avot* and the *imahot* are the fountainheads from which all the remaining blessings and supplications in the prayer flow. Before asking anything else, we first let God know that we remember who we are and who we came from.

That makes stories of ancestral transgression problematic and complex. Of course, the stories of Rebekah and Sarah are hardly the only places where our national epic displays our ancestors as morally flawed human beings. Some readers, I suppose, are repelled by the weakness and occasional infamy of our

---

[32] Sarah says to Abraham, "Cast out that slave-woman and her son, for the son of that slave shall not share in the inheritance with my son Isaac." Gen. 21:10. Earlier, Sarah had mistreated Hagar, Ishmael's mother, out of rivalry. Gen. 16:5–9.

[33] Babylonian Talmud, Berachos *26b.

ancestors, memorably scattered throughout the pages of the Hebrew Bible. The rabbis obviously found it troubling, and the medieval commentary literature is full of interpretations explaining it away – explaining, for example, why Esau and Ishmael deserved to be disinherited.[34] I, on the other hand, am filled with awe and admiration at a national epic that so dispassionately exhibits the founding heroes as flawed human beings, rather than infallible demigods or pillars of righteousness.

But the story of Rebekah, like that of Sarah, does more than exhibit them as flawed human beings. These stories establish that God's covenant with the Jews came about through a series of transgressions of God's own law. For make no mistake – the law of primogeniture, traduced by Sarah and Rebekah, is itself a Deuteronomic commandment:

> If a man has two wives, one loved and the other unloved, and both the loved and the unloved have borne him sons, but the first-born is the son of the unloved one – when he wills his property to his sons, he may not treat as first-born the son of the loved one in disregard of the son of the unloved one who is older. Instead, he must accept the first-born, the son of the unloved one, and allot to him a double portion of all he possesses; since he is the first fruit of his vigor, the birthright is his due (Deut. 21:15–17).

Although the commandment discusses an unusual special case of succession, it informs us that in normal cases the rule gives eldest sons a double portion as their birthright. And the commandment in the special case is itself troubling because the story of Sarah and Ishmael seems to fit it so closely and violate it so plainly.[35] Yet God Himself ratifies Sarah's demand for the

---

[34] Thus, Rashi, the great eleventh-century rabbi who authored the authoritative medieval commentary on the Torah, holds that Sarah demanded the expulsion of Ishmael because Ishmael was committing idolatry, or sexual immorality, or that he planned to murder Isaac with arrows. (Rashi reaches these conclusions by examining other Biblical passages that use the verb *m'tzachek*, "playing" or "mocking," which appears in the Hagar/Ishmael story. Gen. 21:9). The Torah: With Rashi's Commentary Translated, Annotated, and Elucidated: Bereishis/Genesis 221 (Yisrael Isser Zvi Herczeg ed., R. Meir Zlotowitz & R. Nosson Scherman trans., Art Scroll, 1995). Likewise, Rashi explains that on the day Jacob bought Esau's birthright, Esau was returning home from committing murder – and that Abraham died the same day because God did not want Abraham to know that his grandson was a murderer. Ibid. at 279. Rashi's explanation of Rebekah's guile is equally speculative and apologetic. Drawing on Talmudic sources as well as his own creative parsing of the Biblical syntax, Rashi argues that Jacob never actually lies to Isaac; that Isaac knows all along that it is Jacob he is blessing, and consents to the substitution; that Jacob wants the birthright only because it includes heightened obligations and not because he wants the property; and that Esau preferred to be quit of the birthright because of the extra obligations. Ibid. at 280, 290–99.

[35] Of course, the Deuteronomic commandments are given long after the time of the patriarchs and matriarchs, but the rabbinic tradition never doubts that Deuteronomy's version of the birthright codifies rather than overthrows preexisting custom.

expulsion of Ishmael. God assures Abraham that "it is through Isaac that offspring shall be continued for you" (Gen. 21:12). It seems that God ordains and desires the transgression of the law.

But the puzzle runs even deeper than this, for the overthrow of primogeniture and the transmission of divine favor to younger sons over elder forms one of the leitmotifs of the Hebrew Bible. Isaac inherits over Ishmael, and Jacob over Esau. In addition, Joseph prevails over his older brothers, and Moses, "whom the Lord singled out, face to face," is the younger brother of Aaron (Deut. 34:10). For that matter, as Robert Cover points out, God favors Abel over his elder brother Cain, and the human race springs from the third-born Seth.[36] The rise of Solomon to David's throne, like the rise of David to Saul's, and the prophet Samuel's to Eli's high-priesthood, all involve a younger man defeating the birthright of an elder son.[37] In each case the younger man is *ish haruach*, the one whom God has invested with the spirit. The story of Rebekah is unique among these antinomian episodes, because she alone overthrows the law through out-and-out fraud. Yet she too is chosen, and Jacob, whom God names "Israel," is chosen by God through the instrument of Rebekah's trickery.[38]

On Cover's reading, the legalism of the Bible is set within an antilegalistic story. "The biblical narratives always retained their subversive force – the memory that divine destiny is not lawful."[39] For it is nothing less than divine destiny that, again and again, chooses against the letter and the spirit of the law of primogeniture. Cover elaborated the point as follows:

To be an inhabitant of the biblical normative world is to understand, first, that the rule of succession can be overturned; second, that it takes a conviction of divine destiny to overturn it; and third, that divine destiny is likely to manifest itself precisely in overturning this specific rule.[40]

The story of Jewish origins in the Torah is a story of overthrowing the law for the sake of something higher. If Jewishness is "about" origins, then it is "about" the subversion of law. After all, each of these leitmotif stories, each subversion of primogeniture, is a microcosm of the larger story told in the Hebrew Bible – the story of how the "younger" people, the children of Israel, came to do God's will by dispossessing the owners of the land of Canaan of their domains. The Torah story is the story of the overthrow of primogeniture, writ large.

---

[36] See Robert M. Cover, *The Supreme Court 1982 Term Foreword*: Nomos *and Narrative*, 97 Harv. L. Rev. 4, 20 (1983). Cover's great essay is reprinted in Narrative, Violence, and the Law: The Essays of Robert Cover 95 (Martha Minow *et al.* eds., 1992).

[37] Ibid. at 20–21.

[38] That Jacob is chosen by God is clear from Gen. 28:13–15. Jacob's renaming is in Gen. 32:29.

[39] Cover, supra note 36, at 24.   [40] Ibid. at 22.

The Jewish elevation of social justice over property law

If that story was all the Hebrew Bible contains, the Bible would of course be of surpassing interest to Jews, because it would comprise our national epic. Furthermore, its monotheism would still make it a work of surpassing interest to non-Jews as well. But its moral teaching would be troubling, perhaps more troubling than uplifting. A people who have dispossessed the aboriginal owners of land, and put them to the sword, will no doubt tell a story of self-justification, a story of divine election. Outsiders who read the grim tales of genocide that the book of Joshua recounts will very likely draw a different conclusion (not that the Jews are worse in this respect than anyone else). Property may not be theft, but it always begins in theft, and every people's title to its land, traced back far enough, originates in conquest and bloodshed. That is the paradox of property: the law of property protects titles that invariably originated in crimes against the law of property. One might say that that is the point of all the antiprimogeniture stories in the Hebrew Bible.

But the universal moral interest in the Hebrew Bible comes from its second great history: not the story of how the children of Israel took the Promised Land and made it an empire, but the interpretation of its eventual collapse – of the misfortunes and exiles of the Jews. That story, recounted again and again by the prophets, is simple and straightforward: the people became unjust and the wealthy oppressed the poor. Catastrophe overtook the community because God punishes injustice. If the first Biblical theme is the divinely sanctioned overthrow of law, the second is the divinely sanctioned demand that *this* people be just.

The core of Jewish ethics lies in the laws of holiness (*kedushim*) in Leviticus 19: to love the neighbor as yourself (Lev. 19:18), and to love the stranger as yourself (Lev. 19:34) – the law of communitarianism and the law of cosmopolitanism. As the tradition interprets them, these laws center around respecting the dignity of every human being, no matter how poor or humble; and to an astonishing degree, the rabbis elaborated practices for ensuring that the poor should not be humiliated by the rich.[41] Avishai

---

[41] Representative examples include Maimonides' famous discussion of alms-giving – discussed at greater length in chapter 2 of this book – which prefers giving too little money, but graciously, to giving an adequate amount with ill grace, and which praises anonymous giving because it will not shame the recipient. See A Maimonides Reader 136–37 (Isadore Twersky ed., 1972) (excerpting Maimonides, Mishneh Torah bk. 7, ch. 10, §§ 7–14). Other examples include a series of Talmudic strictures requiring the rich to avoid ostentation during occasions of communal mourning in order to avoid shaming the poor who are also present. Thus, wealthy people bringing gifts of food to the house of a mourner should not bring food on fancy plates, or serve beverages in elegant glasses, because otherwise the poor who are also bringing food to the house of mourning will be shamed. Because the poor often cover the deceased's

Margalit's book *The Decent Society*, which proposes that the hallmark of the decent society is that its institutions do not humiliate anyone, stands proudly as a contribution to the mainstream of Jewish ethics.[42] From the prophets on, Jews have located injustice in oppression born of inequality.[43]

Here is one way to understand how the two basic stories in the Hebrew Bible, the story of ascendancy and the story of catastrophe, interlock: community *originates* in a mix of lawfulness and transgression, represented in the Hebrew Bible through the overthrow of primogeniture and the inscrutable notion of divine destiny, of chosenness. But community *endures* through justice. Or, as Jews have traditionally combined these two strands of the story, we were chosen by God, but what we were chosen for was not privilege but obligation – the commandments or *mitzvot* to do justice.[44] In the past, God worked His will through the transgression of the laws of property succession; in the present, God punishes those who place property above justice.

I phrase it this way to highlight that these complementary strands of the Biblical narrative share one thread: an ambivalence, or even skepticism, toward the moral claims of property. And, as we have seen, alongside an exalted regard for the law, the Hebrew Bible expresses an ambivalence about legalism.

I suspect that these deeply ingrained attitudes account, in part, for the attraction so many Jews feel toward political radicalism and political moralism. It is no secret that a remarkably high proportion of Jews are attracted to progressive causes. How could it be otherwise, when our founding stories are about the divinely sanctioned subversion of laws that safeguard the rights of property, and our prophets denounce the humiliation of the poor by the rich? It is a remarkable fact that Christian observers, from St. Paul to Hegel, have so often assailed Judaism for its pettifogging legalism – that is what Pharisaism is all about, and the Pharisees were Jews – but have overlooked the

---

face, which has been discolored through hard work, the rich must cover the face of their dead as well; and the rich, like the poor, must be transported to their graves in plain coffins. Babylonian Talmud, Mo'Eh Katan *27a – *27b. Most striking, perhaps, is another Talmudic dictum: that it is better to throw yourself into a fiery furnace than to humiliate someone in public. Babylonian Talmud, Babba Metzia *59a. I discuss these topics further in a paper about this famous Talmudic passage, *The Coiled Serpent of Argument: Reason, Authority, and Law in a Talmudic Tale*, 79 Chi.-Kent L. Rev. 1253 (2004).

[42] Avishai Margalit, The Decent Society 1 (Naomi Goldblum trans., 1996).

[43] It is not inequality itself. In the Mishneh, Shemos Rabbah 31:5, David asks God why He does not create equality, and God replies that if He did, there would be no opportunity to practice kindness and truth.

[44] This idea that to receive commandments is the same as receiving favors – that obligations are blessings – is reflected in the otherwise curious Talmudic dictum that there is greater moral merit in doing an act out of obligation than in doing it voluntarily. Babylonian Talmud, Babba Kamma *87.

powerful strain of antilegalism, of the subversion of law in the name of justice, that is every Jew's Biblical birthright.[45]

The case for Rebekah

This brings us back to the story of Rebekah. Jacob and Esau are twins, and nothing but the accident of birth-order, the "natural lottery," determines that Esau should inherit the double portion. From Rebekah's point of view, and Jacob's, the law of succession is irrational and perhaps even unjust: it has nothing to do with personal merit, for God Himself has told Rebekah otherwise (Gen. 25:23). Exactly the same thing is true in *Orley Farm*, of course. Trollope presents us with a story in which the law of succession rewards vice over virtue. Joseph Mason, who inherits everything under Sir Joseph's will, is a spiteful, vengeful, baleful, self-righteous prig, and his pathologically tight-fisted wife is the most repulsive character in the book. No characters in *Orley Farm* receive a more pitiless treatment from Trollope. Trollope hurls in our face the question: Why do they deserve Orley Farm, and not the estimable Lady Mason and her flawed but essentially decent son? Only because it was Sir Joseph's will to disinherit Lucius, and the laws of England allow him to work his will and disinherit his infant son, "the brat" (*OF* II.275). Trollope lays it on so thick that he practically compels us to consider that in this case the law is unjust. Lady Mason calls her forgery of the codicil "justice," and even Mrs. Orme agrees that Lady Mason's motive was to remedy "injustice."[46] Furnival's clerk Crabwitz states a more agnostic view that I suspect comes close to Trollope's own: "Who can say what is the justice or the injustice of anything after twenty years of possession?" (*OF* II.249)

For a Jew steeped in the Biblical tales, the subversion of the natural lottery and the law that creates it cannot be regarded as unequivocal wrongdoing. It may instead be divinely ordained, divinely approved wrongdoing, the working-out of a destiny that is higher than the caprice of the natural lottery. There is nothing just about assigning life-chances on the basis of something as arbitrary as which of the twins emerged first from Rebekah's womb.[47]

---

[45] It is Abraham who argues with God about the requirements of justice when God is about to carry out a lawful death sentence against Sodom and Gomorrah – Abraham, who persuades God that carrying out His sentence is unjust. Gen. 18:20–32.

[46] "When he would not do justice to my baby, when he talked of that other being the head of his house, I did it, with my own hands, during the night" (*OF* II.36); later, Mrs. Orme says to Lucius, "Years and years ago, when you were a baby, and when she thought that your father was unjust to you – for your sake, – to remedy that injustice, she did this thing" (*OF* II.263).

[47] Of course, in *Orley Farm* the disposition of Sir Joseph's estate is the result of his will, not of the rule of primogeniture. But Sir Joseph wrote his will to mimic the effect of primogeniture.
    The reason for a rule of primogeniture is based on conservatism, not justice or principle. The argument is that a rule dividing estates equally among the offspring (traditionally, the sons)

A Jew, I think, cannot help regarding the crimes of Rebekah as, at least in one way, *rightful* acts, *justified* acts, acts that were supposed to be done. And a Jewish reader of *Orley Farm* will scarcely share Shaffer's censorious response to Lady Mason. We do not see her as unequivocally guilty, and we certainly do not see her as repulsive. Lady Mason is Rebekah, and Rebekah is *our* foremother – resourceful, quick-witted, strong-willed, fiercely protective, unimpressed by the law when the law works injustice. She is a prototypical Jewish mother, ambitious for her child, and – for all we know – elected by God as the instrument of divine destiny. What is the law other than the instrument by which Sir Joseph Mason and his namesake in Groby Park can horde property for the mean-spirited? Why shouldn't Rebekah break it? In Lady Mason's time, no less than Rebekah's, the law gave a woman no legal power over her husband's right to bequeath family property as he saw fit, whether justly or unjustly. To do justice in a man's world, Lady Mason, like Rebekah, has no alternative but to defeat the law. By presenting us with Lady Mason – a woman of enormous depth and energy, hemmed on all sides by a legal and social order that denies women the power to act – and pitting her against the detestable Mason menfolk, Trollope raises the opposition of justice and law in a distinctly feminist form: women's justice against men's law. He raises the opposition, but he declines to resolve it, leaving Lady Mason broken and defeated at the end of the novel, but no less admirable than when we first meet her.

Thus, when Shaffer begins by saying, "*Orley Farm is* the story of a guilty woman," I think he forecloses an issue that Trollope took pains to leave open. Lady Mason has suffered from qualms of guilt, and there is no doubt that she broke the law. But law-breaking may not be real guilt, and although Shaffer says that Lady Mason is not just legally guilty but really guilty,[48] it seems to me that Trollope places that question squarely before us without presuming to answer it.

---

would prevent the accumulation of large estates because they would be subdivided in every generation. This would make the formation of landed aristocracy impossible. Aristocratic conservatism demands that large estates be kept intact intergenerationally, even at the cost of fairness among the brothers: equality among the brothers is a small sacrifice to gain the salutary inequality among the classes! In societies where the eldest brother customarily assumes the maintenance of his younger siblings, in return for their allegiance, this arrangement would be stable. Once that custom breaks down, the result is that propertyless younger brothers are forced to make their way in the world. This they did by entering the military, or the professions, or the clergy, or the ranks of commerce – or, as in the case of Lucius Mason, by emigrating. The result was a social process in which many sons of the landed gentry abandoned their deeply conservative, static world for the dynamic world of modernity and capitalism. As agrarian society gave way to industrial society, the rule of primogeniture thus created the seeds of its own destruction. *Orley Farm* is set at a time in English history when this self-immolation of the aristocracy is well under way.

[48] On Being a Christian and a Lawyer, supra note 2, at 57.

Now we can see why Shaffer's plot summary of *Orley Farm* is defective. He focuses on Lady Mason's crime, but not on Sir Joseph's will and its distributive consequences, nor on the *de minimis* nature of the injury Lady Mason inflicted on Joseph Mason, nor on the way the law masks and protects moral inequities. Omitting these things, he omits as well Lady Mason's belief that in committing her crime she was doing justice – and he omits the materials Trollope offers us that might lead us to agree.

I sometimes wonder whether Shaffer's conviction that Lady Mason is really guilty derives from his conviction that property and its inheritance are not things to be trifled with (a conviction that he has occasionally expressed in his writings).[49] I also wonder whether his view has changed over the years, as Shaffer has become more explicitly radical. Recently, he has written,

The most significant countercultural witness for Christians is the moral example of an imprudent itinerant rabbi named Jesus who got himself killed by the government. Consider three radical understandings of Christian moral example left to them by this rabbi ... There is, first, an economic reading that subverts all forms of business and of property ownership in favor not of equality, but of distribution to the economic underclass.[50]

This is Shaffer at his point of greatest affinity to the Biblical prophets – not only to Jesus, but also to the Hebrew prophets who denounced the oppression of the poor at the hands of those sharing the outlook of Joseph Mason and his wife. It contains no reverence for property, and Shaffer considers reverence for property (like reverence for the legal system and for the state) a form of idol-worship.

Even more to the point is Shaffer's 1996 reflection on the story of Rebekah. After first noting that Rebekah is a good person, chosen by God, a source of merit for all Israel, and a prophet, he reflects on the lie she told Isaac to win his blessing for Jacob:

The meaning of Rebekah's lie is the meaning to be found in her life and mission, and that had to do with her life of devotion to her family – all generations of it – a family of families – and to protecting her family both from a harmful person and the harmful rule of law that placed too much power in a first-born son and made irrevocable a father's ill-considered testamentary gesture.[51]

Here, Rabbi Shaffer reads Rebekah's story as a Jew reads it. Shaffer vindicates Rebekah's lie. But, as we ponder his vindication, we might find

---

[49] See, e.g., Thomas L. Shaffer, *Men and Things: The Liberal Bias Against Property*, 57 ABAJ 123 (1971).

[50] Thomas L. Shaffer, *Should a Christian Lawyer Sign up for Simon's Practice of Justice?*, 51 Stan. L. Rev. 903, 907 (1999).

[51] Shaffer, *On Lying for Clients*, supra note 19, at 201.

ourselves reflecting on what an apt description it is, in most respects, of Lady Mason as well.[52]

The failure of Mrs. Orme's ministry

Recall Lady Mason's stunning outburst to Mrs. Orme: "No Saviour had lived and died for me" (*OF* II.158). She places herself outside of Christendom and Christian salvation, and perhaps she does so again, despairingly, when she tells Mrs. Orme, "I do not believe in the thief on the cross" (*OF* II.238). This should not surprise us. If Lady Mason is Rebekah, and Trollope tells us three times that she is, then Lady Mason is not Christian but Jewish (at least metaphorically). So too is her lawyer Solomon Aram (not metaphorically but actually), much to the consternation of Lady Mason's proper Christian supporters. And so too, metaphorically again, is her barrister Chaffanbrass. "Mr. Solomon Aram was not ... a dirty old Jew with a hooked nose and an imperfect pronunciation of English consonants. Mr. Chaffanbrass, the barrister, bore more resemblance to a Jew of that ancient type" (*OF* II.100). (Thanks, Mr. Trollope!) The metaphors are plain enough: in Lady Mason's corner we find Jews. Evidently, Trollope took great pains to establish the Jewish credentials of Lady Mason.

That makes her agonized dialogues with Mrs. Orme a kind of dialogue between Judaism and Christianity, in which Christianity prevails. As we have seen, Shaffer writes from the conviction that Mrs. Orme (unlike Furnival) has done the moral thing in overcoming Lady Mason's resistance; he evidently supposes as well that Trollope shared this conviction. I am not so sure on either count.

After all, if Lady Mason is, like Rebekah, a good person who lied in the service of justice, then why is it so imperative that she return Orley Farm? To say that the law requires it supposes, as Shaffer usually takes care not to suppose, that our moral reasons come from the law. Merely to presume that keeping Orley Farm is not just illegal but morally wrong begs the question against Rebekah. That leaves just one possibility. If it was important to return Orley Farm, it must be because the well-being of Lady Mason's own soul required her to return the farm. That is what Shaffer believes, and, at her clearest moments, it is obvious that this is what Mrs. Orme deeply believes as well.[53]

---

[52] But not in all respects, as Shaffer might object. His point seems to be that Rebekah was acting faithfully toward Isaac as well as Jacob, and it would be a stretch to argue that Lady Mason was acting faithfully toward Sir Joseph. But perhaps it is no less a stretch than Shaffer's belief that Rebekah was acting faithfully toward Isaac.

[53] Mrs. Orme also has her less clear moments. When she opines that depriving another of property is in and of itself "a crime of the very blackest dye" (*OF* II.261), she is falling back on the conventional moralism of the gentry rather than responding as a Christian to Lady Mason's sin.

Does the fate of Lady Mason's soul truly depend on whether she returns Orley Farm? The questions of moral psychology here are profound and difficult. Trollope, I have suggested, leaves open the question of whether stealing Orley Farm was a sin. If it was no sin, then it requires no absolution. But matters are not quite so simple, because even if the forgery was the just thing to do, it may well metamorphose into a sin as it eats away at Lady Mason over the years. That is what Lady Mason herself fears when, on the eve of trial, she finds herself burdened by the terrible consciousness of sin:

She had striven to be true and honest, true and honest with the exception of that one deed. But that one deed had communicated its poison to her whole life. Truth and honesty – fair, unblemished truth and open-handed, fearless honesty, – had been impossible to her. Before she could be true and honest it would be necessary that she should go back and cleanse herself from the poison of that deed. Men have sinned deep as she had sinned, and, lepers though they have been, they have afterwards been clean. But that task of cleansing oneself is not an easy one; – the waters of that Jordan in which it is needful to wash are scalding hot. The cool neighbouring streams of life's pleasant valleys will by no means suffice (*OF* II.181).

No wonder that Shaffer comes away with the lesson that it is impossible to make things come out right without suffering.

Two questions arise, however. The first is whether Lady Mason's reflections at this point are true of her. Has her one misdeed in fact poisoned her entire life, or are these the momentary despairing thoughts of an exhausted, humiliated, beaten-down woman facing a terrifying trial the next day, while her own best friend is raising the even more terrifying prospect that she must soon be disgraced in the eyes of her own son? This is, after all, no ordinary night. This is Lady Mason's night in Gethsemane.

I believe that Lady Mason's terrible sin-consciousness is *not* true of her, in the sense that it does not represent any essential fact of who she is. On the eve of trial, in hindsight, it appears to her that the die was cast from the very first moment, but that may be an illusion born of despair. It may be illusion as well when, after her ruin, she takes the same view, that from the moment of the forgery her life had been "one incessant struggle to appear before the world as though that deed had not been done ... a labour that had been all but unendurable" (*OF* II.311). But earlier, tellingly, Trollope places a very different set of recollections in Lady Mason's mind – that for years she had dwelt in Orley Farm "if not happily at least tranquilly ... Her guilt had sat so lightly on her shoulders" (*OF* II.105). This was before her careful plans unraveled. Had circumstances been only slightly different – had, for example, her friend Miriam taken her advice and burned the incriminating papers that Dockwrath eventually discovered, or had Lucius never angered Dockwrath and launched him on his vendetta against Lady Mason – there is no reason to doubt that Lady Mason's life would have proceeded "if not happily at least tranquilly," with no slow poison spreading itself through her soul. Her abjection at the novel's end is no truer of her than her earlier tranquility, the "quiet and repose" of her well-conducted widowhood when we first meet her.

The second question is whether her reflections on the eve of trial are true – whether telling the truth and enduring the suffering that results do indeed make things any better. Here, my answer is more confident. The course of action Lady Mason chose at the behest of Mrs. Orme did *not* make things better for her and did *not* relieve her soul.

We learn this at the novel's end. At that point, Lady Mason has done all that she was asked to do: reveal the truth to Lucius, abandon Orley Farm, and accept banishment from her community. All to no avail. "But the burden had never been away – never could be away. Then she thought once more of her stern but just son, and as she bowed her head and kissed the rod, she prayed that her release might come to her soon" (*OF* II.312).[54] She prays for death because her soul is no less troubled by her crime than before, and now even her son has abandoned her.

A Christian, as Shaffer reminds us, has faith that "the Ruler of the Universe is in charge, that fate is finally benign."[55] But the meaning of "finally" is unclear. Though fate may be benign in the hereafter, it is not necessarily benign in this world, and if Mrs. Orme has ministered to Lady Mason's redemption, it is redemption that, for all Trollope knows, will take place only in the hereafter. That is how I read Trollope's profession of helpless ignorance at the end of his book about whether Lady Mason will ever experience repose again (*OF* II.312). For those of us who accept Trollope's invitation to doubt that Lady Mason has sinned, Mrs. Orme has gambled and lost.

I have suggested that Trollope takes an agnostic stance about whether Lady Mason has sinned, and whether at the story's end she has been redeemed. I now wish to suggest that his stance is equally agnostic toward Mrs. Orme's ministry (and thus, I think, Trollope does *not* take the Christian side in the dialogue between Judaism and Christianity that he so elaborately sets up). The crucial scenes occur at the end of the book, after Lady Mason had been acquitted and Lucius has given back Orley Farm. Sir Peregrine Orme, heartbroken to the point of infirmity by Lady Mason's confession, conceives the hope that he could still salvage happiness from disaster by

---

[54] In a telling turn of phrase, Trollope had earlier called Lucius's justice the most odious virtue of them all (*OF* II.276): "Of all the virtues with which man can endow himself surely none other is so odious as that justice which can teach itself to look down upon mercy almost as a vice!"

[55] *American Lawyers and Their Communities*, supra note 3, at 90.

marrying Lady Mason. After all, he reflects, she has now been acquitted by the law of the perjury charge; and, by returning Orley Farm, she has righted the wrong she did twenty years before. Her legal and moral accounts are balanced. Sir Peregrine has forgiven her, and he knows that Mrs. Orme has as well. Without Lady Mason, he is certain that his life will be over in a matter of months; with her, his vitality would return, and Lady Mason would be rescued from exile and brought into a loving home.

It is Mrs. Orme, none other, who destroys his fantasy. "It would be wrong to yourself, sir. Think of it, father. It is the fact that she did that thing. We may forgive her, but others will not do so on that account. It would not be right that you should bring her here" (*OF* II.307).[56]

At this point, Mrs. Orme is no longer speaking as a minister of souls. She is speaking as the voice of social propriety. Sir Peregrine "would offend all social laws if he were to do that which he contemplated, and ask the world around him to respect as Lady Orme – as his wife, the woman who had so deeply disgraced herself" (*OF* II.307). Theirs is a community of class, and it is the class of people for whom land matters more than character. Lady Mason has stolen real estate and tried to get away with it. For their class of people, that is the one unforgivable sin, regardless of her legal acquittal and her reparations. Bringing Lady Mason into their society would be inappropriate.[57]

Until now, Sir Peregrine has shared his community's outlook. He is a great and pure soul, but his views are the conventional views of his class. Earlier, he regarded Lady Mason's forgery as "great wrong – fearful wrong" (*OF* II.40); "so base a crime" (*OF* II.46); and Lady Mason was "that terrible criminal" (*OF* II.124), "so deep a criminal" (*OF* II.126); "very vile, desperately false, wicked beyond belief, with premeditated villany, for years and years" (*OF* II.152). However, through his own Lear-like suffering, Sir Peregrine has now achieved a glimpse past the prejudices of his class to a vision of redemption through love, redemption for both Lady Mason and himself – until Mrs. Orme brings him to his senses and makes him see how childish his vision is. She conceives it to be her duty to tell him that there will be no renewed vitality for him, "no Medea's caldron from which our limbs can come out young and fresh; and it were well that the heart should grow old as does the body" (*OF* II.307).

---

[56] See also *OF* II.288: " 'Yes, it is all over now,' she said [to Sir Peregrine] in the softest, sweetest, lowest voice. She knew that she was breaking down a last hope, but she knew also that that hope was vain." It is possible that Mrs. Orme's motivations at this point are not entirely pure or selfless. Without admitting it to herself, she may feel threatened by the possibility of being displaced as mistress of the estate by Lady Mason.

[57] I put it this way as a provocation, because Shaffer has written incisively on the shallowness of confusing appropriateness with morality. Thomas L. Shaffer & Julia B. Meister, *Is This Appropriate?*, 46 Duke L. J. 781 (1997).

Trollope voices no judgment of Mrs. Orme, either directly or indirectly. As always in this book, he allows us to draw our own conclusions. The conclusion I draw is that Mrs. Orme is too willing to tolerate suffering so that the proprieties may be maintained – too willing to defer happiness to the world beyond, too credulous of the conventions of this world. If, as Shaffer says, Furnival is too eager to make things come out right, without suffering, I fear that Mrs. Orme is not eager enough. And I fear that the very thing that makes her ministry so magnificent – her hope and faith in the world beyond – leads her to devalue happiness in this world. Mrs. Orme is no model for a lawyer to emulate. Lawyers are given over to the business of this world.

Trollope's ambivalence about lawyers' ethics

That takes us, finally, back to Trollope's lawyers. Are any of them models to emulate? Shaffer thinks that Trollope was scandalized by trial lawyers' disregard for the truth, so perhaps that means the answer is no.[58] I do not think this reading gets at the full Trollopean complexity, however.

To be sure, Trollope voices his outrage more than once, most powerfully when he describes Mr. Chaffanbrass:

He was always true to the man whose money he had taken, and gave to his customer, with all the power at his command, that assistance which he had professed to sell. But we may give the same praise to the hired bravo who goes through with truth and courage the task which he has undertaken. I knew an assassin in Ireland who professed that during twelve years of practice in Tipperary he had never failed when he had once engaged himself. For truth and honesty to their customers – which are great virtues – I would bracket that man and Mr. Chaffanbrass together (*OF* II.277–78).

This is one of the few places where Trollope speaks about the lawyers in his own voice. He does it again when he describes "five lawyers ... not one of whom gave to the course of justice credit that it would ascertain the truth, and not one of whom wished that the truth should be ascertained" (*OF* II.128). Trollope continues,

Surely had they been honest-minded in their profession they would all have so wished; – have so wished, or else have abstained from all professional intercourse in the matter. I cannot understand how any gentleman can be willing to use his intellect for the propagation of untruth, and to be paid for so using it (*OF* II.128).[59]

A bit of conventional lawyer-bashing. But Trollope turns out to be of two minds. In *Orley Farm*, the foil to the truth-despising lawyers is the young

---

[58] See American Lawyers and Their Communities, supra note 3, 88. n. 9.
[59] For a similar sentiment, see *OF* I.91.

barrister Felix Graham, who thinks that law should be about truth, and to whom Chaffanbrass represents "all that was most disgraceful in the profession" (*OF* II.57). The American legal ethicist Henry Drinker, in his introduction to the 1950 edition of *Orley Farm*, described Felix as "Trollope's early idea of the perfect barrister."[60] If Trollope really meant to condemn conventional lawyers' ethics, Drinker might be right. But that is not how Trollope wrote *Orley Farm*.

Trollope introduces Felix Graham as "the English Von Bauhr" (*OF* I.137). Von Bauhr is a German legal scholar, a stupifyingly tedious proceduralist who criticizes the British legal system in a three-hour speech at a conference on law reform. Trollope does not tell us much about Von Bauhr's views, but we learn a great deal about Felix Graham's, and if Felix Graham is the English Von Bauhr, Von Bauhr's views amount to a rejection of adversarial ethics: "Let every lawyer go into court with a mind resolved to make conspicuous to the light of day that which seems to him to be the truth" (*OF* I.141).

What does Trollope think of this theory? If he despises lawyers who defeat the truth as much as the earlier passages I've quoted suggest, he ought to love Von Bauhr's and Graham's theory. But that is not how he writes *Orley Farm*. In an amusing scene, he shows us Von Bauhr in his hotel room after his speech, napping and dreaming. Von Bauhr dreams of "an elysium of justice and mercy," an elysium as orderly "as a beer-garden at Munich," an elysium in which a grand pedestal stands, on which "was a bust with an inscription: 'To Von Bauhr, who reformed the laws of nations'" (*OF* I.136). Trollope comments, "It was a grand thought; and though there was in it much of human conceit, there was in it also much of human philanthropy" (*OF* I.136).

Trollope is gentle, but he leaves little doubt that Von Bauhr is ridiculous. All his reforms, summarized in the dry, unintelligible pamphlet with which he anesthetizes the law-reform congress, are the product of pure theory untouched by human life and untempered by human judgment. In *Orley Farm*, we must realize, Germany represents a kind of theory-besotted Cloud Cuckooland, the antipodes of sound British judgment. Lucius Mason studied at a German university, and came back a conceited, scholarly fool. He lectures to his mother about how he will improve the yield of Orley Farm by fertilizing it scientifically, with expensive, high-quality, imported guano (*OF* I.19). When Lady Mason expresses concern that he will ruin his fields and waste his capital, he loftily dismisses the importance of capital, "speaking on this matter quite *ex cathedra*, as no doubt he was entitled to do by his extensive reading at a German university" (*OF* I.19). Germany is where they

---

[60] Henry S. Drinker, *Introduction* to Anthony Trollope, Orley Farm, at vii (Alfred A. Knopf ed., 1950).

fill your head with expensive, high-quality, imported guano. That, I think, expresses Trollope's judgment about the theories of Von Bauhr and those of Felix Graham.

That leaves Trollope in a standoff. On the one hand, he clearly despises the "unique, novel, and unsound adversary ethic" by which lawyers grant themselves moral immunity for whatever they do to defeat the truth.[61] But Trollope shows no more mercy for the German inquisitorial alternative, which he compares to torture.[62] And he has no sympathy for Graham's legal ethics of truthfulness, because it comes from a theory that has nothing to do with the world in which real people actually live. When Graham argues according to his theory in Lady Mason's trial, Trollope portrays him as a feckless failure (*OF* II.223–24). Trollope's dilemma is one that many of us share. He dislikes the way lawyers defeat truth, and he rejects their rationalizations, but he grudgingly admits that the job they do is an important one and that the way they do it may sometimes be what the job requires.

And what of Mr. Furnival, the central legal interest of the story? Trollope paints him as a lawyer with great powers of discernment in practical matters, and no powers of discernment in his own life – no powers to see how infatuated he has become with Lady Mason, or how badly he is botching his own marriage, or what a calculating, dishonest girl his daughter has grown up to be, or how callous he is to his clerk. Like Chaffanbrass, Furnival is not a pretty sight to behold. If there is any lesson in the figure of Furnival, it is how deeply specialized and disconnected from the rest of life professional excellence can be, even excellence in a field like law that requires careful judgment of other people.

Shaffer thinks worse of Furnival than that, however. Shaffer thinks that Furnival fails even as a lawyer by dodging the truth and trying to make things work out well for Lady Mason. The heart of his criticism is this: "Furnival, as we say, got Lady Mason off; but he could not find a way to help Lady Mason to peace in her guilt or to reconciliation with her family and her community."[63] And again, "Thomas Furnival, barrister, saved Lady Mason from the pain and the promise of being reconciled to her neighbors."[64]

---

[61] Thomas L. Shaffer, *The Unique, Novel, and Unsound Adversary Ethic*, 41 Vand. L. Rev. 697 (1988). When Chaffanbrass offers his own self-justification, Trollope takes care to make it half-contemptible. "I can look back on life and think that I've done a deal of good in my way. I've prevented unnecessary bloodshed. I've saved the country thousands of pounds in the maintenance of men who've shown themselves well able to maintain themselves [i.e., thieves]. And I've made the Crown lawyers very careful as to what sort of evidence they would send up to the Old Bailey." *OF*, II.169–70.

[62] Trollope remarks on "the great practitioners from Germany, men … who believe in the power of their own craft to produce truth, as our forefathers believed in torture; and sometimes with the same result" (*OF* I.91).

[63] American Lawyers and Their Communities, supra note 3, at 88.   [64] Ibid. at 93.

I find the criticism puzzling, however. Mrs. Orme could not find a way to help Lady Mason to peace in her guilt or to reconciliation with her family and her community either. If Furnival pressed Lady Mason as Mrs. Orme pressed her, her defense would have collapsed and the result would have been prison. How would that reconcile her to her neighbors, who shun her even after her acquittal? In the story as it actually unfolds, it is Mrs. Orme's actions, not Mr. Furnival's, that banish Lady Mason from her community and estrange her son from her. Furnival at least had a plan for restoring Lady Mason to her community. Admittedly, it was a plan to restore her on untruthful terms, but they were terms that she had found acceptable for twenty years.

Shaffer is right to this extent: at the end of the novel, only Lady Mason's truthfulness wins forgiveness from Sir Peregrine. Truthfulness reconciles Lady Mason to him – but the cost is that they will never see each other again. And there is little doubt that if Lady Mason had told the truth at the beginning of the novel, Sir Peregrine and Mrs. Orme would never have admitted her to their company in the first place. Truthfulness exacts a terrible toll, and I have argued that Trollope never tells us whether he thinks the price was worth paying. Perhaps he did not want to scandalize his Christian readers with the thought that Rebekah may have been right.

Truthfulness or community?

Jews do not believe that communities are founded on truthfulness alone. In the Biblical story, a family, a family of families, a people, springs from Rebekah's lie. As I have described the Hebrew Bible, it shows us how communities can grow out of moral imperfections. It shows us that moral imperfections do not necessarily poison everything.

Shaffer, I think, believes that communities do require truthfulness. I often teach one of his finest essays, *The Legal Ethics of Radical Individualism*, which he organizes around a husband-and-wife estate-planning dilemma. In it, a lawyer learns that Mary, the wife, has concealed from her husband John her true wishes about what bequests their will should make.[65] She conceals them because she wants to avoid conflict with John.[66] Now that the lawyer has brought the problem to the surface, a messy conflict of interest arises; but Shaffer argues that the lawyer's probing inquiry into deep family issues is a morally good act, not a mistake. "The estate planning issue ... is whether this family is equal to the truth of what it is. The legal ethics issue is whether this lawyer, employed by this family ... is to continue to have anything to do with the truth of what this family is."[67]

[65] Thomas L. Shaffer, *The Legal Ethics of Radical Individualism*, 65 Tex. L. Rev. 963, 968 (1987).
[66] Ibid.   [67] Ibid. at 979.

But what if the family is not equal to the truth of what it is? When I teach Shaffer's essay, I hypothesize some additional facts to my students: before John and Mary knew each other, Mary had a child out of wedlock and placed it for adoption. She never told John. Now, she would like the child to receive a bequest, but she fears that raising the issue after so many years would destroy her marriage.

She may well be right. Friends who are family therapists tell me that family secrets pervade their practice, and the families do not always survive disclosure. That is a hard truth, but an even harder truth is that families whose members do not disclose secrets sometimes thrive. That makes it a genuine question whether the therapist or lawyer should press the family to discover "whether this family is equal to the truth of what it is." I am unsure how Shaffer would answer his own legal ethics question on the melodramatic facts I pose. It seems to me that they are very similar to the facts of *Orley Farm*. But I suspect that even here he favors truthfulness, just as he favors truth-fulness in *Orley Farm*.

Like my therapist friends, I have my doubts. In the best of all possible worlds, Mary tells John about her child, and, after the shock has subsided, they work out of the crisis with their marriage stronger and more truthful. But people have weaknesses, and sometimes good people have terrible weak-nesses, and love does *not* conquer all. The best of all possible worlds may not be available *to these two people*. That leaves two possible futures. In one, Mary tells John about the baby, and he cannot deal with the truth. After two tumultuous years they divorce. It shouldn't be that way. John and Mary should be able to rise to the truth of what their family is. But that is the way it is.

In the alternative future, the lawyer agrees with Mary to let the matter drop without telling John. He draws up a will that includes no bequest to Mary's child, and she signs the will. John and Mary go to their graves after fifty years of marriage in which Mary never tells John about the baby. Their lives and deaths are flawed: John dies deceived, and Mary dies without leaving money to her child. But they live and love together, and they do not die alone.

It is far from obvious which of these is least bad. Therapists and lawyers must reflect deeply on whether they will place their faith in truthfulness, like Shaffer and Mrs. Orme; or whether, like Mr. Furnival, they will try to practice the art of the possible (knowing that what is possible may be morally disappointing). If I read Shaffer aright, he thinks professionals should take the first course. The lawyer should have faith in John and Mary, faith that they can rise to the truth. That entails, however, that Shaffer must be prepared to accept the first alternative future, where the marriage founders, over the second, where the marriage succeeds on false terms. And he thinks that Furnival should have faith that Lady Mason and Lucius can rise to the truth. But that entails a willingness to accept the bitter ending of *Orley Farm* over the alternative that Furnival planned, in which Lady Mason wins acquittal, retains the farm, and never tells Lucius the truth.

In both cases, I incline the other way. My reason for inclining the other way is that lawyers, like therapists, have a responsibility to abjure wishful thinking, and when hope flies in the face of evidence it becomes practically indistinguishable from wishful thinking. Shaffer denies this: he writes that "the virtue of hope can come to terms with and deal truthfully with the certainty that the moral life will cause others to suffer."[68] But if the suffering of others is a *certainty*, where is the hope? Shaffer's answer is one we have seen before: "Hope ... says that the Ruler of the Universe is in charge, that fate is finally benign."[69] Hope is extra-worldly.

Judaism is a this-worldly religion. A few years ago, a Christian friend asked me what Jews believe about the afterlife, and I had to admit that I didn't know. I called my father and asked him whether we (officially) believe in an afterlife. He didn't know either. He called a friend who is deeply immersed in Jewish study, but his friend was unsure. Officially, Jews believe in the resurrection of the dead when the Messiah comes, and recite a statement of that belief near the beginning of the Eighteen Blessings; and the rabbinic literature is filled with folk-tales about paradise and hell, Eden and Gehinnom. But these folk-beliefs are quite peripheral to the religion. "Whatever may be the doctrine of heaven and hell, the central emphasis of Judaism has remained on this world, from the beginning."[70] Abraham's great act of faith, the sacrifice of Isaac, was redeemed in this world rather than the next; so was the faith of Job. A Jewish reader, I think, will look with greater sympathy than Shaffer on Furnival's effort to make things come out right in this world – and with little sympathy on Mrs. Orme's final decree against Sir Peregrine's and Lady Mason's earthly happiness through marriage.[71] I have been arguing that this also happens to be the fairest reading of Trollope's novel.

Furnival, Chaffanbrass, and Aram are unattractive instruments of salvation, but it seems to me that Rabbi Trollope leaves us with the possibility that God works through unattractive instruments. As usual, there is a Jewish joke on the subject.

After many days of hard, continuous rain, the river is in danger of flooding, and word goes out that people may have to abandon their homes. When the river crests, water

---

[68] American Lawyers and Their Communities, supra note 3, at 90.   [69] Ibid.

[70] Arthur Hertzberg, Judaism: The Key Spiritual Writings of the Jewish Tradition 277 (rev. edn., 1991).

[71] Shaffer thinks that Furnival was "so wrong about [his ability to make things come out well] as to have been out of touch with reality." American Lawyers and Their Communities, supra note 3, at 89–90. I do not see why. If Sir Peregrine had not proposed marriage to Lady Mason, precipitating her confession, Furnival's plan might have worked.

pours through the town, inundating houses, and it continues to rise. Firemen are sent in a small motorboat to go through the streets to make sure everyone is leaving. When they come to the house of the rabbi, they find him standing knee-deep in water on his front porch.

"Come on, Rabbi," say the firemen. "The river will go much higher, and you should leave with us."

"No," says the rabbi. "God will protect me." And he sends them away. The river rises higher, the rabbi is forced to go up to the second floor of his house, and now the police come in a motor launch.

"Come on, Rabbi," say the police, "there isn't much time."

"No," insists the rabbi. "I will stay right here. God will look after me." And he sends them away.

Now the river rises so high that the rabbi is forced to stand on the roof of his house. When the National Guard arrive in a large boat, telling him that the river is sure to go even higher, the rabbi says, "All my life I have been a man of faith, and I will stay now, and trust in God," and sends them away.

The river rises, the rabbi is swept away, and the rabbi drowns.

Forthwith the rabbi appears in heaven, where he angrily approaches the throne of God, demanding, "How can You have let this happen to me? For all my life I have kept Your *mitzvot*. I have done what You asked, and trusted in You. Why?"

A voice sounds from the throne: "You shmuck. I sent three boats."[72]

Sometimes, perhaps, God sends three lawyers.

---

[72] Ted Cohen, Jokes: Philosophical Thoughts on Joking Matters 19–20 (1999).

Index

Printed in Great Britain
by Amazon.co.uk, Ltd.,
Marston Gate.